The Collected Oz

Volume Four

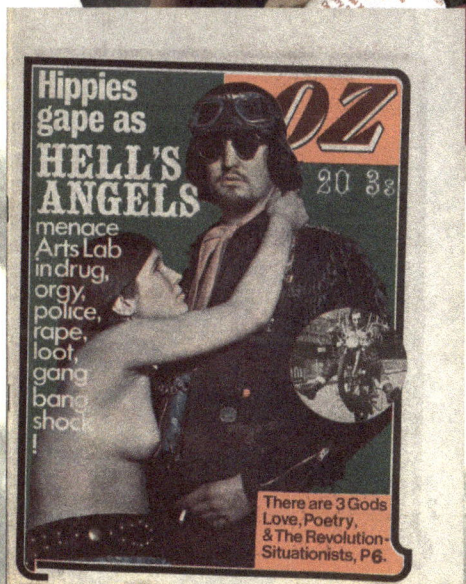

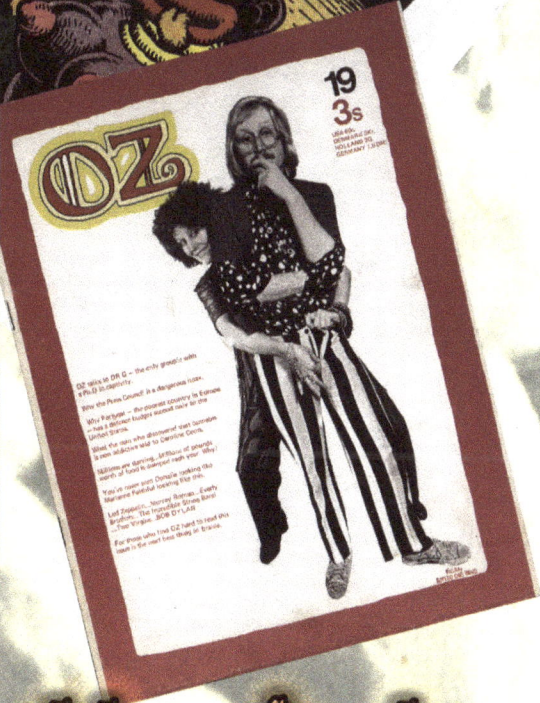

Richard Neville et. al.

Edited by Jonathan Downes
Typeset by Jonathan Downes
Cover and Internal Layout by Jon Downes for Gonzo Multimedia
Using Microsoft Word 2000, Microsoft , Publisher 2000, Adobe Photoshop.

First edition published 2016 by Gonzo Multimedia

c/o Brooks City,
6th Floor New Baltic House
65 Fenchurch Street,
London EC3M 4BE
Fax: +44 (0)191 5121104
Tel: +44 (0) 191 5849144
International Numbers:
Germany: Freephone 08000 825 699
USA: Freephone 18666 747 289

ISBN: 978-1-908728-65-4

For Richard, Felix and Jim

Oz Obscenity Trial Old Bailey London 1971

Trial begins 22 June
Any information contact Friends of Oz,
39a Pottery Lane, London W11. 01-229 5887.

Introduction

Back in the day, and this particular day was about twenty years ago, I was friendly with a notorious Irish Republican musical ensemble known as *Athenrye*, and particularly with their guitarist, a guy called Terry Manton. I was very angry about a lot of things at the time, and quite how drinking with various groups of slightly dodgy Hibernians actually made me feel any better I am not sure, but it seemed to have the desired effect.

On one of their albums there is a song about Éamon de Valera. For those of you not in the know, over to those jolly nice people at Wikipedia.

"Éamon de Valera first registered as George de Valero; changed some time before 1901 to Edward de Valera; 14 October 1882 – 29 August 1975) was a prominent politician and statesman in twentieth-century Ireland. His political career spanned over half a century, from 1917 to 1973; he served several terms as head of government and head of state. He also led the introduction of the Constitution of Ireland.

De Valera was a leader in the War of Independence and of the anti-Treaty opposition in the ensuing Irish Civil War (1922–1923). After leaving Sinn Féin in 1926 due to its policy of abstentionism, he founded Fianna Fáil, and was head of government (President of the Executive Council, later Taoiseach) from 1932 to 1948, 1951 to 1954, and 1957 to 1959, when he resigned after being elected as President of Ireland. His political creed evolved from militant republicanism to social and cultural conservatism.

Assessments of de Valera's career have varied; he has often been characterised as

Lucky man of our times

Chorus
He was loved he was hated he was cherished despised
There were rivers of tears when the chieftain he died
But love him or hate him I cannot decide
What to make of old Dev this man of our times."

And it ended up:

"Now Spain had it's Franco and France it's De Gaulle
We had our Dev and god rest his soul"

It has been many years since I bounced up and down in a weird Gaelic moshpit shouting "Tiocfaidh ár lá" and I strongly doubt whether I shall ever do so again. My foray into such things had more to do with my reaction to the way that I perceived that I had been treated by my family over my particularly scabrous divorce, than any genuine political fervour, although I thought then (and think now) that the British history in Ireland has not been our greatest or most honourable hour. However, today I have had that song going round and around my head, ever since I read an email from Tony Palmer telling me that Richard Neville had died at the age of 74, in Byron Bay, New South Wales, the Australian hippy enclave where Gilli Smyth breathed her last only a few days before.

Now I never met Neville. Our acquaintanceship was confined to two emails about five years ago when I was working on the new edition of Tony Palmer's *The Trials of Oz*. I exchanged a few more emails with Jim Anderson, and had no contact whatsoever with Felix Dennis, so I cannot really be called an insider of the *Oz* scene. But Neville came out with one of my favourite quotes from the counterculture: "There is some corner of a foreign field that is forever Woodstock", and was an undeniably major figure in that much maligned social movement.

He seemed to be someone who brought out strong reactions in people. Whilst I was working on *The Trials of Oz* I discovered that people were either terribly fond of the man or disliked him intensely. I never found anyone who was ambivalent towards him. Even after his death, as I sent emails around the usual suspects asking for their memories of him, most people refused to be drawn one way or the other, with those who had been friends with him at various periods of their lives being totally devastated that they had woken up this morning to a planet on which Richard Neville was no longer alive.

Me? I am no better than any of the others. I have no knowledge of him personally, and whereas I found large chunks of *Oz* unreadable, I was impressed by his book *Playpower* and in the passages about him in Tony Palmer's book he struck an undeniably heroic figure against the same sort of establishment malice which had (as alluded to above) turned me against my parents twenty years back.

His book *Hippy Hippy Shake* was entertaining, even though its hedonism left a slightly bitter taste in one's mouth, but I remember being told that the movie that was made from it was so bad that several of the major figures portrayed refused to let it come out. In July 2007, in a piece for *The Guardian*, feminist author Germaine Greer vehemently expressed her displeasure at being depicted, writing, "You used to have to die before assorted hacks started munching your remains and modelling a new version of you out of their own excreta." Greer refused to be involved with the film, just as she declined to read Neville's memoir before it was published (he had offered to change anything she found offensive). She did not want to meet with Emma Booth, who portrays her in the film, and concluded her article with her

only advice for the actress: "Get an honest job."

So where is this taking me? I truly don't know, but if there had not been a Richard Neville, there might well not have been a *Gonzo Weekly* magazine. I first read *The Trials of Oz* whilst on holiday with my patients back when I was a Registered Nurse for the Mentally Subnormal [RNMS] nearly thirty years ago, and it was one of the sacred texts, together with *A Series of Shock Slogans and Mindless Token Tantrums* by Penny Rimbaud et al, that set me on the path that I am on now. But when I finally read the *Schoolkid's Oz*, I thought it was puerile bollocks, and was massively underwhelmed.

And I too find it hard to adjust to the fact that I have woken up this morning to a planet on which Richard Neville was no longer alive.

So, if I may:

"He was loved he was hated he was cherished despised
There were rivers of tears when the Oz editor died
But love him or hate him I cannot decide
What to make of old Nev this man of our times."

Hare Bol Mr Neville

In Mitigation

So what was *Oz?* And why was it so important?

OZ was an underground alternative magazine. First published in Sydney, Australia, in 1963, a second version appeared in London, England from 1967 and is better known.

The original Australian *OZ* took the form of a satirical magazine published between 1963 and 1969, while the British incarnation was a "psychedelic hippy" magazine which appeared from 1967 to 1973. Strongly identified as part of the underground press, it was the subject of two celebrated obscenity trials, one in Australia in 1964 and the other in the United Kingdom in 1971. On both occasions the magazine's editors were acquitted on appeal after initially being found guilty and sentenced to harsh jail terms. An earlier, 1963 obscenity charge was dealt with expeditiously when, upon the advice of a solicitor, the three editors pleaded guilty.

The central editor throughout the magazine's life in both Australia and Britain was Richard Neville. Co-editors of the Sydney version were Richard Walsh and Martin Sharp. Co-editors of the London version were Jim Anderson and, later, Felix Dennis.

In early 1966 Neville and Sharp travelled to the UK and in early 1967, with fellow Australian Jim Anderson, they founded the London *OZ*. Contributors included Germaine Greer, artist and filmmaker Philippe Mora, illustrator Stewart Mackinnon, photographer Robert Whitaker, journalist Lillian Roxon, cartoonist Michael Leunig, Angelo Quattrocchi, Barney Bubbles and David Widgery.

With access to new print stocks, including metallic foils, new fluorescent inks and the freedom of layout offered by the offset printing system, Sharp's artistic skills came to the fore and *OZ* quickly won renown as one of the most visually exciting publications of its day. Several editions of *Oz* included dazzling psychedelic wrap-around or pull-out posters by Sharp, London design duo Hapshash and the Coloured Coat and others; these instantly became sought-after collectors' items and now command high prices. Another innovation was the cover of *Oz* No.11, which included a collection of detachable adhesive labels, printed in either red, yellow or green. The all-graphic "Magic Theatre" edition (*OZ* No.16, November 1968), overseen by Sharp and Mora, has been described by British author Jonathon Green as "arguably the greatest achievement of the entire British underground press". During this period Sharp also created the two famous psychedelic album covers for the group Cream, Disraeli Gears and Wheels Of Fire.

Sharp's involvement gradually decreased during 1968-69 and the "Magic Theatre" edition was one of his last major contributions to the magazine. In his place, young Londoner Felix Dennis, who had been selling issues on the street, was eventually brought in as Neville and Anderson's new partner. The magazine regularly enraged the British Establishment with a range of left-field stories including heavy critical coverage of the Vietnam War and the anti-war movement, discussions of drugs, sex and alternative lifestyles, and contentious political stories, such as the magazine's revelations about the

torture of citizens under the rule of the military junta in Greece.

In 1970, reacting to criticism that *OZ* had lost touch with youth, the editors put a notice in the magazine inviting "school kids" to edit an issue. The opportunity was taken up by around 20 secondary school students (including Charles Shaar Murray and Deyan Sudjic), who were responsible for *OZ* No.28 (May 1970), generally known as "Schoolkids OZ". This term was widely misunderstood to mean that it was intended for schoolchildren, whereas it was an issue that had been created by them. As Richard Neville said in his opening statement, other issues had been assembled by gay people and members of the Female Liberation Movement. One of the resulting articles was a highly sexualised Rupert Bear parody. It was created by 15-year-old schoolboy Vivian Berger by pasting the head of Rupert onto the lead character of an X-rated satirical cartoon by Robert Crumb.

OZ was one of several 'underground' publications targeted by the Obscene Publications Squad, and their offices had already been raided on several occasions, but the conjunction of schoolchildren, and what some viewed as obscene material, set the scene for the *Oz* obscenity trial of 1971.

The trial was, at the time, the longest obscenity trial in British legal history, and it was the first time that an obscenity charge was combined with the charge of conspiring to corrupt public morals. Defence witnesses included artist Feliks Topolski, comedian Marty Feldman, artist and drugs activist Caroline Coon, DJ John Peel, musician and writer George Melly, legal philosopher Ronald Dworkin and academic Edward de Bono.

At the conclusion of the trial the "OZ Three" were found not guilty on the conspiracy charge, but they were convicted of two lesser offences and sentenced to imprisonment; although Dennis was given a lesser sentence because the judge, Justice Michael Argyle, considered that Dennis was "very much less intelligent" than the others. Shortly after the verdicts were handed down, they were taken to prison and their long hair forcibly cut, an act which caused an even greater stir on top of the already considerable outcry surrounding the trial and verdict.

The best known images of the trial come from the committal hearing, at which Neville, Dennis and Anderson all appeared, wearing rented schoolgirl costumes.

At the appeal trial (where the defendants appeared wearing long wigs) it was found that Justice Argyle had grossly misdirected the jury on numerous occasions and the defence also alleged that Berger, who was called as a prosecution witness, had been harassed and assaulted by police. The convictions were overturned. Years later, Felix Dennis told author Jonathon Green that on the night before the appeal was heard, the *OZ* editors were taken to a secret meeting with the Chief Justice, Lord Widgery, who reportedly said that Argyle had made a "fat mess" of the trial, and informed them that they would be acquitted, but insisted that they had to agree to give up work on *OZ*. Dennis also stated that, in his opinion, MPs Tony Benn and Michael Foot had interceded with Widgery on their behalf.

Despite their supposed undertaking to Lord Widgery, *OZ* continued after the trial, and thanks to the intense public interest the trial generated, its circulation briefly rose to 80,000. However its popularity faded over the next two years and by the time the last issue (*OZ* No.48) was published in November 1973 Oz Publications was £20,000 in debt and the magazine had "no readership worth the name".

We are publishing these magazines in these collected editions, partly as a tribute to the late Richard Neville (1943-2016) and partly because we believe that they constitute a valuable socio-political document reflecting the counterculture of 1967-74. This collection has been made available due to its

historical and research importance. It contains explicit language and images that reflect attitudes of the era in which the material was originally published, and that some viewers may find confronting. However, we have taken the decision to blank out a very few images which would be seen as unacceptable in today's society.

Times have changed a lot in the past half century. The magazine's obsession with pornography, for example, has not stood the test of time very well, and some of the typography is so muddy as to be unreadable. Every effort has been made by the present publishers to clean up the typography, but in most cases it proved to be impossible, so we have left it as it was. The *Oz* readers of the late 1960s were unable to read it. Why should the present generation be any different?

Some of the pictures in the original magazine, especially artwork by Martin Sharp, was printed so it could fold out into a poster. We have therefore included these twice - as per the original pages so they can be read easily, and as extrapolations of the original artwork. Richard Neville stipulated in the extract from the notorious *Schoolkid's Oz* reproduced below that the material in these magazines could be used for any purpose, and we are taking him at his word.

Peace and Love

Ronnie Rooster
September 2016

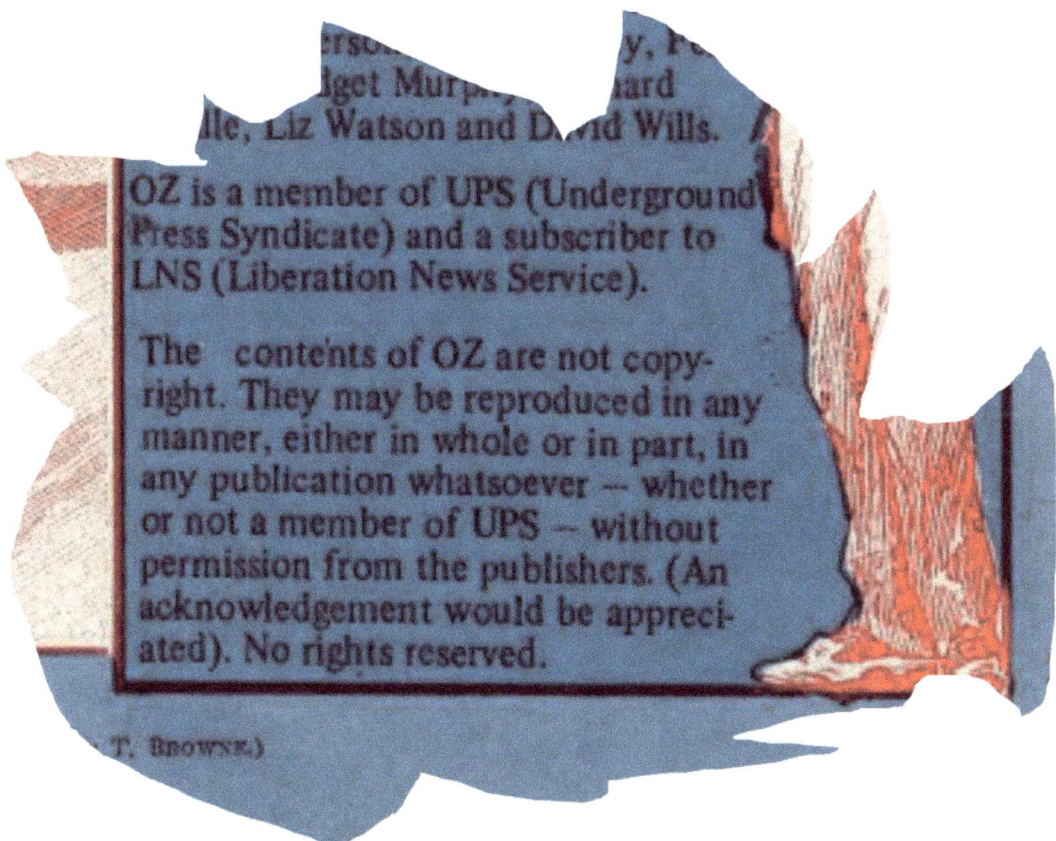

OZ is a member of UPS (Underground Press Syndicate) and a subscriber to LNS (Liberation News Service).

The contents of OZ are not copyright. They may be reproduced in any manner, either in whole or in part, in any publication whatsoever — whether or not a member of UPS — without permission from the publishers. (An acknowledgement would be appreciated). No rights reserved.

OZ

3/-

USA 60c.
DENMARK 3Kr.
HOLLAND 2G.
GERMANY 1.8 DM.

Manfred Mann
Smash Cash
ICA Blast
Indian Ashrams
South African Queen club
Greek Gaols
Don't let your chick blow your Balls
Does Shelter really Shelter
Is Tiny Tim what he eats
Black Eagles
How telly screws up Pop

Robert Whittaker

London OZ is published
approximately monthly by
OZ Publications Ink Ltd,
38a Palace Gdns Terrace W8.
Phone 01-229 4623 . . .
01 603 4205.

Editor: Richard Neville

Design: Jon Goodchild

Writers: Andrew Fisher, Ray
Durgnat, David Widgery,
Angelo Quattrocchi, Ian Stocks.

Artists: Martin Sharp, John
Hurford, Phillipe von Mora.

Photography: Keith Morris

Advertising: Felix Dennis.
REN 1330

Typesetting: Jacky Ephgrave
courtesy Thom Keyes

Pushers: Louise Ferrier, Felix
Dennis, Anou

This issue produced by
Andrew Fisher

Distribution: Britain
(overground); Moore-Harness
Ltd. 11 Lever Street, London
EC1. Phone CLE 4882.
(underground); ECAL,
22 Betterton Street, London
WC2. Phone TEM 8606.
New York DGB Distribut.,
Inc. 41 Union Square, New
York 10003.
Holland Thomas Rap,
Regulierdwarsstraat 91,
Amsterdam, Tel. 020-227 65.
Denmark George Streeto
The Underground, Larsbjørs
straede 13, Copenhagen K.
California Rattner Distributor,
2428 McGee Street, Berkeley,
California 94703.

PSORAKIS

Avant-Garde's "No More War!" poster contest, announced nine months ago, brought a response that swamped our expectations: Over 2000 entries from two dozen countries. The theme most conspicuous in winning posters is a wholesale rejection of militarism, of the military ideal.

winning poster

RON AND KAREN BOWEN, U.S.A.

COUNTER AUTHORITY

by Peter Buckman

Most people haven't read Marx — a sad lot for radicals, all excited by revolution in the air. They are uninterested in the inner mechanics of capitalism, which, like a ratchet wheel, is always supposed to be dying but somehow staggers infuriatingly on. The old strains are broken down, the old analyses out-dated. Here we are in vulgar affluence in the midst of a crisis, and it does not neatly note the rigid logic of the class struggle or the contradictions of capitalism.

What we've got is a crisis of authority. The young, who in America at least will form half the total population by 1970, don't subscribe to any particular doctrine. They theories based on new forms of discipline, not on dogmas founded on the need for alliances with segments of the population — eg 'the workers' — with whom they are totally out of contact. For the new revolutionary, which title potentially includes everyone under 25, the means is the end, with no compromises. The end is the right of everyone to participate in the making of all decisions, political, social and economic, which affect him. The present system — nowhere in the world — permits this. Neither in the socialist countries nor in the capitalist countries,

not even in Cuba, where 500 young people were arrested and banished from the capital for being hippies, is there freedom from oppressive authority. The trouble is that all attempts to replace authority have to rely on discipline, on violence, on coercion — all means which are anathema to the counter authoritarians and which, moreover, have led historically to bureaucratic excesses as bad as any in the precurse system.

The way to enjoy this revolutionary state obviously depends on small, autonomous communities. It should quickly be said that we're not talking about anarchism, at least as conceived by those who label themselves anarchists. Though the feeling of being against authority has a lot in common with Proudhon, Bakunin, and, for that matter, Cohn-Bendit, their beliefs are based, rather romantically, on everyone being members of a community able to sustain itself without rulers. In other words, such a state has to be brought about universally by whatever means necessary in order for 'anarchism' to flourish: it has to be imposed on those unwilling to accept it. Not for nothing was Bakunin close to Marx: both believed in the desirability of violent revolution, the difference being in the methods to be followed.

But the new revolutionaries do not subscribe to anything so

Keith Morris

rigid or systematic as the analysis of Marx or Bakunin. As a matter of fact, Cohn-Bendit was locked into a room at the International Conference of Anarchists for disagreeing with them, so tolerance is not one of their things. Those who are simply anti-authority are individualists,: as members of the underground they believe that the first principle is that everyone must be free to do their thing. Some try this in small communities, but so far history has proved to be against them. Most people don't want to go back to bucolic states of gambolling innocence with no running water. Whatever the new form of social and political organisation that arises in an affluent society, it has to take for granted the maintenance of living standards.

There's no point in regressing, though it's worth pointing out that our notions of what is up-to-date and what is out-of-date have been largely dictated by the system under which we are ruled.

The models of the Third World are inappropriate for those dedicated to a counter authoritarian stance. The Chinese Cultural Revolution is the nearest thing to the permanent questioning of authority known to civilisation, but its excesses, at least as known to the West, are too much for the comfort even of the most radical activists. In China, as in Cuba and other socialist states, the unity of the people to build a revolutionary state from scratch can be relied on. No such unity exists in advanced countries. The alliance between 'workers' and 'intellectuals', though tested and proven in France and Italy in campaigns notable for their brevity as much as for their violence, seems to be the prerogative of a few militants in both camps. As a revolutionary coalition it simply isn't on, especially as the 'working class' can no longer be considered simply as an undifferentiated mass ripe for revolution. Those most disgruntled by the system are those who depend upon it for prosperity, while resenting the way the state interferes with them. They are profoundly anti-revolutionary. The largest class in a neo-capitalist state is that of the consumers, on whom the system depends. All they want is more.

It is this desire which has caused the crises that have so badly shaken the system. All the agitation by the young and the radicals, which has contributed to the break-up of the system's liberal façade, has not in fact brought it to a crisis. That came when the 'workers' demanded higher wages which had to be conceded in some way or other for without doing so the mechanisms of production would have come grinding to a halt. The inflation that was inevitable, and the determination of the consumers not to suffer more than the owning class could, of course, lead to an explosive situation. The probable result will be the advent of a repressive, totalitarian regime. The political Left is simply unprepared to lead a revolution. They have not spelt out what they want and care about, because they think that would be authoritarian. Yet to attract the support of the massively disgruntled — any or all of the consumers, white and blue-collar workers, managers, civil servants, teachers, state and local officials, doctors, firemen, and policemen — a clear statement of the cause and objective of revolution is vitally necessary. It doesn't appear because it runs counter to the dearly-cherished principle of anti-dogmatism, and because no one on the Left is certain of how the revolutionary state would be run, let alone brought into being.

All this leaves the most revolutionary section — those who are against Authority · unmoved. While they don't want much to do with the beliefs of those in authority over them — their teachers, the police, their families — they feel equally alienated from the political Left, with its warring sects, its wild and sometimes incredibly antiquated rhetoric, above all its rigidity. Though I personally believe that for the necessary revolution to take place, a high order of discipline, clarity, organisation, and systematic analysis is necessary, I would be the first to say that what the Left is up to seems most of the time to have little to do with what concerns most people, or to be sadly ineffective. I can understand those on whose cooperation a revolutionary organisation must depend in a crunch — the young, basically — being as fed up with the Left, at least in England, as they are with the authorities who are their real enemy. But if what makes a new revolutionary is his attitude to authority, not his adherence to one dogma or another, what's going to hang him up is how he's to make his revolution. Obviously he can't get permanently high and simply withdraw. By himself he is virtually powerless, though the whole point of the movement is individual liberation. He can express a fuck-you attitude in clothes, actions, or style, but such action is limited, for if he steps too far out of line the system will simply clobber him.

There are two urgent needs. Given that counter-authoritarianism — and I wish someone would provide a good word for it — is what unites today's potential revolutionaries, it is up to the political Left, with its vast experience in agitation, to prove that organisation, analysis, and programmes are capable of being effective in bringing about a revolutionary state, one which will not deteriorate into quasi-Stalinism, as has befallen so many of the socialist countries.

Those who are simply counter-authoritarians, on the other hand, have an equally difficult task. They urgently need to understand that the forms of repression they are constantly encountering, and which they are so against, are all linked to the system we live under. It's not that we suffer under a peculiar and conspiratorial dictatorship, because there's a lot we're allowed to do. But no one is permitted directly to challenge the balance of power between those who govern and those who are governed, and that's what the system is all about. We can protest and wear funny clothes, but when we want a say in making the decisions that directly affect us, whether at school, university, or work, we get no joy at all. Thus to be counter-authoritarian cannot be a series of isolated encounters. They're all the same fight, which to be won requires a totally different life-style, unthinkable under this system. The struggle is political, whichever way you look at it, and the trouble is those who are all involved in politics aren't breaking through the credibility barrier.

It's not possible to be very optimistic. There have been crises of authority before, and the good guys have never been able to take advantage of them. What the political Left has done in America and Europe has been vastly exciting, and it's changed the *climate* of protest, but not the conditions or the balance of power which occasioned it. The most hopeful thing is the really young: the kids at school, who both in France and America are rejecting all forms of authority *and* fighting in the streets with their ageing colleagues at university. Soon these kids are going to be in the majority everywhere. There has never been a greater potential for revolution, but *they* are going to make it, not us, and if we don't do the right thing now, we're going to be on the wrong side of the barricades — the losing side.

WHO MOVED THE BLACK CASTLE
WHO MOVED THE WHITE QUEEN
WHEN GIMMEL AND DALETH
WERE STANDING BETWEEN?
OUT OF THE EVENING GROWING
A VEIL
PINING FOR THE PINE WOODS
THAT ACHED FOR THE SAIL

THERE'S SOMETHING FORGOTTEN
I WANT YOU TO KNOW
THE FRECKLES OF RAIN ARE
TELLING ME SO
O IT'S THE OLD FORGOTTEN
QUESTION
WHAT IS IT THAT WE ARE PART OF?
WHAT IS IT THAT WE ARE?

AND AN ELEPHANT MADNESS HAS COVERED THE SUN
THE JUDGE AND THE JURIES THEY PLAY FOR THE FUN
THEY'VE TORN UP THE ROSES AND WASHED ALL THE SOAP
AND THE MARTYR WHO MARRIES THEM DARE NOT ELOPE
O IT'S THE NEVER REALISED QUESTION

O LONG O LONG E'ER YET MY EYES
BRAYED THE GATES ENORMOUS FIRE
AND THE BODY FOLDED ROUND ME
AND THE PERSON IN ME GREW

THE FLOWER AND ITS PETAL
THE ROOT AND ITS GRASP
THE EARTH AND ITS BUSINESS
THE BREATH AND ITS GASP
THE MIND AND ITS MOTION
THE FOOT AND ITS MOVE
THE LIFE AND ITS PATTERN
THE HEART AND ITS LOVE
O ITS THE HALF REMARKABLE QUESTION
WHAT IS IT THAT WE ARE PART OF?
WHAT IS IT THAT WE ARE?

ROBIN WILLIAMSON

THE HALF REMARKABLE QUESTION
FROM WEE TAM & THE BIG HUGE
BY THE INCREDIBLE STRING BAND
© WARLOCK MUSIC LTD
ELECTRA EKS 74036/37 BY POLYDOR

John
Rutford

OZ 17

Dear OZ,

When WILL IT stop printing 'Periodic Clarifications of Editorial Policy'; when WILL Pete Stansill stop impressing nobody with 'tactical rationality, politico-emotional solidarity, ultimate ecstasy and popular static notions of history:' when WILL the Deviants stop pretending to be The Voice Of The Underground (available at any branch of WH Smiths?); when WILL Middle Earth stop putting up their prices; when WILL John Wilcock stop including comic strip two headed Japanese lesbians in Other Scenes; when WILL Black Dwarf stop printing Che posters/memoirs/diaries/collected sayings and similar crap; when WILL somebody tell Simon Stable that nobody's interested in his phoney fortnightly 'Top Ten Underground Hit LP's,' plastic dream machine and abysmal column, when WILL anybody ever 'come along and do their thing' in an Arts Lab as devoid of creative atmosphere as a British Railways waiting room When? . . . When Pellen Personal and Men it CAN Be Done stop advertising in OZ . . . you know . . . Never.

Love,

Felix
44 Wandsworth Bridge Road
SW6

Dear OZ,

Can a TEEN-AGE PENSIONER bridge the gap between Youth and Age, Us and Them, Student and LABOURER? Or can a Bedevilled SCOTS MYSTIC "Point the Way"?

I LOVE their EDUCATION, their SPIRIT, their desire to right WRONGS: but NOT their fragmentation or lack of PURPOSE. As a MYSTIC I can DO what I MUST for a troubled SOUL: the Establishment can't OPPOSE ME OR DESTROY me or my INFLUENCE. But that is AFFINITY, individual from person to person.

If the WORLD was CHAOS, isolated changes would be possible (as OZ illustrates). But if it is ORGANISED CHAOS for the benefit of the MONEY-CHANGERS, what then? They can sit back at the CENTRE and smile at what happens at the EXTREMES. You have America's THINK-TANK and BRITAIN'S GERMWARFARE.
You have SCIENCE and INTELLECT prostituted by FINANCE and GOVERNMENT — with ABSOLUTE CONTROL of Mass Media. As God in above, I can only KNOW about Student RIOTS, BLACK GHETTOES, VIETNAM, APPLACHIA, if they let me. Do the STUDENTS and TARIQ ALI KNOW this?

Don't the STUDENTS KNOW that TUC and LABOUR PARTY CONFERENCES, are SOPS for the APATHETIC; [illegible] for the selling of TORY LEGISLATION which could have caused REVOLUTION had it come from TORIES? Don't they SEE that 'don't rock the boat' leaves the TORY WACKEYS where they were PLACED?

Let me ILLUSTRATE: as a BELIEVER in SOCIALISM I backed them. As a CHRONIC SICK WORKER I LIVE on four pounds ten, PAY for five essential MEDICINES, where last year I paid NOTHING. More IRONIC still: I retired as a SICK labourer, the DUNCE in my class at School draws seventy pounds PLUS as an MP, and is justly FAMOUS for never having opened his MOUTH in the COMMONS!

THAT, I feel, illustrates the SOCIALISM and sincerity of 'OUR BOYS'.
After years of experience of BRANCHES and CONFERENCES I can assure STUDENTS or MILITANTS that POLICY NOT decided at BRANCH LEVEL; less than 2 percent of MEMBERS actually ATTEND. They have BINGO, overtime, a coupon to fill up, a MATCH they can't miss. These are the PRIORITIES. POLICY is handed DOWN.

Conferences are PLACES I can take the wife to for a bloody good expenses-paid holiday!

What do my friends THE WORKERS 'want'. How can I KNOW if they never attend?

A check-up on HOTELS and boarding-houses in Conference 'RESORTS' will REVEAL the same names year after year. The agenda is PONDEROUS. The effect on Harold and George: NIL.

To succeed at all the STUDENTS must UNITE, win over the apathetic WORKERS and ORGANISE. I with them. I KNOW what they want to pull down, what they want to build.

But surely they KNOW that 'Work for the WORKERS' means the SAME and is more COMFORTABLE, enables My mates to ignore me, ignore VIETNAM, ignore NIGERIA and scream 'Make them BASTARDS WORK'.

As a MYSTIC, I accept de BONO and his LATERAL THINKING. The student must reject him. I accept BABA in toto. But advise: the ESTABLISHMENT first, our NEWWORLD later.

The LAST PLACE youth can go to seek HELP or UNDERSTANDING is MUM and DAD, Principal STAFF. Fifty years of practise (NOT for MONEY) have TAUGHT ME SOMETHING.

ALEX DUTHIE
49 High Street
Innerleithen
Peeblesshire
Scotland

Dear Sir,

I am prompted to write to you by Mr Rogall's letter (OZ 15) about James letter (OZ 14) on revolution. I regard most of this suddenly fashionable talk on this subject as little more than hysterical romanticism deriving ultimately from the anti rational philosophy of Hegel, (as pointed out by Karl Popper more than 20 years ago!

It would be interesting to know what attitude Mr Rogall and all those who think like him have to a seldom mentioned thing called the truth.

If, following Marxist writers like Karl Mannheim, he holds that 'everybody's conciousness is a product of social relations' this is as true of himself as it is of anyone else, 'proletarian' or 'capitalist'. If this is so from the standpoint of truth Mr Rogall's arguments for revolution are to be taken no more seriously than those in favour of the status quo. Presumably along with most Marxist writers he regards myself as one of the select band of mystical brothers who have been vouchsafed a vision of social reality devoid of unconcious bias.

I hold a correspondence theory of the truth, ie. a statement is true if it corresponds to the facts. What are the facts, how do we decide? The only way of arriving at facts is to put forward theories that attempt to explain experience. These theories if they are to be more than merely heuristic must be capable of being rigorously discussion. These requirements as far as I know are never met by anyone who is in favour of revolutions. Their behaviour in this regard seems to me to be what psychologists call 'displacement activity'. They are unable to satisfy some basic drive and vent their frustration by lashing out wildly at everything in sight. That they are unable to satisfy these drives may be due to childhood experiences, lack of love, education, or indeed society as a whole.

But there is no guarantee that violent revolution will resolve either their own frustrations or more importantly anyone else's.

No one doubts that revolutions change things, the question is are they improved? Do we not in reality only change our masters ideas? Then again comes the question which ideas are nearer the truth? Sociological questions should be treated as scientific questions to be resolved by the scientific methods of testing and rational public discussion. Those who advocate violent revolution are condemning to death and injury many innocent people in the hope, and it is nothing more, that things will be better afterwards. The arguments for revolution, tion, such as they are, all have an authoritarian, anti-democratic bias. I regard democracy not primarily as meaning rule by the majority but as being an institutionalised device to prevent tyranny. To stop the strong bullying the weak, and safeguarding the rights of minorities, that is what democracy should be about. Otherwise you are involved in paradoxes of the sort 'what if the majority decide they want to be ruled by a dictator' etc.

Mabe capitalist society is not the finest society that the wit and best aspirations of man can devise, but also maybe neither is a socialist one, ie, I am not ruling out a spiritual development of mankind that has nothing to do with social organisation · a communion of saints?

Yours sincerely,

David Hall
346 London Road
St Albans
Herts

OZ.

You had this fantastic two page I CANT ESCAPE MY PASSION DRIVES. Perfect very beautiful, poetic I guess and perfect then this stupid HO! HO! HO! at the bottom of the page.

I know you know and you should know I know.

It took the edge of the whole work it was like it had never been done. You don't have to give us the knowing nod you almost got the insensitivity award. XX
John & Irene

Dear Friends,

I feel I must expresss disapproval of the sadistic nature of the pictorial section of the advertisement for Magnophall in your last edition (15). Sadism is the fascism of sex and merely another variation of the violence you condemned in yoru Pornography of Violence issue (OZ 10).

I hope that OZ will not raise the same plea as Tony Elliott, editor of the pseudo-progressive magazine . . Unit . . (Whose adverts you have carried in the past), did in reply to my criticism some months ago of the inclusion in that periodical of career advertisements for notorious juggernauts of industry and commerce and even the armed forces! His reply was as follows:

"In any little magazine the bread is so vital that within reason we will accept any advertising revenue that we can. We are not in a position to refuse say £12 from the army".

So, kick this sadism thing OZ before it becomes a habit. Let's have more of the type of beautiful and incredibly endowed nymph such as formed the background to the Pellen Products advertised in OZ 9. Perhaps I'm now out of fashion in still thinking that you can't be both pro-beauty and pro-violence.

Yours sincerely,

Ian Nichol
25 Coronation Road
East Grinstead
Sussex

Dear Sir,

I have never been able to establish satisfactorily whether you lot want authority to remain or not. One article in your magazine serves to reinforce my puzzlement at the chaotic way your minds seem to run ie. "down on the Farm".

In this article we were treated to the joys of communal living and the supposedly ensuing rebirth of individualists.

This was all very good and proper but then the authors advocated 'Underground Banks', 'Trust Funds' and worst of all that omnipresent phrase 'co-ordination of efforts' in other words -

authority. If and when the new order(order see!) has been established will not these 'banks' etc reappear 'overground' to take the place of the old capitalist banks also the 'co-ordinators' will reappear as the governemnt. Back to square one!

This example of the illogicality of the whole movement to gether with this incessant scurrying around after novelty and sensual stimulation means but one thing to me decadence and not evolution as you seem to think.

Quote from the article: 'it is better to light one small candle than curse the universe for its darkness'. Well maybe the candle has been lit but it seems to me that it has been placed on the altar of negation.

I remain dear sir with hopes dashed
yours sincerely
Stephen Timothy Ruittinen

ps pelase print I'd like to see the reaction of your readers and any defense they may care to propose!

Dear OZ,

Visually, OZ 15 has been the best yet. I did find myself in disagreement with two articles, however. As far as 'Barricades around the small screen' goes, surely if you hate a television programme you don't watch it—or does

Wayland Brown think we're all Mary Whitehouses? With Richard Meltzer, you should have taken the advice you got after his first article. With the amount of information he gleans from every word of every song, our pop-song writers must be disguised university professors or something.

Tristan Wood

Roundway House
Colston's School
Stapleton
Bristol

Dear OZ,

In reference to your magazine of November, we think it was an out and out con.

So far we have enjoyed most copies of your magazine, so we would be very grateful if you would refund our money.

Luv
Linda & Jerry

Dear OZ,

In you last edition you said more visually, than you could ever have done otherwise

John Christopher Wakefield

MOTHER FUCKER

6.

 but that wasn't enough. So he retired to think & to work it all out . . . And sooner or later he came up with the correct line. He got paid a lot for going around & telling other people what they should do. But somehow the movement transcended him.

FROM THE BOOK 'UP AGAINST THE WALL MOTHERFUCKER'-LNS

Dear Sir,

What a bloody con, what a take, my precious 3/- back and if I were a subscriber I would divorce you: the chorus of rage and incomprehension that greeted Martin Sharp's 'Magic Theatre' must have gratified everyone on Oz except the accountant. For what on earth can rile that groovily pliant teddy bear, the modish end of the underground audience? Not pot, not denunciations of the Greek colonels or General De Gaulle, not flowers and titties: no matter how challenging a magazine may start out to be, it will usually end by offering 'ideas revues' to an audience which buys to see its attitudes confirmed; this is as true of Oz as of the Observer Colour Supplement or the Watchtower. Thus gentlemen you feel it right that the Times should change its editorial policy but wrong that Oz should change its format; experimenting with the magazine amounts to vivisection of your infinitely valuable leisure time; most of the soothing but tribal identification-points that crop up in a normal issue of Oz and make the readers into a happy family are missing from the 'Magic Theatre', or, more precisely, concealed by a change of medium. I find it ironical that an audience which, at parties, prides itself on being 'avant garde', should be thrown by a mode of presenting images which has been central to modern art since John Hartfield and Max Ernst developed collage fifty years ago. This is old stuff. Only its application to a magazine, in the extended form that Sharp has given it, is new : that is, new to England, in Germany and America it was tried in the 20's. What is more, I think it doubly ironical that readers who, at a guess, spend at least some of their time echoing the usual cliches about instantaneous communication across the global village, the death of the written word and the M being the M should feel such hostility towards one of the first serious, though flawed, attempts to apply the idea of

simultaneity of experience not just to a picture on a wall but to a whole magazine. If you have difficulty with Sharp's narrative collage what problems will you not have with Paolozzi's 'Moon Strips Empire News'? I suspect that the complainers are the sort of people who will parrot the belief that a wired up discotheque is an information-processing centre, while thinking that a collage is not. The reason of course, is that we have magic cliche, communications which is selectively applied: discotheques, T.V and the press communicate, but art objects do not: we have different expectations for them: they sit on the wall, look pretty and go up in value. Martin Sharp, whatever his talents as a pointer may be thought to be, is more affected by this problem than most of his contemporaries: and in a sense it is the subject of the 'Magic Theatre'. Perhaps, in the end, he will not make collages of

all but films, since this is the better medium (as the Surrealists and Dadists themselves realised) for the network of images along which one's mind travels non serially, skipping to and fro in time, that he wishes to project. But the unalterable fact is that this network could not be made with WORDS.

Since magazines are words about other words to be read in a stack of lines from left to right and back again, magazines shouldn't do Sharp's kind of work;
or should they? Why not rupture the medium to look at it? Or do the protestors imagine that spidery little cartoons about flower power are all that graphic design can do for Oz? In the 'Magic Theatre' Sharp has assembled one of the richest banks of images that has ever appeared in a magazine; and if your response to that is to say that it is therefore not a magazine at all, you should

rethink your categories. To my surprise I find myself prepared to ignore the gaucheries, the illiterate Sharp spelling, the word balloons that sometimes read as if they were written by Andre Breton's bastard child out of Grandma Moses ('A Cuba lets loose his bouquet of flowers..... upon the shoulder of a sorceress rich from heaven's feeding alights a dove', and similar bits of hippie embarassment.)
None of that will matter in a few year's time; what does matter, and makes the 'Magic Theatre' the only first class issue of Oz in the last sixteen, is that at last a magazine has broken the mould in a lyrical and decisive way. As a frequent non-reader I can promise you that the readers Oz loses through such an experiment are no loss.

Robert Hughes

WE'VE HAD HORSE POWER, GAS POWER, ATOMIC POWER,
BLACK POWER, FLOWER POWER — AND NOW, THERE'S

FlyPower

HOW DO YOU USE THIS NEWLY-DISCOVERED MICRO POWER
SOURCE? BUILD A FLY POWERED AIRPLANE!

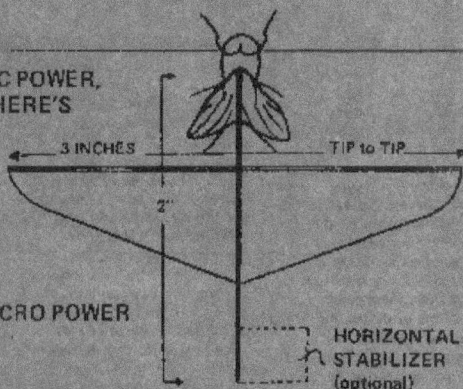

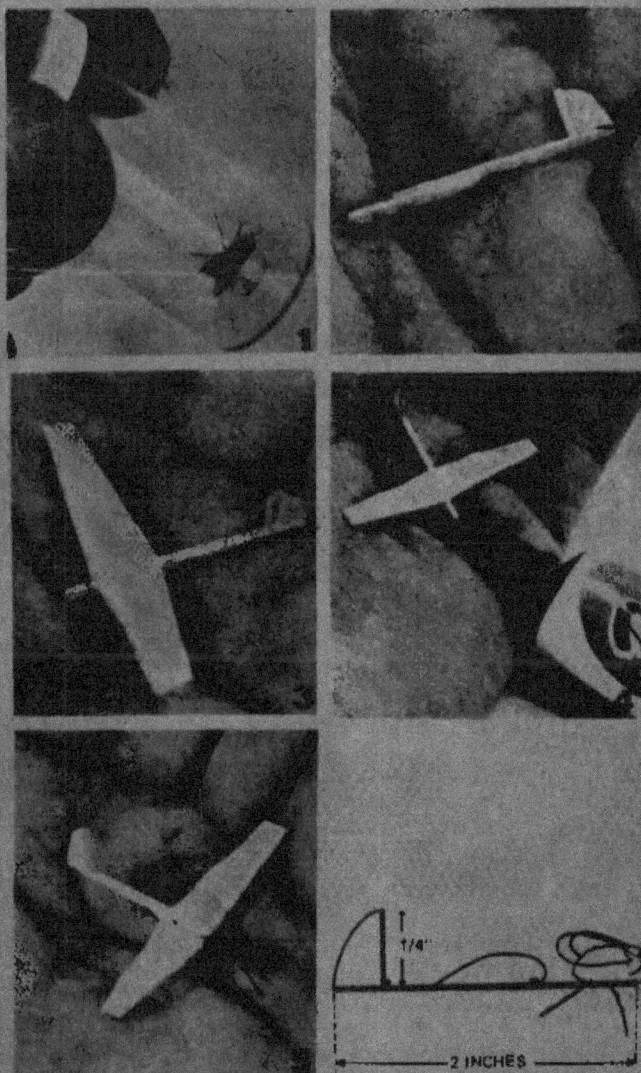

3 INCHES — TIP to TIP

2"

HORIZONTAL
STABILIZER
(optional)

AFTER YEARS of swatting, spray-
ing, etc., we've finally found a use
for the common housefly! The right
fly can become the powerplant for the
wildest, craziest gadget-glider you ever
saw. Here's how . . . .

1. First, out to the local garbage can.
With net, plastic bag or whatever,
catch the biggest, fattest, fly you can
find. Put fly into a container and place
in refrigerator to cool.

2. Get a small piece of balsa or
styrofoam strip. To this piece, glue a
tiny verticle fin, as shown.

3. Using another strip of balsa, glue a
leading edge spar to the fuselage strip.
Then get a piece of tissue (wrapping or
silk) and make a tiny airfoil wing. Glue
the front edge of the tissue to the
balsa spar. Let dry.

4. Touch a dab of Contact cement to
the front edge of the fuselage, as
shown.

5. Take fly out of refrigerator. He may
look dead, but he's just stiff from the
cold, which makes it easy to dab a tiny
bit of contact cement on his bottom
and glue him to the plane.

It takes a few seconds for the fly to
warm up and start moving. Then, after
a few unsuccessful attempts, he'll take
off, dragging the miniature plane. The
added weight will tire him quickly
and, for the first time in his short life,
he'll find he can glide! As he becomes
more expert, you get a great
demonstration of FLY POWER.

Try it . . . It's a riot!

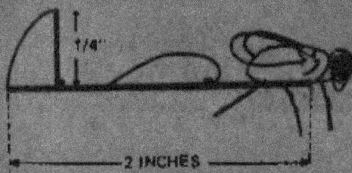

1/4"

2 INCHES

S Whitt Field

Liberation News Service

Poverty Cooking

Beggar Stew

Ingredients:

Ask the butcher, (the shabbiest shops usually sell the best meat), for a shillings worth of mutton neck.

Rob the supermarket of one large carrot and an onion—those who live near a street market or in the Covent Garden area will be able to pick up these for free—otherwise go to the local Co-op grocer. They serve so many old age pensioners with miniscule quantities of vegtables and fruit, (I once heard an elderly lady demand, and get, half a large cooking apple), that the assistant is less likely to snigger condescemingly or refuse to serve you.

Finally, you'll need one large tablespoonful of cornflour or plain flour to thicken, one oxo cube, one and a half pints of tap water, salt, pepper and mustard and a pinch of mixed herbs, (the latter not being essential but at sixpence a packet, worth their weight in cannabis).

Method

Chop up the mutton into mediumsized chunks; slice and chop onion and carrot—not too small or they will dissolve; mix up oxo into a paste with a little water in a cup, then repeat process with cornflour in a seperate cup. Boil up meat, vegetables, cornflour and oxo in the water, stirring as you do so, reducing heat until gently simmering. Add salt and pepper to taste plus a teaspoonful of mustard if you have any. Sprinkle on herbs. Simmer for at least an hour, two hours if you can wait that long.

Golden Rule

A stew boiled is a stew spoiled. Simmer *gently* and stir spasmodically.

Cracked Egg Omelette

Total cost about 9½d an omelette. Cooking time around 5 mins.

Ingredients

Get to Sainsburys early one morning and ask for half a dozen cracked eggs—they're usually sold out by the afternoon, so be warned. They'll cost between 1/3d and 1/6d a dozen.

Method

Recrack three of the eggs into a cup and whip with a half cup of milk, (optional), until creamy. Add ½ teaspoonful of salt and ¼teaspoonful of pepper. Pour this mixture into a hot frying pan which has been greased with a little marg or oil, stirring with a fork until nearly set, then fold over and slide out of pan. *Don't* leave too long—45 seconds to a minute at the outside. Some people prefer to grill the top before eating.

Omelette has countless variations:

Bacon Omelette Fry chopped up rasher of bacon in pan; remove bits with any surplus fat; cook omelette and add bacon just before folding over.

Herb Omelette Sprinkle a handful of mixed herbs into the egg before you beat up.

Potato Omelette Any left over cooked potato? Fry them quickly in an little fat as possible and then pour on usual omelette mixture. Don't try to fold over, it will be too thick.

You'll find you can put almost anything into an omelette—tomatoe, grated cheese, mushrooms, hash, onions, even marmalade or jam if you've got a sweet tooth.

Golden Rule

Speed is vital. Nothing tastes worse than burnt egg. Don't use too much grease and make sure pan is *really* hot.

The Year of the Frog

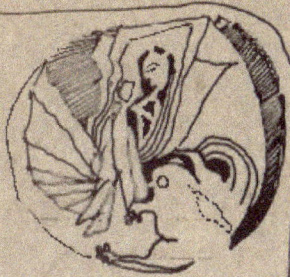

TIME OF NO SPEECH. OUR EYES COMMUNICATE.
THERE IS NO MADNESS. INTENSE IMPATIENT DESIRE
OF KNOWLEDGE. MAKE UNDERSTANDING.
THE ROAD BROADENS. THE GOAL IS THE SAME.
SPEED FREAKS US. CHANGE IS CHAOS.
CHAOS IS PLOUGHING. THE EARTH IN DELICIOUS AGONY.
CHILDREN GROW. WIDE-EYED UNAFRAID.

MOTHER I WANT TO BE WHERE I COME FROM. SING
THE BEATLES WOMEN LOSE THEIR INFANTS

FLESH FLOWER TULIPAN

CLARITY COMES IN WAVES. PEOPLE EXPAND. THEY
SHOW US. A DROP OF ESSENCE FELL ON THE
EARTH. IS SPREADING EVENLY, ALL ENCIRCLING.
ALL ONE.
SOME GO MAD SOME DON'T. ALL IS ONE
AQUASION. AQUARIUS. CLEAR AS WATER
FLOWING CRYSTAL.

I WALK INTO ONE HOUSE AND LEAVE THROUGH THE NEXT

BORN IN THE YEAR OF THE CAT

CAT STORIES PORTRAILING LIFE.
I WAS HELOISE WHO LIVED ON THE ISLAND
SHE CAME FROM EGYPT. I LIVED IN THE HOUSE ON
THE HILL. WENT TO THE PORT... ONE NIGHT IN
MY DREAM SHE WAS NO MORE. RACOON FROM
THE DESERT, THE MOUNTAINS OR ABYSSINIA
GREEN EYED SPACED, A CAT FROM THE TEMPLE
LIVES IN THE CITY, SUBTERRANEAN

I AM THE SERVANT

AND HERE AND THERE IS THE FEAR OF NOT GROWING.
NOT BEING SURE ENOUGH TO BE VISIBLE.

I AM MOTHER AND SOMETIMES I KNOW I AM ALL

SHE CAME FROM FAR AWAY AND SAID
BECAUSE I AM YOUR CHILD. IT WAS A SMALL MISTAKE
AN ERROR IN SOME EGS PART OF COSMOS
MAYBE THE WORLD IS GOING TO LOSE YOUR
SANITY. AND INSTEAD OF
NEW BEINGS, NEWBRAIN,
TO LOVE OUR NEIGHBOR. OR IS IT THAT WE DO
NOT HAVE FAST ENOUGH TO FIT INTO THE COSMIC
GEOMETRY, AND SPACE PEOPLE COME INTO THE
N WHTO
EXPE
NATURE CHANGES WITH THE PASSING
OF ICARUS, CALCULATIONS AND EXCITEMENT.

AND ICARUS PASSED ON A PEACEFUL DAY IN
JUNE. FROM SPACE IT CAME NEAR, AND THEN
THE TENSION AROUND. HE PASSED. YOKO ONO
WILL LOSE THEIR CHILDREN AFTER NEARLY
SIX MONTHS NOW. AND SUZETTE WATCHES
TELEVISION WITH US AND SAYS 'DO THE
PEOPLE KNOW THAT THERE ARE STRANGERS
ON THE EARTH?

I AM IN THE STREETS AND ON BUSES, AND IN
OFFICES, AND IN THE CROWD SUDDENLY A
FACE I KNOW SHINING AND LIGHT, WE MEET
AND MOVE TOGETHER.

DEC 5
SADNESS FOR THE GAMES WE PLAY—
WHY THE TENSIONS—
ANOTHER SOURCE OF ENERGY—

THE FROG   THE YEAR OF THE FROG.

SYMBOLISM

THEY SAY THAT THERE IS YOUR MASTER
TO CHANGE YET STILL COME BACK IN TO US
IN CYCLES, THE CHANGED THE CONFLICTS,
EVENTUALLY SOLVED CORRECTLY, AND
SO THEY PASS FROM
JAPANESE MASTERS AND VISIBLE CONTACTS
OF THE CYCLE.

JULE SACHON

John Wilcock, in India. Other Scenes.

The heart and soul of Pondicherry is the Sri Aurobindo Ashram, focal point for pilgrims not only from India but from all parts of the world. It is an unusual ashram in the sense that its buildings are spread all over the town and some of its businesses provide employment and services for other residents of Pondicherry.

It includes, for example, its own laundry, perfumery, printing press and travel agency as well as bakery, tailors, furniture factory, oil mill and handmade paper workshop.

Right on the town's major square, is a building containing the ashram's central kitchen and there each day almost everybody who wants a meal can drop by between 11.15 am and 12.30 pm and line up for a simple vegetarian lunch sitting crosslegged on the floor to eat stainless silver bowls of rice, curry, yoghurt, bread and fruit. Theoretically non-members are supposed to contribute but nobody presses for the donation.

Sri Aurobindo, born in Calcutta on Aug 15, 1872 (a Leo!) was educated at Cambridge, England, and as a writer and revolutionary became involved in the extremist wing of the Indian Independence Movement early in the century. Jailed by the British for his involvement in a bomb plot (1908) he studied yoga and meditation during his year in prison and by 1910 was in Pondicherry continuing his silent divinations and rejecting political overtures from the increasingly active independence parties.

Four years later a remarkable French woman arrived in this little French town just south of Madras on India's east coast and fell immediately under his spell. She returned to France later in the year but came back to Pondicherry in 1920, married Aurobindo and since 1926 has been in complete charge of the ashram and all its activities under the name of the Mother. Everybody connected with the ashram in any way, and many of the other people in the town, refer to her reverently in this way and in so far as any problems or doubts arise it is confidently assumed by all that 'the Mother will solve them.'

In the ashram's main building, on Rue d'Orleans, which also houses the reception center, is Sri Aurobindo's grave, always covered with flowers and surrounded by meditative disciples, and a framed portrait of both himself and the Mother, both looking about 40 years old and wearing halos. Sri Aurobindo, after a productive life of writing & inspiration, died on Dec 5, 1950; the Mother, who lives more or less in seclusion, is now 91 having been born (a Pisces!) on Feb 21, 1878.

Four times each year on Feb 21, April 24, Aug 15 and Nov 24-- the Mother appears on her balcony and gives general darshan (a sort of papal blessing)—to the assembled crowds, who come from all over the world for the occasion. The rest of the time she utters her pronouncements & preferences indirectly preferring to make her decisions on new applicants, appointments, etc., by studying photographs of would-be adherents. Theoretically ashram members are entitled to a personal audience with the Mother on their individual birthdays.

Membership in the ashram is currently about 1500, including a couple of hundred foreigners, and some of them—an Austrian hotel chef, a former soap company executive, a one-time Madison Avenue designer--were extremely successful in their earlier careers. One wealthy ex-Bostonian now occupies a remote island off the Coromandel Coast growing and processing the ashram's coconut crop. Ensconsed in the biggest of the ashram's numerous guesthouses at any given time are scores of international hippies of all ages, some wearing the gaudy regalia & beads of Haight-Ashbury, others with shoulder length hair and ankle-clinging Indian dhoti.

With the success of its experiment in international harmony assured, the Sri Aurobindo ashram began to think in more ambitious terms of an international city in which people of all races could live and work together. Such a city—Auroville (City of Dawn)--is now planned for a 10,000-acre site three or four miles northwest of Pondicherry stretching inland from the coast to three inland lakes.

On the city's master plan in the ashram's office it looks like a galaxy of stars swirling around a central plaza.

Auroville's planners talk ambitiously of such projects as monorails, moving sidewalks and closed-circuit TV channels which are hard to visualize in the context of the site's present condition: scattered patches of scrub & palm trees sprinkled across the red soil plains.

Instead of building the community's core and spreading out from there, Auroville is being constructed randomly at several points within the 15-mile perimeter, to allow maximum potential for individual effort and different ideas. Within ten years, it is hoped, people from all over the world will have added their contributions to the site including trade or display pavilions from different nations and Indian states. Many kinds of light industry and manufacturing are planned or anticipated—flour & cattle food plants, electronics, leather goods, carpets, canning factory, etc., and a university is also scheduled.

Despite these far-reaching plans for an industrial estate it is hoped to maintain 'a close harmony with nature' so that the community will also be basically rural with orchards, dairy and such crops as rice, groundnuts, mangoes, olives, grapes, dates, soybean and avocados.

The Indian newspapers have referred to the project as 'the first world city' which, when completed within ten years, will have a population of 50,000.

The principles of Auroville will be those that guide the ashram: integrated living and working together of people who seek 'a higher consciousness'. Although all are welcome, with the proviso that 'endurance & perseverance are essential,' it is felt by the community's planners that 'only those who feel they can work in a spirit of self dedication can successfully confront the inner and outer problems which will at every step appear at the personal collective level.'

But perhaps a much quoted aphorism of the Mother puts it more succinctly: 'You are richer with the wealth you give than the wealth you keep in your possession.'

17

We do everything for them...

RUPERT ANDERSON

At this moment there are 100,000 people without homes in this country; a tenth of them are wandering the streets of London now. There is really nothing more I have to say about the subject — the rest of this article is mere wordy and indignant elaboration.

There was a time — between October 1961 and August 1962 — when the problem of homelessness in British cities received a sudden gush of public articulation. The LCC which was the body which governed London before the big reorganisation of the early sixties, announced that the winter of 1961-62 was presenting them with an unprecedented and unexplained increase in the number of men and women who had nowhere to live and who were dependent on welfare accommodation for mere protection against the elements. They had somehow found beds to accommodate 3,000 people and were frightened of the consequences of a further increase. In the late fifties they had only had to worry about a thousand such unfortunates.

There was a huge public outcry at the time. It seemed incredible that at the high-point of what in those days they used to call the affluent society there could be people — 'ordinary decent people', the Times leader called them — who could not afford the price of a roof over their heads. Many of them were not poor, but had fallen victim to eviction-happy landlords, or had families too large to accommodate easily; there were women whose husbands had deserted them or gone to gaol; some of them were feckless problem-ridden people who defaulted on their rent.

In the days before the Labour Government came to power in Britain in 1964 there was a very vigorous Parliamentary opposition, eager to find something to vent its righteous indignation over. The issue of homelessness came readily to hand. Mr. Robert Mellish (later to become the minister responsible for Housing in the London area)

said it made him sick to see such suffering. The Leader of the Labour Party (a Mr. Gaitskell) went personally to visit a number of the reception centres in which those newly rendered homeless were placed. The Conservatives who know how to avoid a hiding to nothing took a responsible investigatory line; Sir Percy Rugg Conservative leader on the LCC suggested a non-party approach to the problem and stressed 'the danger of allowing the awful human problem of London's homeless families to become a football to be kicked around the political arena.' However the blame was generally held to lie with the dreaded Rent Act of 1957 which had destroyed security of tenure for hundreds of thousands of flat-dwellers and the government of the day received an unrelenting drubbing from a string of gentlemen (and not a few ladies) who today adorn the commanding heights of British official political life.

The television and press coverage was overpowering in its concern for the misery of the homeless and fearless in its determination to uncover the facts. It takes many hours, even today, to wade through the files for 1961 and 1962 marked 'homeless.' There was the family that lived in a parked car at Edmonton for six weeks. There was a woman who actually had a baby in a hurriedly-erected tent made of two broomsticks and a sheet. There was a councillor who appealed to the landlords in his area not to carry out a series of threatened evictions until Christmas was over. Encouraged by the mood of the country, tenants banded together and fought against evictions; there were several cases of tenants barricading themselves against bailiffs. The Minister of Housing Dr. Charles Hill was booed and heckled all over the country. His house was besieged by angry evictees.

The Times letter column at that period contained a number of laughable and unheeded suggestions for sudden and dramatic removal of the problem. 'Homeless may be given underground

homes.' 'Why not put them in ships?' The LCC bought a convent and put seventy families in it. They invented the mobile home and placed thousands of them on empty sites all over the metropolis.

But still the figures crept remorselessly upwards. While the fuss was at its height the LCC used to announce the figures once a month. The monthly score used to arouse the kind of fascinated anxiety that the balance of payments figures do at the present time. Just before Christmas 1961 the LCC had counted about 3000 and soon afterwards lost hope that the number would drop much below that level. But by May the following year there were 3700 and by the following Christmas 4000 seemed inexorable. But by the next winter the level reached was around the 5000 mark, and the winter after that 6000. The feverish attention paid by the new Labour Government to the housing problem in the early months had some effect; after eviction was made illegal and the new rent officer system instituted for dealing with rents, the figures actually dropped back to the 6000 level — after climbing up to 7000. There was no doubt that for a short period by running extremely hard indeed the new administration was able to stay at the same spot. But gradually, after 'Cathy Come Home' was transmitted for the second time on BBC television, the swinging dose of conscience-letting had simply reached its limit. The Shelter organisation was born and thereafter its brilliant publicity techniques added a truly professional touch to the coverage; if you look through the files for the more recent years you will find how profoundly Shelter has cast its beneficent shadow over the problem. Pragmatism has filled the aching gap in the liberal conscience; instead of bleating about the problem you can **do** something about it. The figures in London went up to the 8000 level in the winter of 1966-67 and at the end of March 1968, according to an

19

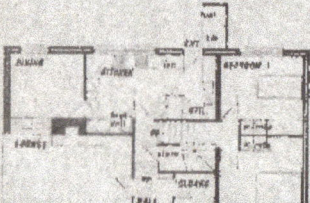

Price £8,800

Prices £6,400–£6,625 (the 971G).
Other properties cost be-
tween £5,500 and £7,825.

Price £4,875

answer given in Parliament there were over 9000 people in temporary accommodation run by local authorities after being rendered homeless. But in the last two years Shelter has provided nearly 700 (seven hundred) homes in various parts of the country for the one hundred thousand homeless people in Britain. The probability is that 'the voice of Britain's homeless' has succeeded in a couple of years of ingenious public relations in not even coping with the increase in the numbers of homeless families while completely taking the heat out of the situation politically.

Even senior members of the Labour Government have been eager to contribute publicly to the work of Shelter. Harold Wilson himself has taken part in a Shelter publicity stunt. Having heaved themselves into power with the aid of the public disgrace incurred by the homeless, they have failed to discover an administrative technique for dealing with the problem; now, without a flicker of embarrassment, they call upon the well-heeled to contribute pennies to the cause. We are not discussing the housing problem which presents an intractable challenge to civilised government in every part of the world. We are discussing the question of mere protection against wind, snow and rain for ordinary people in one of the wealthiest societies in human history. We are not talking about the provision of centrally-heated self-contained homes at economic rents; we are not talking about overcrowding or slum clearance: we are talking about working men and women who have nowhere — this evening — to lay their children to rest.

In London of course there is a significant number of problem families who cannot cope with modern life, with the sheer organisation of a family budget and the arrangement of a family routine. Even when they are housed properly they will almost inevitably bring some disaster upon themselves by not paying rent or running into hire-purchase difficulties; they need a well

organised network of social workers and perhaps — this is surely a technical question — can benefit from a period in a hostel community. But the numbers are being swelled at present with thousands of families who are quite 'normal' and are merely the victims of racial discrimination and illegal eviction. They may be large families but they are not necessarily poverty-stricken.

They could afford a fair rent. They are victims of a situation for which the whole of the rest of society is to blame.

Nonetheless, as soon as a family has reached a position of homelessness and enters into the official system which is designed to cater for their welfare, society begins to take a form of revenge upon the hapless family unit. In many parts of Britain, including much of London, a homeless family will first be forced to divest itself of all males over the age of sixteen. The women are left to cope with their children inside emergency accommodation while the men are left to fend for themselves. In the famous winter of 1961-62 there were 12000 men sleeping in London hostels who possessed no home of their own, another thousand were known to be sleeping in the open air or in railway stations and derelict houses. The number today must be astounding.

The scene in the emergency room at one London hostel recently visited provided an immediate reminder of pictures of an eighteenth century slave ship, just under a score of people in double bunks in a single room. It was a bad night. No one was particularly to blame. No one was able to cope with the deadening task. Of course there is also much hostel accommodation that is bright and cheerful, run by fully trained social workers, with space for the fathers to sleep in. But every borough runs its own system. And how can you design a system to deal with those members of society who have reached the lowest point of social wretchedness in the light of the knowledge that you

are not helping to clear up a problem but are merely contributing to a collectivity of misery that is swelling visibly before your eyes.

It is however worth pointing out some of the ways in which the social scapegoat principle works itself out on the homeless. At one London hostel the conditions of overcrowding are such that the mothers often have nowhere to store food; there are rats and mice. Often there is no hot water available for days on end. The whole atmosphere unsurprisingly is fetid. Many of the mothers keep their children cooped up the entire time inside their tiny rooms — where they have individual rooms — to prevent them catching diseases from other children. When you realise there are anything up to four score people at any time living inside this single old house, you begin to grasp how nerve-wracking the experience can be for mothers who are struggling alone with the occasional help of a visiting social worker to bring up their families without any immediate hope of rehousing. The local doctors refuse to call at the place and refuse to register patients who give the hostel as their address. The local state schools refuse to admit the children. Local employers, unsurprisingly, are unwilling to give jobs to people from the hostel. The wretchedness of homelessness feeds on itself. A woman there recently stabbed her husband and the whole family is now split up; the result of course was inevitably that her children were taken away. The state pays the cost; the expensiveness of the task of destroying these families is incalculable. The cost of hospitals, mental homes, children's homes, welfare workers and later of borstal training for the children, prisons, policework must be many times higher than the price of providing a flat.

The communications gap which exists between the scandal as news and the scandal as administrative practice continues to grow. Most people probably imagine that an improvement has

20

taken place in the situation of the homeless since the days of the really massive publicity; few realise that the old workhouses which have been used as hostels for the homeless have not been removed. The newer hostels and recently acquired welfare accommodation are employed to deal with the increase in numbers.

Take for instance the story of Newington Lodge, the borough of Southwark's hostel for the homeless, a former workhouse which now stands half-derelict in the midst of one of London's huge areas of rebuilding. Once television reporters used to cluster round the gate waylaying inmates in order to extract from them the story of their plight. Politicians used to thunder forth at public meetings in the area about the sickening iniquities which had led to the rising figures of homelessness. Enterprising reporters used to smuggle themselves into the hostel in order to bring the world the inside story of misery, frustration and despair. 12 January 1962 (Guardian) 'The LCC is however determined to go ahead with its plans to close Newington Lodge and all the other homeless family units in the old institutions from which husbands have had to be excluded.' 2 May 1962 (Guardian) 'One result of the increase in the number of families for which the LCC is having to provide shelter is that it has proved impossible to abide by the decision to close the criticised emergency accommodation in the old institution premises such as Newington Lodge in Southwark.' 31 August 1963 (Guardian) 'The LCC is still trying to close its unloved institution of Newington Lodge . . . it is hoped to have ready by October a new reception centre.' 10 July 1964 (Guardian) 'Hopes of finally closing Newington Lodge, Southwark, as a reception centre for homeless families have been defeated.' March 1965 'Southwark, asked by other neighbouring boroughs for more time before demolition can begin have refused to grant a reprieve.

Newington Lodge has been scheduled for demolition for a considerable time. In any case it is not in accord with modern standards.'

It is hardly necessary to complete the story. 'The Lodge' is still used to house the homeless of Southwark – or some of them. Most of its inhabitants are people who have been evicted for non-payment of rent. They are split families, the fathers still being refused admission to the hostel. 'Of course, we are trying hard to close the place down.' the warden will tell you. The women are not given facilities for cooking for themselves. 'We do everything for them' the hard-pressed hostel staff will explain.

The story of the homeless is the tip only of an iceberg of resentment and frustration, that lies thinly concealed under a coating of pragmatic concern and attention. Liberal pragmatism and middle class charity can be seen to be not poles apart; they are allies in a sense. They have a great deal in common, in particular, the way they enclose a problem and shut it off from real public attention. They absorb indignation into helpfulness. They are the lightning conductors for guilt and hopelessness alike. They surround a problem with a cottonwool of needless complexity, and at the same time of spurious professionalism.

But above all they separate giver from receiver, helper from helped, agitators from deprived. The homeless are placed upon a kind of pedestal in the advertising columns rather than the news pages. The enlightened are supposed to worship and dignify them leper-like with gifts, and the result is that they are separated utterly from our understanding. The homeless are not different from the housed; they have merely become victims of the system one way rather than another. The homeless are not available to be coped with. It is their indignation not yours which really matters.

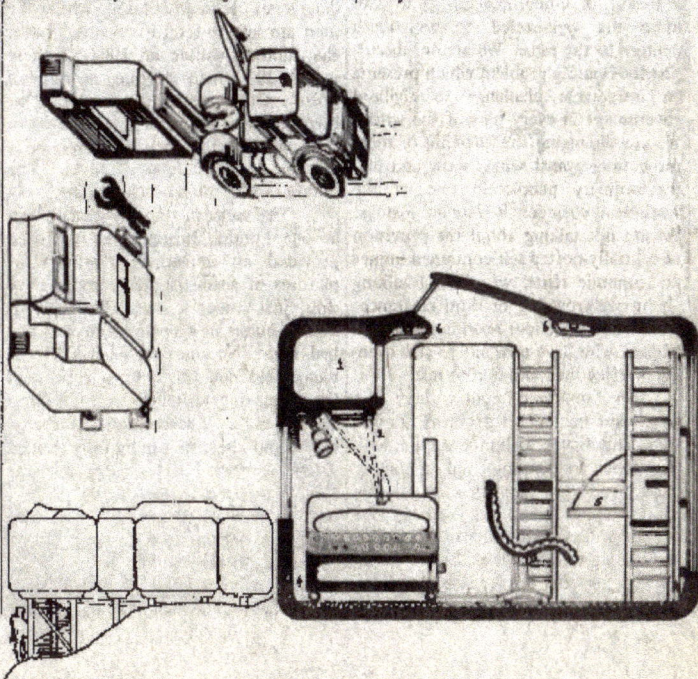

Smalls

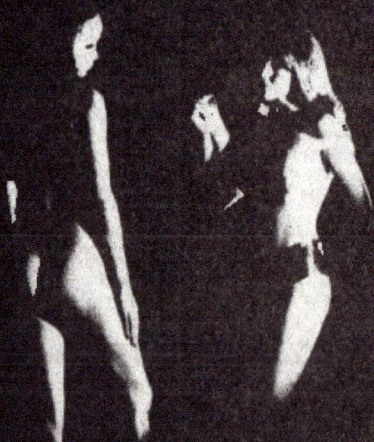

hip ocrates

'Dear Dr Schoenfeld:

A couple of weeks ago my girlfriend and I got loaded and were making love. She told me that she wanted to show me something new that would be a real thrill to me. She said that one of her old boyfriends like to have her to do it to him often, so without knowing what it was, I agreed to let her try it.

What she did was to stretch my scrotum out tightly, then she took a pair of finger nail clippers and cut a small hole in the sac. I began to get scared then but she said not to worry, it was fun and didn't hurt much. Next she stuck a small plastic straw into the hole in my sac and started blowing air into it.

My sac got bigger than a baseball, but surprisingly it didn't hurt much and felt kind of good. I began to worry that it might burst so she stopped blowing and removed the straw. Then she quickly put a piece of adhesive tape over the hole to keep the air in. Then we continued with intercourse and I had a climax that was out of this world.

Afterwards she removed the tape from my scrotum and squeezed the air out of with her hand. Then she dabbed my scrotum with rubbing alcohol (to prevent infection she said) and retaped the hole. When she put the alcohol on it burned like hell. The next day my penis was swollen to about double its normal size and it itched like hell, but two days later it was OK again. What I want to know is could this practice cause me any harm? And what caused my penis to swell the next day?'

Dear Dr Schoenfeld:

My girl friend was experimenting and blew a large quantity of air into my urethra. Well, she says it feels great to her to feel that balloon strike bottom. I do get a thrill from it, albeit a masochistic one because, God, it hurts. Can this form of fun in any way injure me?

Write soon, cause I don't want to stop unless it might really hurt me.'

ANSWER: I hesitated for a long time before deciding to print the above letters about very literal 'blow' jobbs. They appear in print only to point out that pleasurable sensations should be weighed against potential dangers.

To use drugs as an example, shooting (amphetamine) undoubtedly gives great immediate pleasure, but at the potential price of hepatitis, thromboph-lebitis, detrioration of the personality and sudden death through overdosage. Heroin users quickly become heroin addicts. Nineteen known deaths have been caused in the last year by inhalation of freon gases from glass chiller aerosol cans.

If any readers doubt that the practices mentioned in the letters above are harmful, I should point out firstly that more bacteria exist in the mouth than in any other body orifice. Our skin is a natural barrier to bacteria and other microorganisms which are not normally found in the bladder or scrotum. Infections of the bladder (cystitis may continue up the urethra to the kidneys). Infections of the scrotum? Not a pleasant prospect. Even more dangerous is the possibility of an air embolism. Air forced into a closed tissue space may enter the blood stream, go the heart, lungs or brain and cause sudden death or a stroke.

QUESTION: I have a 'condition' which seems to worry my husband more than myself. Ever since my teens my inner or minor vaginal lips have hung outside my major lips.

Because they are not neatly within the major lips my husband believes this could indicate some disorder. What do you think?

ANSWER: There is nothing abnormal about the labia minora protruding through the labia majora. Why some of my best friends . . .

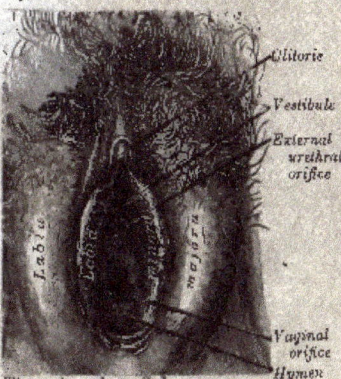

The external genital organs
The labia have been drawn apart.

Clitoris
Vestibule
External urethral orifice
Labia
Vaginal orifice
Hymen

QUESTION: Please don't laugh. I'm serious! My boyfriend has a perpetual hard-on. He is 23 and I've never met anyone like him.

It's absolutely amazing. We make love he ejaculates and still pulls out with a hard-on and wants to start all over again, leaving no time in between.

He could do this all night, if it weren't for my getting sore. It bothers me because I recall reading sometime ago about a physical ailment causing a perpetual hard-on. I also recall it supposedly causes great pain to the male, not to mention the soreness it can cause the female.

ANSWER: Priapism, an abnormal state of continuous erection of the penis, can be caused by several diseases or by trauma to the spinal cord. The condition is commonly observed when a man is hung (literally—not as described in underground classified ads).

One of Balzac's Ribald Tales concerns a woman who brings a hanged man back to life through an unusual method of resuscitation.

But your boyfriend is not diseased—you just turn him on. The use of a lubricant may prevent or relieve soreness.

QUESTION: In the showers I notice all very fat men have a penis barely an inch long. Why?

ANSWER: An aroused (angered) colleague stoutly maintains this is a false observation, caused, no doubt by lack of familiarity with obese people. Increased fat tissue covering the base of the penis accounts for this belief. Have you ever read about Fatty Arbuckle.

QUESTION: Could you please explain what inverted nipples are and what, if anything, is the cure?

ANSWER: Inverted nipples turn in rather than out. The condition is rather common and should cause no concern unless it occurs after puberty. Pregnancy may cause them to evert.

I've also seen a picture of a suction device used to evert the nipples similar to those used to stimulate the flow of breast milk. Some gynecologists suggest having a close friend suck inverted nipples at least once daily to cause eversion. Find someone trying to kick cigarette addiction.

Dr Schoenfeld welcomes your questions. Write to him at PO Box 9002, Berkeley, California. Mark your letter: OZ.

23

HOMOSEXUAL BOERS

Bill

To amend the Immorality Act, 1957, to make punishable the possession or custody of any article which is intended to be used to give sexual satisfaction to a female in an unnatural manner; to make punishable the commission of sexual acts between persons of the same sex; and to repeal section 10 of Act No. 22 of 1898 of Natal;

BE IT ENACTED by the State President, the Senate and the House of Assembly of the Republic of South Africa, as follows:—

1. The following section is hereby inserted in the Immorality Act, 1957 (hereinafter referred to as the principal Act), after section 18:

"Possession or custody of any article which is intended to be used to give sexual satisfaction to a female in an unnatural manner.

18A. Any person who has in his possession or custody any article other than a contraceptive which is intended to be used to give sexual satisfaction to a female in an unnatural manner, shall be guilty of an offence.".

2. The following section is hereby inserted in the principal Act after section 20:

"Sexual offences between persons of the same sex.

20A. (1) A male person who commits any immoral, indecent or unnatural act with another male person or a female person who commits any such act with another female person shall be guilty of an offence.

(2) In the application of the provisions of subsection (1) 'unnatural act' includes any act committed by a male person with another male person or by a female person with another female person and calculated to stimulate sexual passion or to give sexual satisfaction."

3. Section 22 of the principal Act is hereby amended by the substitution for paragraph (a) of the following paragraph:

"(a) in the case of an offence referred to in section 2, 18A, [or] 20 (1) (a) or 20A (1), to imprisonment for a period not exceeding three years with or without a fine not exceeding six hundred rand in addition to such imprisonment, or where it is proved that the person convicted kept a brothel and that unlawful carnal intercourse took place in such brothel to his knowledge between a white female and a coloured male or between a coloured female and a white male, for a period not exceeding seven years with or without a fine not exceeding one thousand rand in addition to such imprisonment;".

4. Section 10 of the Act "To amend the law relative to the trial and punishment of the Crimes of Rape and Indecent Assault and Conduct" (Act No. 22 of 1898 (Natal)) is hereby repealed.

5. This Act shall be called the Immorality Amendment Act, 1968.

The Charges

Lawrence Gandar and Benjamin Pogrund—Editor-in-chief and a reporter of the Rand Daily Mail, Johannesburg—are charged with two counts of contravening Section 44 (1) of the Prisons Act; publishing false information concerning prisons, without taking reasonable steps to verify the information.

One of the allegations made in the article on prison conditions published in the Rand Daily Mail, was that homosexuality was rife in prisons and that officials turned a blind eye to it. The state is eager to refute this as a draft law against homosexuality is going through parliament but has not yet been passed. State witness after state witness denied knowledge of widespread acts of homosexuality, besides giving evidence on other aspects of prison conditions. Evidence was given under the protection of a ruling that witnesses remain unidentified in newspaper reports.

The surprise in the trial's third week was that the judge allowed newspapers to publish the name of former convict Harold John Goodwin. This came after the defence submitted that Goodwin was 'well known, not to say notorious'. Goodwin, who is known throughout South Africa as 'babyface', testified twice during the week's hearing.

His evidence raised the question of whether homosexuality was practised in Pretoria jail. He denied it was rife but under cross-examination admitted being connected with a club since his release which the defence claims was for homosexuals.

He said he was employed as a secretary of a club. Asked what type of people were members of the club, he said it was a matter of opinion and he was 'not prepared to state an opinion'. It was a mixed membership of men and women. Mr Kentridge for the defence said a Major van Zyl of the CID had put in an official memorandum on behalf of the South African Police to the Parliamentary Select Committee investigating the matter of homosexuality.

Goodwin said he had not given evidence before this Select Committee and had not submitted a memorandum although he had sent a letter to the Minister of Justice. He was not prepared to reveal the contents of this letter. It did concern his club.

'Let's not beat about the bush. Was your club for homosexuals?' 'I will neither confirm or deny that.'

He agreed that men sometimes danced together at the club, but said he had no personal knowledge of their private lives.

'You consider it ordinary for men to dance together in a club?'—That is a matter of opinion.'

Questioned about his earlier evidence that he had never heard jokes about homosexuality between prisoners and warders, Mr Goodwin said he had heard jokes occasionally among prisoners, no more or less than outside prison'.

He denied that homosexuality was rife in prison.

Mr Kentridge said that a prisoner called earlier by the state had given evidence that Mr Goodwin was notorious in the prison for having homosexual tendencies.

Immorality Amendment Act

Early in 1968, the South African Government drafted an amendment to the Immorality Act of 1957 making punishable the possession or custody of any article which is intended to be used to give sexual satisfaction to a female in an unnatural manner; to make punishable the commission of sexual acts between persons of the same sex.

In other words male and female homosexuality is to be outlawed and punishable by law. Not only will it increase drastically the penalities for the offence, but it will make lesbianism an offence for the first time.

The Government itself is not entirely happy about the Bill, or about the right-wing behind it. This knowledge and fear of the consequence of the Bill has encouraged the homosexual community to brief lawyers to present their case to the Parliamentary Select Committee studying the Bill.

Club Charade

It so happens that 'babyface' Goodwin is the secretary of a club in Johannesburg called Charade.

On the 22nd February 1968 he wrote a letter to The Minister of Justice. I quote from a photostat copy of the letter:

'Dear Sir,

I am the secretary of a club which is limited exclusively to adults with homosexual or lesbian tendencies.'

He goes on to express the fears of his members and their willingness to make their views known to the Select Committee, and ends the letter by assuring the Minister of his co-operation at all times.

I quote the last paragraph from the Minister's private secretary in reply to Goodwin.

'The Minister also desires me to assure you that your society need not have the slightest fear of being branded or 'listed' as you call

You can draw your own conclusions as to why 'Babyface' Goodwin subsequently turned state witness and lied in the witness box.

DAVID RAMSAY STEELE
Sma$E Ca$E

Abolition of Money! Down through the ages this wild and visionary slogan has been whispered by a subversive few. Ever since human beings discovered cash, they have hated it and tried to rid themselves of it — whilst their own actions have kept it alive. In this respect, money is like syphilis.

Today the whisper has become a shout — though still the shout of a tiny minority. Tomorrow it will be the roar of the crowd, the major topic of discussion in every pub and coffee house, factory and office.

The abolition of money is an ancient dream, the most radical demand of every social revolution for centuries past. We must not suppose that it is therefore destined to remain a Utopia, that the wheel will simply turn full circle once more. Today there is an entirely new element in the situation: Plenty.

All previous societies have been rationed societies, based on scarcity of food, clothing and shelter. The modern world is also a society of scarcity, but with a difference. Today's shortages are unnecessary; today's scarcity is artificial. More than that: scarcity achieved at the expense of strenuous effort, ingenious organization and the most sophisticated planning.

The world is haunted by a spectre — the spectre of Abundance. Only by planned waste and destruction on a colossal scale can the terrifying threat of Plenty be averted.

Money means rationing. It is only useful when there are shortages to be rationed. No one can buy or sell air: it's free because there is plenty of it around. Food, clothing, shelter and entertainment should be free as air. But the means of rationing scarcity themselves keep the scarcity in existence. The only excuse for money is that there is not enough wealth to go round — but it is the money system which makes sure there cannot be enough to go round. By abolishing money we create the conditions where money is unnecessary.

If we made a list of all those occupations which would be unnecessary in a Moneyless World, jobs people now have to do which are entirely useless from a human point of view, we might begin as follows: Customs officer, Security guard, Locksmith, Wages clerk, Tax assessor, Advertising man, Stockbroker, Insurance agent, Ticket puncher, Salesman, Accountant, Slot machine emptier, Industrial spy, Bank manager, before we realized the magnitude of what was involved. And these are merely the jobs which are wholly and utterly useless. Nearly all occupations involve something to do with costing or selling. Now we should see that the phrase "Abolition of Money" is just shorthand for immense, sweeping, root and branch changes in society. The abolition of money means the abolition of wages and profits, nations and frontiers, rich and poor, armies and prisons. It means that all work will be entirely voluntary.

Of course, the itemizing of those jobs which are financial does not end the catalogue of waste. Apart from astronomical sums spent on the Space Race, and the well-known scandal of huge arms production, we have to realise that all production is carried on purely for profit. The profit motive often runs completely counter to human need. "Built-in obsolescence" (planned shoddiness), the restrictive effects of the patents system, the waste of effort through duplication of activities by competing firms or nations — these are just a few of the ways in which profits cause waste.

What this amounts to is that ninety per cent (a conservative estimate) of effort expended by human beings today is entirely pointless, does not the slightest bit of good to anybody. So it is quite ridiculous to talk about "how to make sure people work if they're not paid for it." If less than ten per cent of the population worked, and the other ninety per cent stayed at home watching telly, we'd be no worse off than we are now.

But there would be no need for them to watch telly all the time, because without the profit system work could be made enjoyable. Playing tennis, writing poems or climbing mountains are not essentially any more enjoyable than building houses, growing food or programming computers. The only reason we think of some things as "leisure" and others as "work" is because we get used to doing some things because we want to and others because we have to. Prostitutes despise love. We are all prostitutes. In a Moneyless World work would be recreation and art. That work which is unavoidably unhealthy or unpleasant, such as coalmining, would be automated immediately. Needless to say, the only reason these things aren't done by machines at present is because it is considered more important to lower the costs of the employer than to lower the unhappiness of his slaves.

The money system is obsolete and antihuman. So what should we do about it? In years to come, with the increasing education and increasing misery of

modern life, together with growing squalor in the midst of growing plenty, we can expect the Abolition of Money to be treated more and more as a serious issue, to be inserted into more and more heads. The great mass of individuals will first ridicule, then dare to imagine (Fantasy is the first act of rebellion Freud), then overthrow.

In the meantime, as well as propagating the notion of a Moneyless World, those of us who see its necessity have a responsibility to sort our own ideas out, in order that we may present an intelligible and principled case. We must stop thinking of the Moneyless World as an "ultimate aim" with no effect upon our actions now. We must realise that the Abolition of Money is THE immediate demand. A practical proposition and an urgent necessity — not something to be vaguely "worked towards."

Unfortunately those who want the Moneyless World frequently wade in a mire of mystification. Above all it is necessary to understand the workings of this society, capitalist society (Moscow, Washington and Peking are all in the same boat) if we are to know how to destroy it.

For example there is a commonly held view that Automation is going to settle all our worries, that money will expire automatically as part of a "natural process of evolution." This is quite wrong. As pointed out above, this society only automates to increase profits and for no other reason. Employers even take machines out and put workers back in — if they find that labour-power is cheaper. Any gain from automation these days is more than cancelled out by the waste explosion. Do not imagine that the slight increases in living standards of the last twenty years are the beginning of a smooth transition to Abundance. Another huge world slump is approaching.

A different illusion, also popular, is that cash can be abolished by example, by opening giveaway shops or by starting small moneyless communities which are parasitical upon the main body of society. These experiments accomplish little. Those people, for instance, who open stores to give and receive books without payment, face a predictable result: a large stock of lousy books.

These projects stem partly from a belief that we need to prove something. Relax. We don't need to prove anything.

The defenders of this insane society, it is they who stand accused, they who have to supply the arguments — arguments for poverty and enslavement in a world of Plethora!

All theoretical constructions which relate to wages, prices, profits and taxes are ghosts from the past, as absurdly outdated as the quibbles about how many angels could dance on the point of a needle. "Incomes policy" is irrelevant — we want the abolition of incomes. "Fighting crime" is irrelevant - we want the abolition of the law. "Workers' control" is irrelevant — we want the abolition of "workers." "Black Power" is irrelevant — we want the abolition of power over people. "The national interest" is irrelevant — we want the abolition of nations.

And let no one raise the banal cry: what are you going to put in their place? As though we would say to a research scientist: "And when you've cured Cancer, what are you going to put in its place?"

Then there is the myth of the small-scale. We cannot go back to being peasants and we should not want to. Keeping several thousand million people alive on this planet necessitates railways, oil wells, steel mills. Only by intricate organization and large-scale productive techniques can we maintain our Abundance. Do not be afraid of machines. It is not machines which enslave, but Capital, in whose service machines are employed. McLuhan represents the beginning of the New Consciousness of man-made artifacts. Computers are warm and cuddly creatures. We will have a beautiful time with them.

Many of the worst errors which retard the development of the New Consciousness, the Consciousness of Plenty, are to be found in Herbert Lomas' piece on "The Workless Society" in International Times/43. This at least has the merit that someone is putting forward a case for the removal of money in specific terms. Unfortunately, they are specific non-starters.

According to Herbert Lomas, a political party is to be formed which will take power and proceed as follows. Useless workers in industry will gradually be laid off and paid for not working. The process will be extended until money can be abolished. In the meantime, those being paid for doing nothing will do what they like. To begin

with many of them might play Bingo; eventually more and more would aim at higher things.

What is wrong with this projection? Many things, but chiefly two. First, it fails to take account of the systematic nature of society. Second, it assumes that present-day society exhibits a harmony of interests.

In the first place, Lomas says: "Why are these people working? They are not working for the sake of production, for the truth is that if they were removed production could be increased beyond measure." He concludes that they are working because of their attitudes, the attitudes of their employers, the attitudes of the rest of society. But the fact of the matter is that these workers are working for the sake of production

not the production of goods but the production of profits. The reason why things are "made with great ingenuity to wear out" is not because of the attitudes of the people involved. The management may think it's criminal but they are paid to organize things so as to optimize profits. If they produced razor blades to last for centuries, the firm would go broke. It is not the attitudes which are crucial, but economic interests. If a teetotaller owns shares in a brewery, it does not make the booze less potent.

Which brings us to the second point. Today's world is a jungle of conflicting vested interests. The Abolition of Money will represent the liberation of slaves, yes — but also the dispossession of masters, i.e., the employing class. We cannot view the government as an impartial panel which looks after the best interests of everybody; it is an instrument used by one set of people to oppress another.

On one point Herbert Lomas is correct. The movement for the Abolition of Money must be political, because when we destroy money we destroy the basis of the power of our rulers. They are unlikely to take kindly to this, so we must organize politically to remove them.

For the moment though, what is needed is more discussion and greater understanding. We must be confident that the movement will grow. We must think, argue, and think again — but never lose consciousness of that one, simple, astounding fact: Plenty is here. The Moneyless World is not an ultimate millenium. We need it now.

'The England I know and the England I love is an England of constant change and constant movement of peoples, a proud amorous mongrel race intense and stubborn yet with this wonderful sense of amusement' Ray Gosling's Sum Total.

There is an England undiscovered, its people are violently sarcastic, drink tea and are not all that young now. They grew up in a world of chip shops, library books being overdue, racing bicycle clips, Journey Into Space and tend to look like characters out of Giles cartoons. They grew up in the Fifties and based themselves more on Hancock's Half Hour than the Goon Show; they knew how to hitch and attempt petty crime and from the third form in grammar school it was more or less a race to get expelled and get out to the serious business of buying a motorbike and a girl. I could never see how these people could stomach the Underground, it was precious and they were cynical, it was pretty and they were ugly in an English way, it was American or Australian and they were British, it was exhibitionist and prone to delerium and they were stoic and ran a mile if they thought someone was putting it on.

Occasionally there are explanations of how the two could meet. Ray Gosling, then billed as the talking teenager, wrote one in 1962 called Sum Total. Jeff Nuttall wrote another in 1968. It's called Bomb Culture, and is a quite brilliant social history of this decade. It starts in the pre CND wonderland of the first of David Mercer's plays, of George Melly and Trad before The Observer-and-this-evenings-Art-Critic, that magic time when Alistair McIntyre was still a Trotskyist, when John Berger wrote for the New Statesman, and Cyril Davies and not John Mayall was the father of British Blues. Nuttall stays outside the Underground's mental bathysphere and the awesomely photogenic world of the hippies; he senses this is bourgeois romanticism and serves mainly as a way out of the nastyness of bourgeois utility. Behind the flowers he partially glimpses the hardeyed disinterest and glare of suspicion of the underground, a anatomised 'ritual' characteristic sensibility by Roy Durgnat in an IT centre page spread for which he was subsequently attacked by some underground shaman-moralist for having hangups. Nuttall is suspicious of the limitations of drugs and rejects those who call for reunion with the cosmic: 'I would suggest that not only is this alienation from the cosmos the condition we call human but that such a separation is a vital element in the cosmic pattern, that map is naturally un-natural and that this is an absolute enrichment rather than a psychic tragedy'. The ego, which gets such a bad press these days, is rightly seen as the core of man's strivings and the turning away from Nothing. Nuttall remains compassionate but superior to the majority of the underground and is best of all when talking about CND meetings, American pop and nylons, getting bored up in Finchley (our author has a sizable alcohol habit which is reassuring), the Vicar of St. Martins in the Fields, trad jazz clubs near North Line Tube Stations, and the Young Communist League before it went pop.

Its reviewers have been interesting. Those who know the terrain have gone overboard. Peter Fryer, one of the best of those who left the Communist Party over Hungary, wrote at the end of his piece his terrible need to be a friend of Nuttall's. Dennis Potter, at 33 a bedridden veteran of CND, Oxford and the BBC, reviewed Bomb Culture with a sense of agonising recognition which was almost beyond words. The critical wide boys, noticeable A. Alvarez in the Sunday Beast whose cleverness is in fact mostly belligerence, hammered the book. From the academic-critical greasy pole, even for a critic who has annexed 'extremism' as his analytic territory, Nuttall is too frantic, too painful, not well enough adjusted to the insanity of the present. Lowell and Plath are allowed close to the edge, they are after all Americans, Nuttall's hangups are not permitted.

For those of us who are still angry, Nuttall's gut wrenchings will make perfect sense. There are not two things; how society is organised, how people are conscious and respond to this organisation. The relation of beliefs to action is not external and contingent, but internal and conceptual. What is happening in Vietnam does change the way we use words; the way we use words has an effect on ourselves. In many ways the trough between the end of CND's fruitless non conformity and the beginning of VSC, between post Hiroshima and Vietnam, between Hungary '56 and Paris '68 was a period of being stranded in the unbearable, especially politically.

Looking back on it how it would seem that it took craziness—illness, a political extremism—to get through it and see through it.

The nuttyness of Morgan and Joe Orton's plays, the nudging self awareness of the New British Movie, the metropolitan smugness of Swinging London, these responses differed only in the degree of self-deceit. Hopefully the events of 1968 signal a new future, something more than the brisk merchandising of '63-'67, perhaps we can put the pillow over the cage of pop and get on to something that really matters.

This is, I think, the sense of what writers like David Mercer, Dennis Potter, Adrian Mitchell are about and all of who's work is very specific about the perils of that period and the values of a therapeutic lunacy. Nuttall's conclusions hover, as the book, between tough-sentimental hero and poetic juvenile delinquent; the one headmasterly, the other half barmy with phallic energy. He seems doomed to be saying 'lets at last get down to business' the main message of his My Own Mag editorials and post Trafalgar Square oration letters to Anarchy. But one is followed by the suspicion that, to use Nuttall's own words: 'the most hot blooded insurrectionists hold their role of opposition to a thoroughly secure establishment more important than the overthrow of that establishment'. For much as the idea of revolution in

28

general compells him, any attempt to organise politically is seen as comic opera Leninism (which of course it sometimes is). He quotes a caricature of a Stalinist from Lessing's Golden Notebook as if that proves it. Instead he prefers the garbled halls of verbal anarchism, particularly the tiny Chicago group around Bernard Marzalek and their paler versions in this country, Cuddon's Cosmopolitan Review and Heatwave (now joined by King Mob Echo, the organ of soon-to-be-fashionable-Situationalism). All these groups enjoy a good deal of violence-in-the-head and revolutionary bop prosody and find political or economic theory not worth bothering with; its Wifey who runs American and the telly; beer and mental homes which keep us anaethetised.

The same enthusiasm for apocalyptic rhetoric without any of the dangers attendant to revolutionary committment is visable in the ludicrous over-priase for Maller's last two reports by precisely the people who could'nt see a word of what 'The America Dream' was about. Clive James writing in OZ 14 finds it fairly easy to mock this sort of language politics. He advances the familiar proposition that all revolutions lead to new tyrannies, that these days things are simply too complex anyway and anyway it might upset the bourgeoisie 'the custodian of civilisation in Europe'. Instead he offers hippy fabianism, 'the only way to fight City Hall is by providing an alternative mode of existence and keep it running long enough for the industrial complex to become humanised by penetration and example', in the mean time the Academy will remain the Keeper of the true standard of the 'one literature'. In fact his political condescension is largely misplaced because although hippies don't take a very acute interest in political theory there are many who do, of whom Mr. James, if his citation of Hannah Arendt as a political authority is anything to go by, is likely to be largely ignorant.

As for the 'one literature', it is precisely a conscious rejection of revolutionary politics in one stem of English literary criticism (see Leavis's Scrutiny, a Retrospect) which has produced this exaggerated concern for Cambridge and specifically the English Tripos as the supreme valdiction of literature and human culture. For all the academic muscle bending, boyos and surfing prose and premonitions of social disintegration, James eventually argues himself into a remarkably poky little corner: revolutionary politics are boneheaded because boneheads sometimes talk about them, hippies should grow up, art is forever. James is certainly right to be appalled at the cultural landscape of rank mediocrity, he is wrong to see it as the necessary product of industrialism or those identified as the underground when it is rather the specific result of the nature of British society and the class that dominates it.

What is in fact happening is the convergence of a dissident and political intelligensia with a mass and rebellious youth movement. The previous emmergence of such a genuinely subversive intellectual movement were fin-de-sieacle Bohemianism and, between wars, Stalinism. The 1890s of Beardsley, Wilde and McKintosh ended in Boer War jingoism; it remains the souce of most of the visual plunderings of the underground. The Red Thirties scarcely existed and the swift repatriation of most if its intellectuals to bourgeois society after the Molotov-Ribbentropp Pact demonstrates this, but the Foreign Languages Publishing House prose is still perfectly intact in the arthritic language of Black Dwarf editorials and VSC speakers.

What happened in the era between the end of CND and the beginning of what can be called with justice, the period of revolutionary politics, was the emmergence of both bohemians and revolutionaries alongside. The kind of foklorique anarchism of the underground's politics is an essential stage just as Narodnikism was prior to Bolshevism. 'Where there is revolution there is anarchy, the first stirring, the first cry, the first position before organisation begins. We must greet and welcome anarchy.

'It is not the sword of revolution only its herald. But the herald performs a genuine service,' Peter Sedgwick. This is the meaning of the history Nuttall witnesses; 'The path that leads from moral reasoning to political action is strewn with our dead selves,' Andre Malraux.

David Widgery

1   We demand, full employment for all black people living in the
    United Kingdom.

    We know that black people are being discriminated against in
    employment, and are relegated to jobs that the white man no longer
    wants to do, even though they are well qualified for better jobs.

2   We demand, better housing conditions for all black people and a
    voice in the reallocation of houses for our people.

    We know that white landlords are not giving us housing
    accommodation fit for human beings.

3   We demand an end to police brutality and the persecution of our
    leaders.

    We know that Brothers Michael, Obi, Gideon and Peter Martin,
    have been imprisoned because they dared to speak out for freedom.

4   We demand freedom for all black people in prison.

    We know that our Brothers have not been given fair trials because
    of the very nature of the jury system.

5   We demand that all black people be tried by their own Peer Group
    as is written in the Magna Carta.

    We know that white jury men and women are ignorant of the varous
    dialects of the black people in this country. How could a black man
    have a fair trial if the members of the jury cannot understand his
    means of expression?

6   We demand education for our people that exposes the true nature
    of this racist society.

    We demand education that teachers us our true role in the present
    day society. We know that this educational system is detrimental to
    the free growth of our black children and impedes the creation
    of the new Black Man.

LONG LIVE THE EAGLES!

Ho! Ho! Ho Chi Mall

The gospel according to Ho Chi Mall

Onceuponatime, an outfit called the Institute of Contemporary Arts carried on its smallscale, select, thoughtful operations on a first floor in Dover Street. Its gallery was its lecture room was its bar. Some said it was cliquish, and it did have its own wavelength, but it was a neat, economical, functional format. It was nicely balanced between a Surrealist inheritance and high-powered intellectuality, it was openmindedly eclectic yet selfrespectingly selective. It dealt in new directions and in what was good of its kind.

What policy one wondered, could back the choice of new Mall premises, where no exhibition can cover its costs unless the visitors come pouring in like the rushhour in the tube? It's now apparent The ICA has set itself to appeal to (1) any foundation which will respond to the snob appeal of its past reputation and its new address, like the Arts Council, or Sidney Bernstein, or the Gulbenkian Foundation, or Apple, and (2) the box-office, with a vengeance. It's pop or bust.

For such a strategy the time seems ripe. A new public is appearing. Old brow-barriers are crumbling. All the mini-skirted secretaries and discotheque dollies have learnt to limbo to Vivaldi from UFO and from echochamber soundprocessing to hear structureless sound for its own sake.

So appetising is the grab-allcomers theory that an old showbusiness axiom warns against it. Choose your public, and write for it. Don't try and sit on seven stools at once. You can't be, simultaneously, Queen and Petticoat. If you're eclectic you'll appeal only to eclectics, and there may not be many of them. Of course, an axiom is only a rule of thumb. Overlap areas exist. *The Obsessive Image* romped around in one.

Pitfalls there are, when you try and be a Royal Pop Academy, Tate-cum-hep-Tate-cum-art -discotheque-laboratory. With such a massive rent wrapped like a millstone round your neck it's not so easy to swim between Scylla the love-all, grab-all nonselectivity of the trendhound – and Charybdis – the slack, lowest-common-denominator imbecility exemplified by the Apollinaire production.

Apollinaire. Ah – la belle epoque. Ah, la vie de boheme. Ah, les filles des bordels. Ah, le Douanier Rousseau, ze divine innocent, ze – 'ow you call 'eem?

– peasant Gulley Jimson, no? In Truffaut's Jules et Jim film Jim tells Jules the story of Apollinaire, so the ICA production has Guillaume the spitting image of Jim. With a Strangelove arm. Homage to Truffaut, to Kubrick? No, secondhand, thinking, Banalities. The play is as full of fashionable cliches as of fashionable spades.

What made Apollinaire go establishment? His headwound. Why was he The Outsider? Being a foreign born Jew. Why should we identify with him? Because he was so vulnerable to women and yet full of sexy joie de vivre. What was the Wound in His Soul? All Women Were His Mother, a Haughty Blonde. And when he goes for a jaunt on an automobile (to show how modern he was) it makes period noises and does things like get flat tyres. All the jokey things that seemed new in that 1950 British comedy, Genevieve. Sweet Genevieve. Twenty years on, the ICA borrow from Ealing comedy in a bid for what? Aunt Edna?

Every word spoken or read, proclaim the authors, is from Apollinaire. So what? Such 'fidelity' is treachery when the lines are selected by minds working on the same principles, of two-bit pseudo-psychology and ingratiating martyrology, as the novelists who wrote Moulin Rouge, Lust For Life and The Agony and the Ecstasy. Who bothers so little about Apollinaire's poetry (as opposed to his brand-image) that they get a charming actor to speak it with indigestible flatness. Who are so mesmerised by chronological pedantry that they think the Lumiere programme is an evocation of Paris ca. 1900?

The play is a structureless succession of stagings that had ceased to be avant-garde on the West End stage well before Joan Littlewood. The only critic who liked it was Harold Hobson, and that's no accident. He knows what's safely banal when he sees it.

The ancillary exhibition included many artworks commissioned in homage to Apollinaire. 'In homage to' is current cant for derivative hackwork, 'using the pretext of.' The notion of commissioning little, quick, light artworks, artworks from trendy people is as transparent as it's pitiable. It's the art machine producing little objects to keep itself going. It's the small change of consumer society. The Wimpyburgers of art. It's jobs for the boys. It's 'I'll

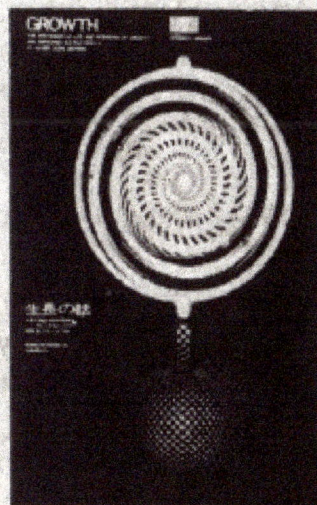

GROWTH

FLUORESCENT CHRYSANTHEMUM
Until 26 Jan.

commission you if I think you're with it.' It's another little one-man Arts Council using the ICA to build up its little sub-empire. It's an old boy net because it's a matter of flip whim, of idle fancy, devoid of merit. The shunting aside, for the sake of the Apollinaire piece, of John Arden's play, about which its author protested, is a case in point. In the first place, the Apollinaire piece should have been offered to theatre groups whose director was not the play's co-author. For obvious reasons. For everybody's sake. As it is, when one thinks that the co-author was once script editor of the Royal Shakespeare Theatre, one is tempted to suppose, either, that he's besotted by his involvement in his play now, or that the Royal Shakespeare Theatre covered up for his remarkable absence of acumen then.

The ICA Bulletin was once a small,

See Back Cover

terse, valuable magazine. The new Magazine is distended by the same ragbag indiscrimination that made the Apollinaire productions so pitiably opportunistic. Now it rambles on about Hornsey, Czechoslovakia, about everything discussed, typically, in The Observer, and here it gets, not analysis, but little inspirational blazons of excited me-tooism. A two-page poem scolds Guatemalan intellectuals whose minds fiddle while the third world burns. So just what does Apollinaire have to offer them? What would it have mattered if his anniversary had been celebrated only by The London Magazine and all the other usuals? Or if it hadn't been celebrated at all? (So Apollinaire was a pornographer! So what? Today everybody's a pornographer. So he welcomed the new! So what? Since pop art everyone welcomes the new. It's the only way bourgeois art can throw up sensational nothings fast enough to make progress look like liberation).

Two issues devoted to the Cybernetic exhibition were a welcome return to thought, in a magazine whose level of universal raving is now almost on a par with The Beatles Monthly Book. The ICA raves so obsessively it's reduced the very notion of enthusiasm to abject tedium. The idea of repudiation also. 'Shit to Institutes of Contemporary Art!' chant the Apollinaire chorus, thus proving that 'Shit' doesn't mean a thing either, because the cry is meant to keep you coming and keep paying its establishment-sized rent. You can enjoy that little sensation of superiority, of jolly twinge of refusal, which snobbery always sells to those who pay for their seat. In trendy mouths, all these 'revolutionary' slogans mean is: 'Anyone for tennis?'. Revolution, like tennis, is offered as a Nice Change. The ICA, meanwhile, will revolve itself ever more firmly into the Mall.

Increasingly the worst in the old art establishment, the insecurely placed within it, cashing in on the revolutionary rave-up. Increasingly the attack on art is also an attack on integrity in the name of the mass produced, easily consumed, throwaway, knicknack objects. Consume faster! consume everything! don't think about anything! Buy art! Buy anti-art! But non-art! You too can be a collector! Buy A History of Anti-Art! Buy an

Anti-History of Anti-Art! Buy the Anti-Art Bulletin! Objects! Institutes! New! Revolutionary! It's All Happenings! Newnewnew nownownow! Wow, zoom, bingbangbollicks! The pseudo-primitivism of the worst pop-art conceals the snatch-and-grab provocativeness of art ' which offers nothing but the illusion of defying art. At a time when the standards of the old ICA are more desperately needed than ever, the newlook ICA like a rotten tonsil, becomes a centre of infection.

Guevara, Paris, Hornsey, all came as if on cue, just as flower power began wilting, to give the same old magazines another set of slogans, of innovations, of trends. It's impossible to respect the Coldstreams and others, who, so isolated in and insulated by the establishment that they don't know what's happening outside it any longer, but who soldier on with integrity about what they do sense or glimpse. It's not so easy to respect the Mr Facing Both Ways who preach spontaneity out of one mouth and commission hackwork with the other, or who cry 'Shit to myself!' in confident expectation for their revolutionary radicalism.

The ICA may get its grants from goodnatured or prestige-hunting sectors of the bourgeoisie. It may also make much trendy todo about reconciling fine art and pop art and pop fine art and avant-garde pop and avant-garde pop fine anti-art and even revolutionary bayonets before cultural butter. To reconcile both strategies has, one must admit, the courage of bluff. One would admire that bluff if behind it were what one senses behind the operations of a Diaghilev or a Darwin, a profound respect for art, and artists, a sensitivity of response, as well as all the survival mechanisms of showmanship, conning and all the rest. The ICA's old style integrity remains, in three of the four exhibitions since its move to the Mall. The filmshows have performed the function, which the BFI still refuses as far as it dare, of accommodating the experimental. Thanks to the ICA, many American phenomena have at last been seen here. And so on and so forth. It would be a great pity if so much that's so promising were stunted or lost because of a too-bold strategy were sabotaged by clumsy tactics, by a cheap, opportunistic tone, by the sacrifice of integrity to an ambition altogether out of its league.

...human figure was draw... ...on of cockpit design at... ...e an animated human figure... ...designer can assess preliminary... ...chair by drawing the outline design on... ...observing its relationship to the human fig... ...this has been done at Nottingham University.

Greek Gaols

'Letter from a Greek Gaol' appeared, unsigned, in OZ 6 and was republished in Underground newspapers throughout the world. It was written by Neal Phillips, an American, who now tells how his guards turned up to interrogate him with a copy of OZ within days of its publication in London. After his release, he was gaoled again in Rome and has since been hounded by CIA officials everywhere.

Cold-sweat flashback to Greek political prison on the island of Aegena, lost somewhere in the Agean Sea. A boatload of secret police called KIP arrive, dreaded gang of psychopaths – from the sadistically selfish oligarchy which robots them to their nameless unknown commander to the lowest functionary, these specialists in mendacity and duplicity, beaters of feet and shockers of balls, pubic-hair pluckers and kidney-kickers, extractors of blood-soaked confessions, these perpetrators of the CIA's dream of a better world. They call me into the usual cold barren office and we're face-to-face again, come certain cool this time but any expert in analyzing these confrontations would see the colour of fear in my aura, even after 38 months in these caves and dungeons and still standing.

A copy of OZ lies opened on the lemonwood table separating us. It is open to a published message I had smuggled out of Prison of Seven Towers in Saloniki a few months before. Shock. There is a 'name withheld' printed under it, it has been on sale in London only four days, but through some unimaginable fuzz-sorcery they've already arrived in the middle of the Agean Sea to confront me with it. Smuggling political information out of prison is five years if they feel polite, and 'accident' or 'escape' if they do not. It's all the same, five years added to my 3½ is death, one cannot live through osmosis acid and will-

power for ever.

They begin their painfully slow and tricky rap with an arrogance which one must hear to know, the heaviest vibe on earth, the God in the White House very definitely is on their side, the world of my prison is shuddering and they are crushing me. They know, they tell me, that John Wilcock visited me at Seven Towers in June, and that he published his 'Other Scenes' jointly with this issue of OZ, and that I had handed Wilcock this message, they'd compared it with my other writings they'd busted through the years and their language-specialists agreed it had to be mine and would certainly swear to it in 'court', and anyway I was the only foreigner in Seven Towers through those months, etc, etc, now please sign this 'admission' and 'all might be forgiven'. I did what one learns to do: remarked upon the strange coincidence in all of this, if the positions were reversed I'd no doubt believe the same as they, but sorry I couldn't sign it, it wasn't me. Crazy laughter. I shot a look which meant that all the tortures and deaths in Greece could not make me sign anything anywhere for anyone, that I could be taken apart piece by piece and NEVER sign a contract for five more years in malnutrition's kitchens and they believed me, although I do not know even now if I flushed them the truth, nobody can ever know.

Three more months pass in frozen misty prison-silence, another deadly winter. New arrivals

daily, all broken and driven mad, condemned to terrible years for thought-crimes. Our unheated little stone room which once held eight now has twelve, then fifteen, now twenty, we are bitterly cold and unwashed and underfed, everywhere there is sickness, and the feeble old doctor who appears two afternoons a week for 1,500 of us has no medicine in his bag. Like the Seige of Stalingrad. Under those conditions those of us with our heads still partly together spend most of our time chasing the vibes of violence out of the air, for life like that is impossible even for the sane, and an eruption in such sad hopeless quarters might destroy us all.

KIP visits again and again, off their OZ kick now, but wanting to know who was publishing those things and bombarding them with those petitions, names and addresses, what organization were they connected with, were they Communists? Dope freaks? They wanted labels; 'friends' would not do. The American Embassy always sent a man with them, not to protect me (an infantile illusion destroyed two smashed kidneys and a face-stabbing before) but to plug my answers into their worldwide fuzz network and classify some more of the underground mind as 'enemy'. No deal.

February comes, and King Constantine, now exiled in Rome, pardons me out of my exile in Greece. Madness. Flight into Rome, five days with the CIA for 'reorientation'. Nights with the Living Theatre. Total acid,

ersed in the acid of the
h. Freedom. We must quickly
ent a new language to handle
infinity of fabulous feelings
ch live in those white-light
ms beyond words. Impossible
ommunicate the power of a
k in the park, alone and
ting free, all senses on
EN, somebody's cut the string
my balloon. There's no privacy
rison, even when asleep or
turbating, the eye of the
e is always at the keyhole.
v each simple walk in the
ets is a blinding parade of
acles. EVERYTHING is an
ısm. Malanga makes a film
ed Recording Zone Operator on
reincarnation of Drakos,
executed cellmate.
rything's too public, Rome is
a village, busted again.
ty months in prison, forty
s' out, busted again for bush.
rybody's complaining about the
on of the Sky Queen in Rome,
to me it's a first class
l — some food, a bed,
tors to repair the old Greek
nds, music, books, letters, a
pathetic and intelligent judge
ed Giovanni who released us
r six months without a trial
thus saved years, said we'd
ken the law but committed no
e, setting up a howl in the
can press and destroying
anni's career.
it's London, in heaven's
er regions and grooving around
our friends. People ask me
y different types of questions
at what is going on in Greece,
what the hell do they THINK
ing on in Greece? How many
s do they have to hear it, in
many ways from how many
ple? Greece was never
, I was busted there in 1964
my first 50 jail-friends had
a falsely convicted of
ime which was a pretext
over political sins which
d not be prosecuted in their
names. Everybody was
ured systematically even
, just generally speaking it
the most twisted social
em anywhere after 20 years of
American political military
omic and moral control, and
before that it was always

bad bad bad. But finally the
Greek Jesus had arrived in the
body of Andreas Papodreau and he
set off Sigma vibrations which
rolled back and forth through the
ignorant terrified streets and
multiplied. The Priest-Palace-
Wealthy CIA–Police–Military
interests which had always
operated Greece to suit their
own obscene pleasures felt the
threat, and together they
launched the Junta upon the
people in it's own name,
attempting to perpetrate the
illusion that the said Junta was
working in it's own name to
continue the enslavement brutili-
zation and mystification of the
Greek people.
There are a couple of thousand
prisoners in exile prisons with
no court at all in their future,
but the Greek Justice-head is
nothing if not tricky. I've lived
in eleven different prisons there
and all of them are full of
political prisoners condemned of
actual 'crimes' and sent to
criminal prisons, therefore they
do not count as political
prisoners, but they are, friend,
thousands. And the Red Cross goes
to Leros and issues a devastating
report of the diet, sanitation,
etc. The food and services which
scandalized the world were far
better than any food or services
I ever saw in a criminal prison.
Nobody knows definitely about
that or supposes that it exists
because the fucking Red Cross
doesn't go there because the
poor people hovering and cowering
in dark corners of their minds
inside are classified and convicted as 'criminal' instead of
'political'.
The deceptions which the
reactionary CIA-controlled
totalitarian state gives the
world as information become ever
more sophisticated and deadly as
the truth of who they are and
their aims and the horrible mind-
crushing nature of the fraud they
have unleased upon the world
becomes ever more difficult to
conceal. They speak of freedom,
but they are themselves enslaved
by their own minds. By the dark
forces which give them their
twisted definitions of what life

is and what should be done about
it. How is it there? Bad, baby,
very bad, like the dark side of
your nightmare moon. When and
how is it going to end? I
know perhaps too much to walk
safely through the streets about
how it happened and what it is,
but the form which the ending
will take I cannot envision. I
only know that it will end when
the America that we know ends,
for a nation of people who are
oppressing each other and
massacring the children of Viet
Nam cannot be expected to
produce Senators and Presidents
who really care that most of the
people in Greece eat garlic and
bread for lunch.
So Greece will begin to free
itself when America understands
what freedom is, and not before—
So I say something now to certain
people who have proved that they
read this magazine. To those
absurd political police who
kept busting me on the streets
of Rome and asking those funny
questions, and the police in
Paris who did the same, and to
the crew-cut philosopher who
cornered me on Tee outside of
Brussells and spoke French like
a lifetime in Iowa tempered by
ten years in Washington and
polished off his education by
six months at the Berlitz school
to learn French) and was
obviously an American CIA
operative riding the Tee in
Belgium and flashing funny
badges there to question me
oddly. To the British Customs
officers who were actually
political police who examined my
correspondence for three hours
and told me that personally they
didn't care how many Greek
colonels I killed — 'it isn't our
show' — to these people and the
others in my future, I say a
couple of things:
We do not kill people, that is
your game and the only one you
understand, nor do we have a
telephone nor a secret organizational chart nor any formal
connection at all with each
other, but there are many
millions of us, we are all
around you, everywhere, even
under the very ground you

tramp with hob-nailed boots. We
do not threaten you, only the
'you' from whom you are dealing
Our political propaganda is
simply to give you a knowledge o
yourselves, a part of your inner
beings which you do not yet kno
exists, and from which you must
live with total integrity and
in freedom when you come to
terms with your discovery. And
if you cannot find your way we
are not going to lock you in
concentration camps and mutilate
your bodies and souls, we shall
simply ISOLATE YOUR MINDS.
This is the movement you feel all
around you and which you canno
understand, the vibration in the
air which disturbs you so, the
thing you slash at with your
swords but cannot kill, and which
is growing until it will engulf
EVERYTHING. And I tell you to
that the information gleaned
from all those years about Litton
Industrie's connection with the
CIA and the CIA's operations in
Greece, etc, is written and
signed in six long and careful
copies and rests with six very
strong and able men. You can
eradicate me if you must have
vengeance, but as for stopping
the release of my deadly data,
you cannot do that, you have
moved too late. We have had a
collective vision of what human
freedom is really all about and
have been given some idea of what
is possible, and we intend to
live those dreams. Now. Right
now.

A section devoted to the
Pop thing, the first of a series.
The Electric Circus is dead.

Mozic

"The Cream is splitting because 50% personal withdrawal and 50% musical difference. I really don't think I could play with a band anymore; it just does not appeal to me to do that kind of thing anymore. It was a big virtuoso kick. I want to lay back. George Harrison and I have clicked a lot together because we are both guitarists and we've thought that we might produce an album between the two of us. He's got more to lose by it. We want to keep his name off it because anybody who hears anything about the Beatles today is bad news. If it got out that George and I were hanging out together we would be queers in the press."

"My future plans are not as vague as they were; they are getting tighter. I've got to cut an album sooner or later which will have different kinds of backing groups. George has opened my eyes to the fact that you can do whatever you want on record. I have not realised that before. I have always been very inhibited in the studio, very limited the different ways to approach a song, whereas George says it doesn't matter you can use strings or whatever. So I'll do lots of different things like strings and brass and small groups. I play with him privately. He wouldn't do a record because he doesn't like his playing that much, that's not true, he wouldn't do it because he would be frightened of inhibiting me."

"Whatever I do now is going to be me because I have been in the other kind of situation too long. Whether or not I am going to be a failure doing me is beside the point, because I've never done it yet. Even with producing I want to work with the producer but I want as much say as he has."

Clapton

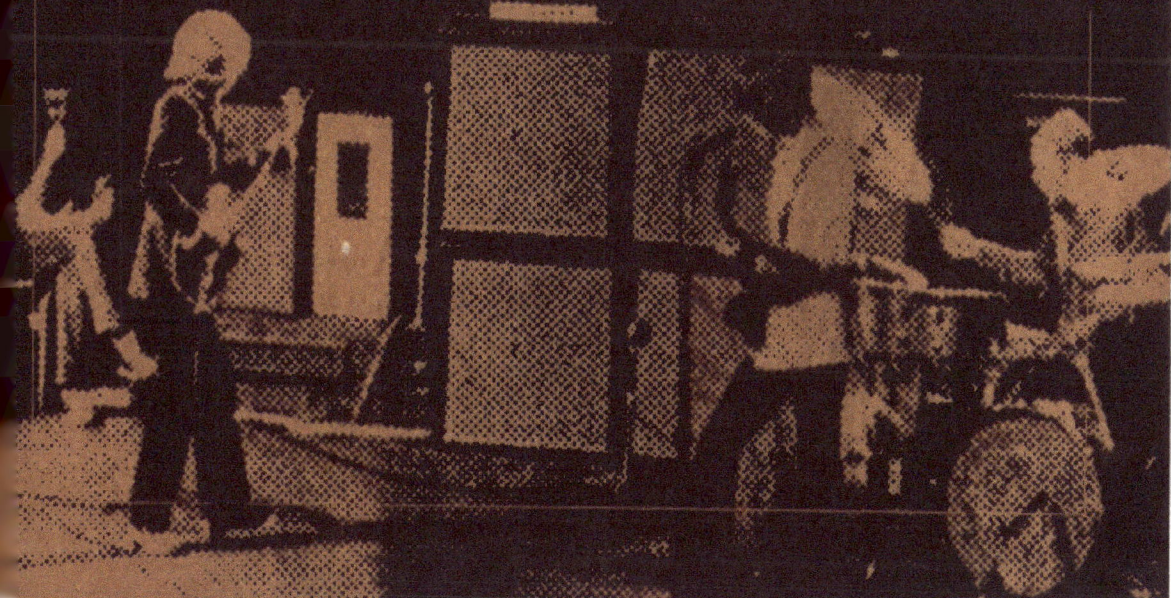

Woodpecker, Woodpecker

Ian Stocks talks to MANFRED MANN, one of the stayers on the British pop scene.

You've been heard to say that you think that music tracks for your TV jingles are better than anything you've done with the Manfred Mann group...
Well I'm not saying that everything is better, but certainly the best things are better than the things we do as a group. Somehow it's generally better music. It's got to do with the fact that the group works as five people — who are together because the group is successful — you get trapped into working in a certain way. But Mike Hugg and I do the commercials together — so we are able to use other musicians who are better suited to the sort of music we want to produce.

So you and Mike Hugg virtually produce the commercials?
We write them, and play on them . . . and we get some guys we like. They aren't all great, some of them are corny, and kind of sweet in their own simple way. And we don't take the whole thing too seriously . . . . it's not a great artistic thing, but some of the music — like for the Woodpecker commercials last year and the Crunchie commercials for next year—stand on their own as pure music. Like this Crunchie commercial that has chocolate being poured over the head of a statue — the track we're using in that one is completely free improvisation on melatron flute, piano and wind chimes that came up one afternoon. There's only 19½ seconds of it on the track but it's exactly what we wanted to do and we're very happy about it.
And of course — it's very well paid, I can see it as a future career. And I really find the whole scene very enjoyable. I know a lot of underground people put advertising down — but we manage to work with a lot of really nice creative blokes.
Fry's Turkish Delight, which have always had a rather corny dated track—we've done that over and now it's sort of pagan chant with soprano sax solo over the top. I think it's really good.

Can you see advertising as a sort of art form?
No, music is an art form, film is an art form and occasionally people get together and make nice things — like the Hamlet commercials, which are great. Some advertising transcends its own thing, and stands up on its own as something worth looking at and listening to — totally apart from the fact that its meant to be selling cider or

whatever. Let's get it straight — it's not something I'm hung up on — I just find I enjoy the short fragments of music, and occasionally one is very proud, and a lot of the time I'm saying, that's nice, that's a really happy sound. It's not like doing a pop track you don't like that lasts for three minutes and takes twelve hours to record — these only take two hours in the studio.

It's been said that you're leaving pop?
Yes, in a very odd sort of way. The Manfred Mann group isn't doing public appearances any more — so Mike Hugg and I are getting involved in our own sort of thing. So I guess in that sense we're not involved in it anymore.

Has this anything to do with the changing nature of pop?
Yes, there's only one way to think of pop in general — it's music which sells to the masses. But now a lot of people are interested in a new sort of music, that's called pop because it derives from pop and because a lot of the people doing it don't want to appear contrived, and there isn't another name.
It's not popular with the masses, so now there are two markets — the pop market, where everybody goes out and buys hit records — and a kind of semi underground market — the people who buy Cream LP's, people who dig Jethro Tull and Brian Auger. People are listening for better music, even though I don't think it *is* necessarily better music.
Mike Hugg and myself have our own thing going — which I'll talk to you about but not to anyone else. Normally I don't like to talk about the thing I'm doing — so many people do it and it never transpires. Ours is not a blues thing at all, though I know there's a big market for blues at the moment— we don't have a big ravey blues vocalist — just us chanting in the background and Mike Hugg singing nicely in a gentle way. An LP for Lyn Dobson. I've put a lot of money into the studio time. It's an odd sort of mixture — a bit of blues, a bit of pop, Ornette Coleman, with avant garde jazz to the fore.
A lot of people are getting involved in the scene, with a lot of synthesis, like the record with Lyn we're doing in there now. What is that music? There's Indian sitar that turns into a bit of a jazz solo, there's bass and drums like they play behind Ornette Coleman and John Coltraine — it's just music, with elements that could come from pop records. It's a long way away from pop, but you could put a little

yeah yeah yeah . . .

melody on it and a vocal and it wouldn't be far away. There's funny kind of thing happening that I can't name

Do you have any particular affiliation with the Underground?
I have no idea what the underground is. Is it giving away flowers and love? – that's probably a very dated view . Or is it the generally violent approach? – worshipping Che Guevara and occupying factories and schools, concerned with overthrowing our evil capitalist community. Even though I like the people in it and sympathise with the attitude, I disagree with both as political philosophy. I'm not a pacifist or revolutionary, but I have to take these people seriously because that's what they want.. The generation that's rebelling today is in a sad state and devoid of philosophy. It's not that we must change things and overthrow evil without anything to put in it's place. Marx worked out a practical system which was a very very wonderful way of organising society. Now that's been in practice in Russia for fifty years. But how can today's genuine socialists look at those places and not see that its lead to a heavy bureaucratic repressive state. Cuba is just the one pathetic hope. I can't believe that Che Guevara is in any way relevant to England today. If you have a real personal or social or artistic conscience then you must see that the system's been found wanting – not because the system is wrong but because people are people and a little bureaucrat will always be a little bureaucrat.
I can't agree with the underground, I'm a terrible realist. I don't even think I fit into the people of the pop world. Perhaps I'm taking the underground too seriously and it's just some load of people who've been given a title. I think really it's a very sheltered generation.

What do you think of music that's arisen through the Underground?
It's the sort I don't listen to al all, though the sort of thing I play would fall within that bracket. I like some of the things I've heard – the Mothers of Invention, the Band, but I don't have the LP's so I can't say that's what I like. I listen to the Beach Boys, Tamla Motown and Stevie Wonder – purely for my own enjoyment, not trying to get high or stoned on it or anything. The big freakout guitar solos just disturbs me. I don't like it, I don't enjoy it. If I want to be serious I put on Bach, or Ornette Coleman. I certainly would'nt go out and buy the Grateful Dead or the Fugs.
For years I've yearned to come off stage, and for people who like good music to say 'Christ wasn't that great, those guys are good'. For years it's been 'Oh I enjoyed the show,' or 'I havent enjoyed the show' more likely, or screaming at the singer, which has very little to do with me personally, or the respect I want as a musician. If you're in the public eye you want some genuine respect for turning out something which is genuinely good, or at least to be judged as either 'They can't make it' or 'They can'. But for years I feel I've avoided the issue, I've been involved in something where I've been judged by something that wasn't me anyway. I'm not putting it down– I've enjoyed it and enjoyed playing in the group and pop music – I've learnt a lot from it, I just don't think that it's the only thing I can do. If I want to play I can't go round and play 'Ha said the clown' can I? I have to play something else.

MFM Productions—Director John Burroughs

LP reviews

DISPOSABLE/The Deviants, Stable SLP7001.

One feels it would be almost absurd to indulge in a strictly logical review of the Deviants new album when the very existence of both group and record is practically an illogical, if inevitable, reality. Neither the Deviants nor their music invite logical explanation, notwithstanding the recent concentration of interest within the straight British press on the London underground/ freak/I-was-a-week-end-hippy scene, which alone ensured the inevitability and emergence of an Underground Group In Chief. Consciously or otherwise, (I suspect the former), the Devi-

ants have clutched and nurtured this title, using it with some considerable success as a springboard for publicity and promotional purposes. Whether without it they would have managed to raise the bread to independantly record and distribute even their first LP, Ptoof, is by now irrelevant and all that should be at issue is whether the group have anything original or valid to offer in the 13 tracks of pure British underground music that constitutes Disposable.

Cuts like Sparrows and Wires, Normality Jam and Somewhere to Go, say they haven't. The lyrics are for the most part pretentious, artificial, clumsily metered and badly sung. With the exception of Dick Heckstall-Smith, who is only credited with playing on Fire in the City and arranging Guaranteed to Bleed, there isn't one outstanding musician to be found within the nineteen assorted people credited as performing on the album. OK so who needs outstanding musicians in a 'mean and filthy' band like the Deviants whose main objective is to tell it, (wait for it), like it is, (like the Mothers, Fugs and Doors have told it presumably?), 'stories of the hung up, the strung up and paranoid 20th century.' So where's the significance of Pappa-oo-mau-mau, the best number on the LP incidentally, Sydney B Goode, without a single credit to the Chuck Berry original, and Blind Joe McTurk's Last Session, a 77 second satirical comment on obscure American country blues artists and their recordings. Where's the significance of Farren's Last Man, an utterly predictable collection of out-dated sound effects, boring lyrics and mediocre arrangement.

The only possible answer is that the entire album is an incredibly cunning joke, calculated from start to finish as a poke in the balls at every potential record buyer. But if this was the intention then why package it so inexpertly—everyone knows it's the graphics that sell LPs these days. Isn't it?

Felix Dennis

40

PLAYBACK/The Apple Tree Theatre, Verve import, FTS3042.

The Apple Tree Theatre say their thing with an even combination of sad amusing sexy sound and articulate a vision of the new scene. Songs Garfunkle would like crampin between acid pieces pieces of conversation.

In the beginning the shouting boring error is thrown out by the whispering prompter and the applause is deafening.

A randy young square stalks a jerky Cole Porter town looking for cunt, a misunderstood conversation with a head cuts his fantasy back to non-reality which is maybe reality and who's crazy?

Two lorry drivers spin a radio dial searching for banality between the static. Its there but everything's tainted so it gives way to a search for some STP amongst the impressive list of drugs they carry in the cab.

Theatre can be an articulate dream sequence trapping and repeating the sounds of the technological society. The Apple Tree Theatre playback what they can remember from their experience. Most pop keeps its sentiments behind a web of imagery and double meaning. Spoken words on records, however short can be very boring. 'I've got blisters on my fingers', is an effective shout of pissed off protest at first. By the 20th time its meaningless and annoying.

The whispered, shouted, screaming voices of the past and the never ending moment have a place. The Apple Tree Theatre mix them with enough nice sounds to make the whole performance bite.

Bryan Willis

JAMES TAYLOR/James Taylor, Apple, Sapcor 3 (stereo), Apcor 3 (mono).

Here is a fine album. James Taylor's songs have a compelling lyrical quality, the words saying what they mean/meaning what they say, never lapsing into artificial imagery and contrasting perfectly, (at times almost too perfectly), with Peter Asher's involved but sensitive production. Oddly, it's not so much what's gone into the arrangements, as what Asher and Richard

Hewson deliberately chose to leave out that puts this debut release into a class of its own. The tightly reined, beautifully timed use of brass and orchestral backing, together with uncluttered chorus work and frugal double tracking all serve to keep the spotlight firmly on Mr Taylor, whose singing, while it may be limited in range is nevertheless refreshingly unaffected and sincere.

Practically all the tracks are linked, usually by studio musicians using Hewson arrangements, and perhaps it is because of this that on first hearing the album tends to sound vaguely 'samey' throughout. It took me at least half a dozen playthroughs before I began to realise how subtley intricate cuts like, Carolina In My Mind, Sunshine, Sunshine and Something's Wrong, really were. Many of the songs are highly personal, introvert compositions, the last track on the first side, Something In The Way She Moves, for example. Here, Taylor sings quietly, alone, sided only by his acoustic guitar playing in perhaps the most moving and impressive piece of the whole collection.

Knocking Round the Zoo, the hardest rock number included, has outstanding lyrics. 'Just knocking round the zoo on a thursday afternoon/There's bars on all the windows and they're count-up the spoons/Now my friends all come to see me they point at me and stare/Said he's just like the rest of us so what's he doing in there?/. . . .' while, Blues Is Just A Bad Dream is a straight twelve bar interesting for its use of threaded discordant violins and orchestration, in a number that might have otherwise been slightly below the phenomenally high standards set by the rest of the album.

It's difficult to bag this recording. It isn't folk-rock or progressive pop, it isn't acidic or electric blues; it's a long playing record by James Taylor. I hope and I'm sure, that it's the first of many.

Felix Dennis

SOUTHERN COMFORT/Walter 'Shakey' Horton & Martin Stone

Two of the sparse benefits produced by the recent British boom in blues have been the release of a number of interesting American imports and the attempts of some major record comp-

anies to float their subsidiaries here. Unfortunately, the mediocrity shown by the foremost of these subsidiaries in their choice of imported release material has so far been matched only by the banality of their home-grown recordings: the Peter Green jokes and pathetic Chicken Shack LP serving as prime examples.

As you read this, another independant company will be making its debut release, not with an acceptable trendy blues breaking band but with a little recorded American harp player and a half forgotten English guitarist. The company, Underground Recording Enterprises, took advantage of the visiting American Blues Festival to combine the talents of former Muddy Waters and Otis Rush sidekick, Walter 'Shakey' Horton and guitarist Martin Stone of the original Savoy Brown band. The resulting album, Southern Comfort, is an odd mixture of strengths and weaknesses. While it contains sustained interest, vocal tracks not only from Shakey but from Jesse Lewis and Jerome Arnold who also play drums and bass respectively, plus a twelve minute raga extemporisation by Stone, it seems unsure of is its own identity, often giving the impression that the technical production and mixing owe more to enthusiasm than to professional skill.

But the band really wails on occasions, especially Shakey with his shouting, while harp on tracks like I Need My Baby, and the Jimmie Roger's Walking By Myself while Martin storms into his own on Jesse's Found Me A New Love and triumphs throughout his complex personal trip Netti Netti.

I will avoid the inevitable comparison with Butterfields East West, (on which Jerome Arnold provided an equally sympathetic bass line), and mention a again only the mixing, which at times resembles nothing so much as a novice producer's demonstration kit: an orgy of reversed tapes, superimposed effects and double tracking. This apart, Southern Comfort deserves to sell, both on its own merits, which are considerable if spasmodic, and as an encouragement to the aforementioned subsidiaries to make a concerted effort in raising the standard of their future British and imported blues releases.

MJ McDonnell

PEWTER SUITOR Tyrannosaurus Rex, Regal Zonophone. RZ 3016.

Haven't I heard it before? No I haven't . . . it's Pewter Suitor and like all other 'Rex numbers can't readily be distinguished from the last, words as usual are reduced to phonetic mutations. But why can't they evolve this sound of theirs? On the lines of familiarity breeding contempt this similarity begets boredom, if a listenable boredom. Perhaps the limitation is that they are two people trying to be a group instead of two people.

Anyway, whatever they're doing it's at least peculiar to Tyrannosaurus Rex and in mild doses, single tracks as opposed to entire albums, can be incredibly effective. Don't confuse their music with the garbage excreted by the pop machine. This folk/rock experiment has an urgency and potential peculiarly valid in these days of the Hump, O'Conner and the Archies.

KEN CORE

Late last year Time Out's ad manager, John Leaver, reviewed a non-existent album 'Heavy Jelly' by the Heavy Jelly. The review set out to send up the worst members of 'Poetian' pop intelligentsia but inevitably created a completely straight demand in record stores all over London. Time Out decided to continue the story by running another full page advertisement for the group in their next issue.

About this time they also agreed to let four well known blues musicians use the title for a forthcoming non commercial experimental blues album, which, for contractual reasons, would have to be recorded anonymously.

Suddenly there are Heavy Jellies everywhere. Heavy Jelly at the Albert Hall just before Christmas and a rush-released Island single from a group calling themselves, surprise, surprise, Heavy Jelly. Chris Blackwell of Island Records lept in quickly it seems. Who are these Island new boys. Shades of Spooky Tooth? The single displays all the worst aspects of today's blues/pop sound, computer formulated and market researched to supply a growing demand.

Meanwhile Granada is reported to have been approached about a film starring Heavy Jelly.

Amanda & the Heavenly Jellie at the Albert Hall.

Why isn't London jumping

Geoffrey Cannon

December 31 1968. My place. Between 8 and 11.30. Incoming telephone call. "Hi Geoffrey? Wynford. Where's it jumping?" Me. "That's my question". Pause for amusement. "There's something in Hampstead: no, two scenes. Forget them. Perhaps in Fulham . . ." Outgoing calls. "Hi. This is Geoffrey. Alan? (Peter? Malcolm? Jo? Joe? Clive? Stuart? David?) What's the scene?" "I thought I'd stay in (I was going to ask you/Not feeling too good tonight/Quiet scene tonight/etc)".

Extract from television and radio programmes. BBC1, 9.05: The Sound Barrier (old movie). 11.0: Cilla Black and Frankie Howerd. 11.50: The end of the year in Llandaff Cathedral. 12.01: Scottish New Year. BBC2, 10.30: Why man creates (film). 11.00: Pick of the Year review. ITV, 10.30: Love Story. 11.30: A show for Hogmanay. Radio 1, 9.15, As you like it (no, not the Shakespeare) 10.00, Late night extra. 11.31: Night ride in Glasgow. Radio 2, As Radio 1 (!!,

as they say in chess problems), Radio 3, 8.25: Handel. 10.10, Haydn. 11.15, Close Down. Radio 4, 10.00, The world in 1968, 11.0: A book at bedtime. 11.45: Service from the Bull Ring, Birmingham. 12.00, Big Ben. 12.02: Forecast for coastal waters. 12.05 Close Down.

Close Down. Close Down. Close Down. Tonite let's all make love in London. There's nothing better to do, and there's pretty much nothing else to do, either.

And yet, there are some recent foreign scenes. Hamburg, offices of Deutsche Grammophon. Horst Schmolzi, chief A&R man "I come to London every four weeks to get my hair cut and to breathe your air. Everyone in London is free; everything is possible. Hamburg is dead." Paris, flat of Philippe Paringaux chief writer for Rock and Folk magazine. Philippe: "I envy you. In London, you can do anything. Everyone is on the scene, everything's moving. Paris has been

killed. Things are worse than before the evenements". London, talking with Andy Wickham, English A&R man and company freak at Warners. He's thinking of settling here with Phil Ochs. California has gone horribly rotten. London. Talking with Stanley Mouse, the designer, and Bob Seidemann, the photographer. They've settled here, because of evil vibrations in California. London again, at Apple. Rock Scully and Danny Rivkin, who work with the Grateful Dead. "I'd like to stay here a long time, and cool out in a sane scene. Let's the get the Dead and the Angels here and have a year's party."

The image of London is that it is the world's most free city. Come on a visit, see the shops, see the people in the streets, see the records on sale, meet nice people, and the image is preserved. Think of what is possible in London: sure, I think anything's possible. But what's really hap-

Continued:

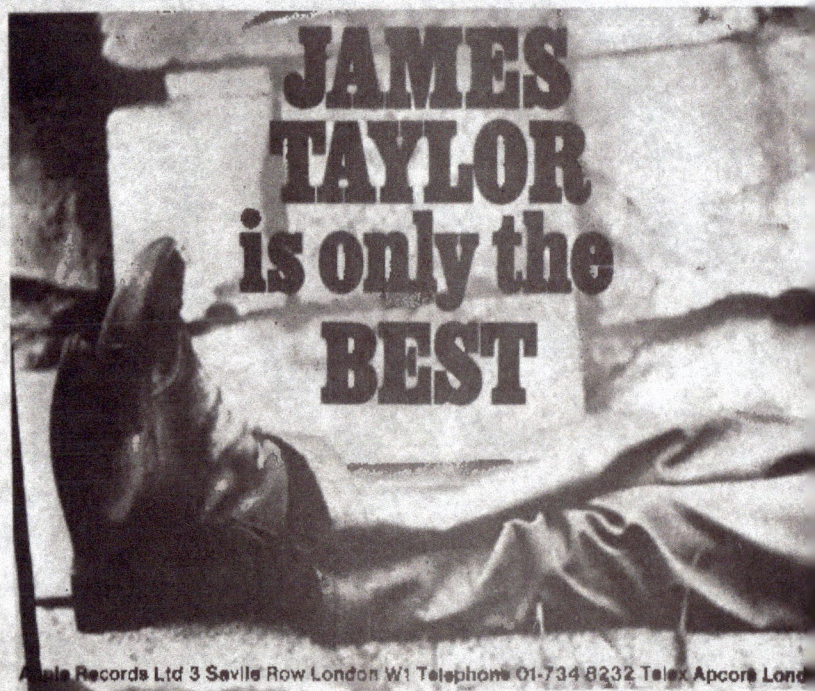

pening; what's for real; what makes you exhilerated to be here; what makes you feel in your political gut, your sensual gut, your being (all the same thing)that here is movement? Where's the electricity? Do you sense it?

Good people in London: there are plenty. Caroline Coon, and Release. Time Out. Jim Haynes and the Arts Lab. The Round House, some nights. IT. OZ. Apple, we would like to think; Derek and George, anyway. Joe Boyd and the Incredibles. Jo Bergman, with the Stones. The

ICA is friendly: Mike Kustow has the chance to pull off a really

big scene, but not yet. And others.

But notice. These are either private people, like all those you know, or else are underground. And by definition, an underground presupposes apathy or oppression above; we know all about that. London is a city which leaves you alone, which is a fresh sensation coming in from Paris, Hamburg, New York, Los Angeles. But you are left alone. The underground flourishes: underground. It is left alone. Where's the electricity?

Down memory lane. Remember the rave at Alexandra Palace? At Olympia? Remember the poetry fest at the Albert Hall? UFO: those were good days. Remember the two good Saturdays in Hyde Park last summer, with "Tantalising Maggie" wreathed in the trees?

Do you remember . . . This must be a joke. What's memory doing in 1968? The Beatles are in their tents. The Stones are in their tents. Middle Earth is being hurt.

And we are in our tents, too. Where's the electricity?

One simple answer: it's in the air. Turn on the television or the radio, and there's electricity. But the air waves might as well be static, for all they do to our minds; they do less for us, and for our parents, and for our grandparents, than electric light. Turn back to that New Year's Eve list of television and radio programmes. Just one evening, sure; but a special, public evening when everyone is caught up by the traditional urge to get stoned (old and or new style). A time of dancing in the streets, of a sense of community, of good thoughts and renewal.

And what did we get? Nothing new. Nothing to do with being in London. It's either the usual mixture, or else reminiscence, or Hogmanay (like in 1965, 1960, 1955, 1950 . . .). Or else the BBC's favourite word: Close Down.

Yes. British broadcasting has a high reputation. Yes, we are

very used to it. Get un-used to it. Think about it. Think about the opportunities. Get enraged. What has broadcasting to do with us? Nothing, at the moment. Everything as it should be.. I don't just mean us as freaks, avant-garde intellectuals, drop-outs, the fringe, post-beats, extra-Parliamentary opposition, or whoever we are. I mean us as people, I mean our friends as people, I mean our families us people, I mean everyone we don't know as poeple. I mean Britain, and, specifically, London. Wake up! We are being swindled. Our lives are being slowed down. London is being rendered invisible.

To get even more specific, thinking about television. London is the hub of the world in rock music. I don't mean rock music as pop entertainment, but as the window to change; the mirror of Paris, Chicago, Columbia; the creator of the new post-scientific, post-technological age; the sounds that tell us how to live. Also, fashion, seen in the same, and proper way: the visual equivalent of rock music here, again, London leads the world. And so I'm not merely using rock and fashion as examples of the state of television, but as the indicator of the rate of movement in television.

Once again, we've got used to what we get. I can't even bring myself to list the shows. They're all geared to 'the market' in the crass sense of the word, just as Radio 1 and Radio 2 are. There's no-one in television thinking. So what we get is what the producers imagine we won't dislike: the old-definition lowest common denominator stuff, with tinsel trappings and go-jo girls. Television is parasitic on what happens to sell best, week by week; and that's no definition of anything. Especially because rock (pop, if you like) is not Denmark Street—remember the old sheet-music sales charts?—but is the visible side of the life-style explosion.

Is Tony Palmer an exception? No. Oh, he was. He has the opportunity, but, for me, he's playing a game of screwing the BBC, marvelling at how many sneaky shots he can get through all those committees. See? Tony's ghost train ride. See? the peasant burning. See? The human skeleton. But I have an interest to declare. I had some part in Granada's show on the Doors, so you must compare the effect of the two shows.

Again, down memory lane. Remember Ready Steady Go? No, it wasn't that good. But it lived, and now dead. What's wrong with London Weekend Television? They are, I am told, planning a mammoth open-ended studio show, not in prime time, but a show where everything that jumps will be seen to jump; and so where the information feedback from the show will put the city in gear, so it can accelerate away. So we can accelerate. A show which has no subject, which doesn't come under any existing department (light entertainment? music??! documentary?!!) and so which will feed into the richness which now passes through London, the biggest ideas factory in the world. We would all run this show. It would be the new music the new styles, the new life, the new politics. We need it, and London Weekend Television need it. Derek Grainger and Humphrey Burton, where is it?

Thinking about radio. But not thinking about the BBC. The BBC is permanently trapped in its history, of which the Musicians' Union, Needle Time, its quasi-civil service concept, the whole Public Service fraud syndrome, is a part. Forget the BBC. Recall, down memory lane again, the pirates. No, again, the pirates weren't as good as we remember. Again, they lived, and are now dead; but, but, their best opportunities are now burst open again.

Because Harold Wilson is thinking of making commercial readio

legal. There is a private member's Bill at present before Parliament which, if carried, will allow the Greater London Council to run its own radio stations. The buzz is that Wilson may calculate that he will gain some critical young votes in 1970 if he allows commercial radio: in which case Radio London will be on the air in a year's time. Or else, if the Conservatives are elected in 1970, then they will bring the Bill forward and pass it, for broadcasting to start in 1971. Of course, if Wilson says no, and is elected in 1970, then no Radio London yet. But let's think to it happening.

Because here is the key to make London jump. An equivalent of American FM stations. The GLC plan four channels, which is perfect thinking. Also, their prime motive is to bring people into London and to promote what's happening in London; also, they'll combine the roles of the government and the ITA relative to commercial television, giving companies franchises, and taking a cut of profits. And, as I see it, the best Radio London will also be the most commercial.

1. There is a demand for good rock music on radio. The BBC will never fill this gap. 2. What's on in London? Not just times of showings, but who's in town, what are they thinking, what are they doing? 3. What's happening now? Evening papers are hours behind; radio can tell it instantly, not by formal news programmes, but by flashes. 4. Who are the people? Let's hear their voices. Not those of 'experts' wheeled in and out to give their half-formed views, but of people who live their thoughts. Certainly there are thousands in London. Perhaps millions. Do you know anyone who you are sure has nothing to say? I don't. But current television and radio work on the principle that only a few hundred people are fit to speak. Let us all speak with each other.

46

you are what you see

The voice you know already, that very eldritch voice, like an Arctic breeze or the breaking of very thin doll's-house porcelain, or the Pierrot of the Minute stepping out of a time capsule . . . so, after the voice, you are dazzled by the hands. With an odd exquisitely palsied flutter, they settle on the mouth, blow swoony kisses, fasten on the breast like a demented dowager calling for the smelling salts, nestle towards the throat like X-Ray photographs of vampire bats . . . Vampires! There is also that hair, snaking elegantly around (Vogue meets Famous Monsters of Movieland) and the face . . .

. . . the actual face . . . Tiny Tim's still photographs do not begin to do him justice. This is Rasputin, or Percy Bysshe Shelley given Dracula's kiss of eternal life, and returned, but after being boxed rather . . . too long.

Anyway it's Tiny Tim, and he gets the nose billing in YOU ARE WHAT YOU EAT, which is a longish short film, and brought to you by Michael Butler (who also brought you Hair) and Peter Yarrow (who brought himself, together with Paul and Mary). YOU ARE WHAT YOU EAT . . . You are what you eat? You are what you watch. What are you watching, eating, here is an exhaustive look at the manners and modes of The Way of Life (The Way of Life being what it's all nostalgically still The Underground. Only recently they understand nowadays that they are looking forward to flying home etc. too).

When I say nostalgic, I mean exhaustive . . . Compendious as an encyclopedia with us from A to Z. Al Jolson to Frank Zappa (but he isn't

on my list of credits, but I swear I saw him!, and taking in data on face-painting, the Electric Flag, surfers, a nude dance by Hamsa el Din, Super Spade, motor bicycles, Harpers Bizarre, all manner of mind stimulants, the Great Indian Desert, several communes and assorted mystics, a hermit, and Father Malcolm Boyd running with his flock along the sea-shore, no hermit he, and excerpts from the Beatles, and . . ., and as the hand-out ends, with disarming honesty into which each head will occasionally stumble — "If or other viewers YAWE C is a trip" — ask yourself what that means, other viewers — and an invitation to see the world through the sensory apparatus of its most vocal and visible citizens".

So why Tiny Tim's head billing? His screen-time is, if not tiny, well, nor is he Garbo in Queen Christina, he is one among many, but — whatever the motives—this one is crucial . . . Indeed, there are the clarifying, indisputably the best sequences, from a scarifying duet with a blonde, with a voice like a bullfrog dipped in honey, in which T.T. takes the Gertrude Lawrence part, to some enveloping material of surreal satire, e.g. an acid, or should I say sharp, piece of reportage involving Plastic Nazi Helmets (Paste on your own hippy decals). Nor was a touch of bitters out of place by this point . . . Everything had been so loving and cosy that I was beginning to get diabetic eye-ball.

YOU ARE WHAT YOU EAT is a documentary, a more or less meaningless definition, and seldom less meaningful than here . . . This is not the product of a polished team of experts, researchers, cameramen, pointing their cameras at a slice of the Assertion, the Nurture of Opium Poppies, Beautiful Caledonia, whatever, and splicing it all together into something which is polemic or poetic, but essentially an object . . . Here is Camera, there is Subject. Here is (hopefully) Audience. This is one of the New Movies in which subject, maker, and watchers, are all splashing about in the same lukewarm bath, soapy with self-applause. This movie is not a construct, it is a pane of glass, transparently honest, and transparently accurate . . . what is good

in it, and what is dull in it, and what is stimulating in it, and what is pretentious in it, is what is good/dull/stimulating/pretentious in the Scene with which makers and viewers identify . . .

What is dull and pretentious incidentally is a good deal . . . Huge passages of inadequate articulation of Great Truths, tapped from the soft underbelly of Mysticism . . . awesomely uninventive visuals, and tiresome sentiments . . . all the bumper home-movie tricks (Look! When I put my face in the camera, the nose swells . . . ad nauseam) except shot in rich National Geographic tones, and none the better for that.

Also I promised myself some time ago never to go knowingly to a film that had the Discotheque Scene, you know, everybody doing that ecstatic jerk, those fashions, so, so wild, and the Inevitable Blonde who is tall, healthy with a sort of icy sparkle, like refrigerated California Grapefruit Juice, and everybody doing the frug, the boogaloo, the whatever, having a wonderful time, and quite sure that you will too . . . which one never does . . . but here it all is. Again, and again . . .

But as I say the movie is transparently honest. It is a New Movie, and what I mean by this is that it is a calculated retreat from art . . . as such it will probably be not liked by most artists, say, and especially critics, because all this long while life has been one thing and art for when another, and it takes training and, preferably, talent. Anyway it is distinct. Otherwise how would artists make any money anyway. But not nowadays . . . this is the New Movie . . . here we are all splashing around in that lukewarm pool of Universal Creativity . . . 'Everybody doing their thing' and if your thing is a tedious thing, well, that's your thing too. But if its Tiny Tim doing his thing, well, that's a different story. Nobody, nobody does a thing like Tiny Tim.

Anthony Haden-Guest

48

3 Shillin **OZ** **18**

USA 60c.
DENMARK 3Kr.
HOLLAND 2G.
GERMANY 1.8 DM.

FINGERLICKIN' GOOD!

SSSSSSSSSSSS Andy Warhol

Lazarus from Liberation News Service is in England and writing for OZ. This is his interview with Andy Warhol made just before he left the States.

Andy of platinum hair and leather fame gets good reviews in Time (I am the Warhol, You are the Warhol, goo goo goo joob) as Holy Mother the Church converts Hard Capitalists to the Belief and brings them to the Factory bearing gifts and offers more . . . much needed as the Spirit of A G Bell wants-his-money-and-he-wants-it-now or he'll foreclose on the Factory Communicators . . . . as the Crew stalls A G Bell (Hullo, Ed's Billiard Hall, Eight-ball speaking), Spaced Out Type with his Hippie-for-fun-and-profit Side Kicks comes for a chance at Superstarring and any odd Hula-Bucks. . . . Elevator whirr whoosh clicks into obscurity as we . . .

Andy, they're here to interview you
Hi, what'd you want to . . .
Andy, telephone, it's your lawyer
Uh, just a minute, okay
Sure, no hurry
Andy says you might be in one of our films, right?
Well, I don't know . . . uh . . .
What's the matter don't you like our stuff? *Chelsea Girls* I liked a great deal . . . his newer stuff, well I don't know
You seen *Joe Dallesandro (in Flesh)* . . . how'd you like that?
Well, it was honest, truth at 24 Ips and all that, but . . . .
It's just a dirty movie, one of them, what'd they call them?
Skin flicks?
Yeah, like stag films, but Andy didn't make that one
No?
No they just . . . just a minute . . .

Sorry about the phone, what'd you want to know?
The film, *Joe Dallesandro in Flesh*, Paul just told me that you didn't make that one . . .
That's right. Paul wrote it and produced it and all; it's his film.
But the Garrick (theatre) . . . the ad's and posters read 'Andy Warhol's Joe Dallesandro in Flesh'
That's right, they just put my name on it

You mean the Garrick? Isn't that the Andy Warhol Garrick Theatre . . . don't you own part of the theatre?
No; they show my films there though, and call it the Andy Warhol Garrick theatre, like they say Andy Warhol's Joe Dallesandro, to bring people in . . .
Andy Warhol at three dollars a head, right? Is that what they charge?
Three dollars. You seem to be amused at that . . . that anyone would pay three dollars to see one of your films, is that too much?
No.
But what about . . .
What's funny is that people pay three dollars because it *says* Andy Warhol, like, you saw the film didn't you? like you did . . . and you take it all in to mean something, like you can *understand* it . . .
But I didn't . . .
I can look at a film and see the film, but understanding it . . . well, I don't *understand* it — it's all usually ad lib, or most of it . . . you know, you really should be in one of our films . . .
Uh, what would it be about?
I don't know yet, we haven't thought about it — why don't you think about it . . . if you get an idea, we'll do it
The ideas for your films, where do they come from?
Oh, someone just comes up with something, or I see someone in the street or hear them talking, or . . . it's hard to

say, but I just think of something.
And your crew, the Superstars?
The same thing, I see them on the street or they come in the office, like you, or something like that — usually they talk a lot — you know, you really should be in our film . . . you could come down some weekend and we'd do it then . . .
Your method of creating, it intrigues me. *Empire* I believe is my favourite; how, or what was involved in doing that —
We filmed a day in the life of the Empire State Building sort of — *why Empire?* I don't know, it just seemed like a good idea, I like it more than a lot of other buildings . . .
Someone, a critic, has said that you bore people, but in a way that, as a defence, they have to try looking at your films in a new or different way . . . boring them into a conscious awareness . . .
I wanted to put it somewhere, where people who walk by and see it would hardly notice any movement — but if they came back and looked in an hour, they would see it had changed, the sun had moved, but if you *looked* for movement, if you watched it, you'd never notice, like a clock . . . it changes, but very slowly. My films though, if they mean anything or have a message, well, I don't know my *message* . . .
When you did the Campbell Soup Cans . . .
I didn't do that either
No?

No.
And the seven canvases by the door of the elevator?
Parts of them, but I really don't know which parts exactly — anyhow, it doesn't matter, as long as I sign them — they aren't beautiful or anything like that, just interesting
Sort of the world within the plastic?
What?
Something Avatar said about you — Avatar?
It's a NY paper, small but quite good, about the best in fact — just after you were shot, they said that, whereas most pop artists took the world and painted the plastic, you took the plastic and revealed the world within . . . would you agree with that?
Well, it's nice
About Solanas; I could shoot you now, anyone could take the . . .
Would you
No, but someone else might, I really

You have a new book, *a*, is it similar to your pop-up, fold-down, peel-off thing, your first book?
Not really; I'm not sure just what it is, someone said it's a novel
Commercially, how did your first book do Sales weren't bad; reviews, well . . .
Getting back to the question of themes . . .
Forget about themes
You say you don't have a message, or at least don't know what it is, but why do you make films
As you say, why not?, I mean I don't know, it's just . . . well, why not?
True enough. There seems to be a trend among what have been called the angry, young film-makers, like Godard, who are trying to say 'Look, this is only a film', to take films out of the hands of a few with the cameras, and let every man make his own life. As Godard said, 'A thousand films from a thousand men', that anyone should and can make a film about life as they know it
Do we?
I see your point; anyone can do it but only a few do, but when you paint your signature onto a canvas someone else has finished, aren't you saying the same thing? I don't know what it's saying or if it says anything

I see, well, I don't really, but . . . what are you doing now?
We just finished a film . . . it's Viva fucking a guy for two hours, but we can't show it Not even at the Garrick?

Whirr Whoosh Click
Andy, dahling, how are you? You look well . . . Andy these men are from the ad agency and they . . . they can explain
Yes, we uh . . . we saw your posters at the Museum of Modern Art and we like what you do . . . we have a client who needs an ad, a poster for a display and we thought you might well we'd like you to do the job, if you're interested . . . here, let me show you
What's that?
It's an idea our boys cooked up . . . you see, wait let me show you, where's a plug? Here's one . . . you don't mind do you if we just unplug it for . . .
. . . it's a good idea, we've already sold it to an airline. Now our artist drew up this idea, and we'd like you to think along the same line . . . how do you like it?
It's nice.
What about you, don't you like it
No, not really
Oh . . . well Mr. Warhol, what do you think. Now like I said, we've seen your things and like your stuff, you certainly know what you are doing, we just wanted to give you a few ideas, know what I mean?
Uh, sure
If you just think about it, we'll give you a ring in a day or two
Uh, could I keep this
Sure, where can we put it
Here I'll take it
Well Andy, I've got to go too, call you later
Bye
Sure

Did you really like the poster.
Uh . . .
Will you take the job though
We need the money, law suits and the phones and all, I'll probably do it. We've done this sort of thing before and
Like the Schraft's 'Underground Sunday'?
Yes, but I really didn't understand the fuss they made over it, it only took half an hour
Andy, I'm going out for dinner, want something
Where are you going . . . I'll have a hamburger and coffee, how about you, want something
Sure, I'll have the same
You can get something different, they have different sandwiches
No, Hamburger is fine, thanks
You sure?
Sure, how much is it
That's okay, I'll pay for it
Here . . .

How's your sandwich
Fine thanks
You got the recorder working again? I'm really sorry about that
That's okay, they're pretty sturdy little machines
It's great, how much does one cost
Somewhere around 70 dollars I guess
Isn't this yours
No, we borrowed it
Just a minute, let me get the phone . . . . . . Sorry about all these interruptions, today's been a bad day. I've got to go out for a while, you're welcome to stay and see some films, then we could talk some more, or do you want to come back some other time?
Thanks, I think I'll wait
Fine, be back soon
Sure

whirr whoosh click

Excuse, me, but do you work here
No, not really, but there's someone in the other room
Thanks, but I'm looking for this girl, my daughter. She left home and we just thought she might have come around, This is her picture, she's a good girl, not bad looking either. She talked about 'Andy' and the Velvet Underground so much, she met him at some party she said, well we just thought that she might have come around here . . .
I wouldn't know, like I said, I don't work here, but if you ask someone they . . .
I don't want to bother anyone, especially

Mr Warhol, but we were just worried about Sue, that's my little girl's name, and my wife has read about Mr Warhol in the Times and, well, she was just afraid my little girl might have gotten mixed up with, well, in trouble
Sure, I know what you mean. Tell you what, write down your name and address and your daughters name and I'll ask Andy about it when he gets back. I'm sure that if he knows anything, he'll get in touch with you
Thanks a lot, I really don't want to pester you, but my wife's been on my back for a week to come down here, anyway, if she's old enough to leave home, she should know what she's doing
I'll tell Andy
Here you can show him her picture, in case she's using another name or something
Sure
Thanks again
I'll tell Andy

an hour later
Hi, sorry I took so long. You like the rushes
What . . . oh, the films
What'd you think . . . you don't shoot do you
Not really, no. How about you
No, these shots aren't too good . . . have any more questions
whirr whoosh click

Enter Spaced Out Type and Hippie Side Kicks
Andy, remember me?
Well, uh no, not really
But Andy, I remember you . . . we met at Maries, remember, last summer
Andy, the phone company wants you
Tell them I'm at my lawyers
We already told them that
Well, make up something
What's That?
A Tape recorder
They say they know you're stalling and that if they don't get their money, they'll disconnect at noon tomorrow
Tell I'm working on it
It's not on is it?
No, its not
What's your name?
Lazarus, what's yours?
My friends call me Billy
Do those two call you Billy?
Oh, they've been taking care of me, and when I told them that I knew Andy, well they brought me down right away. They've been very nice to me
I see
Andy, after all this time, and I'm not even talking to you. Andy, I want to be in one of your films
Sure, uh, what do you mean
Oh, Andy, I feel just like last years flower child . . . that's why I'm wearing a headband, and this shirt is Indian, I mean India Indian
It's very nice, I don't think I've ever seen one in blue before
No, you don't see them much any more. I could get one for you . . .
That's okay, but I'd never wear it
How about the bells
They're nice too
Andy, I feel like I want to take off all my clothes and run naked, you know what I mean
Uh, sure
And I want to be in one of your films like all those other nice people
Oh, I see
I just knew you'd understand, you always did . . . you know, uh I forgot your name
Lazarus
Oh, I know a song about Lazarus, by that Indian girl Buffy St Marie
Yeah, that's the one . . . do you know it too?
No, but why don't you sing it and I'll record you
But you said it wasn't working
It's not, but I'll turn it on, here
No, I couldn't sing . . . what time is it
About six-thirty
Oh, I'm late . . . can I use the phone . . . thanks. Oh, damn, he's not there. I've got to leave Andy, but here's my number and when you need me just call, I'm always at home. Bye.

whirr whhooosh click

OZ

For this experimental format OZ acknowledges the inspiration of San Francisco's great music paper Rolling Stone.

February 1969

London OZ is published monthly by OZ Publications Ink Ltd.
38a Palace Gdns Terrace, London W8.
Phone 01-229 4623
01-603 4205

This issue edited by Andrew Fisher
Editor: Richard Neville

Design: Jon Goodchild.
Writers: Andrew Fisher, Ray Durgnat, Germaine, David Widgery, Angelo Quartrocchi, Fletcher Watkins.
Music: Felix Dennis
Research: Jim Anderson.
Artists: Martin Sharp, Bob Hook, John Hurford, Don Heywood, Phillipe von Mora.
Photography: Keith Morris.
Advertising: Felix Dennis
RKN 1330
Typesetting: Jacky Lawton, courtesy, Thom Keyes.
Pushers: Louise Ferrier, Bridgid Harrison, Casi Pavalko.
Distribution: Britain (overground) Moore-Harness Ltd. 11 Lever Street, London EC1.
Phone CLE 4882
(underground) BCAL, 22 Betterton Street, London WC2. Phone TEM 8606.
New York DGB Distribution Inc, 41 Union Square, New York, 10003.
California: Rattnar Distributors, 2426 McGee Street, Berkeley, California 94703.
Holland Thomas Rap, Regullerdwarstraat 91, Amsterdam, Tel: 020-227065.
Denmark George Streeton, The Underground, Larsbjørn straede 13, Copenhagen K.

Dear OZ,

Khatmandu – 'the place to go to before everybody else gets there' – reads the colour supplement in the Camp restaurant. The walls of the camp are pasted over with pastiches from other places. The banana custard in the Camp tastes of newspaper and the pancakes feel like it, but it is usually full –

of the Doors, of people buying and selling (Dominic sells his rings), medallions of the Tibetan calendar go for 1s.8d. Over the way is the International – of beautiful porridge and toasted cheese sandwiches, winking Christmas tree and chicken chow mein – it's warm and the food is good – Kathmandu is just one long food trip.

New places to go to – the Cabin where hash candies are 6d. a block, one of their hash candies put me on a horror trip for two days and people have been known to run freaking from the cabin; but ganga and chillans pass round and you can score either hash or ganga at the Cabin – they have the best music in town.

The Capital which still cater for Nepalese but is also overrun by Europeans – it's an eating place and good for that – also the Star restaurant. You can also stay at The Matchbox for 2s. a room – that's by the river – there are places all over town to stay.

The Tibetan Blue is still going but no longer makes the scene – it's got 'please to smoke no hash' on the wall. The Globe is defunct with no plaque to mark its demise. Round the corner from the Tibetan Blue is the Government Shop and everybody scores hash here – it's the season for hash.

The cabbage swiping black bulls swipe cabbages and everybody does what they have to – there are a lot of people up here though everybody said that everybody else was going to Goa for Christmas but that was in Delhi. In Delhi you stay in Janpath Lane, or I stayed at the Banerjeer at 18 Fire Brigade Lane – the Cellar is the place to go and I didn't go – exit Delhi.

Benares is the hip place to stay – on a houseboat moored on the Ganges in full view of the prayers on the ghats and the burning bodies. Me, I'm slowly going to Pardichamy and the ashram there and then probably to Bangkok but that's some time ahead. I shall miss the lotus living on the Ceylon beaches.

Love Rosemary.

Dear OZ,

You published a small article about Gary Butler and his girlfriend Kathy in your September issue (I believe) of last year, in reference to a raid on their flat and him being charged with illegal possession of a drug, which resulted in him being sent to the Borstal Wing of Wormwood Scrubs. He is now at South House, H.M. Borstal Institution, Feltham

Middlesex, (his number is 129), where I visited him recently.

He asked me, to convey the accompanying booklet to you with the hope, that you might find something printable he is, not surprisingly, rather depressed under the present conditions.

Yours sincerely
Werner Thomas
22 Rodney Road
London SE17

Here are two extracts from the booklet:

Twas on a cold wet sunny day
They came to take poor me away
Chained by the wrists they pulled me thither
My sweat stained body was all a shiver
He seems to be withdrawn said the fuzz
Quite right
Poor me died six times that night.

To love is to hurt
For love always hurts
Pain tremors, killing hate
Are all forms of violence
Violence: love of
To break someone's head
I hate violence
I enjoy hating violence
It gives me something to do.

Dear Richard,

Whoever you gave two pages in Oz 17 to, to deliver an attack on the ICA and me without having the guts to put his/her opinions is either a) a plain coward, b) someone who nurses such an unutterable grudge against me that they tremble to affix their name to their feelings or alternatively c) a vast international conspiracy dedicated to my downfall.

That's a joke of course, but behind the joke I'm serious: the cloak of anonymity, the use of secrecy for public attacks, poisons relationships, and can lead to 'paranoid fantasies as in c), I'm not normally a paranoid person, but I'll confess that once or twice over the past weeks I've stopped short asking myself 'could it have been X ?...'

Although your brave Sir Galahad of the cultural revolution makes some quite interesting points about ICA policy which under other circumstances I'd be prepared to discuss, I'm not at present willing to wrestle blindfold, or pick combat with a hit-and-run masked bandit.

You were kind enough to warn me in advance that you were going to print a piece about the ICA in Oz 17, and generous enough to invite me to reply to it. It is however unkind and sneaky

to print unsigned onslaughts, a practice more fitting for Beaverbook smut-hounds or totalitarian witch-hunters than for a mag like Oz which proudly pins up the banners of sexual ecstasy (which implies wholeheartedness) and cultural liberation (which implies commitment to your own words and thoughts).

Michael Kustow.

Dear Oz,

Here is an idea for DROP OUT CITY in London. DROP OUT CITY would be a group of run-down slum properties (for cheapness – you guessed) – grouped near each other, providing FREE 24 hour protection from the elements, somewhere to kip in your roll. No rules, supervision or put-downs, equals to a man. During the day, FREE MEALS could be provided from another place, perhaps staffed by participants from DROP OUT CITY, therefore no need to pay them (crude but honest). Later on, more buildings could be aquired for an ART GALLERY, showing produce from any artists, giving them a chance of a semi-permanent show. The same principle applies to other areas of CULTURE (sub or otherwise), e.g. THEATRE, cinema, etc, charging the PIN-STRIPE brigade but again FREE to DROP OUTS. This way the CITY might, just might, pay its way. But here and now, the money to start the thing could come from POP SHOWS or some such, artists CONTRIBUTION to a fund, as in other BENEFIT shows. Am I making a good case? I didn't pass my 11 plus you see, so slightly illiterate. Will somebody please see what I'm trying to say and make a better job of it? You, we, everybody, could start right now, it would fulfill a lot of the things which have appeared in your mag! Workless society MONEYLESS society, SHELTER for the FREE. HELP on details could, would come from SYMPATHISERS in estate agents office's and so on. It needs somebody in a better position than me to have the NERVE and FORESIGHT to start the BALL ROLLING. To my eyes, it seems so possible.

Paul James,
60 Askew Road,
London W.12.

Dear Oz,

In reply to David Ramsey Steele's article in OZ 17. First of all I wholeheartedly agree that a moneyless society would be very groovy providing it was made up of unselfish, loving, compassionate people; qualities which are unfortunately lacking in the greater percentage of the human race. He also calmly assumes that the level of industry would be maintained at its present rate, an assumption which is sadly miscalculated. If you were to offer the average man the abolition of money i.e. incentive and in return for his daily grind food, clothes and shelter he is more than likely to tell you to piss off. This would not only wreck our own standard of living but would do nothing to alleviate the problem of of the world's population starving. Man does NOT possess benevolence towards the underprivileged of this world even with money, let alone

without it. His main concern is number one and that goes for this generation as well as the capitalist one we are all living under.

Even if machines did all the menial jobs, as Ramsey Steele suggests we would still need to import as this country is not self-supporting. I can see the scene now; thousands of people jostling at the dock side screaming 'meat! meat!' as an Argentine boat comes in and meanwhile there is machinery for an irrigation plant in India standing rusting on the quay.

The whole idea is ludicrous.
Love and bewilderment,
Roger Hillier,
60 Fairholme Road,
London W14.

Dearey Oz,

Just a word or two hundred to try and put right any people who think that if we all follow David Ramsey Steele's reasoning in 'smash cash' we will attain a beautiful world.

There is nothing wrong with money as a means of buying and selling goods and services – it is man's corruption of the monetary system that is its downfall – NOT the system.

Can anyone honestly believe that there will ever be enough resources on this minute planet of ours to give everyone in the world what they want. Sure, everyone can have clothes, some kind of house, adequate food, etc , but there will never be enough to let everyone live in a big house, have as much food as they can eat, etc.

The resources of the world are rapidly being outstripped by the global population!

The other main fault in his reasoning was that he said 'abolition of money means abolition of (among other things) nations and frontiers, armies and prison.' – Just think of how many wars between nations have been caused by purely financial considerations. Another quote: 'in a moneyless world work would be recreation and art' – find enough people who regard refuse collection, public toilet cleansing, lorry driving, coal delivery, etc , as 'recreation & art' and you would be OK – but I can't see us getting anyone to do these kind of essential jobs.

It is us, the human race, that is at fault. We cause all the misery, pain, murder & starvation of our fellow beings – no system could corrupt us. It takes a corrupt person to initiate a corrupt system.

Hope you get the message,
love,
Samuel.
6 Wanbleddian Gardens Cardiff.

Dear Oz,

Rupert Anderson may as well gripe at his arse for shitting as at politicians for telling lies.

He criticises Shelter and then suggest the need for 'a well organised network of Social Workers' to help 'problem families'. The well-meaning liberal and the 'fully trained social worker' within the present set-up can do nothing but take the news-worthy stink out of the whole filthy issue of homelessness.

Surely what is wanted most is for the lid to be pulled off until the smell moves the bastards to do something about it, and more important than rhetoric is suggestions as to how this can be done.

EMERGENCY YIPPIE REPORT

Dear friends,

From the Bay Area to New York, we are suffering the greatest depression in our history. People are taking bitterness in their coffee instead of sugar.

It's a common problem, not an individual one, and people don't talk to one another too much any more.

It is 1969 already, and 1965 seems almost like a childhood memory. Then we were the conquerors of the world. No one could stop us. We were going to end the war. We were going to wipe out racism. We were going to mobilize the poor. We were going to take over the universities.

Go back and read some of the early anti-war literature. Check out the original hippie-digger poetry and manifestoes: euphobia, overflowing optimism, and expectation of immediate success. Wow, I can still get high on it.

A lot has gone down since then. The war roars on, the San Francisco scene is gone, pot and acid are being challenged by speed and smack, Nixon has replaced Johnson, and white racism is stronger than ever.

America proved deaf, and our dreams proved innocent. Scores of our brothers have become inactive and cynical.

Still, our victories since 1965 have been enormous. We kicked LBJ's ass. We defeated the Democratic Party. Our history has been marked by a series of great battles: Berkeley, the Pentagon, Colombia, Chicago. We are stealing the youth of America right out of the kindergartens and elementary schools. We are the most exciting energy force in the nation.

It is just because we are striking so deep that, in every phase of the movement, arrests and trials and court appearances and jail have bottled up resources, sapped energy and demoralized the spirit.

This has happened slowly – not the way many paranoids expected, the knock on the door, and concentration camps for thousands of us. Chase that shit out of your head. That's not The American Way.

The American Way is to pick one off here, one there, and try to scare the others into inaction.

So:

Huey Newton is in prison

Eldridge Cleaver is in exile

America's courts are colonial courts, where White America punishes her black subjects. America's jails are Black concentration camps. Every black man in jail is a political prisoner. In America we have Race and Class Justice, pure and simple.

And they have picked off the Panther leadership and driven it into jail and exile without our burning the fucking country down in retaliation.

Oakland Seven are accused of conspiracy

Which means: organize a demonstration which effectively challenges authority and the courts arrest you for conspiracy and tie you up with lawyers and boring shit for years. Is that why so few people are into planning demonstrations any more in Berkeley?

After spending three months there in the fall, I was depressed to see the old Berkeley audaciousness gone. Shit, three years ago we were going to overthrow Washington from Telegraph Avenue. Result: broken dreams for hundreds and hundreds of people. 'Politico' has virtually become a term of insult in Berkeley today.

Meanwhile, the cops are smiling.

Tim Leary is up for 30 years and how many of our brothers are in court and jail for getting high?

Smoking pot is a political act, and every smoker is an outlaw. The drug culture is a revolutionary threat to plasticwasp9-5america.

If you smoke quietly, you won't get bothered. If you smoke in public, or if you live in a commune, or get active politically, or show up somewhere in J. Edgar Freako's computer, you're likely to get busted for getting high.

Through the power of arrest, the cops have virtually silenced the drug evangelists and have destroyed drug communities like the Haight-Ashbury.

Spock faces two years in the pen

When America arrested the Baby Doctor for advising young men to follow their consciences, I was ecstatic: the next day I actually expected thousands of intellectuals and religious folk to stand on soapboxes and repeat Spock's words. Fuck. No one hardly said a word.

The intellectual community was paralyzed by fear. Is it any wonder now how German intellectuals were so easily silenced? Some of the Boston Five tried to beat the rap, re-interpreting their actions into meaninglessness. Where was that moral confrontation with authority that Paul Goodman spoke so oozingly about?

Sorry for the bitterness, but I saw the arrest of Spock as a test case for the government. If they could arrest and convict Spock without much of a backlash, certainly they could exile Cleaver and jail Leary, and eventually get to me.

The government won the test. Now they are willing to try anything.

Campus activists are expelled and arrested

Participants in any campus outbreak now are expelled or suspended from school, and arrested on assorted misdemeanors, if not on felony charges for conspiracy.

Students quickly forget the court cases left behind, and the euphoria of an outbreak turns sour in the hearts of those who go to court and jail alone.

When cops first come on campus, the liberals scream – but gradually the liberals get tired and go to sleep.

Cops and courts never sleep.

War resisters are behind bars

The anti-draft organizations are in shambles. Individuals are left alone to face 3-to-6 year sentences for refusing the draft. Thousands of men have been driven into exile in Canada and Sweden. The bravest men in the army are choosing to go to the stockade rather than eat military shit.

Stockades, federal prisons and courts are full of men who have defied the military, and who now must face the music. Unfortunately, there is no orchestra playing behind them.

Add it up:

Cops and courts have tried to put the national black leadership on ice, knocked the Berkeley white activist movement on its heels, over-run the campuses, wiped out many longhair communities, muted the intellectuals, and given, with impunity, fantastic punishment to draft and GI resisters.

The pattern goes a long way to explaining the malaise so many of us feel. America got where she is by jailing and killing blacks and other coloured peoples. If America's own children – the brats of her white middle class – insist on acting like blacks, well, shit they will jail and kill us too.

Who the hell wants to 'make it' in America today? The hippie-yippie-SDS movement is a 'white nigger' movement. The American economy no longer needs young whites and blacks. We are waste material. We fulfill our destiny in life by rejecting a system which rejects us.

Embarrassed by the national press and the Walker Report, Daley needs a scapegoat in the pen. I am not going to be anyone's scapegoat.

America used to use HUAC to shit people up, but HUAC can only silence a movement that is afraid of itself. Pierson appeared before HUAC in October and said I told him that the yippies were planning to 'assassinate Daley and the other national politicians' and overthrow the government 'within a year.' He sounded like he was on an acid trip.

The yippies love HUAC. For us it is a costume ball: a chance to project to the children of the world our secret fantasies, a la McCluhan. What a gas it was to see the headline: 'HUAC BARS SANTA CLAUS.' HUAC is all bullshit; it has no power.

What is not bullshit is an official government document in which the Department of Justice admitted in December, 1968 to a Virginia appeals court that it maintains 'electronic surveillance' of me. The document, 12660, is signed by C Vernon Spratley Jr., U.S. Attorney for the Eastern District of Virginia, and it was sent to the U.S. Court of Appeals, Fourth Circuit.

It says: 'The government is tendering herewith to this court a sealed exhibit containing transcripts of conversations in which appellant Rubin was a participant or at which he was present which were overheard by means of electronic surveillance.'

Electonic survellance!

The government admits that it maintains either a phone tap or a house bug, or both, of my life. In other words, there is nothing that I can do in the privacy of my own home that does not go into some secret Big Brother tape recorder.

No need anymore for suspicion – it's admitted. And what can I do about it? Nothing.

The New York cops, using an illegal search warrant and phony drug possession charges; the Chicago cops, using an agent provocateur and spy; the Department of Justice, using bugging; and the Chicago courts, using frame-up felony charges, $25,000 bail, and travel restrictions, have joined together in a criminal conspiracy to deprive me of my civil rights. That's about all the shit they could throw at me in six months.

I've got to raise a lot of money to stay out of jail: for everything from lawyer's fees to organizing a propaganda fight against Daley's Neanderthal Republic. A Jerry Rubin Defense Committee is being organized. Please try to help. Make contributions to 'Rubin Defense Committee' and mail to 5 St Marks Place, apt 16, New York 10003, New York.

These are days when one asks himself the most basic questions about the movement: Is it real or transparent? Does it just concern issues, or is it a whole new life style? Could the government break it apart with concessions?

Are we creating a New Man, or are we a reflection ourselves of the bullshit we hate so much? Are we a new brotherhood, or are we just a tangle of organizations and competing egos? What will happen when we reach age 30 and 40?

I am not sure myself, and what I think often depends on how I feel when I wake up in the morning. And this is one of the differences between the black and the white movements. For blacks the liberation movement is a struggle against physical and mental oppression. For whites the movement is an existential choice.

One way to feel whether or not we have something real is to see how people relate to one another in trouble. In the past the movement has left the casualties of the last battle to their own individual fates as it moved on to the next dramatic action.

Many activists have even been forced to turn to their parents for help, rather than to the movement which is trying to overthrow their parents' institutions. How can we ask young kids to take risks in a movement which doesn't defend its own? My brother is 21 years old and his eyes often ask me that question.

The movement is more concerned with ideological debate, organizational games, and in-fighting than with creating a family. But our movement is only as strong as the friendships within it. Our only real strength is in our identification with one another.

That collective identification then becomes the greatest challenge to the cops and courts:

MESS WITH HIM AND YOU'VE GOT ME TO DEAL WITH TOO.

If 1968 was 'The Year of the Heroic Guerrilla,' then 1969 will be 'The Year of the Courts.' We must attack the myths surrounding the courts as ferociously as we have attacked the American myths of war, apple pie, your friendly neighborhood cop, and 'free elections.' Maybe Pigasus should become a judge.

Lenny Bruce put it right: 'In the Halls of Justice, the only Justice is in the Halls.' Courts come on as sacred as churches. Judges act like they just got off the last plane from heaven.

America's courts are the nation's toilets. And in America's jails, human beings are forced to live like animals.

Martin Luther King saw civil disobedience and arrests as moral thrusts aimed at stirring the population and government to action. His death dramatized the death of innocence.

The police, district attorneys and judges use arrests freely: to get activists off the streets, to tie us up in endless judicial and legal procedures, and to serve as a warning to others. Arrests become a form of punishment and detention.

For the cops, an arrest is almost as good as a conviction.

To challenge the courts is to attack American society at its roots. In campus rebellions, the most revolutionary demand, the demand that can never be granted by the administration, is the demand for amnesty. Attacking the society's mechanism for punishing her citizens is attacking the society's very basis for control and repression.

Americans like to believe that this is a country of 'fair play.' We ought to organize tours for the American people of their courts and jails.

An offensive against the courts and jails – including direct action and direct legal and financial aid to the victims of the system -- would be the most immediate link that a white movement could possibly make with blacks and poor whites: the country's shit-on, the "criminal element".

As a beginning let's organize massive mobilizations for the spring, nationally coordinated and very theatrical, taking place near courts, jails, and military stockades.

The demonstration should demand immediate freedom for Huey P Newton, Eldridge Cleaver, Rap Brown, Harlem 5, Harlem 6, all black prisoners, Timothy Leary, the Oakland Seven, all drug prisoners, all draft resisters, Benjamin. Spock, Jeff Segal, Martin Kenner, me, Fort Hood 43, Catonsville Nine and Milwaukee 14, and all white political prisoners, and

amnesty for deserters and draft evaders.

Our search for adventure and heroism takes us outside America, to a life of self-creation and rebellion. In response, America is ready to destroy us.

America, like the Roman Empire, is falling apart. Repression reveals the speed of America's fall. When you challenge the pretty words about democracy, lies a mad, arrogant beast who will tolerate no disrespect or opposition.

I used to know all this in my head. Now I know it in my gut. In the past six months I've personally found out what it's like to live in a police state.

In 1964 and 1965 I was active in campus demonstrations at Berkeley, travel to Cuba, and anti-war actions like stopping troop trains. In those days America thought it could solve its problems with white demonstrators by quickly winning the war in Vietnam.

But we had other ideas, and so did the Vietnamese. The anti-war movement became part of a massive youth movement, student demonstrations spread across the country, and in the summer of 1967 America's ghettoes burned. The solution to rebellion at home became for LBJ a military one, and his administration turned the problem over the FBI, CIA, Red Squads, the cops and the courts.

I guess I began really asking for trouble when, after working as project director for the seige of the Pentagon, I helped organize the youth festival and demonstration in Chicago in opposition to the Democratic Convention.

The yippies were the most public, anarchic and fearless conspiracy the world has ever seen.

It made LBJ very uptight to realize that incredible youth-rock festival was going to be held in Chicago the same week he was scheduled to be renominated. LBJ knew that the one group in the country which had done the most to laugh at him and make him look silly were the hippies.

But LBJ dropped out. Bobby Kennedy looked like he was going to get the nomination and through his charisma put the yippies on the shelf. On June 5, Sirhan assassinated Kennedy, and yippie popped back, as unreal as ever.

On June 13 three New York narcotics detectives, carrying a mysterious search warrant, stormed into my Lower East apartment, angrily tore a Castro poster off the wall, and arrested me for alleged possession of three ounces of marijuana.

They spent 90 minutes in my apartment questioning me about yippee plans for Chicago and going through my personal papers and telephone book.

The search warrant claimed that on June 10 an informer was in my apartment with me and he saw dangerous drugs there. The only people in my apartment on that day were my closest friends. Narcotics police, who use corruption to get high, invented an informer to get a search warrant. Attorney Bill Kunstler is now attacking the warrant.

A Red Squad detective later told a New York Post reporter that this was the first blow against the yippies, whom he said were agents of the Communist Chinese importing dope into the country to destroy American youth.

Virtually everyone under 30 in Manhattan smokes pot. The cops use marijuana busts as a handy club against blacks, longhairs and political activists. If you are a longhair and a political activist, you got trouble. If you are a longhair, a political activist, and black, you got real trouble. (Hello, Eldridge, wherever you are).

The marijuana charge against me is a felony punishable by 2-15 years in the state pen.

When I arrived in Chicago for the yippee festival, I found three shifts of plainclothes cops hounding me day and night. It was typical Chicago police harrassment. Round the clock they tailed the half dozen people they thought were 'leaders.' They were there when we went to bed at night and they were there when we got up in the morning.

For me they cooked up a special treat. Daley sent an undercover cop, Robert Pierson, alias Bob Lavon, to infiltrate the yippies, act as an agent provocateur, spy on me, and frame me on a serious felony rap.

At 10.30 p.m. Wednesday, Aug 28, while looking for a restaurant, I was kidnapped off an empty downtown street in Chicago by four plainclothes pigs. I was threatened with beating and death, slugged and told by the head of the Chicago Red Squad:

'You guys ruined our city. You, you Rubin are responsible. Do you like our city? We hope you do because we are going to put you in jail here for a long time'.

By chance, Jack Mabley, a columnist for the conservative Chicago American, happened to be in the streets when I was picked up. This is how he described what happened:

'No blood flowed in one of the most ominous happenings. Jerry Rubin ... was walking west on Washington ... A girl (Nancy) was with him ...

'An unmarked car with four policemen skidded to a stop besides Rubin. Three men jumped out. 'Come on Jerry, we want you,' one called as they grabbed Rubin. The girl screamed, 'We haven't done anything! We were just walking.'

'I have heard Rubin speak, and he was obscene and revolting. In America a man may be arrested for obscenity or revolution. But Rubin was grabbed off the street and rushed to jail because of what he thinks.

'This is the way it is done in Prague. This is what happens to candidates who finish second in Vietnam. This is not the beginning of the · police state, it IS the police state.'

I was then accused of a wild assortment of charges and bail was set at $25,000,

more than the usual bail for accused murderers.

Two months later, on October 29, the Cook County Grand Jury returned an Illinois State indictment against me on two counts of 'sollicitation to commit mob action,' a felony punishable on each count of 1-5 years in the state pen. Pierson's bullshit provided the basis for each indictment.

Pierson lied by saying that I shouted through a bullhorn, 'Kill the pigs,' thereby supposedly solliciting others to mob action the afternoon of Wednesday, Aug 28 in Grant park. The incident is supposed to have taken place after cops attacked the crowd when the American flag was lowered, during the rally preceding the Mobilization march.

Anyone who was there during that time, including people with photographs or films, and especially people who saw me during that time, please contact my attorney: Frank Oliver, 30 North LaSalle, Chicago, Illinois, 60602.

Whenever I come to Chicago for court appearances the press treats me like a yippie Richard Speck. The Judge has officially restricted my travel to Illinois. (Illinois?) The court system, of course, is under Daley's thumb. It all adds up to a one-way ticket for me to five years in the Illinois state pen and revenge for Richard J Daley.

Remember the legend of Spartacus. The Romans slaughtered all the slaves, but the moral example lives on.

When the Roman Army came to kill Spartacus, they faced a mass of thousands of slaves. They demanded that Spartacus step forward.

'I am Spartacus!' shouted one slave.
'No, I am Spartacus!' shouted another.
'No, I am Spartacus!'
'No, I am Spartacus!'
'No, I am Spartacus!'

With love, Jerry Rubin

(with a little help from my friends, Nancy Kurshan, Martin Kenner, Arthur Naiman, Stew Albert, Gumbo, Jim Petras, David Stein, Sharon Krebs, Robin Palmer, Ken Pitchford.)

What will you say when she asks:

DADDY-WHERE WERE YOU WHEN THE DEAN CALLED THE POLICE?

Why don't we do it in the road

Behind the Barricades or buried in Classes?

These days there's only one place for an active man or woman.
JOIN THE STUDENTS AND CHANGE THE WORLD!
Vietnam talks . . . . . non--proliferation treaties . . . . . negotiations and relief in Nigeria and Biafra . . . . . the world is threatened with peace.
JOIN THE ARMY . . . AND go to sleep.

There are only 7 actual wars in the whole world . . . . and most of these are piddling border skirmishes kept going for publicity purposes, and in which you are not eligible or welcome to fight anyway. But for the man of action, the world still has room. The battlefronts have shifted, that's all. The seat of war has moved to the campus, and now, there is a Korea for you as a *Professional Student.*

In the final analysis, universities depend for their achievements on the human factor — on the intelligence, versatility and strength of character of their student leaders. So, for more than an academic interest in revolution, become a *student.*

Look at what the new student is doing already in the first weeks of 1969, and you will see that somewhere, somehow, there is a rewarding place for you. The year is off to a whirlwind start. YOU as a student, can keep it that way.

LONDON:
Forcible removal at the London School of Economics of gates

Read below where its at. Complete the coupon and send it to your favourite student organisation.

erected by authorities to restrict freedom of student movement. 26 arrests. Confrontation with police at Bow Street. Successful occupation of ULU by students forced re-opening of LSE, closed by director Adams following student protest.

PARIS:
Occupation and sacking of Rectory building following meeting to protest against refusal to show films of the 'events of May and June. Fighting with police, who charged a group of 1000 students. 200 arrests. National Union of French Students has called for mobilisation against police provocation.

BESANCON, NANTERRE, VICENNES, CAEN:
Occupations, strikes, violent clashes with police and authorities. Boycott of elections for university committees of staff and student.

BERLIN:
Hundreds of students clashed with police after demonstrations against the Social Democratic Party and the Greek Military regime. 500 students attacked the Persian embassy in protest against the Shah's regime, and dispersed by police weilding batons. Barricades erected at the Free University. Violent strikes and protest actions caused closure of the Law School.

PRAGUE:
Following upon the death by fire of student martyr Jan Palach, thousands of students have demonstrated their solidarity against the new regime.

MADRID:
Demonstrations following upon the death of a student while under arrest have led to the imposition of a state of newspapers, threw up barricades, and clashed with police.

BARCELONA:
The university is closed until further notice following disturbances in which authorities allege that militant students ransacked the rectors office and attempted to throw him from a window. The students were protesting against the arrest of several of their leaders.

TOKIO:
Hundreds of students held out in the university's Yasuda Assembly building for two days against 9000 police. At one stage students held most of the university buildings. The final police assault took eleven hours. Elsewhere, 1500 students sealed off a square mile with petrol soaked barricades. A total of 443 students were arrested. The students were protesting against close defence ties with America.

KYOTO:
500 students battered down gates to help colleagues in occupation of campus buildings. Clashes with rival students. For the past year in Japan, students have occupied more than fifty campuses.

DACCA:
A march of 5000 students to pray for the sould of a student shot a few days earlier. Barricades raised and thirty injured. Police and army have fired on crowds, and several hundreds have been arrested.

RAWALPINDI:
Six students were injured when police opened fire on student demonstrations. Student violence has created political unrest all over Pakistan.

SAN FRANCISCO:
Mass arrest of 483 students, following demonstrations and strikes at State College. At Berkeley, violent demonstrations involving hundreds of students resulted in the departure of Ronald Reagan's limousine under a hail of eggs and rocks. At San Jose State College, students stormed campus buildings after faculty members threatened with dismissal after participation in a strike.

LOS ANGELES:
At UCLA (as at the San Fransisco campuses) a continual state of unrest amounting to revolution. At New York Queens College, Brandeis University Massachusetts, Swarthmore College Pennsylvania, the story is much the same.

From Montreal to Mexico City, from Brussels to La Paz, students demand radical change. Revolution is being fomented with tactics of confrontation developed in the streets of Chicago last August.

Can you fit into the brilliant, brash, fast-moving action-filled world of the NEW STUDENT?

It is all happening for the NEW STUDENT in 1969.
The Universities need you.

BE THERE.
JOIN THE PROFESSIONALS:
and be a step ahead.

SPIKE File

■OZ has lost its printer. Not because we're broke. Not because we're obscene. Not for any of the usual reasons publications lose printers. But because on October 20th 1968 this item appeared in, for God's sake, the News of the World.

THOUGH Mr Woodrow Wyatt, Labour MP for Bosworth, sports a fancy line in bow ties and select names like Pericles Plantagenet and Petronella Aspasia for his children, he has never been considered particularly avant garde.

It seems unlikely that he would deliberately go beyond the mildly unorthodox behaviour which has made him so much more newsworthy than the average backbencher.

But the fact remains that one of his associate companies is now linked with the printing of the "underground" magazine OZ.

The current issue carries no printer's name, but Mr Wyatt's business headquarters at Banbury confirm that it was printed at Middlesbrough by an associated firm.

Mr Wyatt doesn't have control, but he does take a close interest in the management of this company.

He can hardly have been aware of the true nature of OZ.

How can he fail to be shocked by advertisements which offer do-it-yourself formulas for the drug LSD ?

Can he approve of the obscene poem or of the dirty pictures ? Or of the advice to pot smokers ?

Clearly not.

We then read in the next weeks News of the World this:

MR WOODROW WYATT, MP, tells us that the North Riding Publishing Co., of which he owns 45 per cent, has decided not to print the "underground" magazine OZ in future.

We were officially notified of this decision some time after the News of the World. There was publicity about our problem in the press. We wrote an angry letter alleging breach of contract. As a result Woodrow Wyatt & Co (otherwise known as North Riding Publishing Co Ltd) printed another three issues of OZ. This one is the last.

In January we wrote another letter to North Riding Publishing Co Ltd asking that it continue printing OZ we pointed out amongst other things that OZ had the money to pay promptly, that we had never been prosecuted and that we brought in overseas currency. But the answer was no. we have to find another printer. Which will be difficult because most other printers seem to think like our present lot — which is why we'll probably come out late next time.

■The streets of our country are in turmoil. The universities are filled with students rebelling and rioting. Communists are seeking to destroy our country. Russia is threatening us with her might, and the republic is in danger. Yes, danger from within and from without. We need law and order! Yes, without law and order our nation cannot survive... Elect us and we shall restore law and order. We shall by law and order be respected among the nations of the world. Without law and order our republic shall fall.'
(Excerpt from a campaign speech made in Hamburg in 1932 by Adolph Hitler.)

■We wrote to the distributor who used to handle Australian OZ and asked if he could sell London Oz. This is his reply:
'Many thanks for your letter.

I was sorry to hear 'OZ Aust.' had finished, however the fact that it had to be tamed down the past twelve months, handicapped it saleswise but at least, kept all concerned out of the courts, I suppose.

Regarding your suggestion of me handling London' OZ. Believe me I would really like to say yes, as I think it would sell quite well here.

However the issue you sent me, (No.15) I consider, would be much too hot for me to handle, especially as the powers that be have clamped down solidly on this type of literature.

About the only places where they will let books and newspapers of this type be sold, are in Newsagents shops and of course I do not distribute to Newsagents.

Even in shops they are supposed to be placed where teenagers etc cannot get hold of them.

The Newsagents usually keep them under the counter until an enquiry is made — then they may sell them.'

■RULES FOR THE BLACK PANTHER PARTY

Every member of the BLACK PANTHER PARTY throughout the country must abide by these rules as functional members of the party. CENTRAL COMMTTEE members, CENTRAL STAFFS, and LOCAL STAFFS, including all captains subordinate to either national state, and local leadership of the BLACK PANTHER PARTY will enforce these rules. Length of suspension or other disciplinary action necessary for violation of these rules will depend on national decisions by national, state or state area, and local committees and staffs where said rule or rules of the BLACK PANTHER PARTY WERE VIOLATED.

Every member of the party must know these rules verbatim by heart. And apply them daily. Each member must report any violation of these rules to their leadership or they are counter-revolutionary and are also subjected to suspension by the BLACK PANTHER PARTY.

1. No party member can have narcotics or weed in his possession while doing party work.
2. Any party member found shooting narcotics will be expelled from this party.
3. No party member can be drunk while doing daily party work.
4. No party member will violate rules relating to office work, general meetings of the Black Panther Party, and meetings of the Black Panther Party anywhere.
5. No party member will use, point, or fire a weapon of any kind unnecessarily or accidentally at anyone.
6. No party member can join any other army force other than the Black Liberation Army.
7. No party member can have a weapon in his possession while drunk or loaded off narcotics or weed.
8. No party member will commit any crimes against other party members or BLACK people at all, and cannot steal or take from people, not even a needle or a piece of thread.
9. When arrested Black Panther members will give only name, address, and will sign nothing. Legal first aid must be understood by all Party members.
10. The Ten Point Program and platform of the Black Panther Party must be known and understood by each Party member.
11. Party communications must be National and Local.
12. The 10-10-10 program should be known by all members and also understood by all members.
13. All Finance officers will operate under the jurisdiction of the Ministry of Finance.
14. Each person will submit a report of daily work.
15. Each Sub-Section Leader, Section-Leader, Lieutenant and Captain must submit daily reports of work.
16. All Panthers must learn to operate and service weapons correctly.
17. All Leadership personnel who suspend or expell a member must submit this information to the Editor of the Newspaper, so that it will be published in the paper and will be known by all chapters and branches.
18. Political Education Classes are mandatory for general membership.
19. Only office personnel assigned to respective offices each day should be there. All others are to sell papers and do Political work out in the community, including Captains, Section Leaders, etc.
20. Communications—all chapters must submit weekly reports in writing to the National Headquarters.
21. All Branches must implement First Aid and/or Medical Cadres.
22. All Chapters, Branches, and components of the Black Panther Party must submit a monthly Financial Report to the Ministry of Finance, and also the Central Comittee.
23. Everyone in a leadership position must read no less than two hours per day to keep abreast of the changing political situation.
24. No chapter or branch shall accept grants, poverty funds, money or any other aid from any government agency without contacting the National Headquarters.

■Another item from the Altback. Under the note 'Todays thought: Who so beset him round...do but themselves confound — Bunyan'. Sydneys' Daily Telegraph (one of the States two main morning papers) ran this lead editorial:
The Australian louts in London who are busy organising demonstrations against our Prime Minister (Mr. Gorton), are recruited from an expatriate band of no-hopers whom all normal Australian visitors avoid like the plague.

It is obvious from the placards they are carrying that they are pushing Communist-inspired lines on racialism and the Vietnam issue which they expect some of the delegates to the Commonwealth Prime Ministers' Conference will adopt to attack Australia.

The Communist-slanted pro-Aborigines movement is being whipped up by these renegade Australians who haven't been in this country for years, and have never talked with Aborigines in their lives.

In Mr. Gorton they have picked on the wrong target.

He is a man with an acute awareness of the Aborigines' problems, and has appointed a special Minister to deal with them.

During his tour of Northern Australia last September Mr. Gorton spoke with many Aboriginal groups and displayed a profound sympathy for their welfare.

In fact there has never been a Prime Minister who has had their interest more at heart.

Many of the African delegates to the Conference will undoubtedly press their views on the Rhodesian question on Mr. Gorton, who holds the same views on this subject as Mr. Menzies.

Though Australia may consider some aspects of the Rhodesian situation as deplorable, we are not going to support any black African calls for armed intervention in the dispute.

If it came to the stage where the Conference was swamped by the armed-interventionists, and Mr. Gorton's position became untenable, he would have considerable support if he walked out.

He could then suggest that any such deliberations in the future be limited to members capable of reaching at least a broad basis of agreement, and who see in South-east Asia graver problems than those of Rhodesia and its future.

SYMBOL OF WHITE POWER

OZ has a new office:
52 PRINCEDALE ROAD, W 11,
(the old Release office.)
All subscriptions, magazine purchases, accounts and general business should go to that address only. Telephone:
603-4205
Editorial will remain at
38A Palace Gardens Terrace W 8. Tel:
229-4623.

MICHAEL X

I've always made it clear to anyone coming on physical with me I have only one thing to do – that is die. I know how to die and it doesn't bother me that much.
Anyone coming at me I am prepared to kill him.

First the gaol thing. It was a little complicated in some ways. I'd rather use one person to illustrate it. The deputy editor of New Society, I've known him for a number of years, Brian Lapping, he tells me how he is so very sorry I went to jail and what an unjust sentence it was. But he has a newspaper, an organ, he could have used his newspaper to talk about it, to talk about what he really feels, but he didn't use his newspaper to talk about it, so I don't believe him. Here I get a really clear illustration of what is really happening in England, the gutlessness of the people, the country is in a sense deteriorating into nothingness. Because they talk about being sorry, but they don't feel strongly enough. It all ends up with a lot of rhetoric. He was a friend of mine for a number of years but he didn't feel strongly enough to come and see my wife, how she was, which I find a really inhuman approach. Surely he could have visited to see if my wife had company to talk to for one day during the time I was in prison but their humanity doesn't extend out there. The dehumanising thing of society has got into all of them. So personally I have hard grudges against a lot of people, which I still feel.

In Jail one suffers racism all the time. One of the things about truthfulness is that if you sincerely believe the things you are doing and you're doing it, one does not worry about the consequences like in jail and I've been to a number of them during my sentence, I was in Oxford, Brixton, Bristol, Stafford, Swansea, I kept being moved round from one jail to the next. I finally settled at Swansea. In Oxford, the prison governor was a reasonably kind fellow and there were one or two prison officers who acted like human beings. But there were a considerable number of them who acted like total bararians. Men who would encourage prisoners to have a go and seek out that black savage. Inside, you have to fight your way out of these things, make it clear that you are prepared to act that way too. I've always made it clear to anyone coming on physical with me I have only one thing to do that is die. I know how to die and it doesn't bother me that much. Anyone coming at me I am prepared to kill him. The result was that I had to move from there to Stafford. In Stafford, I don't know what happened there in a way it was frightening. I arrived in the evening when the prisoners are being settled down for the night. The prisoners in the wing knew I was coming there, I don't know how, I could hear them screaming in the night, 'You black bastard, 'we'll get you' and lots of things. But it's not surprising because I hear it on the street anyway. But when you are alone in a cell and you hear these screams from every side it is rather frightening. Your life is threatened in a very real sense. You know in the morning you are going to have to come out amongst these screaming people and you have to come to terms about how you are going to walk. You know fear can be smelled on a person, so you become extremely strong with these fellows. I was there a little over a week. I was shut away in a place called the hole, which was under the cell landings – people shut there are either violent or for punishment or as they say for their own protection from other prisoners. I so I was told was being protected, you can't argue. I wanted to be among the prisoners. I knew they didn't know why they wanted to kill me. I was prepared to work it out in any form with them. But being shut away they can think you are hiding. I talked with some of the others held in the hole when we all went out to empty our piss bowls, they were supposed to be violent men but they saw me as another human being, talked prison talk and were cool. In exercise I had to walk by myself. I could still hear men in the cell blocks around screaming at me. Privileged prisoners also spat at me when I was exercising. I had a cut up with one of them. He followed me into the toilet wanting to punch me up and then split but it worked the other way. He was just a bully, he didn't know anything about fighting. So I was taken away, put in a cell and stopped exercising. Finally shipped to another prison. This happened all the time.

At another prison they wanted me to work in a prison factory sewing mailbags. Now this is a waste of time. Machines can do that. I told a prison officer I didn't want to do it, explained why, which took a lot of time. He said here you have to do what you are told to do. He had weapons all I had is my fists. At the reception desk I knew an officer from Cardiff and he had told me a man in for sex crimes had been cut up in the mail bag works. So I told the governor about this and that I didn't want to go but if I had to I wanted to be in the same department where I could have a knife. I said if I go in there I want a knife and I'll cut up anyone who's aiming to cut me up. He went through the whole scene telling me about accidents and I told him I'd been in enough jails to know what 'accidents' mean. So I was put in the hole again, this time for punishment not for protection. I was not to be given food etc. but that didn't worry me because I wasn't eating anyway, it was

the beginning of the Muslim celebrations and I was on a 30 day fast, which rather confused them, I was supposed to be in for punishment and they didn't have any rules to guide them in my situation. The governor came to see me and talk a number of times while I was there for a month. I told him how I'd like to talk to the other prisoners, maybe I could learn something and they could learn something from me, I could give them other ideas to think about instead of just sitting in the prison factory all day and then in their cells at night. He came on very understanding and said he'd like to help. He was one of the reforming kind and wanted to have new ideas, but then he'd say, you're in prison and there are certain rules we have to go by.

At Swansea I was placed in the execution wing, where the murderers are. I passed through a few prisons on the way and a lot of things happened in all of them. It was rather nice in a way in the execution wing sleeping where hanged prisoners had – outside was the block where their necks were popped off. My window looked over the cemetry too, where they are buried, except it isn't a cemetry but a big lime pit. I would sit at night looking at it in the company of all those dead souls, rather nice, and sometimes write a bit.

After I came out the organisation had gone through considerable changes. RAAS, the organisation I served before I went in was functioning differently because you had brothers like Frankie Dymond or Frankie Y who was in the running of things, and Frankie's methods to say the least are rather unorthodox. So I came out to find a different body to what was originally set up – which was in many ways extremely good. One can then go on to other things. So I drifted around a bit, looking and talking here and there about prisons and about the past year and things because that's what most people really wanted to talk about. Then I ran across a group in London, a very small group which was called the Black Eagles and a very young fellow called Dakus Absou, who is very nice I was very pleased to meet him. He was in Trinidad where he got in trouble constantly, being arrested every so often, sc he came to England to do something serious like study law which he thought would be the right thing to do, in order to understand the law somewhat. Studied and qualified as a barrister, then started lecturing at a couple of Universities. In York, where I first ran into him, he began to want to use his energies and his talents towards people inside the ghettoes, those who had the problems he had when he was 18. When I met him he was 24. This was a few months ago when he was getting these young brothers together and talking to them and they had the group called the Black Eagles. I started spending a lot of time with them. Then Dakus offered me a job, he asked me to be a Minister without Portfolio and relate with him about my experiences in organising. This I did and I still serve as Minister without Portfolio in the Eagles. My latest job with them was to work out a 5 year economic plan. That's what I'm on now, and have been working on this for a month since I came back from the States. My involvement with RAAS still exists, I serve both bodies I don't believe in things like one man one job – like Jim Haynes who does a lot of jobs very well. I have a lot of time to do a number of jobs, probably because I have such good people to work with. Since I went to prison people seem to be better this way, more energy etc. Before I went to jail if I was going somewhere to speak it would take them about 6 days to leaflet the area, now I say I'm coming and the hall is full without 6 days notice.

We must realise how black people have existed over the last 400 years and how they had things going for them that were not in the white community, their terms of reference were different, their sense of values. So the economic plan for them is going to be different than Mr.Callaghan's. We have liberated the young people in their limbs, like in dancing, they can go out now and shake themselves, walking the street has changed a lot, their attire is different, their clothes are not drab and grey like their mothers' were.

All the young kids today, the revolutionary ones running around saying we are going to change the system, when I ask them what will they replace it with they say it will evolve out of us. Well that's not a good enough answer for me, I want to be damn sure and very clear in my mind and break it down to what I am building towards I want to see. I know what is the alternative society, our society has a value system that is quite different to the European value system. The European on the other hand has looked and tried at all kinds of things, like capitalism, conservatism, socialism. We see the alternative society, what it is, one must be clear in your mind what the alternative society is, people may say that that isn't very much but it appears to me like it's all, so I get a different perspective. When people say the area you live in is dirty and degrading I don't believe them because where I live that is home. I can't go measuring my home by anyone else's, which is another of the strange things that happens in white society. If I understand my home and the people inside it I understand all these things, I understand how to exist on very little. I live on very few pounds indeed. I exist on very little. I have 9 in my house and I have to provide their daily bread. It's different for those in bigger houses with fewer people. They live on in a week what I live on in a month. And this is the sort of thing you have to understand to do economic planning, for our Black Nation here, and there is a Black Nation inside of the White Nation and it functions, it really works. My main priority will be human beings, and I can't be indifferent. I'm not like the Black Panthers in America. I don't want to chase round getting a gun because a gun means a bomb, and I don't see why anyone would want to support us or be with us if our ultimate aim is to take Mr Wilson's finger off the button and put mine by in its place. Surely our function is to dismantle that machine which is running riot.

The Black Eagles are completely different to the Black Panthers. Any influences that we have is from the Nation of Islam. We have lived in our communities, we are not looking for any real radical change, we are not looking to fight anybody. I'm most certainly going to defend my home against anybody. Like when the police came to my home recently, the newspapers said I came downstairs with a knife. If 4 men bust into my place I'm not going to receive them like guests. I only fight if I'm threatened, I defend myself. I don't see Enoch Powell's speeches as a threat to me. I'm a threat to him, because I'm showing something quite different than what he can possibly show. His game is one where the Labour party is there and the Conservative party is there and one or the other of them will play games, one will have a go and then the next one will have a go. There is no change that can come out of them because each one complements the other. It is in the interest of each one to make sure the other exists, because otherwise they'd crumble into nothingness. That's their system. Enoch Powell talks about us being a threat to the very core of nationhood and he's absolutely right. Look what we have done to the young people, what we have done to you, surely that's a threat to HIS nationhood. He can see very clearly the change. I understand very clearly what he is saying. He is aware of the change of values of the young white people. I don't see Powell as a terrible man at all I find him one of the most honest. I respect honesty, if some of his proposals were implemented – like shipping black people

back and so on I don't know if that would be such a bad thing because back in my island is an awful lot of sunshine. I think it is in the interests of the people here to shut us in and not let us out.

I've definitely been harrassed by the police. Definitely harrassment. They came with a search warrant to look for stolen money. They only searched for an hour, 9 people, 5 rooms, they knew what they wanted to find and then they left. They were looking for something bulky as well as what they found, like guns, and weapons. I still have faith that somewhere there is honesty. Those police they must have to convince some magistrate that there were guns at my place and surely he or someone will want to know why they came to find something and didn't do it. Why didn't they search for the stolen money they came with the warrent for. I have to live with the problem of the difficulty of communicating in court. But if I allow that to stop me trying then I'm working for nothing. I tried before and now I'll try again. Too bad if I have to go to jail. I'll come out and try again.

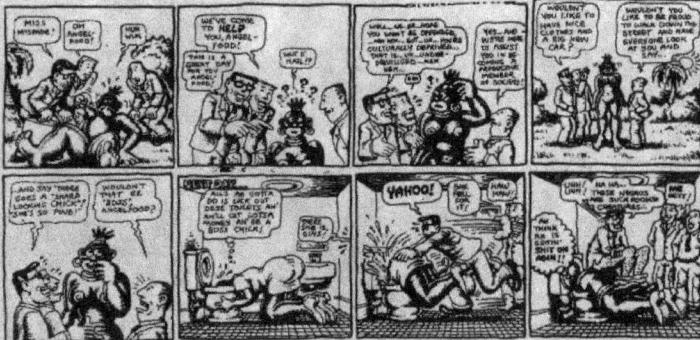

hip pocrates

Copyright 1968 Eugene Schoenfeld MD

Dr Schoenfeld welcomes your questions. Write to him at PO Box 9002, Berkeley, California. Mark your letter: OZ.

Dear Dr.Schoenfeld,

Regarding your column warning about literal blow jobs:

A few years ago, one of the psychiatric journals carried a paper on an unusual accidental death of a woman following coital foreplay.

Her lover had an impulse to blow air into her vagina which he proceeded to do vigorously. She had just stopped menstruating and her vascular system was therefore directly vulnerable. She complained of pain immediately and died within a few minutes – a rather gruesome outcome to what began as an erotic whim.

COMMENT: Or as a well-known Berkeley backgammon expert said, 'No, no baby, blow is just a figure of speech!'

QUESTION: Could you please tell me if there is any other word for 'clitoris'? That's just too scientifically proper for bedroom talk, but neither my boyfriend nor any of my other friends have been able to find one that seems natural to say.

We agreed that 'clit' from 'Candy' was only a little bit better so your suggestions really will be appreciated.

ANSWER: Three syllables does seem out of proportion but I've never heard another word for this unique organ which has pleasure as its only known function. Perhaps there are readers with other suggestions.

QUESTION: I am a single girl of 23 who has a most frustrating problem – I am unable to reach a climax (except through cunnilingus or masturbation) because I have a hooded clitoris.

I know there is an operation to remove the hood, but I am also sure I could not afford it. Therefore I write to you to ask if you might know of any positions that would help me reach a climax.

I have tried all the well-known positions (and other types too) but I'll be damned if I can ever climax through intercourse.

ANSWER: I doubt that a 'hooded' clitoris is the cause of your complaint and surgical procedures seldom are the cure.

Sexology Magazine (a useful source of information – don't be put off by the lurid covers) recently featured an article claiming a useful treatment for this very common problem.

If a woman can reach a climax through masturbation or manipulation by her partner, she is gradually trained to reachorgasm through intercourse. A kind of conditioning takes place. The climax is achieved first when penetration begins and eventually during complete intercourse. (A female's orgasm is almost always caused by clitoral stimulation, direct of indirect).

Patience and perfect frankness between partners is required if this treatment is to be effective.

QUESTION: As a relatively straight guy who showers every day and keeps his hair short, I've never been a great admirer of hippies. But lately I've begun to wonder. With a receding hairline I have become conscious of the scalps of others and yet have seen few bald spots among the hippie population.

Does keeping one's hair long and allowing the natural oils to gather by not washing slow down the fall-out rate of hair? I'll do anything to save myself from becoming bald.

ANSWER: Anything? When I read your letter I immediately thought of two hippies you may not have seen. One is Bob Ockene, a New York Bobbs-Merrill editor and Yippee whose cherubic face seems to be enhanced by his shiny head. Bob's beautiful wife is apprently not turned off by baldness.

The other is Max Scherr, editor of the Berkeley Barb, who seems to have hair growing everyplace except the top of his head. Max's beard reaches to his waist. Sometimes he stuffs part of it under his peaked cap.

The length of one's hair does not hasten or retard normal male pattern baldness so I imagine most of the hippies you have seen are of an age when baldness is rare. And, contrary to popular belief, hippies who long forego bathing are shunned by their fellows, not because of conventional uptight sterility standards, but due to that erotic sense organ, the nose.

Hair grows from structures in the skin called follicles. Each tiny follicle contains an oil or sebaceous gland and an involuntary muscle. 'Gooseflesh', a reaction to cold, fear or other stimuli, occurs when the involuntary erector pili muscles contract and move hair vertically, lift the region around each hair and depress the surrounding skin.

The rate of hair growth varies from one individual to the next and may be slower or faster at times even for one person. But in general hair grows 1.5 millimeters to 2 millimeters per week (approximately 1/25th of an inch). All of the hair except for a small part beneath the skin is 'dead' material. If you think you can spare one, pluck a hair from your head and look at the bottom of the hair shaft – that's the only live part. The rest, in effect, is pushed out or grows from this base.

Recently, I received a letter from a fellow in Los Angeles who had heard that bull sperm could increase the rate of hair growth. I told him it was a lot of bull. No known food or shampoo can increase the speed at which hair grows.

The length to which hair will grow also varies greatly from one individual to another. I've been writing mainly about head hair, but, of course, hair grows all over the body on everyone. Even people who seem relatively hairless have fine hairs which may

be seen on close examination under a strong light.

The hairs on an individual body may vary in length from a few millimeters to almost five feet. Life expectancy for an individual hair varies from 3 to 5 months for the eyebrows to 2 to 4 years for head hair.

Hair becomes more lustrous and fluffy after washing because soaps and shampoos remove oil and dirt particles which coat the hairs and cause them to stick together. The oil is usually secreted from the sebaceous glands of the hair follicles while dirt particles may come from the polluted air of cities or even from rooms densely filled with cigarette smoke.

I know of one Berkley co-ed whose roommates share a common smoking pastime. Her boyfriend claimed he could get stoned just by smelling her hair.

QUESTION: I am a 17 year old buy living with my parents in a small town. I have been hearing and reading quite a bit about THC.

Since it's still legal, it would be a boon to us small-towners who want to turn on but are missed by any drug traffic.

Where can I get some THC?

ANSWER: THC or tetrahydrocannabinol, is thought to be the active ingredient of marijuana. Because the synthesis of this drug is so complicated and expensive, any 'THC' sold on the black markets is almost surely not synthetic marijuana.

Capsules of a drug said to be THC and selling for $1.50/ each were recently collected in the Haight–Ashbury and analysed in the Pharmocology laboratories of the University of California. The capsules were found to contain not THC but a sedative used for treating animals.

Most dealers know little about the purity of the drugs they sell. The most widely known underground (al) chemist believes that a dealer with any feelings at all for other people will use this drug on himself first before selling it to others.

The establishment has no monopoly on dishonest – though they've more than their share of the market.

HOW TO COMMIT **REVOLUTION** IN CORPORATE AMERICA

THE OBSERVER,
2 FEBRUARY 1969

None the less conglomerate power can pose problems and the Monopolies Commission ought to start its inquiry with the guidelines laid down last May by the US Department of Justice.

AND IN CORPORATE BRITAIN

Part One. The Analysis.

There are three aspects, I think, to any good revolutionary program for corporate America. These aspects are closely interwined, and all three must be developed alongside each other, but there is nonetheless a certain logic, a certain order of priorities, in the manner I present them.

First, you need a comprehensive, overall analysis of the present-day American system. You've got to realize that the corporation capitalism of today is not the 19th-century individual capitalism that conservatives yearn for. Nor is it the pluralistic paradise that liberals rave about & try to patch up. Nor is it the finance capitalism of the American Communists, who are frozen in their analysis of another day.

Second, you need relatively detailed blueprints for a post-industrial America. You've got to show people concrete plans that improve their lot either spiritually or materially. There's no use scaring them with shouts of socialism, which used to be enough of a plan, how-ever general, but which today only calls to mind images of Russia, deadening bureaucracy & 1984. And there's no use boring them with vague slogans about participation & vague abstractions about dehumanization. You've got to get down to where people live, and you've got to get them thinking in terms of a better America without the spectre of Russia, rightly or wrongly, driving any thought of risking social change out of their heads.

Third, and finally, you need a plan of attack, a program for taking power. For make no mistake about it – before most people get involved in revolutionary activity they take a mental look way down the road. Maybe not all the way down the road, but a long way down. They want to know what they are getting into, and what the chances are, and whether there is really anything positive in sight that is worth the gamble. In short, I suspect that most people just don't fit the formula that seems to be prevalent in America: get people involved in anything – rent strikes, anti-nuclear testing demonstrations, rat strikes, draft demonstrations, whatever – and gradually they will develop a revolutionary mentality. According to this theory, apparently, people will realize their power & waht more if they win the rat strike, or they will wise up if they are hit on the head by a peace officer at a draft demonstration. Well, maybe that works for some people, but I wouldn't count on it, and I wouldn't rely on it to the exclusion of all else. Actually, most people seem to sink back into lethargy when the rats are gone, or nuclear testing in the atmosphere is abandoned. And I know of no convincing evidence that getting people hit on the head or thrown in jail makes them into revolutionaries – certainly many of those who believe this didn't become revrevolutionaries this routine. So, ponder carefully about this activity for activity's sake. You need a plan of attack, not just some issues like peace rats. And one thing more on this point: that plan has to come out of your analysis of the present socioeconomic system & out of your own life experience – that is, out of the American experience, and not out of the experiences of Russia, or China, or Cuba, all of which have been different from each other, and are different from the U.S.A. The world moves, even in America, and as it moves new realities arise and old theories become irrelevant. New methods become necessary. If you expect to be listened to, you will have to look around you afresh and build your own plan, abandoning all the sacred texts on What Is To Be Done.

An analysis of the system, a set of blueprints, and a program for gaining power. This is the general framework. Let me now say something more concrete about each, admitting in advance that some points will be touched on only lightly and that others, which should be read as friendly criticisms of past & present efforts of American revolutionairies, may be too cryptic for those who have not observed these movements or read about their beliefs & strategies.

As to the analysis, here I will be the most cryptic. The name of the system is corporation capitalism. Huge corporations have come to dominate the economy, reaping fabulous, unheard-of profits and avoiding their share of the taxes, and their owners & managers – the corporate rich – are more & more coming to dominate all aspects of American life, including government. Corporate rich foundations like Ford, Rockefeller & Carnegie finance & direct cultural & intellectual innovations, corporate rich institutes & associations like the Council on Foreign Relations, the Committee for Economic Development and the Rand Corporation do most of the economic, political & military research and provide most of the necessary government experts & consultants. As for the future, well, Bell Telephone is undertaking a pilot project in which it will run a high school in the Detroit ghetto, and Larry Rockefeller has suggested that every corporation in New York 'adopt' a city block and help make sure that its residents are healthy, happy & non-riotous. Adopt-a-block may never happen, and corporations may not run many high schools any time soon, but such instances are symbolic of where we are probably headed – corporation feudalism, cradle to the grave dependency on some aspect or another of a corporate structure run by a privileged few who use its enormous rewards to finance their own private schools, maintain their own exclusive clubs, and ride to the hounds on their vast farm lands. For even agriculture is being corporatized at an amazing rate. Family farmers are in a state of panic as the corporate rich and their coporations use tax loopholes to gobble up this last remaining bastion of 19th-century America.

Much work on this necessary analysis of corporation capitalsim, or feudalism, has been done, but much more needs to be done. It is a scandal, or, rather, a sign of corporate rich dominance of the universities, that so little social stratification research concerns the social upper class of big businessmen, that so little political sociology research concerns the power elite that is the operating arm of the corporate rich . . . indeed, that so much of the social sciences in general concern themselves with the workers, the poor, and other countries – that is, with things that are of interest to the corporate rich. If you want to know anything interesting about the American power structure, you have to piece together the hints of journalists, read the few books by a handful of Leftists who are academic outcasts, follow the research reports of two excellent student groups, and listen to & read Dan Smoot. Dan Smoot? Yes, Dan Smoot. Properly translated, he has a better view of the American power structure than most American political scientists, who of course merely laugh at him. He may not use the same labels I would for the men in charge (he thinks David Rockefeller & Co. are communists or dupes!), but at least he knows who's running the show. It is truly a commentary on American academia that he & one journalist – Establishment journalist Joseph Kraft – have done the only work on the all-important Council on Foreign Relations, one of the most influential policy-forming associations of the corporate rich. While the professors are laughing at Dan Smoot and equating the business community with the National Association of Manufacturers & the U.S. Chamber of Commerce, Smoot is keeping up with the activities of the richest, most powerful, and most internationally oriented of American big businessmen, the vanguard or corporation feudalism.

This really brings you to your first revolutionary act. Research one thing & one thing only – the American power structure. Withdraw your libido from 12th-century Antarctica, historical criticism of Viking poetry, and other such niceties, and get to where you are: here, America, the 20th century. Just turning the spotlight on the power elite is a revolutionary act, although only Act One. Ideas & analyses are powerful, and they shake people up. The problem of would-be American revolutionaries has not been an overemphasis on ideas, but the use of old ones, wrong ones, and transplanted ones. That's why C. Wright Mills grabbed American students & parts of American academia. He had new, relevant ideas & facts about the here & now – he exploded old cliches & slogans, and, I might add without being autobiographical, for Lincoln Steffens & Bertrand Russell had already done the job for me, I think he created more radicals with his work than any hundred Oakland & Los Angeles policemen with their billy clubs.

But analysis is not only important so you can better criticize the system. It is also necessary in developing blueprints & plans of attack. As to the developing of blueprints, to go beyond mere devastating criticism of the system you have to understand it so you can figure out what kind of a better system you can build on it. The most important & obvious point here is that you will be building on a fully industrialized, non-farming system. This means that your post-industrial society can look very different from systems built on pre-industrial, agricultural bases such as was the case in Russia, China & Cuba.

As to the importance of a good analysis in developing a program for taking power, this is essential because it tells you what you can & cannot expect, what you can & cannot do, and what you should & should not advocate. Let me give four examples:

- 1) Corporation capitalism, if it can continue to corporatize the 'underdeveloped' world and displace small businessmen & realtors in the cities, may have a lot more room for reforms. In fact, if creature comfort is enough, it may come to satisfy most of its members. Be that as it may, and I doubt if it can solve its problems in a humanly tolerable way, the important point is that no American revolutionary should find himself shocked or irrelevant because the corporate rich agree to nationwide health insurance or guaranteed annual incomes, or pull out of one of their military adventures. And don't get your hopes up for any imminent collapse. Better to be surprised by a sudden turn that hastens your time schedule than to be disappointed once again by the flexibility of the corporate rich. This means that you should rely on your own program, not depression or war, to challenge the system and bring about change, and that you should have a flexible, hang-loose attitude toward the future.
- 2) Corporation capitalism seems to be very much dependent on overseas sales & investments, probably much more so than it is on the military spending necessary to defend & extend that Free World empire. And even if some economists would dispute this, I think it is 100% safe to say that most members of the corporate rich are convinced that this overseas economic empire is essential – and that is what affects their political & military behaviour. Thus the corporate rich fear . . . nay, more than that, have utter horror of isolationism, and that suggests that you revolutionaries should agree with conservatives about the need for isolationism.
- 3) The American corporate rich have at their command unprecedented, almost unbelievable firepower & snooping power. This makes it questionable whether or not a violent revolutionary movement has a chance of getting off the ground. It also makes it doubtful whether or not a secret little Leninist-type party can remain secret & unpenetrated very long. In short, a non-violent & open party may be dictated to you as your only choice by the given fact of the corporate leaders' military & surveillance capability, just as a violent & closed party was dictated by the Russian situation.
- 4) The differences between present-day corporation capitalism & 19th-century individual capitalism must be emphasized again & again if you are to reach those currently making up the New Right. Those people protest corporation capitalism and its need for big government & overseas spending in the name of small business, small government, competition, the market place – all those things destroyed or distorted by the corporate system. You must agree with the New Right that these things have happened, and then be able to explain to them how & why they have happened: not due to the communists, or labour professors, but due to the growing corporatization of the society and the needs of these corporations.

Now, as to your second general need, blueprints for a post-industrial America. Blueprints are first of all necessary to go beyond mere criticism. Any half-way moral idiot can criticize corporation capitalism, anyone can point to slums, unemployment waste, phony advertising, inflation, shoddy goods, and on & on. To be revolutionary, you have got to go beyond the militantly liberal act of offering some criticism and then asking people to write their congressman or sit in somewhere so that the authorities will do something about the problem. And it is necessary for you to self consciously begin to develop this plan because it is not going to miraculously appear after a holocaust or emanate mystically from the collective mind of that heterogeneous generalization called The Movement. Individuals are going to have to develop aspects of these blueprints, wild, yea-saying blueprints that you can present with excitement & glee to Mr & Mrs Fed-up America. It is not enough to be for peace & freedom, which is really only to be against war & racism. It is not positive enough. As a smug little man from the Rand Corporation – a consultant for the other side – once reminded me, everyone, even him, is for peace & justice. The differences begin when you get to specifics.

G. William Domhoff
from the Entwistle Project.

To be continued

MŌZĪC

The Soft Machine

Joseph Strick to film Pollard in Naked Lunch rumours

When the Corporation sends out their hipster to make a film on Pop he has an easy job on his hands. The previous week he could have been finishing a documentary on PRIMITIVE DANCE & THE NEUROLOGY OF ECSTASY. But the change to a new subject will not be too difficult because Pop has become the kind of cultural compendium where all the birds sing. No editing problems. An image of the Queen (Elizabeth) waving from a balcony is as acceptable as a Russian tank on fire. Total consciousness, baby, and long live Marshall McLuhan.

Our hipster opens with a close shot of Donovan, the shy mystic smile/Cut to blurred focus corn field/Dissolve to cotton, then the cotton pickers/Cut to Negro in Vietnam/Cut to pop singer who says yeah he's got a thing about guns and violence, it's all there in the music.

Images bounce along with the continuity of a conversation led by Eamonn Andrews. Both viewer and critic will find it seductive.

Then the newspapers send out their hipsters for the cosy approach to Pop. Thus — 'I was expecting four Afghan hounds with chocolate drop eyes to come padding to the door, but Paul met me in a Fairisle sweater whose brightness disguised a hangover. In the background I heard Bartok (Yes, I did say Bartok!) playing gently on the stereo.' Or MAUREEN CLEAVE TREMBLES AFTER TALK

SESSION WITH MORRISON, SHE APPROACHES THE MYSTERIES OF THE MYTHIC CROTCH. Then our M C goes on from this experience to the Bachelors, the approach is the same. But not our film maker. He is permanently on the heights of the super-cool where the air is pure ether and there are no horizons.

In his film he will refer to the Soft Machine and/or John Cage, Zen, Satre, Ubu Roi, Phenomenology & others too numerous ... He is bound to mention the Soft Machine because the name itself implies access to the inner sanctum of the avant garde. You don't have to listen to the music — it's enough to know of their existence. So when Kenneth Allsop mentions the Soft Machine in Nova (her Novacaine) the horrible graceless suspicion arises — Has he heard the group? Both journalists and consumers use the name of a group like the Soft Machine as credentials of their complete cultural awareness. This Cabalistic (and cutely — cabbalistic) air surrounds this particular group. They have so far escaped the full treatment from all the journalists who are so determined to communalize the esoteric. (Pop is such a sweet comforting model of the democratic process. Anybody can make out, they don't even have to change their accents. And Kenneth Tynan might offer his high-octane spittle by way of a blessing, e.g. The Beatles are true Marxists in their control of the means of production).

Nobody has made any "all-human-life-is-there" claims for S.M. music. Not yet anyway.

Ten years ago the present members of the Soft Machine were (their own words) obnoxious little hippies in Canterbury. They listened to a lot of Mingus, Cecil Taylor, Webern amongst other classical and modern musicians. They played together at intervals over the next five years but did not come together as a group until the Daevid Allen Quartet was formed (The group was mentioned in Downbeat at the time as part of the stirrings of avant garde jazz in Britain). Their drummer left a straight pop group, the Wild Flowers, to join the quartet. The organist, Mike Ratledge, came down from Oxford, mistimed an application for Ph.D course and started playing with them. Daevid Allen was doing Jazz/Poetry, Electronic music and Indian-influenced material.

They ran through the usual little black book of names and ended up with the Soft Machine, a group which began playing tightly-controlled pop tunes before moving into looser improvistional work. Club and College gigs piled up in the first year, the obligatory commuting up and down the M 1

Left stranded for work in the first summer, they moved to the South of France, playing at a polystyrene club designed and built by Ian Knight and Keith Allburn. The

French police came down on the club for 'attracting undesirables.' They moved along the coast. Then a combine of promoters (Victor Herbert, Jean Jacques Lebel, Allan Zion (director of film Who's crazy? with The Living Theatre) got them to perform at the Picasso play, La Desir sitrape par la queue. French television showed followed, gigs in Rotterdam, the occasional live British show. Daevid Allen, lead guitarist, was banned from the country for work permit reasons (he later left the group).

During this time they attracted the attention of people not directly concerned with the pop world. American composers such as Earle Browne said 'The S M are playing the music I want to write.' Mark Boyle provided the light-shows for the group's work from the beginning. They came back from France, move with M B's Sensual Laboratory to Edinburgh, followed him to Paris for the Biennale where M B won the sculpture prize. There they played on a happening called 'St Genevieve et le tobogan,' accompanying the dance of Graziella Martinez.

An American tour with Hendrix followed directly on this. They worked there for three months. In New York they recorded their first L P with Tom Wilson (Producer of Mothers', the Animals and the first man to put Cecil Taylor on record). There was another three month tour, again with Hendrix.

The group have returned to this country where they are working on the second L P. They hope to avoid live performance and tours after the American experience, with the exception of possible Continental tours with Ronnie Scott & Roland Kirk. They are at present rehearsing for the L P. A new bass player has joined the group.

The first L P has not been released in this country. Copies were available in the import sections of shops like Music Land in Berwick Street, Soho.

INTERVIEW

Mike Ratledge, organist with The Soft Machine.

The interviewee prefaced the text below with the fact that he had no opinions on any subjects. It was 'ridiculous to attempt an interview.' The tape recorder was switched on. The interviewer gives the impression of being both stupid and innocent — which is quite genuine. For him, pop begins and ends with the Four Seasons & the work of Phil Spector — a fact of no particular relevance.

F W: Are you an Underground group?

M R: That can mean two things. Are we regarded as the subject of cultisms in the Underground? The answer to which may or may not be true, it is not for me to say. The second thing is whether that is desirable. I would say that none of us wish to be a cult in the Underground. The Underground is basically what Taylor Meade described it as — 'Doing something for nothing.' And that's what it's turned out to be. When you're asked to do an Underground benefit, and the promoter starts talking to you in terms of the art you're offering, you know very well that you won't get any money for it, you'll even have to pay your own expenses. It means no organization, the stage will be a shambles, the P A will be hopeless and everything else. But good things have still come out of the Underground. The U F O was good when Hoppy was running it. It

was well run. But the Underground is usually shambolic.

F W: Would you like to be disociated with the Underground, move out, make a lot of money, a lot — like Hendrix?

M R: I'd hate to have the position of Hendrix in terms of his work schedule and what it's doing to him. I'd hate to be on the road months at a time, working every night and never rehearsing. I mean, still playing numbers like Hey Joe after three years to an audience that shows it doesn't listen to what you're playing because the applause at the beginning of a number when it identifies it is louder than the applause you get at the end. That's all they're interested in.

F W: Off-stage sounds like a nightmare. What's it like?

M R: Exactly as they say it is — working with Hendrix it is anyway.
And travel in the States with a pop group is like a luxury purgatory. You stay in Hiltons, then a Cadillac Fleetwood takes you to the airport first thing in the morning. Another Cadillac Fleetwood meets you, takes you to the hotel. You wash, the Cadillac Fleetwood takes you to the gig and back to the Hilton. You sleep. In the end it completely destroys your sense of geography. You're manipulated like a piece of baggage. You have no control over the direction your life takes. It's like those experiments where they deprive rats of control over their bodies. In the end you suffer from depersonalisation, loss of identity. It sounds heavy but it does happen like that. There is no longer any 'I' that travels, the travel subsumes you, there is no such thing as place because air destroys that as a form of travel. And America is constructed in such a way that it denies any individual differences from place to place. This is the blueprint for America.

F W: Alright.

M R: What do you mean alright? I haven't finished yet.

F W: O K What about American groups?

M R: There are the Mothers' and the Spirit. They were the only two groups I was interested in, or impressed with at all. (pause) There are four types of groups. Firstly, the group that has technical proficiency on their instruments and have got ideas of their own. The Second has ideas but no technical proficiency. Then those that have no ideas of their own but have the proficiency. And lastly, those who have neither ideas nor technical proficiency.

F W: But they have publicity.

M R: Yes. The Mothers and the Spirit come into the first group. There are thousands of other groups that have either technique or proficiency. Or blues groups doing blues arrangements better than the people did them originally. Then there are weird underground groups in places like Chicago who have ideas but no proficiency — like the M C Five. But most are not worth mentioning because they are so

technically bad.

F W: What about the Doors?

M R: The Doors I can't really see, except as a sociological phenomenon. The Doors are a chance for all the little teenyboppers in the States to think they're digging something avant garde when they're not at all. They have got all the symptoms of being avant garde. They've got the proselytising lyrics, the sex figure of Morrison who masturbates on stage, so he's really iconoclastic and you're worshipping an iconoclast — who is not actually moving the art forward in any way. They go into old blues riffs, none of them are proficient, they have no authority on stage, their sound is appallingly weak. In all the ways that pop music has broken through in five years, they don't possess any of these features that caused the breakthrough. Hendrix contributed a new searing sound. But they have no sound identity. They're contributing nothing musically.

F W: Groups like the Jefferson Airplane — how do they fit into the scale you just suggested?

M R: The J A and the Big Brother Holding Co. are big cult figures on the American underground.
I've never seen the J A live, but apparently they're much better than on record. They're too tidy on record for me and the soloists aren't what they're reputed to be. They have strong voices sure. But there's still a blues tyranny in America basically. To be a substantial hit you have to be a blues group. B B & T H C are not an avant garde group. They're just a big super-charged, super-heat blues group. You read in the papers in England about the avant garde in America, their names — when you hear them they're just blues groups.

F W: You started as a straight jazz group and moved into pop. This isn't typical, because the usual group starts with blues and ends up with an avant garde reputation. But you never were a blues group.

M R: This jazz/pop thing is very difficult. There are two types — the jazz group that goes into pop, and the pop group that goes vaguely into jazz. Don Ellis and Gary Burton have gone into pop. And in a peculiar way they tend to lose something. Whereas pop groups going into jazz don't. Jazz groups going into pop tend to misconstrue what the actual excitement about pop is. They tend to simplify their structures, but what makes pop is the sound. The excitement of the sound is something which somebody like Don Ellis hasn't got, nor Gary Burton. So they lose both ways. Whereas pop groups in jazz, if they're any good, maintain the excitement of the sound. The best example of this is the Mothers', although they're not really a Jazz/Pop group — there's no such middle stream. But they use devices as in jazz, and they have jazz soloists. But they still have the tough rock sound. The Spirit is another example of this.

F W: Do you have a tough rock sound?

M R: It's tough. I don't know whether it's rock. It's very distorted and individual.

F W: If somebody who manufactures hits (like Spector used to) came to you and asked to record for him — would you?

M R: No, largely because you can't calculate a hit ever. It's chancy. So you'd be left recording something which is neither a success nor a pleasure to perform. The only thing to do is to do what you really like doing. (pause) Supposing Jim Webb came up to me with a song. That's a better example. I wouldn't mind doing it if I liked the song — but not as the Soft Machine. That would be unfair on what little public we have. But I love playing with other people whatever music they play. If Kevin in the group did a pretty-pretty single I wouldn't mind playing on it with him. But not as a Soft Machine. It just confuses the consumer.

F W: How do you react to pop journalism?

M R: The basic trouble is that all journalists are outside us. i.e. they don't play instruments, they've certainly never played in a pop group. They probably, until recently, haven't listened to pop music, not until the Beatles. They're not equipped in terms of musical knowledge to make any kind of judgement. If they confined themselves to saying who they liked and didn't like that would be acceptable. Unfortunately, they try to give musical reasons why they approve. These musical reasons tend to become a series of clichés that people bandy around, which usually have no relevance to the people they're talking about. A specific instance is Tony Palmer who claims qualities for The Cream which they don't possess. He says they expand the structure of common pop song chords, whereas they're still using blues structures basically, and more than any other group around. It's the same for all groups designated avant garde. It reminds me of the beginning of jazz where they tried to make jazz respectable by comparing jazz musicians to Stravinsky & Schoenberg & Bartok. But this is confusing the form because each medium has its own syntax. To make cross-judgements is confusing. It doesn't respect the identity of the medium, like all people writing film criticism in terms of theatre. Thereby you miss the basic point of what cinema is. So Tony Palmer and the rest of them — when they talk about the Beatles being better or as good as Schubert or Schoenberg or whatever are missing the point about what makes Pop special and different from these people. Cross-judgements simply confuse rather than illuminate. Apart from not being really desirable.

F W: So how would you evaluate the Soft Machine in your musical terms?

M R: It's difficult. I think we're using a lot of things that modern jazz is now using. The most recent numbers use time-signatures like 13/4 and 9/4. We're tending to get more onto a completely compositional basis and not the idea of the

cyclical song that's repeated. We're getting away from the idea of a song as a repeated structure A B A. And more onto song as complete composition. With our definite structure, the structure is a straight fifteen minutes which doesn't actually repeat, which is more of a classical procedure if you like, but then that's not saying that we're jazz/pop or that we're classical. That simply confuses it. We have a straight pop sound inasmuch as it's very abrasive, direct and immediate.

Most criticism tends to be based on this pointless comparative system. To say we're like Coltrane or like Cecil Taylor doesn't really help all that much.

F W: Well, you particularly sound like those people to me.

M R: Sometimes it might. But I know that everyone in the group has liked Coltrane at some stage, and the group feeling he got was something one liked. But I prefer to think that we had assimilated it. Because what makes it worth talking about us, or any other group, is what makes them different from the people they've been influenced by.

F W: Is there a pop-musician who even approaches Coltrane as a musician? I'm sorry.

M R: Certainly not in the terms of technique. But they have things which Coltrane doesn't have, and vice versa. I personally don't think that pop has got to the stage where I'd rather listen to any pop group than Coltrane. I'd rather listen to Coltrane any day. You see, you idiot, I don't see that there should be this exclusive choice. Everybody tries to set it up in terms of exclusive preferences.

F W: What of the present claims for pop music, claims which I find pretty screwy, that it is the complete reflection of our time, pop singers being its best interpreters.

M R: As MacIntyre would say — That's either trivial or false. Either you make it tautologically true in terms of retrospective criticism that every artist has always reflected his age — he has no choice. Or it's false because certainly the people one meets in the pop world have no motives in

those terms of expressing this thing.

F W: Some of them make these precious claims for themselves.

M R: So do a lot of other people. We all over-estimate our importance, and quite often this is necessary to survive. If you didn't think that you were doing something worthwhile you'd never do it, so again that's inevitable.

F W: I think pop music's importance is over-inflated. Why is there this importance attached to it?

M R: In the last ten years it's been possible to get a lot of money from pop. It was always true of people like Presley. But now the 'star' thing isn't so strong. Today it's friends next door who make a record and become successful or make money. There can't be a person living who doesn't know through somebody or other a pop group that's actually made a lot of bread. So it draws more and more people into it, like supposed intellectuals and everybody else. There's this possibility of so much money to be made. And in the early fifties there was a beginning of a whole concern with the gap between the cultures. Michael Tippet used to have a big thing about the high brow and low brow culture. With this concern the gap began to narrow. At the same time things were becoming more available.

F W: So if poetry made people a fortune, we'd probably now find thousands of poets – is that what your reasoning?

M R: If you could make a huge amount of bread from writing poetry it would work this way. Money means a/ you'll be a social success b/ you have dozens of chicks c/ it means amazing publicity d/ money must imply a large audience because nobody makes a lot of money without a huge audience e/ it would have to involve a personal confrontation.

If all these conditions were satisfied you would find poetry practised by thousands of people.

F W: What about you?

M R: I'd do whatever I like doing. It sounds strange but I don't do things for economic motives. I fantasize about doing

things for money like robbing banks, or huge advertising cons, or writing a con novel. But I never do it.

F W: Why not?

M R: Because I'm too fucking lazy, and I have no real conviction that they would ever work.

Both questions and answers ran out at different points in the interview. To start things off it was necessary to establish what the Soft Machine were NOT doing. As below.

M R: There is nothing to connect us with people like Cage in terms of operational procedures. We don't use chance methods like throwing the I Ching, or I.B.M. random charts, or throwing coins or that stuff. Occasionally we have written a piece which is written by chance in that every note and the rhythmic structure of the piece was written by chance. But that's not our basic working procedure.

F W: You play a long number though called WE DID IT AGAIN? What was that all about? For five or six minutes, or more.

M R: Everybody in the group saw it in a different way. Robert saw it as a chance to do soul drumming for thirty minutes or whatever it was. Kevin saw the whole idea of the repeated figure as being spiritual liberation, the ultimate effect.

F W: Being boring?

M R: It was his idea that if you find something boring, a basic Zen concept, then in the end you find it interesting. And there is something in that if you listen to something repeated in the same way your mind changes the structure of it each time, the ear either habituates or forces a change on it itself, which is similar in a way to the stuff Terry Riley's doing. I saw it mainly as an irritant source.

F W: For yourself or the audience?

M R: I saw it directed at the audience. And the only times I wanted to use it was when I felt like saying fuck you to the audience. But Kevin wanted to use it at any time possible. And Robert saw it as a gesture too. Kevin saw it half way between this spiritual liberation thing, and showing how hip we were. These ostenato techniques, I saw it as an irritant source though mainly.

Fletcher Watkins

Michael Broome
Mary Moore

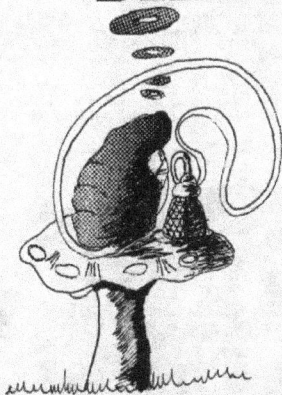

The MC5 kick out the Jams!

Hands clapping, fast as boots marching at the double.

Then the hoarse preaching roar of Brother J C Crawford. This is a White Panther church. Brothers and sisters, I want to see your hands up there. I want to hear some revolution out there. It's time to testify. Are you ready to testify? I give you a testimonial. The MC5!

This is a record. The real thing is in concert. Feel yourself at Fillmore East, crushed in heat and light. Then at this moment, Rob Tyner, the MC5 lead singer, sprints on stage, leaps high in the air, his body writhing through the strobes; then, as he hits ground:

KICK OUT THE JAMS, MOTHERFUCKERS!

The MC5 album will be released here in a couple of months, on Elektra EKS 74042. While you're waiting for it, buy a pair of stereo headphones. On the day, invest in a considerable sized piece of dope. Put the volume on full through the headphones; bass three-quarters round to full, treble neutral. Be sure you are already stoned.

During the next 40 minutes, any vestiges of attraction 3000 years of western culture may have for you will be burned and smashed out of your head. The MC5 provide the definitive trip. They fuck your mind with a white poker, and they stay in. And at a certain point, primally aroused, you move too, they melt in your head seething and shaping. You pour with sweat and energy, the jerks forming into your own unique rhythm, which takes over from the music. It wraps you; then you wrap it, surging electrically and chemically. Now you can feel how it would be to live at the point of orgasm every day. Now you are a microcosm of the world.
You are on fire. Burn!

When the police went beserk in Lincoln Park, Chicago, breaking people with clubs, one band stood firm and played, the MC5. Norman Mailer was there, and this is what he felt (Miami and the Siege of Chicago, published in Penguins on 27 February):

A young white singer was taking off on an interplanetary, then galactic, flight of song . . ., the sound screaming up to a climax of vibrations like one rocket blasting out of itself, the force of the noise a vertigo in the cauldrons of inner space – it was the roar of the beast in all nihilism, electric bass and drum driving behind out of their own non-stop to the end of mind. . . There was the sound of mountains crashing in this holocaust of the decibels, hearts bursting, literally bursting, as if this was the sound of death by exploding within, the drums of physio-logical climax when the mind was blown, and forces of the future, powerful, characterless, as insane and scalding as waves of lava, came flushing through the urn of all acquired culture and sent the brain like a foundered carcass smashing down a rapids, revolving through a whirl of demons, pool of uproar, discords vibrating, electric crescendo screaming as if at the electro-mechanical climax of the age.

'Hey, think the time is right for a palace revolution/ But where I live the game to play is compromise solution' sings Mick Jagger in Street Fighting Man; and we think of Brian Jones, ashen and alone in the dock. But Detroit (Motor City: Motor City 5: MC5) is solid and militant. The hippies and the Panthers dig each other, share mores, and are politically bonded. The MC5 are now the emblem of Detroit in insurrection. They turn on blatantly; and the police know that if big arrests are made for smoking, then Detroit could be in flames again, as it was in summer 1966. Eric Ehrmann in Rolling Stone:
'There are more politicized hippies in Detroit and its surrounding areas who have helmets, gas masks, tear gas and home made Mace along with other ordnance paraphernalia than any other city currently in insurrection'. Peace is up to the police. Meanwhile, in freedom, the MC5 liberate their energies, and ours.
The MC5 have been playing in and around Detroit for some years now. Their surge started in March 1966, when Allen Ginsberg, fresh from India, appeared at a big Detroit concert with them. The bridge was John Sinclair, then a post-Beat entrepreneur/writer/poet. Sinclair connected Ginsberg's energies, new to America, with rock and roll energy. Beat meets beat. Sinclair was then running a local artist's workshop, which then changed its name to Trans-Love Energies. And these new energies became focused after the summer 1966 Detroit fires. The MC5 are now the band of Trans-Love Energies, and live in a big house in Ann Arbor, from which a violently radical sheet, Fifth Estate, is produced by Sinclair, who combines being their manager and being Minister of Information for the white Panther party – Eldridge's equivalent.

White Panthers? Sure. The revolution is now, and carries no passengers. Panthers are not racists. So what do White Panthers stand for? Maybe there's too much echo of Ginsberg and Corso in Sinclair, but this is what he says in the Berkeley Barb:

I heard Stokely Carmichael in 1966 call for '20 million arrogant black men' as America' salvation. And there are a lot of arrogant black motherfuckers in the streets today – for the first time in America – and for the first time in America there is a generation of visionary maniac white mother country dope fiend rock and roll freaks who are ready to get down and kick out the jams. Our programme of rock and roll, dope, and fucking in the streets is a programme of total freedom for everyone.

What kind of programme is that? The revolution is its own programme. What kind of revolution is that? Hear some more MC5 sound.

Detroit is the machine city: a place where you can only win or lose. The MC5 harness these ruthless rhythms. They thrust raw chunks of Hendrix, theWho,Screaming Jay Hawkins into their sound, melting and binding them with Detroit's incessant pulses of metal, engines and fire. Picture drummer Dennis Thompson, stripped to his pants, sweat streams flickering off his body. The noise doesn't let up. The band modulate only at maximum volume. The point at which you take over the sound is the point at which you rock with it, roll with it, know that it is the level at which we all live after breaking through to the other side. It takes a brave man to listen to the Velvet Underground when stoned, because they do more than break through. They describe their own world on the other side: horror trips of worms and canker and no connections; and this world can fasten on you. The MC5 only break through. They are the only band ahead of the action. Their jet stream of energy directs, focuses and releases your own energy, for you to use for your own needs and desires. This is what Sinclair is saying his way. This is what Rob Tyner screams ecstatically, out of his mind at 130,140,150 decibels, piercing the pain level, the amps shaking and roaring, his audience becoming with him, in him, so that he is their shaman, possessed by his own forces to fuck and purify and whirl himself and them and us into the vision of all our worlds, clear, unblocked, and moving fast as light:

'Kick out the jams, yeah, kick out the jams, KICK EM OUT KICK EM OUT'

The rest is our affair. Whose else?'

At a lower energy level, Jim Morrison has this quality (and his own personality). And, like the Doors, the MC5 are going to be very big in America in 1969; and hardly known in Britain ('Cos in sleepy London town/There's just no place for a street fighting man'). And, like the Doors, the MC5 are an enormous hype; much like Christ. They are a young band, with the utter lack of hesitancy of 20 or 21. They will probably become a teeny bopper band. Good. Then, They'll zero straight into kids' heads. Rock and roll never destroys: it creates mental autonomy. Grow up with the MC5, and no-one will ever pull a fix on you; no politician will masturbate your mind. Sandy Pearlman, describing the recent MC5 riot at Fillmore East in Village Voice:

Rock and roll is no political instrument. It's autonomously powerful. Politics is a phase and an inspiration to rock and roll. Rock and roll's forms autonomously tend toward energy release and focus. In the competition of energy scenes these forms are, in fact, more efficient than those available to the American Revolution.

Taoism is what we need. To a Taoist, nature (=, to the West, personality) and nature (=, to the West, the world) are indivisible. And, for a Taoist priest, emblem of the people, if the world is wrong, then, inevitably, his personality must be wrong, except, for him, there is no way to speak separately in this way. So, for the world to be put right, he must first purify himself. The act is more than symbolic; it is the only way. And this is our only way, also. We must strip the world of abstraction, of rationalisation, of principles, of idealogies: of all verbal and institutional power structures. We must make the world us-sized. Then we move; then it moves; then we are people again, and the world is human again. The MC5 speak, They speak for us. Of our own autonomy, and potential autonomy.

Stoned? Got the album on? Can you get more volume?
Hit it. KICK OUT THE JAMS.

G C.

LPREVIEWS

EXPRESSWAY TO YOUR SKULL
Buddy Miles Express Mercury 20137 SMCL

'The Express has made the bend . . . He is coming on down the tracks. Shaking steady . . . Shaking FEELING — Shaking LIFE!' . . . enthuses Hendrix on the liner notes. But something went wrong at Sunset Sound, Hollywood, last October. Something that probably doesn't notice live; not with a thousand watts of shattering Wrap It Up it wouldn't; not with the demented High Priest of the Electric Church storming the stage like a berserk Sherman tank it wouldn't. But it's there, the question mark, the nagging doubt — Is Superspade really a super spade? Can he make it on his own? Is Buddy Miles really James Brown, Arthur Conely and Otis Redding rolled into one monstrous, ugly genius. Bloomfield used to say he was. A lot of people used to 'know' he was. But on Expressway To Your Skull that's just not what comes across.

Of course he's good. Of course he can play superbly. Listen to the only instrumental on the album, Funky Mule. Here, as on no other track, the band is incredibly together. Miles is in his element, effortlessly displaying all the qualities of the gutsy, funk drumming that made his name in the Flag; a masserful display of technique and emotional feel. Here too, Jim McCarty on guitar breaks out to solo brilliantly, the snorting repetitive brass of Herbie Rich Marcus Doubleday, Virgin Gonsales and Bill McPherson piling up the pressure, forcing the pace; and all the time Buddy is there, pounding, thrashing, flailing like he owned eighteen limbs. On this track the seeds sown in the ashes of the Electric Flag reap a rich harvest.

So why doesn't it all work? It doesn't work because Buddy can't sing like Redding, Conely or Brown. He has a good voice, but it's just not *that* good. And it doesn't work because Buddy is superspading three quarters of every number. The other members of the Express hardly get a look in. It's sad to see a brass section as competent as this reduced to unimaginative honking on tightly reined riffs and used only as a vehicle for B M's grunt-grunt vocals. Their solo potential is enormous and amply illustrated whenever the opportunity arises. Like at the close of Wrap It Up where the whole band merges into a free-form cacophony of discordant 'Coltrane' one tastes for a moment the promise of what hopefully is to come.

Perhaps it would be as well to remember that Expressway To Your Skull, now over four months old, was recorded pretty soon after the groups formation — perhaps a little too soon after — since which time, if the Atlantic grapevine is to be relied upon for once, they have been, 'going thru' changes'. Let's hope that one of those changes is related to material. By the fourth cut I was beginning to sick up on another helping of 'Good God Almighty. .Uh. . .Uh. . .My baby's comin' back/back down the railway track . .Yes she is. . . ohhhhhh. . .Yes she is. . .nah, nah nah, nah, nahnah', especially as the album only consists of seven numbers. The Buddy Miles Express is a great band, all it basically lacks is someone who can tell Buddy Miles when to button his fat pussy and make with the machine gun he uses as a left hand.
Felix Dennis

BRIAN AUGER & THE TRINITY
'Definitely What' (Marmalade 608 003)

There are two types of group in London. To see one type of group you get stoned and go to Middle Earth; to see the other type you get drunk and go to Blaises. Brian Auger & the Trinity fall into the latter category.

Brian Auger's image used to be in the same bag as that of Zoot Money's in the days when he had his Big Roll Band, did numbers like I Go Crazy and took his trousers off on-stage. On Definitely What, which features Brian Auger & the Trinity without Julie Driscoll, there are some good examples of Zoot Money's slightly anachronistic type of humour.

However, although two numbers on the album (George Bruno Money and John Brown's Body) show signs of this type of influence — one is, in fact, dedicated to Zoot Money — the other show that Brian Auger is making a determined attempt to break away from leaping music.

To this end the group is augmented on many of the tracks with brass and strings. Sometimes the arrangements work — on Far Horizon, for example where the brass creates a moody, nostalgic backing to the reflective vocal — and sometimes they don't. Day In The Life, for example, goes on for too long without enough variation. Bumpin' On Sunset on the other hand, another instrumental number, succeeds because more care seems to have been taken to make the various instrumental parts hang together.

In a couple of places, however, the album really explodes. On Red Beans and Rice, Brian Auger's pyrotechnic organ-playing and his really superb rhythm section generate as much excitement as, say, the Cream do on Spoonful. The bass and drums don't just lay down the beat, they drive it along as if they were trying to outdo one another.

The self indulgent bits (like George Bruno Money) apart, this is a very good album, worth listening to because, if nothing else, it demonstrates that Brian Auger and The Trinity deserve wider recognition in their own right with or without Julie Driscoll.
John Leaver

LOVE CHRONICLES. *Al Stewart.* (CBS 63460)

If Al Stewart's first album, *Bedsitter Images*, was less than perfect it was because of the over-produced, anything-and-everything- goes musical arrangements. *Love Chronicles* is his second album and, if anything, there seems to have been a reaction in the opposite direction; now the arrangements, by comparison, seem positively subdued, with suitably restrained drumming and, on most tracks, a rather unambitious mixture of acoustic and electric guitar, the latter whining away at mundane linking phrases like a dog worrying a well-chewed bone. All in all, then, nothing very exciting and it all serves to highlight Stewart's voice, ever-dominant, which unfortunately doesn't always live up to this showcase (albeit a slightly dusty showcase) treatment; its nasal quality sometimes irritates (some of the tracks sound as if Stewart had a head cold when he recorded them) and its poppy slickness

doesn't seem entirely suited to the subject matter of the songs.

The songs, of course, are the redeeming feature of the whole affair. They elevate it from just another pop-folk LP to a major and important one. Stewart knows better than anyone else on the scene today how to write effective narrative folk lyrics. He's remained uncomplicated where Dylan has gone off into ellipsis, and where Paul Simon has floated off into whimsy and romantic fantasy, Stewart has remained with his feet in a tangible and intriguing reality: 'Maurice,' said Renee, 'Why didn't you say that you'd be so late,/The supper that I made is ruined again./Is there anything you'd like?'. 'No, nothing,' he replied/Standing by the stairs, not looking in her eyes, so stupidly Male.

There are six tracks on this album. In Brooklyn, Old Compton Street Blues, Ballad of Mary Foster, Life and Life Only and You Should Have Listened to Al are all longer than usual and the sixth is the eighteen minute magnum opus Love Chronicles itself. Described variously as a love story (by Stewart) and a sexual odyssey (by his publicists, who are prone to that kind of thing), this is in fact a confessional song about sex which subtly and creditably avoids the conceit and sexual-bragging of Don Juanism. It's tender, its thoughtful and it's an original experiment in pop music to compliment the assured genre writing of the other tracks.

It would be a pity if this album became memorable only as the first pop LP to feature the word 'fuck', when there are so many other good and equally memorable things about it.

Graham Charnock.

CRUISING WITH RUBEN AND THE JETS. *Mothers of Invention.* VERVE IMPORT. (V6 5055 X)

The Mothers are doing something different. Perhaps the cynicism has disappeared or the irony become more subtle, Zappa always gives the impression of being formulated in what he does. In Rubens songs he is doing just this. None of the hard acid freakout here.

The impression that the record seeks to create is of nice quiet kids singing nice quiet little rock songs. The big bad freaky boys don't do it anymore anyway they do it in a different way.

Their own description of this music is 'greasy love songs of cretin simplicity! 'They sing these they say because they like to sing them. The songs are nice to listen to, sweet beat, unremarkable sentiments. 'We made a wish and threw a coin/Since that day our hearts have been joined. I gave you all my love/Theres nothing left for me to do but cry. Stars in the sky they never lie/Tell me you need me/Don't say goodbye.

Ruben is everywhere though you might not recognize him in his space helmet and bombed out shades. He likes to bop, eat ice-cream soda in the drugstore, ride in space ships, play hell in Vietnam and throw coins in the fountain of love.

The mothers are singing harmonious space age rock and roll with dwardy - doop/oh wah pulsating rhythm and funny junkie articulations of parodied virtue. The shadows of the fifties when we used to hold hands in the back rows of cinemas and make it in the parking lot. Deseri is the grooviest chick around and jelly roll gum drops are good to eat.

Memories are trivial, only experience is meaningful. Time is present; ghosted with the spectures of everything. So the beat goes on.

So where are the ticket stubs to the chemical gardens for rusty shit people? Are the ashen faced heros of all the grooves sitting on the birdshit spattered fence and whistling for true love through the bars of the 7th cage on the left.

Bryan Willis

TIM HARDIN *LIVE IN CONCERT.* MGM Verve Forecast (VLP 6010)

'You know this' says Tim Hardin as he drops the opening notes of Misty Roses. He's damn right you do. You've heard it on the first album. You've heard it at the Albert Hall if you went to his first concert in England last July. You've heard it if you

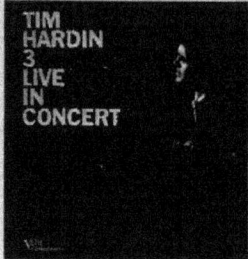

were at the New York Town Hall on April 10th last year you'll hear it again if you buy his new LP.

It's a beautiful record with sound that washes over you like gentle water then rears in rasping protest at a pain so personal that it excludes the listener. But apart from an eulogy to friend Lenny Bruce, the songs on this album are no more *new* than Don't Make Promises was when released last year to coincide with his English concert.

How long can you play that song again and still get the same applause? From the claps wedged in between each track of Tim Hardin 3 it seem's he's still getting it from the fans. A tribute to his ability to weave new magic with old songs. But it isn't enough to freak out an amalgam of oldies with the tinkle of a hippy bell from the drummer, Donald Macdonald, and one new song.

Private sorrow may be the merchandise of poets, but we look to poets for constant creativity and Tim gets bogged down by his insatiable appetite for excess. He pours out his love-songs with the same generosity (self-indulgence?) as rum and coca cola and as with rum and coca cola or whatever, you either dig it and turn on or don't and cut out. Presumably there are those people who are so dedicated to the Hardin myth that they'll dig his music from here on out. But Tim Hardin sells Tim Hardin's pain with a label spelling MGM, profits to Koppelman and Rubin, and he's in dire danger of drowning in it. His tribute to Hank Williams is both elegant and moving. We know you've been places he's been, Tim – but Lenny Bruce was a brilliant comic head not just a tragic figure and the words to the song don't match the strength of the music.

I know Tim thinks Misty Roses his best song, but its the fact that he can erupt out of maudlin introspection into something as funny/witty as Smugglin Man which makes him great.

That ruthless sense of humour should produce more than just one song and it's time he wrote something new.

Danaë

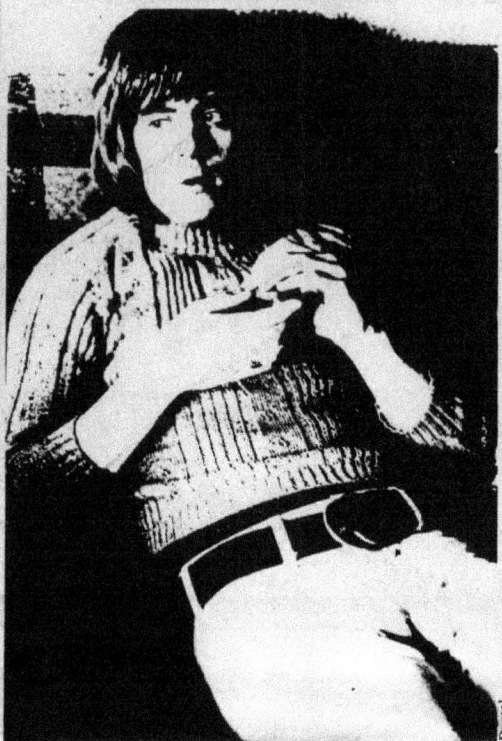
Terry Reid had just returned from his phenomenally succesful tour of the States when he recorded the following interview for MOZIC last month. Accompanied by Pete Shelley on organ and Keith Webb on drums this nineteen year old former member of Peter Jay's Jaywalker's had been electrifying American audiences for the past three months, playing alongside, and holding his own, with established names like Country Joe And The Fish, Buddy Miles Express, Procul Harum, Jeff Beck, Canned Heat and The Cream.

Reid's music is not 'progessive'. It is joyful, uninhibited, hard core soft rock, brought across with a combination of naivity and sweat, (it is not usual for Reid to pass out on stage), and aided by the group's ability to exactly gauge an audience's mood and adapt their performance accordingly. If Reid was a painter he would be Constable; if he could write he would be Fleming.

How exactly did you come to get your present band together?

Well, I was with Peter, (Jay), for around two years playing hard and mostly on the road, when I got to this stage where I felt like I had to get a band of my own. I guess every musician wants to do that at some period, and that's what happened to me. Must be about a year or so ago, Christmas before last, and I met Keith through this organist guy . . . Pete came later, just before the tour, so really he's only been with us for just over three months, but already he's got his own thing together . . . as it turned out I was bloody lucky, both those guys are fucking good musicians.

And the US really helped us, almost forced us, to develop musically. You know, America is a great place for making a band; or breaking it of course.

Did you notice any immediate differences between audiences here and those you played to in the States?

Differences? Oh yeah, there are differences alright. Like sheer quantities, you know? That theory about everything over there being bigger is definitely not a hype. It's not a hype, it's a way of life. Like for instance here, in Britain, you might play to a few hundred, maybe even a few thousand in the Albert Hall or Wembley, but in the U S that would be ridiculous. You get used to playing to thousands, six thousand, ten thousand even twelve thousand and that could be in almost any major city. The Cream show at Madison Sq. Gardens pulled over 21,000 and at the Miami International Pop thing there were almost five times that over a period of three days. I mean 100,000 people is a lot of people. I would say size was the major difference.

Then there's this other thing you know. Take here; if you're top of a bill but you play say medium to poorly, well, you're still almost certain to go down better than the rest of the show. It's almost a tradition. But that doesn't apply so automatically over there. Kids will listen to you; you get more of a chance. We found time and time again that if you play well and play for your audience you can steal a show. Jeff Beck he did that.

Do you think maybe that's why you did so much better in America than you have done here, up to now?

Yeah, that was one of the main reasons. Bang-Bang helped too of course.

Were you satisfied with Bang-Bang?

Well, that album was produced with the tour in mind, it was designed to coincide. We needed something to take over with us, that was why it was only released in the States, and consequently the whole thing was rushed. We didn't spend enough time on it and I . . . well, lets just say it wasn't as good as it could have been. Anyway, it certainly won't be released in Britain now, although I understand that it has sold well in America. We'll be recording a new album for release here in the very near future.

Your producer, Mickie Most, has been quoted as saying, 'There is no art in gramaphone records'. Do you agree with that statement?

I don't think that you can say that. I'd be prepared to, like, to accept that a small proportion of today's pop, say one or two of McCartney's songs, might in a hundred years time be recognised as . . . as art. But

only time can tell. Anyway is it that important? Surely what is important about pop music today is it's role in our generations lives. Isn't that, like, more relevant? Man, I believe that rock, pop, whatever you want to call it is a vital release. I think kids in America, here, all over the world are using it to escape from the daily shit-grind. It's a turn on, a gas, a happy thing. That's what it should be too, a happy thing. The 'progressive', or so called progressive scene is bogged down in doom, people are sick of wrucking their brains trying to figure out what the words mean. Kids want to be entertained not preached to . . . it's all got out of hand. When I perform am I producing art? Am I fuck. I'm trying to turn kids on, trying to make people happy . . . that's what I'm here to do, that's what I'm paid to do.

So you wouldn't agree with John Peel's statement about pop being the warning drum of an imminent social revolution?

No, I wouldn't agree. He's . . . well, like, he's coming on too strong. Man, Lennon and McCartney's songs may have caused so many million wet knickers but they won't produce a 'social revolution'.

OK. Leaving wet knickers and revolution behind us temporarily, what bands really impressed you during your tour?

Oh wow, that's very difficult. There are so many good groups in the States. Procul Harum are just too much. They are so good live, incredible from start to finish. The whole band is together, and the guitarist . . . ridiculous. Cream of course. We caught them several times, played on the same bill a few times. The split was beginning to show though. Sometimes they were brilliant, sometimes they were fucking miserable. Buddy Miles has got together a nice scene now, they are so loud! Canned Heat the same, loud, but excellent, Then there were the GTO's. Girls Together Occasionally that stands for, Three chicks in LA, very freaked out; never seen anything like these, They were really good, and good to us! The only nice thing about Christmas was the cake they baked for us. Some cake.

The Grateful Dead I didn't dig too much. In fact I couldn't believe it, they were so bad. And Country Joe etc were a disappointment. Probably because we caught them just before they split.

Did America appear to be a violent country to you?

Yeah, in many ways I guess it is. Though it's amazing that it all the gigs we did I never saw one fight break out in the audience. That's something you wouldn't get in this country . . . man, I'd rather play the Appolo Theatre, Harlem than Glasgow anyday. We nearly got bottled in Glasgow one time, not because we were bad like, just because they didn't like the looks of us. There were no scenes like that in any of the gigs we did in the US.

The cops? Oh, just about as uptight and corrupt as in Britain. You're more likely to be damaged permanently in a tangle with the American fuzz though, if you see what I mean. And there are some cops there, like over here, who seem to have a fair understanding of the kids. Like in Atlanta, which is basically a very, very uptight town, there were cops at the concert we played there who were gently leading away a bunch of kids tripping out. No rough stuff. No arrests like. Just gently leading them out.

I think that some of the cops in the States are beginning to realise that kids are going to smoke and take acid no matter how the law stands . . . anyhow, I'm sure that pretty soon one state or another is going to try legalising hash. It's too late for them to stop it now; the number of people that smoke in America is ridiculous. This is true, listen. I met a 15 year old girl, the daughter of an FBI official who was turning on really regularly. At 15 she could roll a perfect joint. I'm not saying that's good or bad man, I'm just saying like there it is.

Will you be going back to America in the near future?

Oh yeah, almost certainly. The bread is there, you can earn up to 4000 dollars a gig without too much trouble. There's nowhere in this country you can earn that sort of bread. But right now it's just good to be back. Three months is a long time to be away.

FD

THE RAT GAME

Angelo Quattrocchi in Paris, end of January:

Kids are forced out of schools and beaten, while you are told of Che Guevara, Vietnam and other shows. High school kids rebel to their teachers-jailers.

Daily they perform the rites of the next revolution, by desecrating authority.

The armies of the state beat them up.

Unmask a teacher, you'll find a copper.

The show retreats further into the land of unreality, where soap bubbles ads are reaching paper cunts. Here, we ignore those who want to die stupid.

Breakfast, tube, job, telly, sleep, breakfast. .

Deface their advertisements, ridicule their teachers, laugh at their Parties. Since our first raid in May, they live in fear, we in hope.

They have bought five thousand new coppers.

We have acquired tens of thousands young workers, who despise their Trade-Union leaders.

Hundreds of thousand are doubtful, doubtful that one penny more can change the misery of their daily life. If you don't listen to telly, you'll soon hear the police sirens, rapists of dreams.

If you don't read the papers, they'll send you a party member home.

If you say no to your parents, they'll put you into the army.

How long can they last?

In their supermarkets, you still buy their last dead god, parcelled in merchandise.

Where will it snap?

In university-factories, in factory-universities, there were the assembly lines of the canned minds your waste.

Or in the churches-supermarkets where they buy time of your life and give you survival in exchange, and boredom.

The king is naked, shivering.

Strip the king and strip the teachers and strip the manager and the banker.

In the caverns of housewives' minds the rats are squealing. Omo is washing their life away.

The rattling of coins exchanged from dead hand to dead hand has for too long covered the gentle and piercing cries of orgasms.

Much has been learned.

The millions of private tragedies, exposed to the sun, have revealed the nature of the collective fare.

Who can endure it?

The more I want the revolution, the more I want to make love, the more I want to make love, the more I want to make a revolution.

Do not drop out. Drop in. Drip in. Fuck your neighbour, fuck him well and slowly, with determination, on the common pavement, then together you can go shopping, for fun.

Don't listen to those who want to teach you how to make a revolution, or how to make love, they are dry priests.

They sell you Marx in grocery shops, as long as you stay quiet. Lenin you can buy at the chemist, as long as you wait till tomorrow.

Here, in Paris, we amuse ourselves by defacing their ads, laughing to their faces, playing with the rat, which, when prodded, takes always the shape of a copper.

Not before long, it will be time for the festival again, when we'll take over their concetration camp factories and their universities, releasing them finally from their long fear.

From Action, newspaper of the movement in France.

What has made the bourgeoisie tremble, what gives them cold sweat? France is melancholic. Like always, politicians lie, but without much conviction, out of habit, excusing themselves for using too trite devices to mask the truth.

Because truth is too clear: the bourgeois are done in, dead.

Big trusts still control the state, De Gaulle their servant, the coppers are at every corner, stolid as ever, sinister clowns perform daily on telt, reciting rosaries of irrelevant nonfacts.

Unctous managers of ignorance, called professors, administer carcasses of myths, handling dollars of examination papers.

It is undeniable.

But something bigger, an innocent blinding reality is laid bare to stupefied millions of citizens: the bourgeoisie has the power, but it stinks.

Even its faithful servants murmer it in private, only they console themselves with the knowledge that it stinks elsewhere too, the american and russian bourgeoisie stink as much.

It is a cancer, which May has revealed, suddenly, and for ever.

The ruling class is drowning in shit. Hiding its head in its own vomit, where it's choking to death. All that helped its digestion is now filling its throttle, its knowledge of itself, its discovery of its unreality, the realization of his absurdity.

When, everywhere, a son despise his parents, a student refuses to stuff himself with solemn lies and questions the teacher, when the workers refuse to be conned by their leaders who betray them, when artists don't want to be clowns anymore, then the cracks in the wall become so big that even the moles see them.

WIND UP BLACK DWARFS

The present generation of revolutionaries are precisely the people who are unwilling to be specific about the conditions of the immediate revolutionary future – the subject about which, as Orwell once contended, every revolutionary is forced to lie. Faced with the assertion that the liberties embodied in this country's institutions should be protected in the first instance, the revolutionaries proclaim those liberties meaningless by continually widening their definition of 'system.' British liberties are thus not *really* liberties because of the Americans; American liberties are not *really* liberties because of the Vietnam war; everything active in the system, even that which criticises, limits and modifies the system, is just part of the system – except the revolution.

The historical strength of the classic Left in this country has been its practical recognition that society can be, and has to be, treated bit-by-bit even though an intellectual commitment to an ideology apparently insists that anything less than a total upheaval is meaningless. The revolutionaries, these newest of new brooms, noting only the failings and writing off all actual improvements achieved over the last century as a movement of history for which nobody is responsible and for which credit need consequently not be given, are able to present this strength as a weakness, and to suggest that a great number of honest men and women have been wasting their time.

This is a persistent and extremely unenticing *failure of the imagination*, usually ascribable to conceit but in the case of the better part of this generation, I am sure, ascribable to a generous passion. This revolutionary generation, overwhelmed by the fact that a lot of people are still getting hurt, saves its maximum rancour for anyone who suggests that a total solution might hurt even more people and hurt them worse. If your creed is all or nothing, the man you hate most is not the man who offers nothing but the man who offers something. Suppose you accept the premise that Vietnamese children are frying in their own fat because of something intrinsically murderous in the American capitalist 'system'; and accept further premise that the British 'system' bolsters the American; and the further premise that the overthrow of our 'system' is a *required gesture* against the American 'system' and on behalf of those children. Then the man you hate is likely to be the man who tries to break down this chain of consequence – the man who says that the continuity of British society has an absolute virtue independent of the welfare of the Vietnamese children and that to contend otherwise is simply to be rhetorical. A man talks like that is bound to appear a demon, since he scorns directly the most self-consciously generous of all youthful sympathies – the sympathy that says, like Eugene Debs, 'while there is a soul in prison I am not free.'

Now that sympathy, and not much more, is to the credit side of the ledger. On the debit side the entries are densely packed and piling up fast. Leaving aside the greater part of the Underground which is content to enjoy its practical existence in a non-theoretical continuous present, hasn't the remarkable thing about this particular revolutionary generation been that it advances its own innocence, its own impatience and its own ignorance as positive qualities? There seems to be this general impression that society doesn't *have* to be analysed or understood in its dynamism, that it is in fact static and needs to be replaced holus-bolus by a new and true dynamism in which all values will have their genuine beginning. In the fervour of this general impression, the objective nature of intellect as regarded as a drawback; the analytical heritage is reduced to symbol-ridden myth in which Rosa Luxemburg becomes a swinger in a maxi-skirt; and the emotional initiative passes to the 'invisible international', the gentle people who are supposed to be everywhere and will effect a universal change of heart once they solve the problem of asserting their will without coercion. But as you can see already, merely to expound is to expose. This new revolution, while relatively (not wholly) guiltless of philosophically justified brutality, is nevertheless *characteristically* anti-intellectual, ahistorical and obscurantist. Ideology, pared down to a mood-determined minimum of 'ideas' and all the more powerful for being free of analytical determinants, attains a new spreadability, like butter left a long time in the sun. Anyone can have a go. If you feel young and all the world looks wrong, you're in. The residual dislike of the bourgeoisie, though vociferous, is determined by rejection of mores rather than analysis of class-function. This is why classic Left figures like Grass in Germany and Pasolini in Italy were unable to discommode the young student revolutionaries by accusing them of being what they in fact were – well-heeled sons of daddy and mummy. The revolution as a whole, rather than having 'objective class-enemies' in the old Stalinist sense, only has *objective intellectual enemies* – people who feel broadly what the revolutionaries feel but think differently about the revolution. It's a sweet set-up. If you want a revolution, no matter how much of a bastard or idiot you are, you're part of this most popular of all popular fronts. If you *don't* want revolution, no matter how deep your concern for liberty, mercy and justice in individual cases and in society at large, then you are part of the system – this static system which has never *really* changed, until last year in Paris and of course next week here.

The classic Left in this country over a long period has largely managed to free itself from ideology by realising that 'society' is simple a word doing limited linguistic duty for a complex actuality that *always* changes. Gradually it has abandoned the notion of stasis (along with its counter-notion, crisis) and come to see that society is merely coherent – it is not rationally interrelated and is therefore not subject to being totally changed any more than it is subject to being totally described. This is not a mud-hut country where you leave to break up the ceiling in order to make furniture; nor is it a high-rise country in which the bourgeoisie suddenly falls into the basement to re-emerge, black with dust, as Nazis; it is a *mature* society much more complex than any metaphor which can be thought up to describe it.

The huge upheavals which look total in other lands, in this land are held closer to the surface and squeezed further into time, giving the apocalyptic revolutionary, whose hunger is as much for brute experience as for justice, the opportunity to say they never happen. In fact these upheavals cannot be stopped happening – except, paradoxically, by revolution, which really *can* arrest history in Hegel's definition of the word (the story of liberty growing conscious of itself) or anyway slow it down to a crawl. The revolutionary approach to politics, fastening on the superficial similarities of our society and say, Batista's Cuba, recommends revolution *here* because of its necessity *there*. But these supposed similarities ('capitalist') are absolutely nothing compared to the differences between the two places as *states*. Britain is so immeasurably more advanced that it is practically indescribable – which is most of the trouble.

The logic of the thing is ruthless. Since all the world is the system and nothing in the world is not the system, the countries which naively offer the maximum of tolerance may be regarded as its weakest points. The complex countries, the centres of revolutionary *thought*, while not immediately the most vulnerable to revolutionary activity are certainly the most hospitable. This ought logically to mean that they are the last places one should try to start a revolution, but no, it has come to mean the opposite. Retaining from classical Marxism only a vague notion of capitalism as a social concept, and inflating this notion into an even vaguer interpretation of the *state* (a job Marx himself never systematically tackled), the revolutionaries inflate *that* into a vision of the world where justice, love, peace, creativity and sanctity cannot *really* exist until everything is changed. The grimly ironic thing is that it's exactly the way the Americans think about Vietnam, where they, too, are trying to impose an interpretation of reality on reality itself. And of course it is killing them. Like a fire-breather who has taken too much fuel into his mouth, they have ignited a flame which is running backwards inexorably towards its trembling source, and their own steadfastness can only concentrate the inevitable explosion. But if American society is wrecked, must ours be wrecked with it? Isn't this just the time to realise that Britain is an inherently pluralist society with its own uniqueness to protect against both American *and* revolutionary interpretations of reality? This country is a centre of *civilisation* – which is a phenomenon complex and valuable beyond any sociological opinion which can be formed of it, beyond any political concept which can be derived from it, and beyond any single idea which can be had in it. At present it is being held in contempt by young people whose love of justice is unquestionable but who do not realise that to a certain extent this is a passion they were bred to feel here, in these islands.

Clive James

WHAT **PAUL GETTY**, THE **FREAK HORSEMAN** OF THE DJMAA EL FNA, AND THE **NUDE TEXAN GIRL** FROM THE ALBERT HALL ALCHEMICAL WEDDING DID LAST MONTH

Typically, I was a day too late for the first annual Love In held at the local park in Marrakesh, Morocco, on Christmas Eve, where hundreds of European/U S heads freaked out on acid punch and a potent repertoire of improvised narcotics, including Marjoon – walnuts and peanuts, honey, cream, coffee, yoghourt, chocolate, pomegranates and other mysterious substances compounded into a fudge with the leaves – not the buds – of the keif plant and which offers a stunningly faithful impersonation of old fashioned Western LSD. Some of the more voracious Christmas trippers developed de-hydration symptoms (incessant pissing) and landed in hospital where the very un-Florence Nightingale Berber nurses apparently proved an effective ant-acid.

This Love In was convened by Lee, who had published an open invitation in IT and had created a special passport stamp to commemorate the occasion, reading 'Brothers of Eternal Love'. Lee and I met as soon as my bags were unpacked and he took me immediately to his crash pad in the Mellah, the Jewish section of town which is renowned for its Kremilinists – unlike, as it turned out, Lee's residence.

Upon arrival Lee flourished a keif-filled Indian chilum, whereupon some of the inert cadavers who littered the crash pad floor came to, well not *life* exactly, but to a ghostly characature thereof, a state of befuddled vegetable life expectancy, as the water pipe was passed from communal hand to mouth. Cream's Wheels of Fire was on the cassette, but rotating wearily because the batteries in Marrakesh are from Shanghai, called White Elephant, and they are not joking. A friendly neighbourhood policeman called by to share the pipe and improve his English. Inger, a bald headed Swedish girl, sat in the corner mumbling and scratching. ("Shaving is the only way to get rid of head lice known" said Lee, who had wielded the scissors.) Mahommed, a westernised local, passed around the fried fish and bread. A Danish couple projected a light show on the ceiling, the usual confused homage to abstract expressionism, a quiet Australian wrote poetry in the corner. And so a pot cloud descended, within minutes of arrival, and all attempts at retrieving a few unstoned moments for the next few weeks proved fruitless. Which is as it should be. Staying cool in Marrakesh would be like Alice not falling down the hole.

It is said that 57 per cent of Moroccans officialy smoke keif and certainly none of the other 43 per cent ever seem to show up in Marrakesh. A small packet (about three tablespoons) costs 2s. The ancient popeyed, grinning Merlin who sells candy to the kids on the way to school, distributes hash cookies in the Medina at twilight for 1s.8d. each. You can score blue cheer acid all the way from the West Coast for £1 per capsule. It is the most unparanoid drug scene this side of Kathmandu, although as I was leaving there were familiar rumours of Hippie purges. Some speculate on the home market by exporting keif stuffed camels, but cheques are difficult to clear in Marrakesh, even if the mail survives the Arab postal gauntlet. All my letters were either lost or opened by local postal authorities. (One last hazard: the girl at Poste Restante has an eccentric command of the alphabet.)

The great central square, Djmaa el Fna, is a combination market place, play ground, circus and freak show which rarely closes: percussionist families, snake charmers (the cobras are toothless but don't tell the fat rich tourist), magicians, mystics, shooting galleries, soup ladies, pin heads, and the galloping clove-foot gentleman, who wears a saddle, whips himself and neighs. (Sometimes, I am told, he plays the carriage. . .)

In the market you can unearth rich velvet caftans, antique leather Berber satchels, gay striped blankets, the priceless jewelry now the rage of Paris, embroidered sandals, baskets and carpets. Or bathe, like you never have before, in a dark steamy dungeon under wooden buckets of hot and cold water, among writhing silent black bodies.

Mohammed found me a suspiciously cheap four-roomed Moroccan house, built around a tiled courtyard, with orange and lemon trees and sparrows. I traded a transistor radio for a table and settled down to work, but not for long. A friend warned us that the house had a crazy landlord attached, he was now in hospital but if he ever escaped our lives were in danger. We were further unnerved when the Arab lady upstairs began affixing great bars to our shared doorway.

Meanwhile, Lee kept calling to make sure I stayed high.

Biographical Digression:

Lee is a prodigeously bearded lice-ridden dishevelled deserter from the American Way of Death, thirty-six years old, but looks older, from California. His philosophical change of life was ushered in with LSD. 'I first took acid when I was thirty-three and instantly became one of Sergeant Pepper's Band.' Before then, Lee had served with the United States Army in Korea; from where he returned home to marry an heiress. Marriage did not purge him of his life-long addiction to pederasty. He spent two years and much of his wife's money bribing himself out of goal after the first conviction. In the early sixties, when pot began to raise its head on United States campuses, Lee was a police informer. He was later converted after unexpectedly catching some of his best friends rolling joints. By 1967 he had discovered acid and he decided to drop out to Kathmandu, Nepal. The decision was not entirely unconnected with a scheduled court appearance in a few days time on another child molesting charge.

Lee arrived at Buddha's birth place with tons of money and a record player. He headed straight for the Blue Tibetan Coffee House, the appropriate H Q at the time, hooked up his machine and blew Sergeant Pepper to the Himalayan Sherpas and the stunned assembly of hippies (this was 1967, remember). Lee Pied Pipered the entire Blue Tibetan clientele on to a passing tourist bus and headed far into the foothills. When the driver lost wind, Lee bought the bus on the spot and continued to the edges of Dhulikhel, nineteen miles away, where he discovered a paradisial Himalayan hill top and established a commune. Lee equippod this with tents, sleeping bags and assorted camping gadgets.

After a few idyllic weeks, they were visited by the men from Reuters and the consequent publicity set up disastrous results, providing an apt parallel to the press's simultaneous corruption of Haight Ashbury. The commune was scattered by the usually docile Nepalese, Lee was arrested and frogmarched, hand-cuffed, through the Kathmandu streets from the Blue Tibetan to gaol. Where he spent 10 nights before being loaded aboard an outward bound flight . . .

Lee had lived in Morrocco for a year and he lived by the absence of his stolen passport: 'I am the happiest man in the world without that document, the Poste Restante gives me my mail, the bank cashes my cheques'. This last item has now petered down to $10 or $20 a month, from the $500 bus-buying days, but Lee still gives it to down-and-outs with equal abandon. He somehow scrapes together enough money for a house, and he accommodates and feeds anyone who needs it. A sincere relic from Hippieland, Lee hasn't molested *anyone* since taking acid, much less little boys. He is warm friends with many Moroccans and a gifted guru to those passing through.

He knows the Tibetan Book of the Dead, the Book of Tal, Sergeant Pepper virtually by heart, has renounced wordly posessions, uses water instead of Andrax and probably has the unhealthiest chromosomes this side of Timothy Leary. For some of his entourage the going is too tough. Three weeks after the Love In, Inger could still mouth only one sentence "I don't know", and the last I saw of her was twiching aboard the Casablanca bus with friends who were shipping her home to hospital. Apart from this hard core beat community, mystical and moneyless, the scene splits further into a) the Paris, healthy, East Village, Haight Ashbury, drop out, artists, writers, stray Living Theatre members and pretty blacks who live in the Hotel de France (7s. per night) huddling high around Beatleful cassettes: and

b) Vógue and gin upper class freak outs who orbit around Paul Getty's holiday house and sip coolness in the twilight shade of outdoor cafes.

The Madman first came at 4 a m, hurling his empty wine bottles at the reinforced door, which happily did not give in (the only bad Arab is a drunken Arab, which is why alcohol, not keif, is discouraged, Mr Callaghan). Neil Phillips, (who wrote the scary Greek gaol piece in the last Oz) came to town and I quickly moved him in for protection. (Sorry about that, Neil.) Two exotic witches from the Hotel de France began feeding me with extraordinary hallucigens which they had extracted from a man called Ackmed from Tangier, who is famous for turning on Mick Jagger, among thousands of others. It was in the drugged haze of these last few days that countless clowns began popping out of the mirages. The blonde Texan lady who I had last seen naked inside the Albert Hall flowed into the courtyard one afternoon and giggled tumultuously. A soft gentle trio of Americans, Michael, John & Rick (who slept in a walnut factory) wove spells of magic and mystery. Breathless Bill Butler, of Brighton's Unicorn Bookshop, brought urgent and nonsensical gossip from London. A long time resident came with tales of local fuzz busts and warnings of mass deportations.

Finally, inevitably, on the last night, the madman slid silently into my courtyard while I was engrossed, with friends, in the ceiling shadow patterns projected by a parrafin heater. There was a brief struggle, which I lost, and he carried inside a whale-like Moroccan prostitute in a white petticoat and flamenco lipstick, then he proceeded to cunilinga in the court yard, much to the dreamy fascination of my stoned companions. I danced around like an epileptic faggot, ordering someone to go find the cavalry. Why was I so afraid? The madman was harmlessly exploring the bowels of his beauty, on my porch now, and offering extra portions of the house rent free if only I would turn up "zee moozic". His grinning maiden lumbered towards my petrified genitals, whereupon someone returned with a solo rescuer, who took one look at the chaos, boggled incredulously and fled. The madman spotted some Western flesh and was anxious to barter. Perhaps we could have even reached a deal, but marjoon has a habit of making even the mundane sensational, so that this particular evening's not uneventful circumstances were rendered, to say the least, farcically incomprehensible. And this was just the prologue to a night rampant with insanity.

I know that the madman kicked in the door of a nearby travellers commune and that the police raided my house, leaving when no one opened the door. Lee strayed into the dream, somehow frightening a pregnant Moroccan, getting locked in a room and beaten by six outraged relatives. (Sorry about that, Lee.) Friends bundled us on to the Casablanca bus, the tambourine man pressed a hash cookie in my hand. The watch said four hours, but we knew the journey took ten minutes. Next we sat in a Paris transit lounge being laughed at by Jet Set stockbrokers, and woke up in London in bed with Marrakesh flue – something Alice never caught.

Richard Neville.

OZ

19

3s

USA 60c.
DENMARK 3Kr.
HOLLAND 2G.
GERMANY 1.8 DM.

OZ talks to DR G — the only groupie with a Ph.D in captivity.

Why the Press Council is a dangerous hoax.

Why Portugal — the poorest country in Europe — has a defence budget second only to the United States.

What the man who discovered that cannabis is non addictive said to Caroline Coon.

Millions are starving...Millions of pounds worth of food is dumped each year. Why?

You've never seen Ophelia looking like Marianne Faithful looking like this.

Led Zeppelin...Murray Roman...Everly Brothers...The Incredible String Band ...Two Virgins...BOB DYLAN.

For those who find OZ hard to read this issue is the next best thing to braille.

VIVIAN
BONZO DOG BAND

OZ

LONDON OZ is published monthly
by OZ Publications Ink Ltd.
52 Princedale Road, London, W11.
Phone: 229 7541. Directors:
Richard Neville, Andrew Fisher.

Editor: Richard Neville.
Design: Jon Goodchild, Virginia.
Writers: Andrew Fisher, Ray
Durgnat, Germaine, David Widgery,
Angelo Quattrocchi, Fletcher Watkins.
Muzic: Felix Dennis.
Research: Jim Anderson.
Artists: Martin Martin Sharp, Bob Hook,
John Hurford, Womack, Phillipe
von Mora
Photography: Keith Morris.
Advertising: Felix Dennis.
Pushers: Louise Ferrier, Brigid
Harrison, Cosi Pavalko, Lyn Richards.
Typesetting: Papyrotype.
Distribution: Britain
(overground) Moore-Harness Ltd,
11 Lever Street, London, EC1.
Phone: CLE 4882.
(Underground) ECAL, 22 Betterton
Street, London, WC2. Phone
TEM 8606. Transmutation, Guildford 65694.
California: Rattner Distributors,
2428 McGee St, Berkley,
Calif. 94703.
Holland: Thomas Rap,
Regulierdwarstraat 91,
Amsterdam, Tel: 020-227065
Denmark: George Streeton,
The Underground, Larsbjorn
straede 13, Copenhagen K.
Printed by: OZ Publications Ink Ltd.

OTHER
SCENES

NEW YORK:Lower East Side types all disclaiming knowledge of where the several thousand neatly-rolled joints came from — the ones that arrived in New York homes on St Valentine's Day accompanied by a heart-encircled fact sheet which declared that 'marihuana is not habit-forming any more than are the movies' despite the 200,000 arrests for possession last year. The anonymous donors promised that more joints would be sent out Mother's Day 'to persons selected from the phone books.' Yippie Abbie Hoffman, sometime spokesman for the Tompkins Square community, says: 'Wish we knew who did it; we never got any. My theory is that it's the American Tobacco company. They know that with all this pressure on tobacco that cigarettes will be declared illegal soon. They've already registered names like Acapulco Gold and Panama Red and now, they're looking around for ways to test new products.'

Ford's Theatre in Washington spent thousands on installing hard-bottomed seats, replicas of those in the theatre when Lincoln was shot, only to discover (after complaints from patrons) that asses are apparently not the same shape today. Red velvet cushions have been ordered . . . DC's radical newsletter Mayday (now seeking suggestions for a new name because Mayday has been previously copyrighted) says the Federal government is growing marihuana for "testing' purposes on Senator James Eastland's Mississippi farm . . . Senators Albert Gore and Everett Dirksen are feuding over whether the iris (Gore's choice) or the marigold should be proclaimed the national flower. Meanwhile, Rome burns . . . The men's john in the Supreme Court building dispenses watered soap . . . No news is Agnew.

Everybody's into the movie thing these days with techniques often getting more attention than the actual content. Montage or collage films, for example, popping up on all sides with various methods aimed at the same results. Two projectors with different films combine beautifully on one screen (Warholish) but you can also get the same effect in the processing (as John Chamberlain does in his "Secret Life of Hernando Cortes"). And you can even do it in the camera by rewinding the film back to a certain point and double exposing as you shoot a different scene over the first. Ed Seeman specializes in this method with his mind-blowing Frank Zappa footage (now being edited by Zappa for release in the spring). Chamberlain, by the way, has also screened a color movie called 'Wide Point' which displays fragmentary scenes and images on seven enormous screens at once. Fascinating to learn how much more one's eyes can be forced to absorb simultaneously. Then there are the Maysles Brothers whose latest epic is about a team of bible-salesmen touring the south, making their pitch at some gruesomely suburban homes. The Maysles

technique is to hang around so close for so long that everybody gets used to you and you end up with film as close to real-life as you can get. In the case of their "Salesman" it works marvellously.

Universities were described as "mere trade schools for the 'military-industrial complex" by California delegates to a recent Peace & Freedom party conference at Venice. Committees were set up to study lowering the voting age, institute free public transportation and change the present penal system . . . Charter flights to Africa for $460 roundtrip are being organised by Jimi Daniel, 1853 New Hampshire Ave NW, Washington DC 20009 . . The NY Post and other straight papers around the country are currently on a salutory kick — interviews with the families of slaughtered GIs who invariably 'didn't want to go to Vietnam'. Presumably the reporters didn't think it cool to ask the obvious question, 'Then why did you let him go?' And none of the stories chooses to make the point that if a kid willingly goes off to a foreign country to kill complete strangers without asking 'Why?', then neither he nor his family has any kick coming if he doesn't come back. 'Poems are too spiritual for Americans" (Greenfeel a commune magazine, 25c, from Box 1037, Carmel, Calif. 93921).

The California firm, Computicket Corp, that's replacing those old-fashioned gaudy-colored theatre tickets with a standard computer-punched one, book European theatre tickets within seconds . . .

Nixon's foodtaster is stoned most of the time . . . Bantam Books often to pay expenses involved in setting up press conferences between its author and college newspaper editors . . Why does Douglas Fairbanks call himself 'Junior'? Does he still see himself as a child?

What may have killed Ramparts was its hang-up on glossy paper, full-color photographs, general extravagance. Ramparts' top brass threw money around from the beginning like a drunken sailor; on that budget almost any competent newsman could have kept the mag going for at least four times as long. Ramparts' problem was that it always had more money than experience (or commonsense) as became only too sadly clear when they had SF virtually to themselves during the newspaper strike and filled the gap with a subcollegiate tabloid that nobody bothered to buy or read . . .

William Buckley's rightwing National Review gave a glowing testimonial to Boston's Avatar which, unlike most undergrounds says NR writer Anthony Dolan, is 'patriotic' . . . Sad that Bill Graham's Fillmore had to go the slickpaper route with his pocket-size program that looks like a replica of Broadway's Playbill. It could have been a creative product. But then one sees all the ads (20 out of 24 pages) and remembers that friendly Bill Graham isn't in this business to be creative, right? . . . Courses on belly-dancing, medical aspects of drugs, gourmet cooking, rock music, stained glass art, witchcraft and communal living are offered by SF's Heliotrope (Free University) which adds that courses 'generally take place in the warmth and comfort of the instructors home . . . but they may meet at the beach, or in a tree'.

to discuss things or even help if I can.
I wish OZ all the best.

Agnes Diannent

Commite d'action de langues
Sorbonne/lensier.

Dear OZ

I belong to a 'commite d'action' at
the Sorbonne and we were all upset to
read: "Unmask a teacher, you'll find a
copper" (Angelo Quattrrochi – OZ Feb
69). The other day, 200 teachers
occupied the Sorbonne to protest
against repression and students being
sent to the army because of their
political action. Most teachers want
revolution; its obvious, as during our
active strike; we interrupted some
lectures to explain this strike, and most
teachers didn't object — though some
students did.

Also, I don't like this RMS idea if
those people talk of "Professionals" or
of "part-time Revolutionary Militant
Student". Revolution is not a new

game or fashion – it's very serious, and
if one really believes in it, anything he
does or says is revolution. I was quite
upset too to read the French addresses
given by the RMS at the moment, only
the "commites d'action"can be
powerful as they unite all
revolutionary tendencies. And we're
precisely trying to get rid of the PSU
and other Unions, because of all they
do is make a lot of publicity – even
abroad, as OZ print it for their own
little pointless Unions – Unions have
proved to be useless before May. May
was an action of the masses (and not of
the Unions) and Unions like those
mentioned in OZ won't make a
revolution.

If Angelo Quattrrochi or anybody
from OZ is still in Paris, I'd like to
meet this person as I quite like OZ
(except what I mentioned) and I'd like

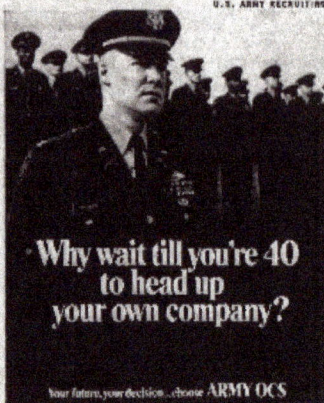

Why wait till you're 40 to head up your own company?

Your future, your decision...choose **ARMY OCS**

Dear Oz,
What is happening? What's with all
this violence? These Poor Bastards are
sick. Let's stop now before these
phoney cunts blow the whole scene.
Everybody knows that a social
Revolution is just underway. Our
attitudes have changed radically in the
last 5 years. More sweeping changes are
yet to come. Grass *will* win the day
we hope we have the control to achieve
the aim's of most. A peaceful society.
A love community. Naked and
unafraid: 'What do the petrol bomb
mob want, Stalin!? A policed state.
That's great for the States. They're
that already. What do they want in the
words of the Prophet? Fuck knows!
If they want to kick shit in the face
of the establishment, there are nicer
ways.
In the spring when the gardens are
reborn lets go out into the streets
Naked. Make love in the streets. On
Buses in Trains. Fuck in the Parks and
Squares. Give flowers and grass to the
fuzz. Lets do it in the road! Fuck for
peace. You must agree its no more
ridiculous than throwing molotov
cocktails at policemen, and if its
publicity that they're after they'll get
it; look at the spread that the nude at
the Albert Hall got, and John & Yoko.
But please, don't lower yourselves to
the violence that typifies the grey
world that surrounds us. Don't imitate
it like a bunch of sheep. Kids have got
more sense. Let's have a revolution by
all means but lets not act as sick as the
rest of the Alf's.
Dear Harold & Papa God Nixon
included.
I hope somebody feels the same and
rewrites this better than I have.
Love
Pete

Sir,
It has come to my notice that a
disgusting and pornographic
publication called OZ is being mailed
to this address.
Take notice, that under no
circumstances are any further copies of
this filth to be delivered to my
daughter at this or any other address.
L A Bidmead
46 Onslow Road,
Burwood Park,
Walton-on-Thames,
Surrey.

Comrades,
I dont know where comrade
Buckman got his information on
Anarchism – from the columns of the
"Guardian" perhaps, being charitable.
Malatesta defined anarchism as
"Society organised without Authority"
In what respects could that differ from
"counter-authoritarian society?'.
On the charge that "Their beliefs
are based ... on everyone being
members of a community able to
sustain itself without rules" I would
reply, firstly, that this differs not at all
in essence from his own concept of
autonomous communities (unless by
revolutionary state he means
revolutionary Stage, which is
particularly a contradiction in terms).
Secondly, it is not necessary to
overthrow the State before carrying
out liberation activities.
Counter-authoritarian activities can be
carried out here and now by anarchist
and liberation groups. The East
London Libertarians, active in the
London Squatters Campaign (and
elsewhere) are a case in point.
It is possible that some such
libertarian groupings could act as
base-units for Comrade Buckman's
autonomous communities,
co-operating and helping each other on
"Mutual Aid" – for, as he himself
admits, "If [the individual] steps too
far out of line the system will clobber
him" Collective action is necessary in
Leftie jargon – its called "Solidarity".
He further accuses the anarchists of
"imposing" their system on those
"unwilling to accept it". Yet he regards
the Left generally as potential allies –
and is thus put in the position of
singling out for authoritarianism
precisely the one tendency of the Left
which is uncompromisingly
counter-authoritarian, and enlisting
the aid of groups whose belief in
Authority is complete, (as long as they
have the authority). They are also
dogmatic, despite comrade Buckmans
ideas about them – the S.L.L. and
certain Maoist groups are notable in
this respect.
As to the Corrara Congress; perhaps
I should quote 'Freedom'; "after all
old revolutionary movements there is

always a residue of the old faithful who have come to regard themselves an establishment." There was a division between those who wanted an institutionalised adherence to a doctrine, and those who wanted freedom of revolutionary action. The British delegate indeed opposed 'the idea of national delegations, as accepting those "bourgeois concepts which destroy the roots of international revolutionary solidarity" (Freedom, 21-9-68).

Many of comrade Buckman's concepts are unclear — I would presume that by "discipline" he means self-discipline (as opposed to externally imposed rules of behaviour) — an essential in all anarchist thought. But what does he mean by "organisation"? Too many people on the Left equate organisation with bureaucracy, ennabling them on the one hand to justify their own bureaucratic excesses as "organisation," while condemning the anti-bureaucratic anarchists as being, therefore, anti-organisation.

I would agree on the inadvisability of merely "dropping out" in the purely emotional involvement of the "hippie". Quite apart from such an action's impotence in the face of repression, such involvement without a defensive basis of theory, can be dangerous (Hitlers adaptation of the "Wandervogel" of the twenties to become the Hitlerjugend of the thirties, and the Maharishi Mahesh Yogi, are two cases to think about).

Finally, while agreeing wholeheartedly on the inappropriatness of Third World models, I should like to end with a quotation from the "Red Book" (CH.26)

1. The individual is subordinate to the organisation

2. The minority is subordinate to the majority

3. The lower level is subordinate to the higher level

4. The entire membership is subordinate to the Central Committee

So much for the questioning of authority implied in the red-book waving Red Guards (although the situation in China is complex). Those who would ally themselves with British Maoists, please note.
Fraternally,
Mike Don

Oz Baby,
It seems really sad to me that in order to create Drop out city, (Pauls letter Oz 18) the method suggested involved founding it with bread derived from shows etc. surely this is just bloody hypocritical.

How the hell can any society be justified when its founded by one of the main things it opposes? By doing that we would be indistinguishable from warmongers who say in order to have peace there must be a war.

The whole idea of drop out city is beautiful, but free meals, never, someone has to pay for them in a place like the smoke.

Why not take over a deserted stretch of coast line and make shelters of branches or driftwood, grow all necessary food and all excess trade for things that Mother Nature doesnt provide, only then could it be a moneyless society.

Love to those who want or need it,
Tesse.

I'm really just sitting here listening to Bobbie Dylan.
I had a friend called Keith, he wrote a poem called 'Bob Dylan My Idol'.
This was to be a lengthy piece . . . no, piece, of writing, but will now I just don't know.
Bob Dylan's pretty good, some of lyrics really screw me up, I think he's a druggie, I also think, no believe he's a horse addict.
I wish I had an object in life but I have'nt it doesn't really matter I suppose.
This is rather meaningless I know, but, well, I just a meaningless guy, sorry.
I was going to end there well you know how it is.

Dedicated To No One . . . . . Sorry
Alan Hunter

Dear OZ,
The reproduction of Eugene Schoenfeld's proclivities in OZ 17 could only be dismissed as iniquitous filth. Pages like this no doubt create pretentiousness, perhaps necessary for such a publication but this issue did not in anyway compare with the Sharp-Von Mora tacit well implied "Magic Theatre."
Jeremy Hinds, Manchester 10.

Dear Oz,
Smash capitalism, violence, corruptness, stagnation, injustice, they all cry.
And how are they going to do it? With violence, hash, acid, and their own form of injustice, intolerance.
Policeman, nice guy, no harmful whims what to do? Kick him in the face, belly, anywhere, call him fuzz.
Yes. Trample on all who are in the way, no clear sight here.
My dear God. How many must be hurt by the herd with warped ideals, before somebody sees the light.
BN.

Dear Friends,
I was a little surprised by the criticism of David Ramsey Steeles' Smash Cash article. Anyone who works with money will realise the amazing amount of trouble cash in all its various forms can cause.

In the past month the following things have effectively loused things up for me. (I am a salesman in an Electricity Show room). First of all a guy walked in complaining about getting a letter demanding that he pay two outstanding HP payments on his refrigerator. He said he'd paid them. The following day he was in again with 38 pieces of paper which were receipts for each of his HP payments. Checking through these I discovered he was in fact one short, and another receipt was invalid because it had not been machine printed through the shops till machine. This receipt had however been written out by me and I saw it as my responsibility, so on the spur of the moment I decided to offer to pay the payment in place of the invalid receipt.

My charitable action however was not seen as such by our head office, and the following week one of my numerous superiors appeared with an accountant. I then found myself on the carpet — for offering to pay the money in myself — it was then suggested that at an earlier date I had accepted the money from this guy, for myself by not making a permanant record of it by stamping the guy's receipt form. They then suggested that I had virtually confessed my crime by offering to pay the money in myself, at this later date.

The whole thing is now I think cleared up, though I'm assured any further anomalies concerning my cash will be considered along with this one at a future date. And as you can imagine I'm sick to death of the whole money thing, I'm not employed as a cashier anyway, but due to staff shortages I have to look after as much as £500 a day. And further more I can work like hell all day, and all I have to show at the end is a pile of bits of paper I'd like to leave now and see if I can get a less frustrating — and dangerous job, but if I leave now I imagine I'll get a lousy reference, so all I can do is stop on in the hope of being lucky and keeping on the right sides of the twisted valves of the land.

I was going to give you a list of

some of the other problems I've had with money recently in the hope of showing what a stupid system the whole currency thing is however the final comment I will make is this one. There is plenty for all, at least in this country. Only money allows so few to have much more than their fair share, and I find only when people are very hard will they beg and get something that isn't theirs.

Love to all from the centre of a stupid battle of great sadness and bewilderment.

Terry Kidd.

Dear Editor,
Isn't this just the time for Clive James (wind up Black Dwarfs, Oz, Feb. 69) to realise that sometimes, just occasionally, we dull, classic members of the British working class master the intellectual strength to digest his brilliantly reasoned column in Oz, and sometimes, just occasionally, have the impertinence to disagree with him?

'Britain is an inherently pluralist society.' Thank you for the information. Tell us of a society which is not. He talks of the 'anti-intellectual revolution'. Now then, Clive, principle down a bit here. The revolution only seems anti-intellectual to you, because you obviously see intellect as an entity valuable entirely in its own right with no necessary relevance to anything except itself. No intellect, not even our stunted working man Socialist tradition, even developed without something into which first to get its teeth. Give any man a steak and he will chew it. To be anti-intellectual now is the healthiest attitude a thinking man can have. Try to understand the real intellect of the historically hard-bitten century-old grass roots mostly uneducated international left and you will be helping your own brilliance to perhaps develop a little further.

Does the 'classic Left' have 'only objective intellectual enemies'? Well, to be brief, the present student struggles are directly relevant to chipping away once again at our old enemies — the blind, selfish, albeit "civilised" councillors, politicians, financiers, businessmen, soldiers and all other heads of men who, once they have succeeded in grabbing something from the rest of us, wish to make bloody sure we don't ever get it back. And if all that Guss of Germany, Pasolini of Italy and James of Great Britain (or is it Australia?) can see as enemies of the revolution are their fellow-intellectuals, then you must be in an extremely fortunate, secure, well-heeled and blissful situation, and I wish you good luck.

So, Mr. James, please continue to delight us with your frolics, thereby making an Emerald Isle, I assure you, even more cultured and civilised than it already may be. However, seeing that we both have the pleasure of living in the same nauseating, over-civilised city, may I recommend you to spend the odd evening out in the Newmarket Road pubs with us and our discontents, which are legion, and forget for a moment the plush Common Rooms and effete Satirical Clubs of the University, where more hot air is dispersed nightly than in the Mill Road Public Baths?

Yours fraternally,

Stuart Clucas.
(Vice-chairman, Cambridge University Branch of the National Union of Public Employees)
13 Fair Street
Cambridge.

Sir/Madam,
I don't have any money, but I have more sense than to eat the sort of food recommended in your feature, 'Poverty Cooking'. On a diet of recipes like Beggars Stew, Cracked Egg Omelette, or Ballsed Up Bolognese, I would remain poor, physically, and spiritually, as well as materially, all my life. Being without money is often unavoidable, perhaps even laudable, but there is absolutely no need to eat poorly. 'Poverty cooking', no matter what variety of recipes turns up in subsequent issues, is wrongly conceived. Cheap, no doubt, beggars stew is. Delicious it may be (in a degraded sense — but this sort of concoction is ten times more delicious if it is made ten times more expensively) but these are hardly the two most important criteria. Is it rich in protein? Is it good for you? and the answer is of course, no. About as good for you as a meal you might buy in a Wimpy Bar of a Golden egg or any other cheap restaurant chain in London — nutritive value, nil. Just platefuls of shit for those at the bottom of the heap. Shit to give you, bad skin, bad breath, constipation, piles, baldness, and generally to keep you running along at about half pressure. The droppings from the Fat Honky's table. Tenth rate imitations of some of the gastronomic delights of western cuisine. A cuisine which is thoroughly decadent anyway. An attitude to food which by ignoring the nature of man and what is good for him, and concentrating on appearance and taste, has most of its adherents diseased in some way by the time they are forty. The average life span in the west is about sixty five. For this longevity, of which it is so proud western civilisation relies not on the sensibility of its dietary habits, but on the brilliance of its surgeons, and the dubious efficacy of its drugs. That is the *best* that can be expected — and 'poverty cooking' represent that same attitude at its very *worst*. On beggars stew, life will be very short and very unhappy. Racked by disorders, both psychological and physical, you will be an easy prey for the vultures of capitalism and the overground. Don't beg, don't scrounge cracked eggs from Sainsbury's don't buy cheap spaghetti from cheap supermarkets, *OPT OUT.* Don't let your lack of bread turn the getting of enough food into a middle class hang-up.

Revolutionise your whole philosophy of eating — you are what you eat. Brown rice, fresh vegetables in small quantities are what you should start with; make every day a trip, spend less, go macrobiotic. Macrobiotics is simple intelligence, common sense and natural foods. The authors of your column should read up on the theory of yin and yang before digging deeper into the garbage can. Roast Trafalgar Square pigeon might, just might, be OK, but you would probably be better off eating the 6d carton of grain. Doses of strontium-90 all round.

Richard O'Sullivan
5-7 Earlham St
London WC2

Dear OZ,
Sprats yes. But why potatoes and spaghetti? Cheap food can be nourishing For instance, MUESLI can be made for under 2s. per pound as compared to 6s for a packaged brand. It contains oats, 2/6 2lbs; millet, 3/6 lb; wheatgerm, 2/- lb; barley kernels, 1/6; soya flour; nuts; Sainsburys walnut pieces are 1/5; sultanas 1 lb, 2/2; sea salt.

It can be made as a porridge as normal. Or, with milk and fruit, There are endless cheap combinations.

Vegetable soups are also very nourishing. Winter vegetables: carrots, onions, turnips, parsnips, cabbages, leeks, swedes, sprouts all combine well. Heat up thicken with soya flour of wholemeal; garnish with cheese. With wholemeal bread this is a good meal. You can make enough for 8 for about 5s bread inclusive. Lentil broth is another good stand by. Lentils cost about 2s per lb, simply soak overnight heat up, flavour with herbs.

If your real interest lies in helping folk buy and eat cheap and nourishing food, why not put people in touch with wholesalers, or open a distribution centre for goods at almost wholesale prices, thereby avoiding food manufacturers con. By buying wholesale you can save from 15 to 50%. Cereals and vegetables are the cheapest foods.

Yours,
Anthony Lovell,
UEA, Norwich.

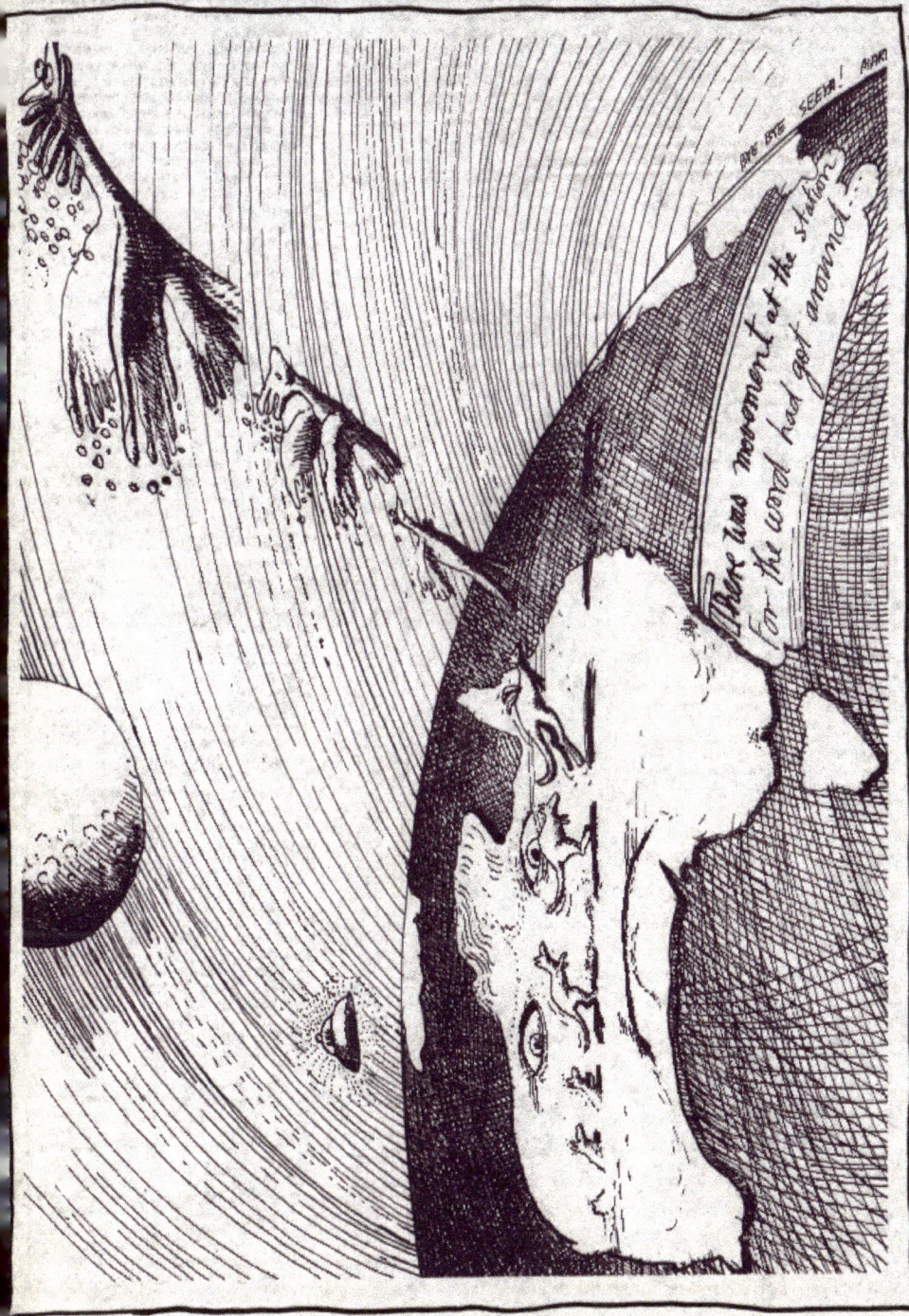

5

the Editor's

SPIKE

Those who ploughed through the typist's idiosyncracies in my report from Marrakech last month may recall Lee, a charismatic International hippie consul who gives freely his love, food and accommodation to those passing through. On Feb 24, he sent me this message through a friend:

"...enclosed with this letter is a witnessed copy of a letter I received from Sandy Stephenson, the kilted Scot you met in Marrakech, it sounds only too authentic. We do not know what is happening to his friend Winfred Hanck, aged 22-23, but fear he might be in the same position... Cops are roaming around Marrakech stamping passports, controlling visas and the like, being very unpleasant to those who don't have any. Like Lee, Roy, Inger and a few others...".

This is the letter enclosed with Lee's message:

Dear Lee, Winfred got busted yesterday, and I got busted about 3 or 4 weeks ago. I had 350 grams hash in my room and they came and searched my room and found it. I've been living in pure hell for those 3-4 weeks, and now I'm deported and repatriated. They decided right away that I was selling stuff and not smoking it as I told them, and to make me admit it, they tied my hands and feet and hoisted me on a length of steel scaffold between two desks and let me hang there by my arms and legs, they took my shoes and socks off and whipped the soles of my feet with a cowhide whip, they also tied a towel around my head and poured water onto it over my mouth and nose, this went on for half an hour every morning and afternoon for 3 days, while they shouted at me "you were selling it weren't you". I managed somehow to keep from admitting that, don't ask me how, I am 26 years old, and it's the first time I've cried I think since I was 10. I was thrown into a cell about 10 ft squ.

with 11 other people and a toilet, we had to lie on top of each other all night, and were eaten alive by lice. I am going to write to Time Magazine about it and will send you a copy when I do.

Winfred had ½ kilo of stuff in his sleeping bag, and I managed to pass a message on to my friend in Rabat to remove it, he promised to do so this morning, so I hope he has. My advice to you right now is to get out of Morocco as soon as possible, as my Consul tells me they are arresting people all over the country, about 30 were deported from Agadir recently. I realize you have no passport, and if you know of any way I can help you write and let me know, I will be living in London.

My sentence was one month imprisonment suspended sentence and as they knew I had 250 DH (£2-18) they fined me that, but that wasn't the end of my troubles. The Prosecutor for the King wasn't satisfied, and wanted to keep me in prison for another 3 months for another trial, and was going to give me two years. That's what I think Winfred will get if they find the stuff.

I don't advise you to go and try to see him, because they will arrest you too, and no matter what you tell them, they won't believe it, and will not make any enquiries about it either. They decide what they will charge you with, and torture you until you admit it. Then if you don't admit it, they write out your confession and make you sign it anyway. They said in mine that I bought a little to smoke and the rest was for sale. To see Winfred in prison, you have to go and get special permission from the Tribunal, and they really HATE Hippies, so don't do it man, you might fuck it up for him.

Don't forget to write if I can help you in any way. I did all I

could to help Winfred, as I was escorted out of the country by a Police Inspector. Maybe if you sent somebody who looks a bit straight just to be sure that his stuff is removed, don't go yourself, you are sure to be arrested, they only ask to see your Passport, and that's enough.

You may think I'm raving a bit, but believe me I have good cause to, I wonder that I didn't go completely crazy.

Good luck again,
Sandy
On the boat
Ceuta Algeciras.

Sandy is in London now. In Rabat the British vice-consul asked him to warn 'hippie travellers' that Moroccan pipe dream days are over. The country is being cleaned up for tourists.

STOP PRESS:

An organisation called KK has just been formed by Tom Cartwright (who was busted with Neal Philips in Greece) with the co-operation of Release and Bit. It has three main purposes: 1. To help those doing time or awaiting trial by sending bread, books, clothes, etc. and providing legal advice. 2. To collect information on busts, severity of sentences and prison conditions, to publicise such information and bring pressure to bear where necessary. 3. To act as an association comprising of bust-survivors, their friends and helpers, which will be a morale booster for those in jail.

Anyone who can help with information, bread, clothes, books, letters or visits to prisoners, contact KK, Release Office, 50a Princedale Road, London, W.11. Tel: 01-229 7753.

Abbie Hoffman's 'Revolution for the Hell of It' is the most important book yet to emerge, or rather, leap out of the Underground. Along with Paul Krassner (of the Realist) and Jerry Rubin (Of the Berkeley Free Speech Movement), Hoffman was a founder freak of Yippie! (Youth International Party, see OZ 10).— the anti-organisation which invented Chicago. This acid gamester is an intuitively brilliant media tactician, a tireless psychic guerilla and a profound dialectician of new style politics: 'Political irrelevance is more effective than political relevance... A be-in is an emotional United Nations.... If you want to begin to understand our culture you can start by comparing Frank Sinatra and the Beatles.... The Viet Cong attacking the U.S. Embassy in Saigon is a work of art ... there is no programme — a programme would make our movement sterile'. Revolution for the Hell of It (written in three amphetamine days) is an epigrammanifesto for the only revolution possible in an age where there 'are no more political solutions, only technological ones... all the rest is propaganda' (Jacques Ellul), and as

such is a total repudiation of New Left political beauticians and their hoary Marxist utensils. His strategy I would call the Politics of Play, a concept which, along with his book, I hope to discuss in the next OZ. (Revolution for the Hell of it. Dial Press Inc, 750 Third Ave, New York, NY 10017; $1.95 . . . some extracts appeared in IT 51).

OZ urgently requires an amazing comic-strip artist. Send samples of your work to 52 Princedale Road, W11 for Jon Goodchild, or contact him direct at 352 7258 (evenings).
Some readers may have detected an improvement in the quality of this magazine. Those with broad tastes may also have noticed Zeta's catastrophic slump into a mire of witless incomprehensibility. These two events are not un-connected. Paul Lawson, once our assistant editor, left OZ some months ago for the bounteous pastures of London's most unnecessary tit magazine. We wish him luck.

Piper Greene seeks 'reviews, articles, editorial or stray facts' on John Mayall: write to Box 193, Kerhonkson, NY 12446, New York.
High school age, mindblow writings on drugs, revolution, life, arts, race, the generational war, ecology, etc, are being anthologised by Keith Lampe (of Yippie and Liberation Magazine) and David Herres (of Liberation and WIN Magazines). 'People whose things are accepted eventually will receive tiny loaves of bread floating slowly back.' Send to — 10th Floor, 5 Beeckman St, New York City, 10038.

It is doubtful whether the abovementioned yippie editors could extract much revolution from UK students, let alone schoolchildren, if a survey published in the latest issue of Sennet, the University of London Union newspaper, is to be taken as a guide. Sennet (Feb 26) has completed a survey of almost one thousand students, which they say is an accurate mirror of opinion at England's largest university. 'If Parliament were to be elected to-day', 32% of students would vote conservative, 30% Labour, 16% Liberal, although they would prefer Harold Wilson as Prime Minister. 41% are satisfied with the present political system, and 60% have changed their views since attending university. Of these 60%, 30% have shifted to the right. The survey concludes that students are 'parochial and insular.'After reading Sennet, I came to the same conclusion — not about students, but about student editors.
Why are British student papers so bad? Most of them look like trade journals for the asbestos industry. Even the best of them slavishly imitate traditional newspaper lay-out styles (bold intro pars, justified type, column heads etc). The prose is plank Fleet Street, the issues stubbornly provincial. Student journalists droop with surprise when it

is explained that their publications lack one single, distinctive or original feature (good or bad) and that they have somehow managed to resist the sweeping technical and aesthetic printing advancements which rendered their efforts obsolete twenty years ago. The editorial mood is coy, soporific, unchallenging.
A week after I joined a student paper in Australia in 1962, the editor called for the Vice Chancellor to resign, published highly confidential and scandalous minutes of Senate meetings, exposed Security links with the administration and created an outcry that reverberated around the lecture halls and newspaper columns of every city in the country. In Australia! In 1962!
A few years later the same newspaper (Tharunka, laugh, it's Aborigine for 'message stick') was prosecuted by the Sydney Vice-Squad for obscenity, and its editors fined. Meanwhile, the editor of a nearby student paper Honi Soit) campaigned for the abolition of the student union and the substitution of a student-wide anarchist commune. The British editor's stock answer to any suggestion that they should ease their publication into the nineteenth century is: Oh! The printer wouldn't let us do that.
Change the printer.
'But' they say, recovering their composure, 'they've been printing us for 25 years.
Change the printer.
'But he does it as a favour very cheaply'. Cheaply and badly. Change the printer, improve quality, boost circulation and advertising revenue. Oh yes, advertising. For all their demolition of iron gates, students are only too meek before the insane restrictions of bucholic agency hacks who even dictate the position of their hideous pieces of 'College Scarves' art work, (often on the front page).
Most of the papers are printed on collapsing letterpresses and could easily be transferred to any of the numerous sheet-fed offset machines which at half the price, are hungry to print these uncontroversial parish rags. Pages could then be designed totally by students, like paintings or even sculptures, instead of left to molten-lead robots. No-one wants the papers to imitate OZ, merely to develop their own personality, like the 100 members of the Underground Press Syndicate, which share a family resemblance yet exhibit individual variations. Typically, few of the students have ever heard of the UPS or of such famous pioneering tabloids as Other Scenes, East Village Other, or the Berkeley Barb.
The editors of the Buffalo Chip, from Omaha Nebraska, were in London recently. They produce a 20 page tabloid for £150 an issue and often set their type on nothing more sophisticated than an Olivetti portable. Their only two advertisers withdrew after being threatened with violence by outraged Nebraskans. Their brave and

fiery little tabloid makes Cherwell and Varsity seem like the prose prostitute's training-beds they really are.
Student editors seem completely ignorant of the world-wide proliferation of Underground alternative publications - which, from Dallas (Notes) to Zagreb (Paradoks), from Wellington (Cock) to Saskatchewan (The Carillon) from even Curacao (Vito) to Bombay (Anti/Pro) are light-years ahead of the sad, trite, grey banalities of undergraduate role playing. Recently, when I was showing the staff of Sennet samples of these amateur, indigent and much harrassed newspapers, they at least had the integrity to be embarrased. But one of them asked plaintively, as she inspected the world's most beautiful newspaper, the San Francisco Oracle, 'WELL, suppose we did try and turn Sennet into something original. What would Fleet Street editors think? They might prefer Sennet like it is'. A question which reveals, I think, the reason for the contemptible standards of student publishing.
We wish Private Eye goodluck with their libel fund and offer congratulations on their move to palatial three storey offices. Now the editors on the Wilton-carpeted top floor ring the secretaries on the cord-matted bottom floor for endless cups of tea - with which they scurry upstairs past the pleasant, always-on-the-verge-of-being-fired, Tony Rushton.

The last Australian OZ was published in February. From its first issue (April Fools Day, 1963) Aust-OZ was a semi-digestible stew of satire, short stories, caricature, pertinent Hansard reprints, inside news and gossip. It was the only magazine to ever reveal the real cause for the unexpected resignation of Sydney's Archbishop Gough (who now presides over the smallest parish in Britain) and it once published a remarkable Guide to Sydney's Underworld with an accompanying pop Top Twenty chart of local hoods. (Unfortunately the latter precipitated such a flood of underworld jealousy that there were several bashings and one near fatal gangland shooting). Regular outbursts of police atrocities were recorded under the title 'The stiff arm of the law' and a 'This month in censorship' feature was dropped as examples became too commonplace. The magazine exposed that sacred car, Holden, produced for Australia by General Motors ('At 60 miles an hour the only sound you can hear is the rust') the dishonesty of the press, the cowardice of the Australian Broadcasting Corporation and the abominable bellicosity, racialism and Rugby Club morality of the Government.
A Sydney magistrate, Gerald Locke, once ruled that 'the publication would deprave and corrupt young people or unhealthy minded adults so injudicious

SMALLS

9

as to fancy it as literature and so misguided as to cultivate the habit of reading it'. He discarded the testimony of seventeen 'expert' witnesses who were so injudicious as to consider the magazine had literary merit and so misguided as to dispute its tendency to deprave and corrupt. Martin Sharp, art editor, was sentenced to four months hard labour and editors Neville & Walsh to 6 months. The prosecution had spent many court hours establishing whether a pun contained in a cartoon, 'Get Folked', was in fact a pun– which is some indication of the prevailing level of intelligence.

Following the verdict, one of Australia's most popular news commentators, the late Eric Baume, had this to say. 'And I was very pleased indeed to see – and I don't care whether these people who talk about liberties and so forth jump in the lake – I was very pleased to see that three young men were gaoled on charges of publishing an obscene publication, OZ magazine. Well, that's a good thing – to wipe OZ out will be one of the best things for the country, A dirty little rag with filth in it'. Two years later Mr. Locke's verdict was quashed on appeal.

The Australian OZ team are now to publish a monthly newsletter which will compensate for the infuriating vagaries of local media. £1/10/-; Box H143, OZtralia Square, Sydney, Australia.

One of the more depressing memories of Australian OZ days, if readers will forgive the persistently autobiographical tone of this month's Spike, is the panic tour of print shops. I once saw about fifty printers in three days with proofs of a forthcoming issue (I still recall its cover picture of a British policeman verbally offering Profumo his sister, (sorry). The original printer had been scared off by police action and was anxious to unload the metal. It is not an enviable feeling, tramping streets with the hard-fought proofs of a magazine that may never be printed. Almost at the point of abandoning the whole OZ project, we visited – with a resigned jocularity – the Anglican Press, who, to our utter amazement, accepted the job without question. This experience of seeking out printers, with the desperation of a junkie haunting pharmaceutical warehouses, has occurred ever since, with the relentless consistency of the trade cycle.

We have no idea what press – indeed, if any, this OZ is being prepared for. One printer (London Caledonian) reacted with such unsavoury hysteria to a Sunday Times news item linking our names, that, as you will see from their outburst below it was pointless proceeding with them - although a price had been agreed and a production schedule established. While generally admitting an absence of legal obstacles, printers' reasons for rejecting OZ include:

1. It will upset other clients ('we print lots of religious material').
2. It will upset the unions ('too revolutionary').
3. It will upset the tea lady ('tastelessness').
And, incredibly,4. one printer last week said, 'we'd love to do the job but we're too near Windsor'. Windsor? 'Yes, the palace you know. They might not like it'. Even the printers of Fanny Hill refused to quote for OZ.
There will be no free press in this country until OZ, Black Dwarf, IT, Hustler, and the Running (late) Man establish their own printing company.

Dear Sir, re.– Oz.
We act for London Caledonian Press Ltd. In the Sunday Times of 23rd February, 1969, there appeared on page 15 an article which stated that 'OZ' was 'fixed up now with the London Caledonian Press'. Our instructions are that there is no truth whatever in this allegation and we wrote accordingly on 27th to the Sunday Times. In reply they have written in their letter as follows:–
'We have made inquiries of the editor of the magazine and have been assured that such arrangements have been made'.
Our clients inform us that they had in fact been approached by you and had submitted a quotation but that the question of publication was subject to a number of assurances to be given by you. In this connection, a Mr. Freedman, who informs us he is a partner in the firm of Accountants which act for you, telephoned us on 19th February. We discussed with him the question of certain assurances and indemnities which our client would require, and he said he would get in touch with your solicitors. Since then we have heard nothing from them, from Mr Freedman, or from their solicitors, or from yourself.
Mr Blatt of the London Caledonian Press informs us that on Friday evening last, 28th February, you telephoned him at his home in connection with our letter to the Sunday Times. He made it quite clear to you that there was no arrangement for publication of your paper, and would not be until certain assurances had been obtained. In these circumstances, we must ask that you write to the Sunday Times immediately confirming that there has in fact never been any agreement by our clients to publish your paper. We must also ask that you let us have a copy of your letter to the Sunday Times, and we must make it clear that our clients reserve their rights against you in the matter.
We are by the same post sending a copy of this letter to the Editor of the Sunday Times.
Yours faithfully,
(Unreadable)
Seifert Sedley & Co. Solicitors, 14, Tooks Court, Cursitor St, Chancery Lane, EC4.

Needless to say, it was thought better to suffer a production set-back than to enter into any sort of professional relationship with such people.

UPS

THE UNDERGROUND PRESS SYNDICATE is an informal association of publications of the "alternative press" and exists to facilitate communication among such papers and with the public. UPS members are free to use each other's material. A list of UPS papers is available by sending a stamped self-addressed envelope to UPS, Box 26, Village P.O., New York, N.Y. 10014. A UPS Directory containing ad rates, subscription prices, wholesale prices and a great deal more is available for $2. A sample packet of a dozen UPS papers is available for $4, and a Library Subscription to all UPS papers (about 50) costs $50 for 6 months, $100 for one year. The above offers are available from UPS, Box 1603, Phoenix, Arizona 85001.

Would-be members of UPS are requested to first send $25 membership fee and then ten consecutive issues of their publication to all members of UPS, after which time their membership will be granted automatically, assuming that a majority of the members have raised no objections.

From our correspondent :
December last year, 'Time Out, our very own, hip, What's On In London, staged a successful non-event. They invented a West Coast blues bank, Heavy Jelly, reviewed their non-existant album and promoted it with a full page image advertisement. Harmless, adolescent, if perhaps weary stuff (OZ 17). The trendier half of London's underground smirked, (or yawned,) self indulgently at what soon became an open secret and Island Records moved quickly to cash in on the resulting publicity, (a mention in the Melody Maker Raver's column), releasing a single by a group of the same name.
Next issue, Time Out used another half page to explain to their doubtless

10

bewildered readers exactly what had happened. Under the heading, The Heavy Jelly Affair, they stressed that their advertisement had no connection whatever with the Island group as the name had already been promised to 'some very good musicians from several groups who want to record together but could not do so under their names because of contractual reasons'. They rounded off by saying, '. . . when these musicians produce *their* L P . . . it should be an important event in British Blues'. Well, Head Records are soon to release this 'important event' with African drums, due out in the first week of April. The title of the record is interesting though; wait for it, yes, it's Time Out (The Long Wait). *(FD)*

Incidentally, this brave new team of pop predators has taken to censoring its advertisements with such prurient enthusiasm that they are fast becoming known as the Mary Whitehouses of the Underground.

ANSMUTATION CO-OP ROJECT 1. DISTRIBUTION OF PHOTO/TYPOGRAPHIC INFORMATION. (OZ, ROLLING STONE, I GANDALFS GARDEN,etc) HELPERS/FUTURE ASSOCIATES? WITH VANS OR CARS — OR OTHER INDIVIDUAL THINGS. COMMUNICATION EXPLOSION — CONTACT AT c/o 27, Endell St (IT) phone 836.3727 or 727.1868.

Is the girl in this picture a tart? Yes! says Jimi Hendrix, who wouldn't be seen posing with her for OZ. It's the lovely Caroline Coon. When she arrived at Jimi's - especially tarted-up for a groupie parody - an acolyte muttered: 'Jimi's the only one around here who's allowed to wear frizzed hair'.

'Yes', added Mr. Hendrix, 'you don't have to prostitute yourself'.

In that case, thought Caroline, I'll leave. Which she did. Followed by a sympathetic Noel Redding and Mitch Mitchell. Recalls Caroline: 'It was an awful Experience'. Teeny rave bop OZ

11

FRELIMO

Examining the struggle in Mozambique between the Portuguese colonialists and the local inhabitants is like re-reading some mediaeval history book. All the hoary (and gory) ingredients of an old-style colonial war are there. Fine cities set along the East Coast of Africa have become fortress of privilege for the settlers from Lisbon.

Perhaps there's a touch of the Crusades in it too: the noble sons of Portugal — 70,000 men-at-arms — travel to Darkest Africa to bring Christ and Portuguese culture to the 'uncivilised'. (Especially Christ. A tourist just back from the capital Lourenco Marques said, 'The Portuguese are very religious. Whenever they kick or strike an African they cross themselves afterwards as an apology to God.' As an after thought he said, 'And you see a lot of people crossing themselves in Mozambique.')

The task of freeing Mozambique from Portuguese exploitation is in the hands of Frelimo, the Mozambique liberation movement which operates from the neighbouring state of Tanzania. Before discussing Frelimo's chances of wresting power from the Portuguese, it is appropriate to study the nature of the power of the oppressors.

Portugal itself is an economically and socially bankrupt country. It has Europe's lowest Gross National Product (GNP) and the lowest literacy rate. But it manages to maintain colonies in Africa (Mozambique, Angola and Portuguese Guinea) many, many times its size because it believes in fascism, and fascism is a safer alternative to communism — particularly if you are an American State Department official or a gnome in Zurich. And since 1926 when Dr Salazar came to power fascism has kept Portugal (not to mention Spain) an impoverished, yet stable, country.

Then, of course, Portugal belongs to NATO which means her colonial aberrations give her the tremendous military backing of the United States and Britain. Although the treaty is specifically directed towards peace-keeping north of the Tropic of Cancer, the Portuguese find no difficulty in shifting vast quantities of NATO guns, ammunition and bombs to the war zones in Mozambique.

Portugal's trump, but unplayed, card is her close association with the appalling regimes of Balthazar Vorster (South Africa) and Ian Smith (Rhodesia). As Vorster so glibly put it two years ago:

'We are good friends with both Portugal and Rhodesia. Good friends do not need a pact. Good friends know what their duty is when a neighbour's house is on fire.'

Apart from heavy economic investment in Mozambique, South Africa sends 'advisers' to the fighting areas and hands over a steady supply of arms to help fight the 'common enemy' — kaffirs.

Since UDI the rebel Smith has also become a hero figure to the Portuguese settlers, and they have responded to his cause by permitting sanctions-busting traffic to the coast with tobacco and metals. Eighty thousand Rhodesian tourists a year spend their holidays in Mozambique where their passports and currency are still valid.

No one in the liberation movement has any illusions about the might of the enemy. But there is a curious belief that the rightness of their struggle will transcend these massive obstacles to freedom and independence.

Frelimo began in 1962 as a response to a horrible massacre carried out in the northern province of Muada.

On June 26, 1960, the peasants of the region held a peaceful demonstration to protest against the extreme economic hardship posed by the settlers' labour laws. Portuguese soldiers opened fire on the unarmed crowd killing 500 Africans, more than eight times the number massacred at Sharpeville in South Africa in the same year.

At the first major conference Eduardo Chivambo Mondlane was elected president, a post he was to hold until he was assassinated in Dar es Salaam in January this year.

As a child, Mondlane was peculiarly fortunate. He was able to go to school which was rare for an African. He went to university in South Africa and eventually completed his studies in the United States where he obtained a doctorate in sociology. He then spent five years in the trusteeship department of the United Nations. In 1961, however, he left the soft options of American university life and the corridors of the UN to return to Africa and engage directly in Mozambique's liberation struggle.

It is necessary to spend so much time on Mondlane's background in an attempt to show what special qualities he brought to bear on the character of the movement. As a sociologist, Mondlane was an intense humanist. He saw the role of the party not as strictly speaking a military weapon to stab and slaughter the existing tyrannical order. He fought for a coherent revolutionary strategy of integrated activity in the military, political, economic, social and educational fields. Mondlane always insisted on the importance of education, both academic and political. Through the Mozambique Institute set up in 1963 by

his American wife, Janet, young Mozambiques are trained in educational, medical and social programmes. This year there are 200 students who have been assisted by Frelimo studying at university level overseas.

In the brief years of struggle Frelimo has been successful in securing the northern province of Cabo Delgado and Niassa. In these areas one can get a glimpse of the New Order proposed by Frelimo. One of the first reports from the Frelimo-controlled areas said: 'One of the most urgent problems Frelimo is facing is to make good the years of neglect in education. The first step has been to organise primary schools where children can be taught Portuguese, basic literacy and arithmetic, and be given an outline of the history and geography of Mozambique.'

The next stage of the liberation was to set up small clinics and first aid posts; the job of the Frelimo Public Health Department. By the end of 1967, 100,000 people had been vaccinated against smallpox while smaller numbers had been immunised against typhoid, tetanus and tuberculosis. Somehow this programme of revolution seems unreal to twentieth century revolutionaries who have lived with the purges of post-czarist Russia, the anti-revisionism of Mao and the ruthless determination of Ho. But Eduardo Mondlane, blown to pieces by a time bomb, was a different sort of revolutionary.

How successful was he? In July last year the party held its first national conference *inside* Mozambique. In jungle clearings the leaders and

13

delegates sat down to discuss the future of the struggle. At one time Portuguese aircraft spotted their meeting place and bombed it; but the talks merely shifted to another site and no one was injured. After a week of debate the Frelimo men melted back into the jungles to continue their work – but they had proved to the world that their strength was real.

The only way to break Portugal's colonial grip, however, is to smash economically or politically the regime back in Lisbon.

Mondlane's tactics of military harrassment were certainly helping this process. Under Dr Salazar defence spending reached a peak of £145 million. This year with conscription extended to all men between 18 and 45 and the serving period increased from two to three or even four years, the defence budget is likely to eat up 50 per cent of the national budget. The serious effect of this expenditure is reflected in the balance of payments. By the pruning of essential social services, this is still kept in surplus. But the £52 million credit registered at the end of 1967 was down to £25 million for the first nine months of 1968.

How long will this depressed society take these enormously heavy overseas commitments? And as the battle sharpens, what effect will the heavy death toll have on the national conscience? (The Portuguese have officially admitted to 378 dead and 3,500 wounded in fighting to mid-1967. The Johannesburg Star suggested, however, that Portugal is now losing an average of 100 men killed in action each month).

Frelimo's immediate job is to re-group around the Rev Simango, the new president and deliver more decisive military blows on the Portuguese garrison. For this she needs more military support from the Organisation of African Unity, Russia and China.

In Britain, support can only be of a specialised kind. It must be of a political nature and aimed at ending Britain's bland acceptance of Portuguese colonial rule in Africa. There is a long-held tradition in this country that Portugal is 'our oldest ally'. This must end. As Mondlane himself wrote: 'It is not that a change of attitude on the part of the West will alter the outcome of the struggle. But it could, we feel, help to determine the time it may take for us to win.'

INDEPENDENCIA OU MORTE – VENCEREMOS!

For further information on the Mozambique liberation struggle, write to:
Miss Polly Gaster
The Committee for
Freedom in Mozambique,
1 Antrim Road, London, NW3.

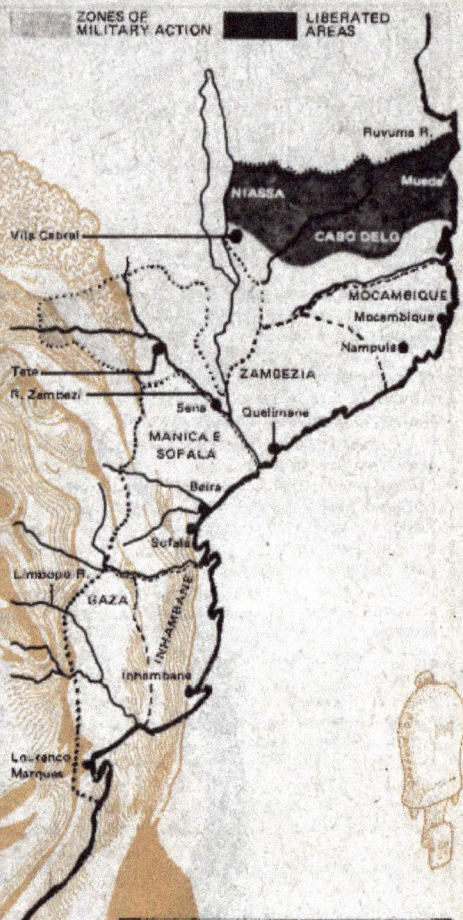

ZONES OF MILITARY ACTION

LIBERATED AREAS

Ruvuma R.

NIASSA

Muede

Vila Cabral

CABO DELGO

MOCAMBIQUE

Mocambique

Nampula

Tete

R. Zambezi

ZAMBEZIA

Sena

Quelimane

MANICA E SOFALA

Beira

Sofala

Limpopo R.

GAZA

INHAMBANE

Inhambane

Lourenco Marques

FOOD EXPLOS· ION

There is too much food in the world. Far too much. And the surplus is growing at a terrifying, uncontrollable rate.

Governments try to tackle this crisis by all sorts of restrictions on agricultural output — the most famous of which is the American practice of paying farmers to leave their land uncultivated:

Areas to be cultivated for particular purposes are fixed farm by farm, and are subject to inspection by officials who have grown increasingly anxious, as surpluses have mounted, to check on anyone who is inclined to cheat. On occasion the inspection has taken on features of a military exercise, with the government men engaging in surprise aerial reconnaissance over suspicious fields of corn. Even so, the great flood of produce coming off American farms has not been checked.

In other words, even though the farmers are restricted in the acreage they can cultivate, the problem of excess food still gets worse, because they manage to produce more and more from a smaller and smaller amount of land.

When other means fail, the last resort is destruction. Fields of sugar cane are burnt, baby pigs slaughtered by the million, milk poured down mine shafts, wheat tipped into the sea. Crops are ploughed back into the ground, and fruit left to rot on the trees.

Remember that publicity campaign to keep the Biafran children alive until Christmas was over? Well, just up the road from Biafra, in the Ivory Coast, they were systematically destroying 100,000 tons of coffee. And in Europe, two immense (but by now familiar) crises were coming to a head: the French fruit glut (an annual affair), and the Common Market butter problem.

In France over half a million tons of fruit and vegetables had to be destroyed. Fruit was tipped on to the roads by the lorryload, and tourists having to drive through this sticky mush were handed free gifts of peaches, together with protest leaflets. Grapes were dumped into rivers, abandoned at the roadside, and occasionally thrown by frustrated farmers at government buildings.

As for the Common Market's dairy problems, the Financial Times commented: 'the butter surplus seems to be a problem almost beyond the wit of man to solve'. What could the EEC farm bosses do about their 350,000 tons excess butter? They thought of feeding it back to the cows, but that would cause the cows to supply more milk, resulting in a worse situation. Even as things stand, next year's dairy surplus is expected to be more disastrous than ever (ie: bigger). They thought of getting rid of the stuff at half-price, but people in Europe are already eating enough butter, and couldn't consume much more, even if it was that cheap.

They thought of turning the butter into something that couldn't spread, then presenting it as some new product and trying to sell it that way. They still haven't sorted the problem out, and sooner or later they will almost certainly be forced to slaughter a lot of dairy cows — probably four million out of the Common Market's 22 million.

Of course, we all know that there are quite a few hungry people in the world, and for this reason talk of 'too much' food being a 'problem' seems ludicrous and bizarre. Those who admire Black Comedy can be recommended to read almost any material on agricultural economics. It is usually wildly hilarious, to a degree only possible with an undertone of stark horror. Picking on a couple of standard economics textbooks at random, I find the following gems:

'Unfortunately, with the help of fertilizers, modern chemicals and irrigation, some farmers managed to maintain their normal output on reduced acreage and receive the federal payment too.'

It's the 'Unfortunately' that kills you.

(The restrictive Agriculture Acts of the early thirties were) 'merely interim measures until the bounty of nature again became an embarrassment.'

A beautifully coy way of putting it.

Quotes such as these are beyond the imaginative powers of a Kafka. Capitalism's insanity is so systematic, and such an everyday thing, that it is impossible to satirize. It is its own caricature. My favourite quote of the lot is from a 1958 Press Release of the Food and Agriculture Organization. Here, the problem of too much food is described as though it were a dangerous epidemic, a Black Death sweeping over the world:

'The 30th session of the Committee on Commodity Problems ended yesterday after almost two weeks of discussions on what it termed a grave situation for international commerce in agricultural products.

The discussions of the 24-member committee have stressed the concern of delegates at the deterioration of the world agricultural economy. Accumulation of surpluses, contraction of international markets, the fall of world prices for most products and the slowing down of general economic activity were the chief factors involved. It was also noted that the chronic presence of surpluses had spread to new products and additional countries. The outlook was rather dark, and the attention of governments was drawn to the urgent need for measures to alleviate the situation. . . .At the same time it was recognized that from now on the problem of surpluses should be considered as a permanent characteristic of the world agricultural economy.

If there is too much food, if there is a volcano of

plenty threatening to engulf humanity, it would seem to follow that the thing to save the situation would be a colossal natural (or unnatural) catastrophe. And this is in fact the case. The present system of society, choking in its own abundance, would be perked up no end by a world-wide series of super-earthquakes, or some disastrous fallout of nuclear pollution. Anything that destroyed men, machines and materials in a really big way would provide a welcome shot in the arm. You cannot sell something unless it's scarce.

As a matter of fact, that isn't as fanciful as it sounds. The big American drought of 1934 was a tremendous boon, reducing the wheat crop more effectively than any government action, and letting Agriculture Secretary Henry Wallace off the hook. It was reported that he:

'breathed a sigh of relief; it would not be necessary to write about the logic of ploughing up wheat while millions lacked bread'

That, of course, took place during a depression. 'Overproduction' has always been a feature of slumps. What is new about the modern overproduction of food is that it is permanent, chronic, continuing through boom and slump alike. In 1947 Marx and Engels described the crises of plenty as follows:

'In these crises there breaks out an epidemic that in all earlier epochs would have seemed an absurdity — the epidemic of overproduction. Society suddenly finds itself put back into a state of momentary barbarism; it appears as if famine, a universal war of devastation had cut off the supply of every means of subsistence: industry and commerce seem to be destroyed, and why? Because there is too much civilization, too much means of subsistence, too much industry, too much commerce. . . And how does the bourgeoisie get over these crises? On the one hand by enforced destruction of a mass of productive forces; on the other, by the conquest of new markets, and by the more thorough exploitation of the old ones. That is to say, by paving the way for more extensive and more destructive crises, and by diminishing the means whereby crises are prevented.'

The reason for today's permanent surplus of food in all the advanced countries is rather different. If governments stopped interfering in agriculture, food prices would dive and farmers would be going broke all over the place. Farming would become a permanently depressed sector (as it was in America during the twenties boom). Men, machines and land would move out of agriculture into other uses. This would keep on until food prices rose again to a profitable level. Governments are not prepared to let this happen, for various reasons, so they 'support' the farmers and prevent food prices from falling.

This sort of policy can have laughable consequences on a world sale. Thus, European governments subsidize the growing of sugar beet. At the moment the Common Market has a big headache with its million ton sugar surplus, whilst in Cuba they've just introduced sugar rationing.

I suppose there will be someone innocent enough to ask: 'How can there possibly be too much food in the world, when so many people are starving?' Such a person has not yet realized that in a buying and selling world, a world which produces for the sake of cash, human needs can go and get stuffed. Money talks; hunger is dumb. People are starving all right, not because there isn't any food for them, but because they've got no money to buy it. In other words: 'too much' means 'too much for a profitable market' not too much for human needs.

Actually, starvation isn't as widespread as a lot of people think. Those who put it about that there is some sort of 'overpopulation problem' still bring up the old myth that 'two-thirds of the world are underfed.' It would be truer to say that two-thirds of the world suffer from malnutrition — one-third from under-eating, one-third from over-eating.

The idiocy of the money system is illustrated by what happened when America decided to give some of its surplus wheat away to India. This is just the sort of thing some woolly-minded Humanists advocate. The effect was, of course, to hinder the development of Indian agriculture, and also to keep out exports of rice from Burma and wheat from Argentine, aggravating hardship in both these countries. Ironically, both Burma and Argentine get American aid. When surplus American corn was handed out in Israel, this cut the price of Israeli eggs (Hens eat corn). Israeli eggs were exported at prices so low that the European egg market was upset. Giving things away, within a buying and selling system, doesn't work.

In a Moneyless World there would be no difficulty about improving farming in backward areas, and transporting food out to them at the same time, but under Capitalism these two obviously sensible actions are in direct conflict with each other.

Similarly, I suppose most people are now aware that there's a certain amount of starvation in the USA, the richest nation in the world's history. The Observer mentioned this last August, and incidentally gave us another gem for our collection of Real Life Sick Gags: a Senator James Eastland opposes welfare hand-outs which he calls 'giving something for nothing', whilst he gets £1,000 a week from the government for not growing cotton on his plantation.

Why can't the US government simply open its granaries to the poor of America? Because even the poor, if they eat at all, pay for what they eat, and if they get their food free, they will no longer spend money on food, so the price of food will tumble down and the farmers will be hit. You can't operate bits of sanity inside an insane system.

DAVID RAMSAY STEELE.

Sources: Andrew Shonfield, *Modern Capitalism, The Times*, 30.11.68; *The Scotsman*, 16.8.68; *Financial Times*, 30.10.68; *Guardian*, 19.10.68; P d' A Jones, *The Consumer Society*; A J Brown, *The American Economy*; FAO Press Release, quoted in: *Proceedings of the International Conference of Agricultural Economists, 1958*; G N Peek, *Why Quit Our Own*, quoted in: Brown, *The American Economy*; K Marx and F Engels, *The Communist Manifesto*; C Clark, *Population Growth And Land Use*; R Bailey, *Problems of the World Economy*; *Observer*, 18.8.68.

Late one afternoon, Harvard's Professor of Social Relations sat cross-legged in his sitting room floor, saying goodbye to a stream of LSE students who were using the off-Kings Road house as a temporary home for their tutorials. Professor Norman Zinberg 'possibly the World's greatest expert on the smoking of cannabis', (Sunday Times) had decided not to drink the Martini that is a customary tonic prior to his frequent journeys – the next morning he and his wife were off on African safari – until after he had finished talking! The American magazine Science has published the results of the first truly scientific test ever made on the subject of pot, and after meeting Professor Zinberg, who is in England as Visiting Professor of Social Psychology at the London School of Economies, it was not difficult to see that he will play a significant role in bringing the issue into the open – then the myths about pot will not persist and Government Officials will *have* to revise their attitudes to the so called 'problem' of 'drug' use.

Z. Let me tell you something which I think will interest you about experimental work in this area. Not only is there an overwhelming problem based on the legal position making it very hard to start any kind of research, but people suspect you because you're doing research in this field. The other night* the first question I was asked was 'Do you use pot?'

I felt that this was the most definitive question of the evening it was really a question of establishing your credentials. If you are a drug user then anything you say cannot mean anything, and if you're not – are you afraid of it, of what? It's one of those questions where you start pissing on the toilet seat. You know, you're damned if you do it, and damned if you don't. I find, in this field it is difficult to establish yourself as a reasonably objective person. Arguments are thrown at you at every possible chance and in every possible way.

We found, in working with naive subjects, (those who had never seen or smoked pot) and chronic users (those who had smoked pot daily for at least two years) that, instead of working like alcohol, where people have to learn to hold their liquor, with marijuana, as you become accustomed to its effects, it takes less, down to a specific base line, to enable you to get high. This is what is known as 'reverse tolerance'.

We felt, on the basis of the information from users and from our experimental data, that it wasn't question of chemical accumulation with chronic users. It was too consistent. They took just about the same amount, depending on body weight and what-have-you, to get them high. It didn't seem to matter how many years they had smoked.

C. Hardin B Jones, Professor of Medical Physics & Physiology at the University of California, argues that there is strong evidence for physiological, mental and social deterioration associated with prolonged use of Pot, and that accumulation of small doses injures the body and mind.

Z. I think it would be very difficult to postulate an accumulation hypothesis given the kind of data we recovered after our experiments. To have such a hypothesis you would have to postulate a very complex chemical retention system – only retaining so much and no more – roughly on the basis of enzymatic action or endocrine action, or what-have-you that it was bound to a certain tension level. A very difficult hypothesis!

C. What action do you think cannabis has on the central nervous system?

Z. I don't really have a clue.

But I do think we know a lot about cannabis and I do hate it when people say, "Well I can't have an opinion because we are so ignorant.

We know a lot of things, and a lot of people have used cannabis for quite some time, and if we don't know enough it's because we haven't allowed ourselves to look. On the other hand when it comes to the actual action – what makes up intoxication – what brain centres are involved – I think we truly don't know. For that matter, we don't know that much about alcohol.

We felt, from our experiments, that it was probably the higher brain centres that were affected – the centres that control abstract and reasoning capacities rather than the brain centres which tend to be more automatised and control lawfulness, regularity and what-have-you. That might explain why a chronic user could do a test like the Digit Symbol Substitution Test (that is replacing numbers with symbols) rather well, and perhaps would do badly in the Speech Sample, when he turns back on his own imagination and abstract thinking – but that's all hypothesis.

C. From your experiences could you say whether alcohol was physiologically more harmful than cannabis?

Z. Well, physiologically I would think that cannabis is the less harmful. The thing is that it's hard to compare dosages. We take in a great deal of alcohol – we ingest it for one thing – and with ingestion we have much less ability to judge how much has been taken in. By the time you have absorbed it and it has gone to the blood

---

*at the meeting of the Society for the Study of Addiction
where Professor Zinberg read the second part of his paper,
Clinical and Psychological Effect of Marijuana in Man.

stream then to higher centres of the brain, you have taken in a great deal more than you think – I don't know if it has happened to you, but it has happened to me once or twice!

When you have smoked cannabis you really know rather quickly how much has been absorbed and what the response is, probably in a very few minutes, so you are unlikely to take a consistent over-dose. The only way you would be able to make a valid comparison between cannabis and alcohol, is if you really gave people consistent over-doses of ingested cannabis over long periods of time, to see whether or not, at that level, it would have a great deal of effect relative to all the various physiological effects. I think the comparison of alcohol with cannabis doesn't really get anybody anywhere. If I were to say that cannabis is less harmful than alcohol, people would say, 'But under what conditions'. The conditions under which people smoke cannabis in this country – the average user – I would say, takes cannabis only once or twice a week, and considers himself a regular user – what is smoked amounts to only a very small dose. If you consider that regular use, occasional low dosage, you are talking about quite a different phenomenon from even the man who has three drinks before dinner every night – and doesn't in any way consider himself as an alcoholic!

C. In that case, why is there such hysterical reaction to pot from the general public?

Z. Well, I guess that the only offering hypothesis prevalent at the moment is that it threatens peoples concepts of social order, individual psychic order, and that it offers some concept of hedonism, and so on. I don't think this is true, but I think in a way pot users have sold this idea to the other people, and I think they have also promised more than is true to themselves and to others. This whole idea of mutual disappointment has a lot to do with the kind of pressures that are involved. I don't really understand it yet, and it's what I want to find out.

If you try to talk to people who are intelligent and reasonable or in legislative positions, they say that cannabis is bad because it releases aggression. You say, well no, it is really more of a tranquilliser. Then they say, it leads to other drugs. Then you point out – I point out – that from the findings of my experiments it results in 'reversed tolerance', and for cannabis to lead to other drugs would mean increased tolerance

rather than decreased tolerance. Therefore, it is unlikely, in the classical sense of a drug progression, – growing tolerance, dissatisfaction & greater craving – that it does lead to other drugs. On the other hand, in the sense of so called 'horizontal' drug use, that is, where you are thrown in with other people and obtain your cannabis in a certain way so as to be in contact with other drugs, and if you are a curious person, you might want to try other things. Then, they say, 'what is going to happen to society if everybody uses drugs and drops out?' Then you have to differentiate! Are they dropping out because they use drugs, or does the use of drugs in society result in people dropping out? A hard question to answer. It's a result of the present social situation, not a cause of it. I don't think at this point we can answer in a Yes or No way.

Certainly the other half say that people drop out and use drugs because they feel depressed and are concerned about the social situation. The fact is that, increasingly, I've seen so many *middle-class*   people who do use drugs, and don't drop out. They don't get picked up by the Law. Their drug use is discreet and careful. They think that their chances of being in trouble with the law, except by the greatest kind of fluke, are as close to zero as possible. Therefore, when you do find a group who use their drug use as a reason to drop out, you have to look further and deeper which is not all that simple.

Each year I think this is more true, and for some reason it seems that these people that drop out, *do* find something for themselves in the definition of being deviants which has been put upon them, and once it's put upon them, somehow or another it fits.

C. It seems, from what you have been saying that the 'Pot culture' could be described as an expressive social movement.

Z. Again, that involves a differentiation between the actual effects of the drug, the personality of the user before he becomes a user, and then the impact of the person being defined by his larger society as a social deviant, of how this eventually affects his definition of himself. There is, I think, a lot of evidence that the third hypothesis, if not explanatory of the whole situation, is certainly a very important point. It is a problem of a self-fulfilling prophecy and I think I may make myself very unpopular by saying that the thing that most strikes me about it all is how opinionated people are on both sides, and how difficult it is to have a relatively objective view. But certainly the authorities who are still uptight make it impossible for anything to happen and I'll tell you a funny story.

The other night I was invited to a dinner party to meet a very prominent English Minister. There were six men in the room as I walked in, all of us having separated ourselves from the ladies for coffee & brandy after dinner! I walked in and he was introduced to me. In a friendly and generous manner I was introduced as being here to do a study on drug use. The famous man then turned to me and asked me, in a very pleasant way, whether I thought there was any important difference in drug use in Great Britain and the United States. And I said inoccuously: well, to tell the truth I think there is astonishingly little difference – I have

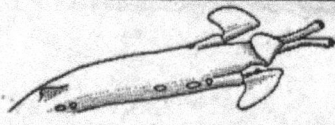

been surprised at how little difference I have found. At which, he turned on me, and screamed, ridiculous! — the only reason why we have drug use in Great Britain is because the Americans and the Chinese and these chocolate coloured babies show up and bring in the drugs. You find me a real Englishman from my constituency (which shall remain nameless) and not one person uses drugs — I assure you, not one person! All these awful things are only done in ports, where all these people come to from outside. And so on and so forth. He went completely wild and really felt that my comment had been an accusation of him and all Englishmen, and that any right-thinking, moral, decent person wouldn't possibly do it. A very famous man, a very influential man.

I think it gives you some idea of the extent of the prejudice in that direction. Now to go to the other side of it.

Recently I was talking to somebody who you would, I guess, have to describe as a head, and I said; 'I do think that some of the people we work with like the chronic users have gotten too far out. I can't tell whether they were far out when they started using it, but they had been using some form of cannabis almost daily for three to four years, and I have had trouble talking to them. You know, we didn't really quite connect, in the sense that sometimes people connect. They were intellectually sound, they were working and doing okay, but I'm sure they felt the reason we didn't connect was my fault. The kinds of images they used — and it wasn't just pot like images — but the philosophical images around Zen and abstractions — I found circumstantial and I found it difficult to establish communication'. This Head got mad at me too, when I said that.

He said that I was really sticking to Western thought and western civilisation, and that my interest in talking to him was scientific. Science was the cause of all the trouble and it indicated that there was an invariant reality and the truth was that there wasn't an invariant reality — and he went on like this. And so I couldn't really talk to this man any better than I could talk to the Minister on his moral grounds.

I still don't understand why everybody is so up tight about the issue, and really what I'm trying to do is study this and try to understand why it has become such an emotional issue. If in fact the drug, as you suggest, and lots of people suggest, is a relatively mild drug — let's say that it is — than the fact that on both sides people are so uptight about it, becomes even more remarkable.

A Notice to all !

Ours is the only His Majesty's Government liscence holder firm to have business of Hashish and Cannabis—Induces (PAHADI CHARES and GANJA). No other firms and black—marketeers are allowed to have business of these goods. His Majesty's Government will take action against those who go against this notice.

For purest, cheapest and not to be cheated please do not forget to keep contact with us in the following address.

Krishna Lama,
Sole Stockst, Whole—Sale and Retail
Centre of Hashish And Cannabis-Induces
9/465, Khilba Tole, Bhedasing
Kathmandu, Nepal.

21

Part Two: Blueprints & The Plan.

Blueprints

What could this post-industrial society look like? I want to emphasize that it is on this project that so many more people could become totally involved in the revolutionary process. If it would be by & large intellectuals, academics and students who would work on the analysis & critique of the growing corporation feudalism, it would be people from all walks of life who would be essential to this second necessity. You need men & women with years of experience in farming, small business, teaching, city planning, recreation, medicine, and on & on, to start discussing & writing about ways to organize that part of society they know best for a post-industrial America. You need to provide outlets via forums, discussions, papers and magazines for the pent-up plans & ideals of literally millions of well-trained, experienced, frustrated Americans who see stupidity & greed all around them but can't do a thing about it. You need to say, for example, "Look Mr & Mrs City Planning Expert trapped in this deadly bureaucracy controlled by big businessmen, draw up a sensible plan for street development, or park development, in your town of 30,000 people". "Look, Mr Blue Collar Worker, working for the big corporation, how should this particular plant be run in a sensible society?"

And, you need not only to discuss & to develop these programs, you need to make them clear to every American, not only to the ones you might win to your side because the present system disgusts them morally, or exploits them, or ignores them, or rejects them. No, even more, you need to reach the many millions more who, once they did not fear you or distrust you, would be willing to live under either the new or old system. And make no mistake about their importance. When people talk about the small percentage of Bolsheviks who took over Russia, they often forget the overwhelming numbers who passively accepted them, in that case out of disgust with war, despair, and the lack of a plan of their own that they really believed in.

Let me repeat to make its importance clearer: the neutralization of large masses should be a prime goal for a program to develop & present blueprints for a post-industrial America. To this end it should be personally handed by some one revolutionary to every person in America. Each person should receive a short, simple, one-page handbill especially relevant to his situation or occupation. It would begin, for example, "Policeman, standing here protecting us from Evil at this demonstration, where will you be after the revolution?" And then, in a few short sentences you will tell this bewildered soul, whom you embraced after handing him his message, that there will still be a great need for policemen after the revolution, but that policemen will tend to do more of the things that they like to do - helping, assisting, guiding - rather than the things that get them a bad name, to wit, faithfully carrying out the repressive dictates of their power elite masters. You will tell him that you know that some policemen are prejudiced or authoritarian, but you know that's neither here nor there, because orders on whether to shoot ("to do whatever is necessary to keep 'law & order' in this ghetto") or not to shoot come from officials higher up who are intimately intertwined in the corporate system.

Similar handbills should be prepared for every person. Some would hear good things, like more money & better health. Some would hear things that would surprise them or make them wonder, like:

'You won't be socialized, Mr Small Businessman producing a novelty or retailing pets on a local level, because the socialized corporations can produce more than enough; and furthermore, keep in mind that government in a post-industrial America couldn't possibly harass you as much as the big bankers who won't lend you money, the big corporations who undercut you, and the corporate-oriented politicians who overtax you'.

Others, for whom there is no good news would get such cheery messages as Mr. Insurance Man we hope you have other skills, like gardening or typing;' 'Corporate Manager — we hope you like working for the anonymous public good as much as you liked working for anonymous millionaire coupon clippers;' 'CIA Man — we hope you are as good at hiding as you are supposed to be at sneaking'.

Perhaps most of all, there has to be a consideration of the role of Mr John Bircher, Mr Physician, Mr Dentist and others now on the New Right. They who are put off or ignored by the increasing corporatization have to be shown that their major values – individuality, freedom local determination – are also the values of a post-industrial America. This does not mean they will suddenly become revolutionaries, but it is important to start them wondering as to whether or not they would find things as bad in the new social system as they do in this system which increasingly annoys them, exasperates them, and ignores them. They must we weaned from the handful of large corporations & multi-millionaires who use them for their own end by talking competition while practicing monopoly, by screaming about taxes while paying very little, and by talking individualism while practicing collectivism.

What would a post-industrial America look like? First of all, it would be certain American institutions writ large – like the Berkeley food Co-op that is locally controlled by consumers, like the Pasadena water & electric systems that are publically owned like the Tennessee Valley Authority which has allowed the beginnings of the sane, productive and beautiful development of at least one river region in our country. In short, the system would start from local controls and work up, as it used to before all power & taxes were swept to the national level, mostly by war and the big corporations. And, as you can see, it would be a mixed system, sometimes with control by consumers, sometimes with control by local government, sometimes with control by regional authorities, and sometimes – as should be made clear in the handbill to certain small businessmen – with control in private hands. For many retail franchises, for many novelty productions, and, I suspect, for many types of farms & farmers, depending on region, crop involved and other considerations, private enterprise may be the best method of control.

The question will be raised – is this promise of some private ownership pandering to a voting bloc? Is it like the old Communist trick of the United Front? The answer is a resounding NO. Any post-industrial society that does not maximize chances for freedom, flexibility and individuality is not worth fighting for. Given the enormous capabilities of corporate production, the economic & cultural insignificance of most small businessmen, and the very small number of family farmers, there is simply no economic or political or cultural reason to socialize everything. There is no "kulak" class, there is no "petty bourgeois". Pre-industrial societies may have had to socialize everything to defend their revolutions against hostile forces, but that is only another way in which your situation differs from theirs.

I have left the most obvious for last. Of course the corporations would be socialized. Their profits would go to all people in lower prices (and thus higher real wages) and/or repair to local, state and national treasuries in the amounts necessary to have a park on every corner (replacing one of the four gas stations), and medical, dental, educational or arts facilities on the other corners (replacing the other three gas stations – there being no need for any but a few gas stations due to the ease of introducing electric cars when a few hundred thousand rich people are not in a position to interfere). But how to man this huge corporation enterprise? First, with blue collar workers, who would be with you all the way in any showdown no matter how nice some members of the corporate rich have been to them lately. Second, with men from lower-level management positions who have long ago given up the rat race, wised up, and tacitly awaited your revolution.

The Plan: Psychic Guerilla Warfare

I come then, finally to the third necessity, a program for taking the reins of government away from the power elite in order to carry out the plan developed by revolutionary visionaries. It is on this point that there is likely to be found the most disagreement, the most confusion, the most uncertainty and the most fear. But I think you do have something very important to go on — the ideas & experiences & successes of the Civil Rights & New Left & Hippie movements of the past several years. If they have not given you an analysis of corporation capitalism or a set of blueprints, which is their weakness, they have given you the incredibly precious gifts of new forms of struggle and new methods of reaching people, and these gifts must be generalized, articulated and more fully developed.

I have a general term, borrowed from a radical hippy, that I like to use because I think it so beautifully encompasses what these movements have given to you: "Psychic Guerrilla Warfare" — the "psychic" part appealing to my psychologist instincts and summarizing all hard-hitting non-violent methods, the "guerilla warfare" part hopefully giving to those who want to take to the hills enough measure of satisfaction to allow them to stick around & participate in the only type of guerrilla warfare likely to work in corporate America. For make no mistake about it, psychic guerrilla warfare is a powerful weapon in a well-educated, sedate, highly industrialized country that has a tradition of liberal values & democratic political processes. And it is the kind of guerrilla warfare that America's great new acting-out girls can indulge in on an equal basis with any male anywhere. It is the confrontation politics of the New Left-teach-ins, marches walk-ins, sit-ins, push-ins, love-ins, folk rocks and be-ins. It is the non-violent, religiously-based, democratically-inspired confrontation morality of Martin Luther King, and it is the unfailing good humor, psychological analysis and flower power of the Hippy. Together they are dynamite — what politician or labor leader can fault confrontation, what true Christian or Jew can react violently to non-violence, and what disgruntled middle-classer can fail to smile or admit begrudging admiration for the best in American hippiedom?

How do you direct this dynamite to its task of destroying the ideological cover of the corporate rich? First, you start a new political party, a wide-open, locally-based political party dedicated to the development of blueprints for a post-industrial America guerrilla warfare. It should be a party open to anyone prepared to abandon all other political affiliations & beliefs — in other words, it would not be an Anti-This-Or-That coalition of liberal Democrats, Communists, Trotskyists and Maoists. In fact, ignore those groups. The best members will drop out & join yours. For the rest, they have non constituencies and would soon fall to fighting the Old Fights among themselves anyway — Communist & Anti-Communist, Pro-Soviet & Anti-Soviet, and On & On ad tedium. No, you don't need that — it would destroy you like it destroyed them. In fact, they need you, for if you got something going the party would be big enough for all of them to work in without seeing each other or having to defend the old Faiths.

Fantasy? Perhaps, but don't under-estimate the cynicism at minor levels of the techno-structure. I have spoken with & to these groups, and there is hope. They are not all taken in, any more than most Americans are fooled by the mass media about domestic matters. They are just trapped, with no place to go but out if they think too much or make a wave. Now, "out" is easy enough if you're young & single, but it's a little sticky if you didn't wake up to the whole corporate absurdity until you were long out of college and had a wife & two kids. Cultivate these well-educated men & women whose talents are wasted & ill-used. Remind them that the most revolutionary thing they can do — aside from feeding you information & money so you can further expose the system, and aside from helping to plan the post-industrial society — is to be in a key position in the technostructure when the revolution comes. You may not win many of them percentagewise, but then it wouldn't take many to help you through a transition.

Then too, part of the corporate system would disappear — one computerized system of banking & insurance would eliminate the incredible duplication, paperwork and nonsense now existent in those two "highly profitable" but worthless areas of the corporate economy. Corporate retails would be broken up & given to local consumer co-ops, or integrated into nationalized producer/retailer units in some cases. Corporate transports (air, rails, buses) would be given in different cases to state, local and national government, as well as to, on occasion, the retailers or producers they primarily serve. The public utilities, as earlier hinted, would finally be given to the public, mostly on the local & regional level, probably on the national level in the case of telephones. The only real problem, I think, is manufacturing, where you have to hold the loyalty of technicians & workers to survive a transition. Blue collar control — syndicalism could be the answer in some cases, regional or national government control in others. Here, obviously, is one of those questions that needs much study, with blue collar & white collar workers in the various industries being the key informants & idea men.

In addition to declining offers of coalition, and instead seeking converts, such a party should reject as inappropriate the Leninist "democratic centralism" for an American revolutionary party. Not that all the Old Lefties would give it up — some would probably join your party and try to "caucus" or "bore from within", but the open give & take of ideas and the local autonomy of chapters could handle the little organizational games they have become so good at while organizing & reorganizing each other over the past 30 or 40 years.

So what does this party do besides present a constant withering critique of corporation capitalism and build blueprints for a post-industrial America? It practices all forms of psychic guerrilla warfare whenever & wherever there is a possible convert. Eventually, and on the right occasions, it even enters elections, not to win votes at first, but to win converts. In making its pitch, it doesn't ask men & women to quit their jobs or take to the hills, but rather it asks them to commit their allegiances to new socioeconomic arrangements, to help develop new social & intellectual institutions, to financially support the growth of the party, to read party-orientated newspapers, to convert & neutralize friends & neighbours, and to stand firm if the corporate rich try something funny.

After building chapters in every town or city district in the country by word of mouth and small group contact, you would gradually begin to participate in local elections to gain further attention. Then you would enter legislative elections, both to gain converts and to win seats, for the more legislative seats you hold, state & national, the better for the sudden takeover that will come later. You avoid like the plague winning any executive offices, for to be a major or governor when you don't control the whole system as meaningless and a waste of energy. You couldn't do anything liberals won't eventually do until you control the presidency. In other words, I'm not suggesting a gradual takeover, which would wear you down, compromise your program and *(Jesus, what CRAP! Ed.)* perhaps allow you to develop an ameliorist mentality as you got used to a little bit of influence & status. Indeed, the British Labour Party should be as sad a lesson to you as any other recent experience, and you should not repeat their failure to force a total & complete change the minute you take power. If they couldn't do it, well, you can, because once you take over the Presidency in a one-election shot, there is enough power concentrated there to accomplish drastic changes overnight. In short, the corporate rich are absolutely dependent upon the executive branch to keep their economic system from depression and collapse.

I don't mean to imply that you would only control the Presidency, that you would only move on the national level. Actually, you should move on the whole system at once, for each local chapter would have developed parallel governments that would also enter elections for the first time when you decided you had the popular support to win the Presidency. All members of a given chapter would train themselves to fill some government job at local levels — they would be like the shadow cabinets of British politics only more so. The transition would be sudden — one election — and it would be total in the sense of taking money power and status from the corporate rich.

*G William Domhoff
From the Entwistle Project* (If the Revolution means prose like this, let's LOSE!)

23

VERB editions

poems PETER MAYER   typography ALAN RICKMAN

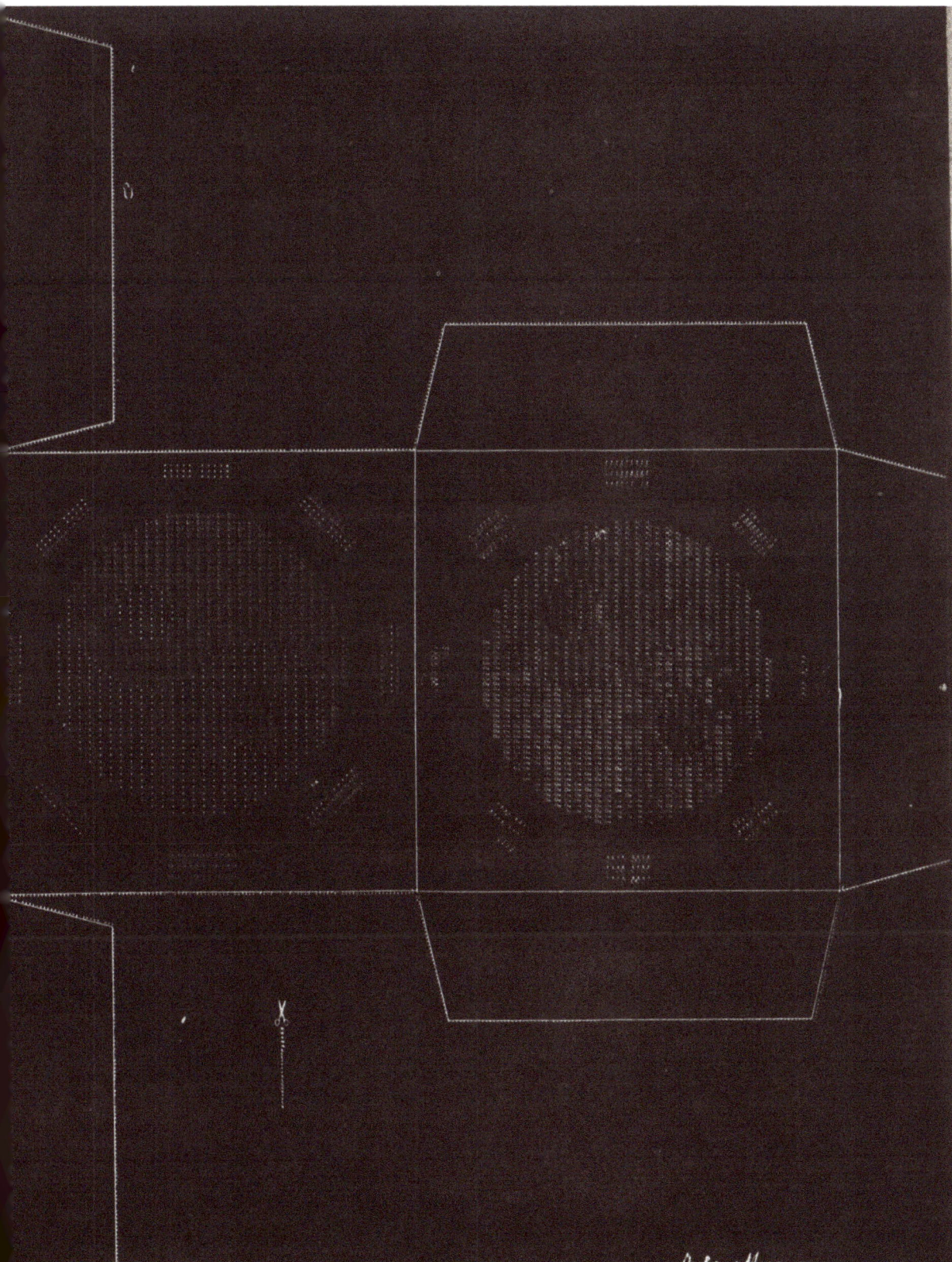

Peter Mayer

Why the Press Council's a Fake

A startling expose of the methods of the Press Council is contained in a recent Solidarity pamphlet 'Damned' by Andy Anderson. Anderson is secretary of the Friends of King Hill, a direct action group that scored a notable victory over Kent County Council's treatment of homeless families in 1966. The group exposed official callousness, victimisation and inhumanity in hostels that one MP compared to concentration camps.

At the height of the campaign, The People newspaper ran an article headed *Don't Waste Your Pity On This Phoney Martyr.* The puff for it said:

[Everyone was sorry for poor Mrs Mills, the man in the hostel row. But read the full facts . . . Today for the first time. The People reveals the full story about Mr Mills. It exposes him as nothing more than a phoney martyr. (2/1/66)

With the tone safely set in the best traditions of the Sunday press the article proceeded to attack Mills – who had squatted in one of the hostels with the support of the Friends of King Hill.

The article described Mills as a 'sponger'; asserted that in eight years 'Mr Mills and his family have received more help than any other family in the country'; described Mills' propensity to 'fix the electricity meter wherever possible'; and gave a general impression of filth and degeneracy, concluding that 'Mr Mills is the despair of all the people that have tried to help him. And yet he dares to play the martyr.' The article also attempted to show the patience and forbearance of the Kent County Council in putting up with him for so long. It ended with a plea that the KCC 'should do one more act of kindness – they should put the Mills children into a home. Then they should kick Mrs Mills out of the Hostel.'

The article, apart from setting back the Campaign some weeks, had a profound effect on Mrs Mills. She had just come out of Chatham Hospital. When she read the article, she collapsed. Locking herself in the dingy Hostel, threatened with the loss of her children, she refused to go out. Her children were jeered at in the streets, and some weeks later she was admitted to a London hospital, on the verge of a nervous breakdown.

Such is the power of the People – THE PAPER THAT FINDS OUT!

Mr Mills, with the help of the Friends, began an ill-fated libel action against The People. Money was donated and borrowed, but after about £150 had been spent, it became apparent that excessive amounts would be involved, and the action was dropped. The People's editor refused to discuss the matter, so an agit-prop pamphlet campaign was started, refuting the most flagrant of the articles' allegations. Odham's Press was picketed daily, and two of the Friends were arrested for obstruction.

With few illusions about the outcome, the Friends decided to see what the Press Council would do with the situation with 39 complaints against the People article. This correspondence piled up over eighteen months and 17,000 words before a decision was reached.

The Friend's general complaints about The People article were:
1. the bulk of the article contained lies, half truths and insinuations.
2. it was unwarranted, misleading and disgraceful comment.
3. it was highly defamatory and malicious.

In the Friend's document – five statements were signed supporting allegations about lies in the People's article. Three people categorically denying statements attributed to them in the article. Each was witnessed by two out of four people – including a doctor, a teacher, a computer programmer and a civil servant. In addition, one section (39) contained attested statments on the methods used by Patricia Elston in compiling

The People article. This was an additional cause for complaint.

Noel S Paul replied for the Council on 13 Feb, insisting that all complaints should also be represented to The People editor Robert Edwards. This had already been done, but further copies of all documents were sent to Edwards on 14 Feb 67.

Edwards replied on 14 March 67 saying that he was 'fully satisfied' that the article on Roy Mills 'was accurate in every particular, was fully justified . . . . was fair comment on a matter of public interest . . . and The People was thoroughly entitled to take the view it did.'

A copy of this letter was sent to Noel S Paul a press council secretary, who replied by asking that the complaints sign a 'legal document' releasing the People from any legal complaints arising from the matter, and insisting that the campaign against the paper be halted.

The Friends signed this document on 8 May 67, reasoning that if they didn't, the complaints would never be represented to the Council, and that in any case the document was not morally binding.

Three days later they received an astonishing 1700 word letter from Paul. He had arbitrarily split the complaints into three categories:—
A Substantial complaints which might or might not be subject to adjudication. (8 complaints).
B. Complaints 'consequential in character' to the first eight, which were not 'challenges of statements of fact' but complaints about 'unjustified comment'. If the council 'sees fit to adjudicate' on the first eight it would 'naturally' deal with some or all of the eight complaints in this category.
C. 'Complaints about which I (Paul) am unable to find anything substantial' and which would not be presented to the council. Twenty–three complaints were relegated to this category.

It was an appalling situation. Not only had the Press Council, through Paul, claimed to be the final arbiters of the matter–(by insisting that the Friends signed the 'legal document') – but it was painfully apparent that the complaints would go under the virtual censorship of Noel S Paul, and against whose decisions there could be no appeal.

We have a selection from the correspondence limiting it to the original People statement, the Friends complaints and the subsequent and awe inspiring acrobatics of Mr Noel S Paul, in selecting which of the 39 complaints were to be considered. Mr Paul, at the time a 'secretary' to the Council, has since trodden the primrose path to 'assistant Secretary' (1967), and in 1968 he was appointed Secretary in place of the retiring Col W C Clissit.

Category A

1. 'A series of well-wishers gave them (the Mills family) accommodation.' The People, 2.1.66.

Untrue. No-one had ever given the family accommodation, there had always been rent to pay. A Mr Hopkins put the family up, and asked for 'about 10s per week' towards gas and electricity, which the Mills paid. Paul produced *no other case* of 'free' accommodation.

2. A complaint about words attributed to Mr Hopkins, who was quoted as saying that he let the Mills family one room in the house and . . .

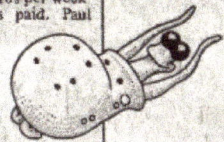

27

... *when they left, our new settee and the mattresses and bedclothes had to be destroyed. The People, 2.1.66.*

This was a flagrant lie. Hopkins made the following statement to two of the Friends on 9 Jan 66:

I, Brian William Hopkins of (address) have at no time stated that after Mr Roy Mills and Mrs Mildred Mills left my house, 'our new settee and the mattresses and bedclothes had to be destroyed' as stated in The People on Sunday 2 January 1966, nor is it true that because of the Mills family I had to destroy a settee and matresse and bedclothes.

In a letter to the editor of the People Hopkins made a similar statement, but the Press Council made no further reference to this complaint.

3. *'A stream of social workers and welfare officers have tried to help the Mills family. Their aid has either been ignored or thrown back in their faces . . .'*

This too was a distortion. No social workers or welfare workers ever visited the Mills.

4. *'A woman social worker called on Mrs Mills to help her plan her household budget properly. When Mr Mills discovered this service did not include the lady doing the family's housework and shopping, he told her to go.' The People, 2.1.66.*

Another lie. The woman was in fact a Home Help, forbidden by the terms of her employment to help with budgeting or to handle money. Elderly and untrained, she did little housework. Mrs Mills real problem was budgeting, and although her husband made a special request for expert help it was never provided. When Mrs Mills got a job, the Home Help was removed because it was against the County's rules. Even Mr W E Allison, the Kent official who gave so much information to The People, said later 'the service was *withdrawn* because Mrs Mills declared her intention to go to work in a factory.'

5. The People article stated that a Mrs Molly Riley had said that, when the Mills family were homeless, she had let them two rooms in her house. According to The People, Mrs Riley said that she and her husband had been through some hard times themselves and . . .

' . . . we felt we ought to help this family. We decided we could let them have the two top rooms in the house. The rent was 30s. a week, plus half the gas and electricity bills. The Millses stayed for six months, paid the rent intermittently and contributed a total of £1 to the gas and electricity bills. The People, 2.1.66.

The Friends accusation that this passage contained downright lies was supported by a statement signed by Mrs Molly Riley on 9 January 66 and formally witnessed by the doctor and the civil servant referred to above.

Mrs Riley completely denied having made a number of the remarks attributed to her in The People article. She said:

'I, Mrs Molly Riley, of (address), do hereby state that Mr Roy Mills and Mrs Mildred Mills were not our tenants at any time and that there was never any question of them paying rent to me or my husband. Nor was there at any time any agreement about paying for the gas and electricity . . .'

Category 'B'

6. Some of the complaints in Paul's category B were just as serious, but these too were to be rejected by the Press Council (if, in fact, they ever saw them.) Here are two examples.

'. . . Over a period of eight years Mr Mills and his family have received more help than any other family in the country. The People, 2.1.66.

This was patently untrue, a sweeping statement for which there could be no evidence. However it certainly shows The People's heavy hand in developing the picture of Mills as a 'phoney martyr.'

7. *'Mr Mills 'fixes' the electricity meter whenever possible.'*

This sweeping statement is based on one conviction some years before. It neglects to add that at the time Mills was suffering severe injuries, and had been unemployed for some months. While digging in his garden, he set off a wartime cannon shell, and suffered shrapnel injuries. The court

recognised his difficulties and sentenced him to two years probation. The People made no mention of this, but the malicious intent is obvious.

Category 'C'

Finally, some examples of the complaints Paul rejected, and which therefore would not be presented to the Council. His excuses are threadbare to the extreme.

Objection was raised to People reporter Patricia Elston's methods in gathering material for the article. Facts were distorted or omitted, in line with the general editorial instructions she had received. Elston visited Mr Mills, and after telling him that the article would be a hard-hitting description of the plight of the homeless, she got her interview. More seriously, she visited KCC officials, who broke their own rules in giving private information about the homeless. She attributed statements to people which were the very opposite of what they had said to her.

Paul's answer to this complaint was short – 'I am unable to find any grounds on which to seek an adjudication.'

Another complaint was directed against The People's claim to be giving 'the full facts' about Mills, which was very far from the truth – for example the following quote:

'Then Mr Mills had an accident and was off work'. The People, 2.1.66.

the paper's passing reference to Mills cannon shell accident and resulting long period of unemployment. The incident itself had serious repercussions in Mr Mill's life. But Paul's reason for rejecting this complaint:

'What comprises a 'full story' is entirely a matter of opinion. That a 'full story' is not in someone else's opinion of sufficient extent does not provide grounds for complaint.'

'Mr Mills is the despair of all the people who have tried to help him. And yet he dares to play the martyr.' The People, 2.1.66.

This was quite untrue – another sneer at MR Mills. For a start, the 40 members of the Friends of King Hill did not 'despair' of him. Paul's reply –

'. . . many people may have a high opinion of Mr Mills and his family, but that does not extinguish the newspaper's right to make the statements here given.'

'The Kent County Council gave him a council house. Eventually, even the council's patience was exhausted and in 1962 Mr Mills was turned out for non-payment of rent.' The People, 2.1.66.

This was a false fact, designed to restore the Kent County Council's tarnished image. In fact the house belonged to Maidstone Borough Council. Important facts were omitted – Mills was still suffering from the shell accident, and that the arrears were only £20 (and paid in full 3 weeks after eviction).

Paul's reply: –

'Although it may be (I have not investigated the point) that the wrong housing authority has been named, the error, if it is one, clearly does not inflict injury on anyone.'

The Friends wrote back angrily that the complaint illustrated the general inaccuracy of the article, in that the council was hardly 'patient' under the circumstances.

'Again the Kent County Council took pity on them and allowed Mrs Mills and her children into the West Malling Hostel.' The People, 2.1.66.

Another attempt to restore the Kent County Council's image. There was no 'pity' involved. The KCC had a statutory duty under the National Assistance Act to provide accommodation.

Noel Paul's excuse for excluding this complaint was that . . .

'. . . the expression 'took pity' in the context, even if it were considered inappropriate, would not be a substantial matter of complaint.'

'Mrs Mills has three rooms (in King Hill Hostel), with cooking facilities and the use of a communal room.' The People, 2.1.66.

In fact there was no communal room. The Friend's campaign demanded the provision of such a room. One MP had described the Hostel as 'like a prison camp.'

Paul's reply:

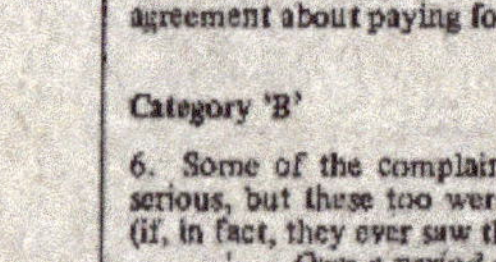

'The only challenge here seems to be in respect of the communal room. The injurious nature of this statement, if it is incorrect, is not apparent . . .'

'Kent County Council should do one more act of kindness – they should put the Mills children into a home. Then they should kick Mrs Mills out of the Hostel.' The People, 2.1.66.

The KCC had already been pursuing this policy for years – setting an all-Britain record for children in care over the past 14 years. The King Hill Campaign put a complete stop to this inhuman policy. This too, was totally false and misleading.

Paul's reply –

'The newspaper is entitled to take the view that it would be an act of kindness to put the children into a home, just as your organization is entitled to take a contrary view.'

'Mrs Mills has been in the Hostel longer than the three-month maximum period – so the Council does not take the £1 2s 6d rent. Her husband is staying with yet another kind-hearted well-wisher – and he pays no rent either.' The People, 2.1.66.

Another distortion. Mrs Mills was defying the rules by staying in the Hostel, and the Council could not accept the rent because it would nullify trespassing charges being brought against the squatters. At the same time, Mr Mills was paying rent where he was staying, and a statement was produced to this effect.

Paul's reply –

'The facts do not appear to be challenged.'

'Yet he is not slow to cash in on someone else's misfortune. At one time the Mills family was renting a house at South Avenue, Rochester, Kent, for £4 10s a week. Yet Mr Mills had the nerve to charge a woman £5 rent for one room in the house.' The People, 2.1.66.

This was false and distorted. The Friend s produced a statement from the woman in question to show that the rent was much less than £5, and for it she received full board for herself and her two children (whom the People had not mentioned.)

Paul's reply:

'It would seem appropriate to describe a lady with two children as a woman. The failure to mention the existence of the children does not affect the accuracy of the statement in the newspaper.'

In any case, no further reference was made to any of these complaints, though some were easily as justified as those Paul included in his first category, and supported the Friend s accusations of 'malicious intent', insinuations and disgraceful comment'.

THE ADJUDICATION

Six months passed. Despite letters and phone calls, the Friend s elicited only one piece of information: Paul's assistant, a Mr E Harrison, said that although he could give no information about the progress of complaints, he would say that the matter 'had become a nightmare for Mr Paul and no-one was more anxious than Mr Paul to get it off his desk.'

On 28th July 1968, the Council's 670 word statement was published.

Their adjudication was:

'The Press Council is satisfied that the article in The People contained no substantial inaccuracy and the complaint that it was vicious, malicious and grossly inaccurate is rejected.'

As far as is known, The People was the only national paper to mention the adjudication Under the heading End of a Vile Campaign – The Paper that Finds Out on the front page of the 28 July issue, Editor Robert Edwards indulged in an orgy of self praise.

'It was, in fact, a masterpiece of good reporting' 'Once more The People has lived up to its reputation as the paper that finds out and publishes the facts as they really are.'

'A group of agitators' had 'initiated against Pat Elston and The People a filthy public campaign . . . . one of the most disgraceful smear campaigns ever launched against a newspaper.'

With such strong convictions, it's odd that The People have never bothered to sue the Friends for libel. Certainly the financial problems wouldn't be too great. IPC's profits at October '68 were up to £6,236,000. Compare this with the Friend's failure to raise more than £150 for their first abortive libel action on behalf of Mr Mills.

But the real importance of this case is that it exposes the Press Council as a complete fake.

The Council is composed of at least 80% journalist, all dependent on the industry. All the Constitution has to say about lay representatives is that Representatives of the Public shall not exceed 20% of the total to vote. The same anachronism exists in the much-criticised Police Tribunals.

Of course, the logical solution is contained in the Constitution of the Press Council. We quote Section 16: Dissolution:

'The Council may at any time terminate is existence if it appears to the members that the Council's voluntary nature and independence are threatened.'

It's obvious to us that the Council never had any 'voluntary nature and independence' to begin with – by the very nature of it's Constitution.

THE UNIVERSAL TONGUEBATH
A GROUPIES VISION

Staff writer Germaine talks to Dr G, a celebrated
(and over educated) international groupie.

Musicians, like other men, have always had women, but something in their way of having them was different by virtue of their being musicians, like it would differ again for airline pilots and lighthouse keepers. In the years BB(before Beatlemania) there were two kinds of musicians' birds, the musos' old ladies and the scrubbers. The rock-and-rollers picked up and put down the local goers like meals, perhaps storing a little woman at home, protected from the knowledge of her husband's promiscuity and lunatic fringes of his sexuality. The scrubbers suffered all his aggression, all his loneliness and self doubt. The Jazz musicians had a different scene. They toured less often and less spectacularly, and played to a discriminating clientele which came to listen. They were deep into their music, and so perforce were their women. Marriage was not common, but monogamy was the rule. It was a hard life for the birds, because they never went out at night except to sit out the old man's sets. There wasn't much money so they worked in the daytime, and fought fatigue and loneliness sitting in a dark corner where the clubowner would not find their presence intolerable. They came to listen instead of waiting a t home in bed because musicians were not often verbal in those days of separated media, and the only way they could hear the message of love was through the music. But cool jazz was cool. The message was often cold, inner-directed, and musos often lost their birds, not often to each other. Some of them took up a pose of embitterment, and took it out on the scrubbers. Lots of them drank or pilled up. One or two kept a wife in the suburbs. And took that out on the scrubbers too.

'The first boyfriend I ever had' said Dr. G, the Daytripper,' 'was a jazz drummer, the best. I was with him for a year, and I never danced with him: that was one of the things it meant. I couldn't even dance to his music, in front of him. Seems like I sat that whole year. In the end I became the hatcheck girl in the club. Then he took a long gig in another state. On his last night in the club he sang a blues just for me, about having a girl tenfoot tall, and I cried myself blind in the hatcheck room. The rag merchants talked all through it and then they all clapped their hands'. She knitted her brows. 'Then somebody told him I had been with somebody else, 2,000 miles away, and he just dropped me cold without another word. Can you imagine that?'

But the post Beatle era was dawning and the media were drawing closer to each other for the fusion which is now. Music became commercial and creative, not only notes but words, not only sound but physical onslaught, sight, movement, total enviroment. The jazz musician's love affair with his instrument moved out of his head and met the rocker's violent cruel sensuality at tenderness junction, and the girls sitting wiped out against cold nightclub walls in quiet clothes arose with their listening eyes and danced alone, opened out their beauty in the various light and sex flowed back into the scene and lapped all around them. Where all the currents intersected and flowed forward and back, there he was, the musical revolutionary-poet calling all to witness the new order and achieve the group grope, astride his thousands of volts, winding his horn while the mode of the music changed and the walls of the city fell and everybody burst out laughing. The women kept on dancing while their long skirts crept up, and their girdles dissolved, and their nipples burst through like hyacinth tips and their clothes withered away to the mere wisps and ghost of draperies to adorn and glorify, and at last the cunt lay open like a shining seapath to the sun.

So who did it happen for? Not for everybody. For the musicians it happened, and for those same girls who dragged out their lives flattened against a leaf of sound, for their sisters and their daughters. The women who really understand what the bass guitar is saying when it thumps against their skin, a velvet-hard glans of soundwaves, nuzzling. To understand and face the possibilities of annihilation OM without flinching. To be limitless, Infinite. Bounty as boundless as the sea, and love as deep. Here's how it happened for one.

'I was very slow to turn onto pop. I turned down an invitation to a party for the Beatles. I moved from jazz through blues, skirted folk music, and ended up with Bach and Buxtehude. Monteverdi and the great madmen. Hobnobbed with guys who were called composers and wrote operas and ballets and stuff. Started to go to concerts of contemporary music and talk about it. Sang Carl Orff. The song that made the difference was I can't get no satisfaction and the original resensifiers were The Stones. I pay attention. The walls of the city began to shake.'

'It was evident that there was a pop conspiracy to blow the minds of my generation. I was interested but not involved. I only began to understand the group symbol when I met Simon Dupree and the Big Sound in a TV Studio. The place was full of smoothies and groovers being cool and calculating every move. The

31

sounds of sucking filled the air, when these little guys blasted off, singing what was already an old number, *Reservations*, I remember, and his underpants showed. And he sweated a lot. And his sound blew out all the crap and BBC gumshoes and I knew I was on his side. You know what its like; all the technicians regard rockstars as freaks, the management regards them as charming, grubby mental defectives. They are *their thing and don't give a Fuck. The message is sent. When I was being dressed for some change or other in some tight little thing that squeezed all my boobs up, I looked up and they were all looking at me...* with a kind of hot innocence, and I suddenly realised that groupiedom was possible. But the stitches were still in. Just say, it occurred to me. They all went off and took a train to Aberdeen or somewhere, some gruelling bloody awful tour

'The first popstar I actually pulled was an entire accident. I was at this ball in the country (the best scene for a calculated 'hit' now I come to consider it) and I was having a dreary time because my bloke was utterly spaced out, so I made myself mildly conspicuous .
(We should point out that Dr G's six feet and other freakish attributes make inconspicuousness a more significant achievement)
'- and sure enough in the first break the lead singer of the group turned up next to me and stayed there, which was alright except it was a nowhere group who were not getting it together and I didn't dig him. I started to kind of edge away and I walked into the lead singer of the star group and we went into this crazy improvised routine, as if we'd known each other for years. When it's right that show it is. You recognise each other, and you play in tune. Because you meet that way there are no hang-ups, no ploys, well, no ways of exploiting each other. If you fuck, you do it with the carnal innocence of children or cats or something. When you've watched a man cailing his call and you've heard it and know what it means, there are no limits; the night you spend together is limitless too...you might go off for a few days to a few places, but it's immaterial if you're still together... Sounds like a poor line in cheap mysticism, but that's how it can be. Usually you separate quite soon, because there are things to do, more things to have and do, and maybe it happens again a few times, maybe months apart. It's a bit like a jam session I suppose .Or a super group. Maybe he's married or got an old lady: that's like his regular scene. He knows he can blow good things when he's with you, sometimes, things he can only blow with you, so you get together. That's how I like it. Monogamy is death for me.'

She's laughing but she means it. She explains that she's very promiscuous but out of the hundreds of guys that she's made, relatively few are popstars, but most of the popstars are names to conjure with.

'I guess I'm a starfucker really. You know it's a name I dig, because all the men who get inside me are stars. Even if they're plumbers, they're star plumbers. Another thing I dig is balling the greats before the rest of the world knows about them, before they get the big hype. Because I have to follow my judgement, not the charts, you dig? Now take Magic Terry, he's a star which your telescope hasn't picked up yet We met at a party in New York, and he said he wanted to come and read poetry at my apartment. I believed him, although it seemed unlikely and he came and did this amazing thing, this ENORMOUS poetry, which he's going to do soon (if he doesn't die or something) with the best hard rock backing money and his judgement can get, and that is the best. When it happens it will all happen to me too, whether I'm there or not. The great thing about starfucking is that every time you play a record, or just dig his thing again. it's all there, like he was there.'

I spy on her by looking through the records scattered round the turntable: they are the names I expect, with a few notable exceptions. I had seen her sharing Jim Morrison's spotlight at the Doors concert so I asked why there were none of their records there.

'I suppose I went there to get some Jim Morrison. I never know until I experience the thing properly whether it's a good thing or not. Jim Morrison was a terrible bring down. I mean, he was there coming on like a fucking sex kitten, pouting and wiggling and slipping out of his clothes. He thought he was singing to teeny-boppers and kept throwing them the drumsticks and stuff and everyone froze with embarrassment. The vibes were so bad that he started to have trouble getting it together. He went upstage and tried to bring himself on jigging the maracas up and down with his elbow down here so he'd have a

stand to show the customers, and then he goes leaping down to show it to everyone and it's gone.'

'Most commercial groups are a terrible bringdown: it must be like fucking a whore, you know. You watch them standing there slapping their instruments with these terrible fixed expressions. Can you imagine sex with Andy Fairweather-Low or that podgy guy from the Amen Corner or is it the other one? Jesus, I never know which is which. That night the Doors communicated their impotence to all of us, and we sneaked home furtively, separately, ashamed of liking that LP so long ago. What a disgusting hype they are.'

Most groups are hypes sure. That ought to be irrelevant. Like you and I both publish to earn a bottle of wine, you write The Wanker's Manual and I write Reality Sandwiches. But when a group is nothing but a hype, as I believe the Doors are, when they make love and revolution *commodities* , assassination is called for. Mind you, there are other kinds of motives for starfucking. Maybe if someone turned Jim Morrison on properly the Doors would open. But I'm really not a groupie-reformer, for God's sake.'

'But do you know I find Englebert very horny-making. He's so evil you know, getting all those lonely housewives to cream their jeans, with his tight highfronted shiny mohair trousers with just a touch of rubber hose. So fucking evil'

She's still laughing, and I start her off on a different tack and she stops.

'I don't know. I mean everybody uses the sacrament Acid, most people some of the time. I only ever once went with anyone on horse, and I remember it as absolutely magical. I nearly turned on myself. He was as strong as a hawk, as light as a feather. His breath was a sweet as a child and his skin was hot and smelled like sunlight. He slept and woke and made love and slept as easily as if it was happening every day instead of every hour. He was amazingly high energy, and unutterably tender. I thought it would be all monkey-on-my- back stuff, but it was unbelievably potent and delicate. I still feel very involved with him although I never see him. I heard he fell off a bandstand the other day and cut his head. He gets sick a lot and he's unhappy I think. That's a drag, not being able to help. I guess it's unemancipated of something but I won't call him. I only hope if it gets really bad he'll think of me...I love him you know, him and a thousand others as they say.'

She is laughing again, but I am glad when the phone rings, and I put on a record while she talks.

What a *bring-down*...

When she comes back ... I ask my last question. I phrase it awkwardly and the Doctor squeezes her fleecy hair up in her hands and laughs again.

'It's not a matter of *minding* balling the whole group. They're not like the ton-up guys who'd hold a girl down while they all fucked her: that's the fascist sort of homosexual kick, like where the leader fucks the girl in the glare of their headlights and they all jack off and stuff. I'd never be likely to wind up in that situation. But I'd love to be one of a group in a loving sexual situation. I just don't know very many groups who can get it together. The Airplane seem to love and listen to each other a lot, but Rolling Stone tells me they get uptight about sharing birds. Now RS is not always right anymore than a penis is called a *Hampton Wick* , but   I haven't often come across groups that were so together that they could make that scene. Probably the MC5 are near it. I had to go to sleep in their hotel after Elektra had had to ring me up to get Rob Tyner to a conference, and they slept two to a room with the doors open and everyone walked through. I found out I really *really* liked being able to hear other people balling very close to me while I was, and I was very pleased; you see, the group fuck is the highest ritual expression of our faith, but it must happen as a sort of special grace. Contrived it could be really terrible, like a dirty weekend with the Monkees!

'When you asked me that question, you made like you thought that it was a kinky sort of thing, well it isn't you see, because kinkiness...it's the great British disease. Kinkiness comes from low energy. It's the substitution of lechery for lust. You don't really feel desirous so you turn yourself on with cute variants like rubber mackintoshes and nuns' habits... Lots of popstars run a sort of playboy scene where they lie about, being the rich tycoons, having skilled whores go to work on them, sort of refining sensations like learning about caviare. Look at the image Tom Jones puts out on his TV show, a sort of fat noseless Hugh Hefner, real consumer sex in selfseal plastic wrap. But the groups I dig, and who are likely to dig me, are high energy, high voltage tenderness! There are no taboos, you can do anything anywhere, from excess to excess. Rolling Stone speak true when he say The Happy Nation sucks. Frank Zappa's an odd case though: I fancy him like mad. Have you seen the photo on the American sleeve of Ruben and the Jets. Here they made it too little, but the big photo reveals that Frank Zappa is a Grade-A-High-School-Prom-Heart-Throb!

I dig everything he does, except when he goes into his paranoid why – am – I – explaining – you – don't – care – or – understand routine, but I'd think twice about balling him because Ed Sanders told me that he has the same perversion as Tyrone Power on *Hollywood Babylon* and somebody else told me that that means he's a shit fancier! How do you get that together for Godsake? I don't really believe it. It's probably meant to frighten off all but the brave and resourceful. Still, maybe I'm not that brave and resourceful. Nevertheless, because I really respond to his vibes, I want him, shit or no shit, because that's how it is if your body and soul and mind are hooked up. I'd fuck Shakespeare, except that he specially asked that his bones not be disturbed.'

She jumps up to get ready to go eat at the Macrobiotic (because she likes it!) and rattles on while she fluffs out her hair, about the cafe-au-lait groupies of New York, brittle and loveless, but beautiful and

'YOU MIGHT THINK IT'S A LOAD OF OLD COCK, MAN, BUT THAT'S YOUR HANGUP'

TWO VIRGINS Yoko Ono/John Lennon. *Apple Records.*

Come to think of it psychedelics, macrobiotics and just plain idiotics have bowled over an awful lot of musicians these past few years. You know the sort of thing. 'Man', that was just the grooviest gig of my life' says the third-eyed drummer boy whose holy sticks never actually made contact with his kit during some transcendental solo which, horrors, threatened to go on for a week. Or the spaced-out singer who's always mixing up the words and melody of his last and next songs with the one he's supposed to be into. And then falls into the orchestra pit.

The luckier ones, so their claim goes, and mine, wake up forever. A world in a grain of sound is their first fabulous discovery. From that moment on the steps might lead anywhere or nowhere but they'll seem new steps and they'll seem revolutionary steps and they might be. Melody, harmony, rhythm die as we've known them to be reborn, perhaps. Those aged, exhausted imperatives, the G7 to C, 4 x 4 = 12 – The Blues syndrome can never again quite seem the limit of music's possibilities. Some even get into the aleatory kick, that one musical territory where advanced pop, jazz and "classical" musicians can meet, fuse and come up breathing the same musical language.

Aleatory (sometimes called 'chance' or 'random') theory finally and crudely boils down to a kind of anything goes as long as it works for someone, somewhere. Its criteria, to say the least, is vague. To bore the pants off an audience is often considered desirable. 'Inner tension' is perhaps the universally favoured expression of praise. Unpredictable factors like the creaking of a chair three rows from the back of a concert hall can become a crucial ingredient of the performance, equal in musical status to any a pre-planned, notated instrumental sequence.

Way back when flowers and love and doing your own thing and smiling at the fuzz were all in bloom I took part in what was probably the first attempt here to put aleatory principles into practice in a pop context. The result was that best-forgotten first LP by Hannah and the Coined Coat. I doubt, however, if the Pye Recording Studio people will ever forget it. Every manner of banged, plucked, stroked and blown sound producing device was put at our disposal. There was one instruction only, from the rather excited sessions producer, 'Blow', he would say, frantically dashing from one well-intentioned group to another, 'Blow, baby, blow.' For the next three hours, with increasing timidity, possibly 100 people banged, plucked, stroked and blew and looked as if they were on the worst trip of their lives.

An American friend of mine used to play the same lousy trick. You'd be settling into a nice scene at her place when suddenly, without warning, she'd produce an equally bewildering array of instruments and utterly obliterate your high by saying in her New York kiddies, Martha Graham-modulated, dance instructress voice, 'Come on. Everyone can be an artist. Technique is the refuge of the insecure. Let's just forget all about our self-conscious little egos and create beautiful, beautiful sounds.'

Just as the dancers go on and on about how the traditional concepts of their art are mere deformations of spontaneity so the new musicians talk endlessly of their need to disentangle themselves from "Bourgeois" procedures.

There's lots of talk too about John Cage, that most discussed jazz listened to maestro of modern music. [Those wanting to join in might first read Silence – Calder & Boyars, 34', or the more recent A Year From Monday – also C & B; 35/–.]

Where in relation to all this do Two Virgins of Miss Ono and Mr Lennon stand? Do they know their Cage? Does it matter? Many of the new politicians couldn't care a gruff about Marx so we might as well excuse their musical equivalents if they choose to ignore the teachings of their predecessors. After all a Cage could be a cage.

For my money Two Virgins is not the pretentious bore most of the established critics have complained about. Neither does it seethe with the magical insights claimed for it by others. Better to welcome it on its own ground as a genuine happening to sound, crude and naïve if compared with the tried and tested master of the avant garde, certainly less boring than some, more uncertain than most. It fascinates, like the best bad art, not because of an independent aesthetic life of its own but because it is the creation of those two splendid creatures on the sleeve about whom we know, superficially at any rate, more than we ever did about any Bach, Beethoven or Boulez. It's a far from unpleasant way of extending that knowledge. And Parkinson's Law operates, I for one can hardly wait for the coming of the Third Virgin.

If by some chance you're still interested in things aleatory pay a visit to the Arts Lab Tuesday nights, 8 pm. There you'll find English music's true street-fighting men, the AMM group. They fucked their way out of virginity years ago and are today to be reckoned with from Cologne to California.

For them, as with most revolutionaries, whether in politics or the arts, the question is Freedom. How much real freedom can you have and survive?

Translated into the language of the new musicians this mostly becomes a question of how much say the contemporary composer will allow his performer in determining the music's final shape and content. In other words the traditional authoritarian concept of hero-composer lording it over humble interpreter is being challenged. A struggle over power no less. The analogy with current political debate is obvious and fascinating. The performer insists on a bigger share of the creative cake. Sometimes he wins complete control. Composer abdicates or rather composer and performer become one and the same and a group like the AMM is the result. Their members include the one super star of the local avant garde, Cornelius Cardew, Prof of Composition at the Royal Academy and three ex-Mike Westbrook band jazzmen. Don't miss them.

Sebastian Jorgensen.

35

LP REVIEWS

**LED ZEPPELIN Led Zeppelin.
Atlantic 588171**

Very occasionally a long-playing record is released that defies immediate classification or description, simply because it's so obviously a turning point in rock music that only time proves capable of shifting it into eventual perspective. (Dylan's Bringing It All Back Home, The Byrds Younger Than Yesterday, Disraeli Gears, Hendrix's Are You Experienced? and Sgt Pepper). This Led Zeppelin album is like that.

Before joining the now sadly defunct Yardbirds Jim Page was acknowledged as one of the best session musicians on either side of the Atlantic. Here it's clear why. Few rock musicians in the world could hope to parallel the degree of technical assurance and gutsy emotion he displays throughout these nine tracks. Exactly eighty-four seconds after the beginning of Good Time Bad Times, the first cut, side one, Page does things with an electric guitar that might feebly be described as bewildering. From then on it only gets better.

Lead vocalist, Robert Plant, is a blue-eyed-soul merchant furious when he isn't being Winwood—living proof of the You Don't Have To Be Black To Sing The Blues theory, formerly with a Birmingham based group, The Band of Joy, as is the Zeppelin's drummer, John Bonham. Bonham's technique is interesting. It's nice to be able to listen to a drummer whose use of bass pedal and cymbals is intelligent without being studied or contrived and at the other end of the stick, powerful without deteriorating into frenzied, feverish thrashing.

John Paul Jones plays bass and organ for Led Zeppelin. It's enough to say that of both instruments he is an experienced, resourceful master.

This album makes you feel good. It makes you feel good to hear a band with so much to say and the conspicuous ability to say it as they feel it; to translate what's in their heads to music. It makes you feel good to hear Bonham and Jones working together, creating those deep, surging, undercurrents of rhythm as Page again and again molest the more vulnerable areas of his Telecaster. Good to listen to Plant with his ugly, angry vocals, bellowing to his woman that he's leaving her – right after the next fuck. Good to dig completely spontaneous but so, so beautifully controlled breaks in How Many More Times, or Jones running amok on his Hammond keyboard in Willie Dixon's You Shook Me and to sway, entranced with Page's droning, mantra-like bow guitar in Dazed & Confused.

It makes you feel good because it is good; and in places much more than that.

Of course, as a result of this album we'll lose the group to the States, and almost certainly within the month the M M letters page will headline 'Is Page BETTER Than God?!!' – and then the BBC will begin negotiations on a feature film . . . . . but there's more to it than that. There is a phrase nobody uses anymore, (not since we de-freaked our hair, handed back granny her beads quietly disposing of kaftans and joss sticks to jumble collectors). That phrase exactly sums up Led Zeppelin's debut album, Remember Good Vibrations?
Felix Dennis

RHINOCEROS. Elektra EKS 74030.
A decorated Rhinoceros with sort of multi-coloured scales, strewn with shells and beads. Very pretty.

Inside seven cats looking serious or Western Movie Style mean. They have hats, rings, hair on their faces and scarves around their necks. They come from the Electric Flag, The Iron Butterfly, The Buffalo Springfield, The Mothers of Invention and there is a cat from some music school.

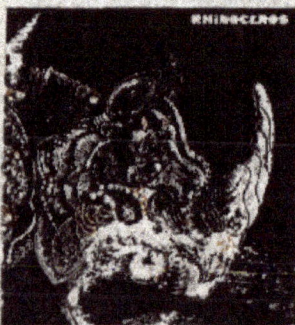

Sometime, somewhere they have been together in a recording studio to try and put something between the pretty coloured Rhinoceros.

The results of their efforts don't take long to hear. The first time I played it I had to take it off again it was so bad. But the record came from Elektra, so I tried again later.

After the sounds become familiar it's not so bad and occasionally a little bit of it nearly comes together, but then it is possible to become accustomed to things that are really quite unpleasant. Usually unpleasant things are best avoided. In this case it's easy. I still have my copy. One of these days somebody will get the hot eye for the pretty cover and take it away. That's how it goes.
Bryan Willis.

'PROJECTIONS'. The Concert Ensemble, featuring, John Handy, Michael White, Mike Nock, Bruce Cale, Larry Hancock. CBS.

Since first hearing John Handy at Monterey, I have very much enjoyed hearing and seeing all his albums. So far CBS have released four of them, Monterey, 2nd Album, New View, and Projections.

In 1965 Handy recorded Spanish Lady and If Only We Knew. These were live recordings, and on this occasion the quintet consisted of Handy, also; Mike White, violin; Don Thompson, piano and bass; Terry Hahn on guitar, and Terry Clarke on drums. On this occasion seven thousand people gave Handy a standing ovation.

On his second LP, Mr Handy gives us five very different themes to work on. Dancy, Dancy is a simple little tune, in the Bossanova beat, with some really nice drumming by Terry Clarke. Scene X, on the other hand is more serious, and is in 5/4 time, while Blues For A High Strung Guitar is really beautiful, featuring Jerry Hahn on guitar.

New View was recorded in 1967, and the line-up is completely changed. This time Mike White is not featured at all. Instead, Bobby Hutchinson, courtesy of Blue Note Records, plays vibraphone. This is not such an exciting sound, rather it is a sad sound, and was recorded at The Village Gate in New York, some three weeks before the death of John Coltrane. In fact, Handy dedicates a track to that memory. This is more serious Handy, and requires a much more concentrated attention.

Projection is the latest release and is very much more like the first album. Mike White is back with Handy, and the tracks all have a much lighter air about them.

MARIANNE

The track Projections itself is in waltz time, composed by pianist Mike Knock, featuring some excellent double stops and exchanges between Handy and White. I think the track that reminds me most of Monterey is Senora Nancye because the opening is again unaccompanied sax and the quartet come in with the same feeling. The album lasts forty-two minutes, and is well worth the 37/6d that I paid for it. If you can afford it, try and make up the set as it is always possible that CBS may decide to delete the earlier recordings.
Simon Stable

ROOTS, The Everly Brothers.
Warner Bros. Seven Arts Records WS1752

Roots by the old Everly Brothers is a dandy bucketful of tunes that'll bring that renegade Cowboy Spirit back home. The album sleeve notes explain that the album is an attempt by the brothers to trace their roots or something like that and it sure does, sort of. They've sprinkled the album with some very short bits of tape done by themselves along with Mom and Dad Everly, the whole family pickin' plunkin' and singin' away on their old radio show somewhere

up in the Kentucky boondocks, wherever. The tape effect provides us with a ready reference for the progression of the Thing as a whole: it measures the exact distance that down-home hillbilly bluegrass could come if it wanted to.
Roots is a smooth kind of thing like ethnic tennis balls bouncing down a mossy rock garden and the Everly Brothers, like the True Cowboys that they almost are, never expend too much energy. Roots rolls nice but it don't never tumble.
Only once in the album do the brothers become a little too enthusiastic. Throughout and especially towards the end of T For Texas the electronicality gets to be a trifle obnoxious but after a few listens, one realizes that Don and Phil are carelessly constructing a special tin-foil and plastic platform of discord from which to dive straight down into

the eighty-seven bars of the introductory guitar solo of 'I Wonder If I Care As Much'. This solo is a pure modern amplified coyote's lament, the song is a great old hit risen from the grave, its rhythm is heavy tribal Cherokee and the result is one of the finest modern Cowboy songs in captivity.
Side two has two cuts worth quietly shouting about.

The third cut deserving a special mention might well be the high spot of the album. It's the Merle Haggard composition, Sing Me Back Home. The arrangement on this is so tight (!) that the consequent tension provides some kind of wierd dimension that really makes this tune bite! Sing Me Back Home is the key to Roots and to Country & Western and it fits like a finger. On the back of the key it says: You can do what you may to a man but you can't tear the music from him, it was around long before he got there.
'Sing me back home,
before I die . . .'
G B P

YOU CAN'T BEAT PEOPLE UP & HAVE THEM SAY I LOVE YOU
Murray Roman Track 613 007

America never had music hall as such. It had saloons in frontier towns, and later it had silent films, prohibition and speakeasies. None of these are really ideal environments for the stand-up comic, the patter merchant who flourished on the British stage, and it wasn't until the advent of an electronic, tv-orientated age that the USA really got into the swing of this kind of humour. Once it did, however, it produced some notable talents: Stan Freeberg, Shelley Berman and Bob Newhart among them. Murray Roman works in this tradition but uses the West Coast freakout idiom. Whether he's an entirely natural product of his time is arguable (he has groovy friends like Tom Smothers who count against him) but outside the bounds of this review; if he *has* cut his clothes to suit the style of the day then he's done it so well that none of the seams show. The patter is very neat.
One of the faults of this album (it's as riddled as gruyere cheese) is that, if anything, the patter is *too* neat. Roman obviously believes a comic can get by on idiom alone, an idea so daring it hasn't been attempted since George Formby. Fuck content, Roman seems to be saying, a thing, *anything*, has only to *sound* funny to get you laughing.
Even the relatively lucid ,straight tracks bow to this abnegation of content: canned phoney 'soul' music clatters in the background, swelling and fading, intercut at random to destroy any idea of sequence or cohesion; the traditional devices of humour, the juxtapositions,

the interplay of tensions that provokes laughter, are spread pretty thin; at all times the style's the thing. All very well, but can you really get laughs by declaiming sotto voce and with echo: 'Smoke your draft card'? Well maybe, but not by paying the same kind of shallow lip service to psychedelic effect and serious modern preoccupations (such as drugs and race riots) for two entire sides of an LP. One can't blame Murray Roman for trying, I suppose, but having tried he should have had the grace to acknowledge the experiment a failure. I think it's Shelley Berman in disguise.
Graham Carnock

TOUCH
—' Deram. Mono DML 1033. Stereo SML 1033.

When your organ gets out of control, pop-pickers, beware. No other instrument can compare with it for volume, variety or sustaining power. Equally no other instrument in the history of music has attracted so many meglomaniacs, pedants and bores.
Only an organist (Al Kooper of Dylan backings and Super-Session fame) could bring out an album called "I Stand Alone". Probably the most sinister thing about the Right Hon. Edward Heath is not his tendency to keep us with the Powells but the fact that he's an accomplished player and a fully paid-up member of the Royal Society of Organists.
So watch that organ.
Don Gallucci is the somewhat

overwhelming organist with this new group from California. Listening to Touch you get the feeling that he's very much the boss, that he's academically clever (probably a Julliard graduate or something) and that if only he'd work more at his piano he might end up a considerable jazz soloist. Some of the nicest things here take place when he shifts from key-board pipes to key-board strings. Despite blurb claims of "unique individuality" however, the other four members of "Touch" don't amount to much except as glorified organ stops for Maestro Gallucci to pull and shove. Nevertheless they are kept extremely busy.

Touch is very tight, together and troubling. Apart from easy-going tracks like We Feel Fine, The Spiritual Death of Howard Green and Miss Teach the music has the character of a ritual funeral wake, all spooky organ riffs and stately drum beats. On the credit side however I've not heard a record since "The United States of America" which so boldly and effectively tackles the problems of avantegarde pop.

There may not be much joy but there's musical adventure galore.

Eschewing the blues altogether and indifferent to the devices of straight pop "Touch" attempts a synthesis of post Sergeant Pepper esoterics twentieth century classical music and jazz with just a dash of electronics and musique concrete. Heady uncommercial stuff, heavily arranged and multi-multi-multi-tracked, pretentious certainly but not unattractively so.

The lyrics are dreadful (Wake up and feel it in the air/It's a time of hope for man/Jesus was right/Sensitivity Reigns/But yet the fighting and the hatred goes on and on and on) but the organisation and distribution of the vocal parts is often brilliant and original. Seldom have voices been used with such austere theatricalstyle in a pop context. On second thoughts though it could also be said that seldom have voices (the same is true of the lead guitar) sounded so much like they came from the organ.

Drat that organ.

Sebastian Jørgensen

THIS MAN IS DANGEROUS

Detective Sergeant Norman (normal) Pilcher is London's deadliest male groupie. Originally from Chelsea police station, he's now the Scotland Yard drug-squad's chief head-hunter. That's why big time dope criminals are rejoicing. Pilcher is a publicity junkie, who likes nothing so much as to bask in the limelight of celebrity arrests. Banal racketeers are not for him. For a cop, his tastes are amazingly hip. Twice he has beseiged the home of Brian Jones.

Last year he lumbered into the bedroom of John Lennon and Yoko Ono. On the day Paul McCartney got married, Pilcher delivered a wedding present in the form of his own intruding person to the home of George Harrison. One day last year the intercom buzzed in a Chelsea studio: "Postman here, special delivery"...up the stairs came Pilcher and the boys puffing and panting and screaming "where's Eric Clapton, where's Eric Clapton?" Out, luckily, so the co-tenant was bagged instead. For God's sake, someone, give Pilcher a lead guitar and build a group around him. Sergeant Pilcher and the Great Alf Conspiracy. It might catch on. At least it would keep him off the streets.

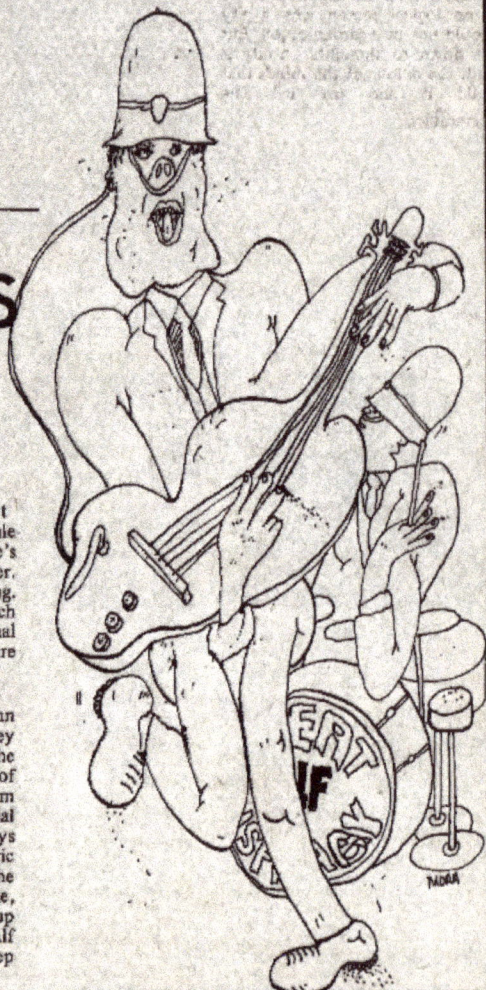

41

THE ONLY LIVING
DYLANOLOGIST

Recently The East Village Other has been featuring articles by A.J.Weberman, in which the self-styled 'Dylanologist' dissects at length the songs of Bob Dylan and of others (such as Hey Jude) which he feels he can relate in some way to Dylan. The articles have produced, not surprisingly, some outraged letters from EVO readers, containing comments ranging from outright abuse ("A J Weberman is an ass-hole") to the restrained irony of 'soon he will be finding a meaning in such obvious nonsense poetry as Mother Goose.' Weberman is shortly to publish a book about his findings in connection with Dylan. Dylan's new LP is due out sometime in April. The 'definite last word' on John Wesley Harding which follows, provides amusement, and a warning to those who want, at any cost, to load a simple song with significance and meaning. The text is taken from an interview with Weberman by Gordon Friesen, contributing editor of Broadside Magazine, which appeared originally in Graffiti.

G: How about JOHN WESLEY HARDING? How does it stack up to his other work ?

Alan: First of all, in this album Dylan has changed his style of poetry. In the other recent LP s he used surrealistic, 3-dimensional, multi-layered imagery in order to get across what he wanted to say. Now in JOHN WESLEY HARDING we have what are apparently meaningful songs o n one level. But on this level the meaning is kind of trivial - 'John Wesley Harding was a friend to the poor' and all that crap. It's enough for many people; few people look for irony anymore since they tend to take Dylan quite literally; and the stories on JOHN WESLEY HARDING make sense on this level, to some degree. They make more sense than the material on most of Dylan's previous albums, especially Bringing It All Back Home and Blonde on Blonde. You know that the cat isn't going to write this simple kind of poetry. Everything is going to have an ironic meaning. As Dylan says, 'Don't under estimate me and I won't under estimate you.' This album is full of irony even though you might not be able to find it at first glance. I happen to believe that the whole first side is autobiography, Dylan talking about his career including the time he had the motorcycle accident. 'John Wesley Harding was a friend to the poor, he travelled with a gun in every hand'. Here we apparen tly have the Robin Hood superman outlaw. 'All along this countryside he opened many a door'. He took off a lot of people. 'but he was never known to hurt an honest man'. He only ripped off the dishonest rich. But when I hear it, it's a song about the old Dylan, i e. the Dylan of the TIMES THEY ARE A-CHANGING days, who was 'a friend to the poor', that is, a proletarian songwriter who wrote songs about the poor - 'Hollis Brown', 'Hattie Carroll', 'Only a Pawn in Their Game' and so on. So he was a leftist songwriter, 'a leftist poet,' he travelled with a gun in every hand'- gun is guitar in this context because Dylan says 'in every hand' and you generally play a guitar with both hands (unless you're Jimi Hendrix,that is). Woody used a similar metaphor when he wrote on his guitar case; 'This machine kills fascists'. And here's something funny: Teen Star Time Magazine said April 1, 1966, 'Bob Dylan, who sings his own compositions, wears blue jeans and has little to do with barbers, and is armed with a guitar...' (my emphasis). So that's weird. The whole melody and layout of this poem is extremely Guthriesque...' all along this countryside', and why 'all along'? Every word that Dylan uses has ironic meaning. 'All along the watchtower/Princes kept the view'; why ' all along '? If anyone has any ideas on this write to me in care of Broadside, 215 W 98St, NYC 10025. 'This countryside' is the USA where ' he opened many a door'. ' Opened the door' is a phrase used by some commercial trade publications to describe Dylan's effect on the music business around the time of ' Blowing in the Wind'. For instance CASHBOX Magazine on Oct 5 1963, said: 'If the Kingston Trio opened the door of the folk boom, then Bob Dylan has opened the door much further with Blowin' in the Wind. Others with Dylan's perspective can now get a chance to be heard and display their musical wares. So whether pro or con Bob Dylan, one cannot deny that he is a major force to be watched and reckoned with'. So Dylan borrows this phrase from the commercial pop music publications. ' But he was never known to hurt an honest man'- the singers whom Dylan replaced were dishonest in the sense that they didn't sing the truth, what was happening to them or going on in their minds; they sang almost exclusively about true love and that sort of bullshit often entirely divorced from reality It was down in Chaney County ' -- down south in Mississippi where Chaney, Goodman and Schwerner were slaughtered. 'A time they talk about' --- they don't talk about it in the movie Don't Look Back, where Dylan is shown in Greenwood, Mississippi with Seegar and Bikel singing to a black audience. 'With his lady by his side'- at first I thought this line referred to Joan Baez, because in Oxford Town ' Dylan says,' Me , my gal, and my gal's son,we got met with a teargas bomb'. I kind of erased the information that Joan has no son and wasn't with him in Greenwood. But then I remembered that 'Lady' was Dylan's symbol for the oligarchy in some of his previous poems and when you reminded me that the Feds were behind the Civil Rights voter registration I realised he may have meant: ' With the Federal Government on his (political) side ', ' He took

a stand '—a microphone and a stand on the issues—' And soon the situation there was all but straightened out '. He went down south toprotest the murders and brutality going on (Dylan was very sincere - in Don't Look Back, if you look at his eyes while he sings ' Only a Pawn in Their Game ' you will see tears in them). But the Civil Rights linked murders went on the same as before—in fact, it was after he went to Mississippi that Chaney, Goodman,Schwerner, Viola Liuzzo and others were killed. And so, Bob Dylan - in combination with our great Federal Government—didn't really help the situation at all. ' For he was always known to lend a helping hand ' -- Dylan attributed this lack of success to the fact that the hand fate dealt him wasn't high enough to straighten out his own problems, let alone those of the black people, and when combined with the hand of the Federal Government was a stoned loser. All across the telegraph ' - make those capital ' T's '. The Telegraph, a protypical American newspaper - ' his name it did resound ', Dylan received a lot of publicity in the press media. ' But no charge held against him could they prove '. The press slandered him - many of the articles written about Dylan were derogatory. For example, Time Magazine had one entitled ' Not quite a Genius Genius And Newsweek printed an article accusing Dylan of getting ' Blowin' in the Wind ' from a New Jersey High School student named Lorre Wyatt.

' As I Went Out One Morning ' has to do, I think, about what happened when Dylan got the Thomas Paine Award from the Emergency Civil Liberties Committee. ' I Dreamed I Saw St. Augustine 'deals with Dylan the poetic political activist pretty much as he was during the Bringing It All Back Home Days. This is a good example of what happens to listeners if not set to get into Dylan. It sounds like some semi-religious mystic poetry sufficient unto itself. But if you are hip to where Dylan's head is at,then you'll find that what appears simple is actually a lot of irony with hidden meaning. ' All along the Watchtower ' -- at first I thought this was about Dylan's friend Ginsberg. ' Two riders ' - writers - ' were approaching and the wind ' - Dylan's most promising symbol, the wind - ' began to HOWL '. - Ginsberg's autobiographical poem . I want to make a confession. I even went and asked Ginsberg and he said, ' No, it never took place. It never happened '. So I decided that Dylan is talking about when he became electrified, though I'm still not sure - ' the wind began to howl '. Like ' the ghost of electricity howls in the bones of her face '. It follows, because he then goes ahead and tells about his experience as a rock singer in the ' Ballad of Frankie Lee and Judas Priest. ' Which is very funny - a series of misunderstandings between himself, his manager, andthe folkniks. It's the longest cut on the album and from rapping with friends I gather that it's the most talked about cut. A very interesting riff. ' Frankie Lee ', Frankie Lane, Frankie Lyman- it's Dylan the rock and roll singer. Dylan, when he was making records like ' Positively 4th Street ', ' Like a Rolling Stone ', ' Please Crawl out of Your Window '. And Judas Priest is none other than

his manager, Al Grossman. It could be any kind of commercial character but it seems to be Grossman. The last cut on the first side ' A Drifter's Escape ' is Dylan telling about his motorcycle accident. The whole side shows that Dylan is getting to be more autobiographical and more concerned with what is going on in his head.

G. You haven't had time to get into the second side ?

A. Not really. I've only been playing the record five times a day now for seven months. But I have some ideas. ' Dear Landlord ' is I think, addressed to a Dylan critic or interpreter. ' I am a Lonesome Hobo ' is a very personal song. ' I pity the Poor Immigrant ' is, I think, about Viet Nam. ' The Wicked Messenger '- this song is a very short history of Dylan's career from a radical standpoint. ' There was a wicked messenger, from Eli he did come ' . Dylan is the wicked messenger, and Eli is the Old Testament from which he draws so much of his symbolism. ' Down Along the Cove ' is another very personal song. And ' I'll Be Your Baby ToNight ', I feel,although I'm not sure, is Dylan saying that he is going to stop protesting. What makes me think that he is laying a 'message' on us is its position at the end of the LP. Dylan often saves the last cut on an album to tell us what he's going to do on the next one. He did it with 'Restless Farewell', announcing he was going to change; he did it in 'Sad-Eyed Lady of the Lowlands', where he wasn't sure he should continue being a recording artist. So I felt that in 'Baby To-night' Dylan is giving us a hint of what his next album is going to be like. It's going to be very simple. Perhaps he is not really going to stop protesting, just seem to stop. The irony will still be there, only it will be in a different form of poetry. I'm beginning to wonder if Dylan's not running out of autobiographical things to say -- he's said it all - given his ideas about politics,leftists, rightists,man's condition, universities, the mass media, war, religion, philosophy, science, idealism, everything. A whole lifetime of ideas - he's really offered what amounts toa complete systematised ideology, a complete world view. But then, Dylan has a way of presenting the same ideas in new forms. If you want to understand JOHN WESLEY HARDING you have to understand all of Dylan You have to take his first record BOB DYLAN, play the two original cuts on it, then go on and listen to every record, albums and singles Dylan has ever released, in chronological order. And to really understand Dylan you have to be a revolutionary - youhave to have an extreme dislike for our present society and a strong desire to overthrow it.

G: Alan, how does your system of interpreting Dylan work ? It sounds quite complicated.

Alan: First, you've got to get thoroughly acquainted with Dylanology. That means, among other things, you have got to realise that everything the cat says is packed with irony.If you can't find the irony that doesn't say it isn't there; it means only that you can't

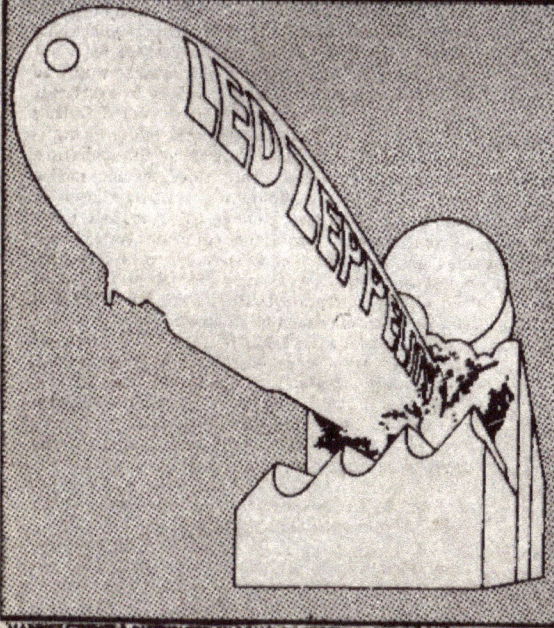

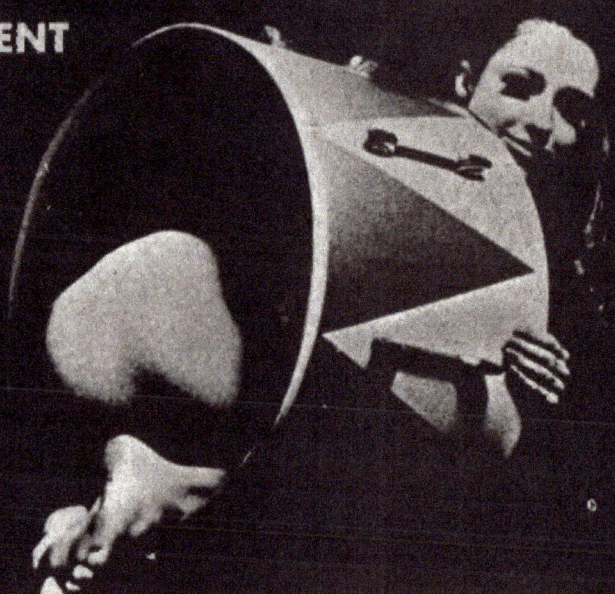

find it. Next, once he has decided on a symbol, he tends to use it pretty consistently. Take the symbol 'lady' which came up before. Remember 'With his lady by his side/He took a stand'? The reason I said it meant oligarchy in that context was because I had looked at Dylan's use of the word in several other contexts. You see, my brain is this computer, programmed with Dylan's poetry, so when I hear the word 'lady', I think of 'Sad-Eyed Lady of the Lowlands' — 'In the empty lot where the ladies play blindman's bluff with the key chain' and 'And the ladies treat me kindly and furnish me with tape'. And 'As lady and I look out to-night from Desolation Row.' When I substitute the word 'oligarchy' for 'lady' in those lines, I get a coherent interpretation. Dig it, Gordon? 'In the empty lot' - America - 'where the ladies' - the oligarchy - 'play blindman's bluff with the key chain' - plays meaningless games with the nation's wealth. 'And the all night girls' - the poor - 'whisper of escapades' - are forced into an existence where sex becomes another form of escape - 'out on the D-Train.' 'Train' is a Guthrie symbol which Bob uses. Remember, 'This train don't carry no gamblers, this train'? I think Woody meant this 'life', the life cycle. Well, Dylan means the same thing. But 'D' is Death, so the D-Train becomes the Death Train, and this is a very apt metaphor since the D-Train used to go through the Lower East Side, Bedford-Stuyvesant and Harlem, where death is prevalent all around. Hey, I better cool myself before I run down my whole book. **Of his new LP Dylan himself has had this to say: 'I can't remember too much about how I wrote the new songs It depends on where I am, what the weather is like and who is around at the time. The music is a little of everything. You'll know what it is when you hear it...The new songs are easy to sing and there aren't too many words'**

continued from page 33

entertaining, and the softer girls who still hunt among the minstrels the familiar lineaments of a husband and cry by silent telephones in lofts along the Bowery, of the necessity of being into your own thing, of getting back into your body so if you understand and admire an artist your nipples erect when you read a line of him or hear a bar of his music (like berries under the brown gauze of her long dress whipped with old lace) so Norman Mailer's penis blossoms in her head, stopping suddenly to swoop and kiss me on the mouth with her hand cupping my breast as naturally as a nest a bird, a kiss full of promise for a day when we shall come to life among the flowers of Beulah, 'rejoicing in unity In the Four Senses, in the Outline, the Circumference and Form, for ever in the Forgiveness of Sins which is Self Annihilation', and I notice that she has changed the record.

I'm so glad, I'm so glad, I'm glad, I'm glad, I'm glad.

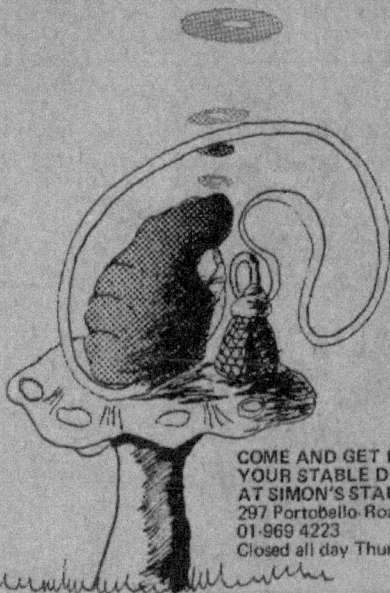

Hippies gape as HELL'S ANGELS

menace Arts Lab in drug, orgy, police, rape, loot, gang bang shock!

OZ

20 3s

There are 3 Gods Love, Poetry, & The Revolution - Situationists, P 6.

OTHER SCENES

The tremendous pace at which the so-called sexual revolution is moving leaves us all a little dizzy. It's only a matter of weeks since Jim Buckley & Al Goldstein broke away from The New York Free Press to found a new unabashedly sexual tabloid called Screw. After seven issues it is selling 60,000 copies (at 35¢ each) & is about to go weekly. The New York Review of Sex, whose major assets have been high-quality paper (better reproductions) & such mind-blowers as a close-up of Ultra Violet's snatch & Sam Edwards' pseudonymously-written column about sex-&-politics, is close on its heels to both circulation & potential income. Marvin Grafton, the Rat's ad manager, launched another sex tabloid named Pleasure & a fourth, Kiss, is on the way from the Evo stable. Inevitably there'll be others & just as inevitably the fast-moving world of offset publishing will move into & exploit other neglected areas.

Meanwhile, poet Lennox Raphael & producer Ed Wode try to figure out what all the fuss is about over 'Che!' Just because they put on a play which has fucking in it — which is where everybody is at right now — there's all this commotion & old-fashioned legal shit. All you had to do was go to the special performance that was put on for the press after the initial bust to see how important this story is: at least 100 'members of the press' crammed into the tiny Free Store to watch, drool over & record in minute detail this precedent-shattering production. Miles of film was shot, hundreds of stills were taken but all that was seen in print or TV were the same old 'safe' shots (no tits of ass) that have always been shown.

Where is the Establishment press at? One of the answers, of course, is somebody like Helen Gurley Brown who was hired as Hearst's sexpert-in-residence, after her book 'Sex & the Single Girl' proved she knew a little more about sex than the average typist (but still considerably less than anybody the slightest bit hip).

As the years have gone by, the gap between what Helen Gurley Brown knows about sex & what is really happening has grown so much wider that today she sounds like some naive high school chick* (except, of course, that high school chicks these days are fucking when they're 12 years old). It's fitting that the Hearst organization should regard her as an authority because it confirms that they're still at least two years away from what's really going on. Why do dinosaurs like Hearst publications fold while young, vigorous, new papers spring up & expand so rapidly? Well, you don't need an answer to that question unless you're very naive.

But, to return to the play 'Che!' for a moment, author Lennox Raphael says that he regards it as merely a curtain-raiser, a sort of tantalising hors d'ouevres so to speak, & you should see the NEXT two plays, he's already written. Obviously it's not going to be long before people who go to the theatre will be attending a fuck-in, just like you might have gone to the Roman baths for the evening with your groovy, uninhibited friends.

Which brings us to the movies. While the squares are being repeatedly conned on 42nd Street by 12-minute beaver pictures (you'd think they'd at least overlay the straight girly shots with a fantasy sequence) or hyped-up nudist frolics, the little old ladies and Cosmopolitan readers are lining up to pay $4.50 for an excruciatingly dull Swedish film containing one brief fucking sequence. Sally Kirkland & Rip Torn look like being the first two stars to actually demonstrate sixty-nine in a commercially released flick, although it's rumored that the producers of that little epic are quite uptight about the sequence.

AP ran its annual wire story on millionaires who don't pay taxes (21 of them last year because of depreciation deals and other swindles) but as usual didn't name any names or follow up on what might be done about it.... Manhattan Tribune calls underground papers 'semi-pornographic' which is a stupid putdown with about as much meaning as 'half pregnant'.

Is Eldridge Cleaver dead? A victim of CIA agents? That's the suggestion made by Chicago's militant Resistance Press in the first issue of their new paper, The Free Chicago Graphic scheduled for publication next month...

Bill Hutton's 'A History of America' (Coach House Press, 671 Spadina Ave, Toronto, Canada, $1.98) will definitely give you a different perspective than you learned at school; latest casualty figures in Vietnam & concluding with PRAY FOR PEACE are being distributed by the group called 'Clergy & Laymen Concerned About Vietnam'. Figures are updated with a new poster each month & you can subscribe to a 12-month set for $3 (475 Riverside Drive, New York 10027)...

As noted in this column before, Meher Baba is likely to be heralded much more dead than alive. His was a rather exclusive cult & very little he did or said (virtually nothing) could shift or alter the allegiance of his disciples. It is interesting, though, that it's easier to sell a dead god than a live one... The Underground Press Syndicate Directory is the most comprehensive reference book on UPS papers so far. It lists size, frequency, ad rates etc and costs $2 from Orpheus, Box 1832, Phoenix, Ariz, 85001...

First underground paper in Australia, since AUST OZ folded there, is the multi-colored Ubu News (25¢ from Andrew Reed, 54 George Street, Redfern, NSW 2016) which used to be the newsletter of the underground film freaks in that country... New Zealand booksellers are getting uptight about an underground mag named Cock (50¢ from PO Box 2538, Wellington, New Zealand).

In the introduction to his book of columns, 'Notes of a Dirty Old Man' (Essex House, $1.95) poet Charles Bukowski reminisces about turning out his column for LA's late, lamented Open City: 'For action, it has poetry beat all to hell. Get a poem accepted & chances are i... ... ms out two to five years later, and a 50-50 shot it wi... ... ar, or exact lines of it will later appear, word for wor... some famous poet's mouth, & then you know the world ain't much. Of course, this isn't the fault of poetry, only that so many shits attempt to print and write it.' ... That celebrated paper writer George Plimpton has been under fire from Harry Smith's Newsletter for allegedly favoring his own magazine, Paris Review in much over-touted delettante coffee-table quarterly) with grants he was supposedly administering to benefit little mags and unknown writers. You can bet your hippy that nothing with guts — neither an underground paper nor any truly underground writers — will attract Plimpton's eye favourably; he's too careful of his image to allow that to happen...

Philadelphia's Distant Drummer reports that Drew Pearson's column about gangster-tainted Walter Annenberg was blacked out of Philadelphia papers. Annenberg, owner of two Philly papers, plus TV Guide & a bookie wire, has been named as ambassador to Britain because he's NIXON's kind of guy... Peter Hutchinson (John Gibson gallery) deals with 'super-saturated chemical solutions that yield crystals; tubes filled with fermenting materials that produce yeasts & moulds' and John Van Saun (feigen) who specializes in demonstrating the properties & potentialities of fire through burning Sterno pots, sizzling steel wool and melting candles.

Thousands of people, mostly students, have been officially ordained as ministers in the Universal Life Church. It's within everybody's grasp to become ministers by mail order thereby getting half-price fares, a break on taxes, exemption from the draft & all those other groovy extras that clergy seem to accept as their birthright. Trouble is that when 'ordinary' citizens start claiming these benefits the authorities get very uptight. There'll be a test case in San Jose, Calif on May 5 when Universal Life Church primate, Rev Kirby J Hensley goes on trial for 'violating the State Education Code' by issuing doctor of divinity licenses.

Dear OZ,

When I heard about the Squatters 'Home' at Bell Hotel, Drury Lane I was enthusiastic. I thought something was really happening. I was going to move in. Luckily I took a good look round & didn't.

These are the developments from what I heard & saw. The Arts Lab had its eye on the place & some guys from there climbed through & started clearing up. When they were spotted they opened the front door & got everyone then in the Lab to move in & start clearing up. At this point KYLASTRON who was deputised by Jim Haynes made no effectual explanation of the Art Lab's intentions

for the place. It was christened the 'home' & a notice was put on the door telling people without homes to move in & clean up. The one tramp already there was allowed to keep his room which he cleared up. He moved in one of his mates next door. KYLASTRON later explained to me that the Lab wanted the place as a cheap hostel for 'Artists & creative people, unmarried mothers, ex-junkies. Six rooms would be kept locked for travelling theatre troupes performing at the Lab.' The sanitary inspector came & pronounced the place unfit for human habitation. Hell's Angels were moved in on the 3rd floor as a protection against external aggression. After the 1st few days precious little clearing up was done & a levy of £1 per head was imposed. When the talks broke down on matters of internal discipline . . . who should stay . . . who must go. KYLASTRON resigned but returned a couple of days later by popular(?) demand. He is well in with the angels & started using them to evict people who would not come clean or who refused to pay their £1 per week. KYLASTRON organised a 3.00 am raiding party which threw out anyone found smoking or refusing to pay. The angels knocked on every door. Who's there? no answer. Delay. Door opened. Sniff sniff, 'right you lot — out' . . . in the case of a lot of my friends. KYLASTRON appeared from time to time & when he was criticised he would turn & say something like 'Look man, this is my place — morally if not legally, & if you don't like it go & find your own place & do your own thing there. This isn't a fucking dosshouse. Go on, just get out.' & in the event of trouble the angels were never far away to help the evicted tenant on his way.

After the Saturday bust KYLASTRON & the others from the Arts Lab gave up & pulled out. The place was reoccupied on Sunday & the ground floor barricaded. Access was by ladder to the 1st floor & most of the people turned out previously moved back in. On Wednesday workman broke in & smashed the place up because

... ASSESS WHAT IS THE DINOSAUR'S CASE..

ITS MY TURN NOW!

OUR CALL FOR AN 'AMAZING COMIC STRIP ARTIST' PRODUCED A FLOOD OF SUGGESTIONS, SOME OF WHICH (ABOVE) AL- MOST MADE IT VISUALLY. BUT IN THE MAIN THE STORY IDEAS WERE TOO BANAL. HOPEFULLY WE'LL HAVE ONE FOR OZ 21.

A blast from the Nationals

THE GUARDIAN
POP MUSIC
by Geoffrey Cannon

The second enterprise is "Time Out," which I judge to be the most exciting and admirable magazine launched within the last year. To over simplify, this magazine is a what's-on-in-London for avant-garde, experimental, and electric events.   It covers rock, blues, folk and jazz events with particular thoroughness. It's already indispensable. "Time Out's" rock record reviews are pretty good, too.

3

it was 'unfit for human habitation.' What KYLASTRON had hoped to do was get everybody working to clear the place up, turn out the junkies & get the place properly legal. His methods created a microcosm of state which he readily admitted but claimed was the only way of securing the place for any length of time. Was a place run along fascist lines worth securing anyway? Would it have changed? It's arguable, but doubtful. KYLASTRON did express the hope of setting up an office to organise the taking over of other properties by squatters.

He wanted this to be the precedent. To get this legal & then get people moving in on empty houses on a large scale. Now marches & petitions are under way. Also a petition demanding employment for those discriminated against for unusual appearance or behaviour, now this may give some idea of where the arts lab crowd are at I mean what about those that don't want employment & want to smoke & things, I mean . . .

I seem to be going on a bit so anyway I haven't a point to make especially except some people are so happy playing along with the straights that they're probably happier being straight anyway & it don't make no difference what they look like, & its sad. Honestly I don't know where I am so why don't I just keep quiet?
Love
Steve Burke
28 Roland Gdns
London SW7

Dear Editor,
I compliment you for printing such a fine article as Germaine's on Dr. G. It was beautifully done.

It brought one thing clearly to my mind, in this world saturated with violence, physical, mental or spiritual, it is infinitely better to have a good fuck.
Yours sincerely
C. E. PHILLIPS
31 Cumberland Mansions
Brown Street
London, W.1.

Dear OZ,
Pure & eurhythmic, clear & polymorphic. I wonder if anyone realises exactly how content a glass of water must be?
Paul, Frank & Zettusa
Farnham Close,
London N20.
P.S. Except Robin & Mike.

Dear OZ,
I wish you well in your campaign against capitalism and hypocrisy, but permit me a cynical middle-aged observation: LSE was a nice simple symbolic target to pick; what about the big stuff next time? why don't all you hairy teenagers boycott the pop music industry? what about a self-denying ordinance for twelve months, no albums, no magazines (other than OZ, of course), no transistor radios, no discotheques; how about a march down Charing Cross Road to Denmark Street, to smash a few windows there? Not that I've anything (much) against pop music,

I can take it or leave it, like Vivaldi, Beethoven, or Sibelius: but I puke when I see the love & sympathy flowing towards Biafra & Vietnam, whilst the money from your hot little pockets all flows in the opposite direction. But here's a little bit of both for OZ.
Yours faithfully,
P R Bridger
Happy Island
Pwllmelin Road
Cardiff.

Dear OZ,
There is an article entitled 'Psychic Guerilla Warfare', in which someone named G William Domhoff from the Entwhistle Project, attempts to air his plans & views for a political takeover in good old decadent America. Towards the end of the article the editor, Richard Neville (xxxxxx), has resented two comments 'Jesus, what CRAP! ed.' & in parentheses at the bottom of p 23. (If the Revolution means prose like this, let's LOSE!). After reading Mr Domhoff article & finding these two 'gems' from Mr Neville at the bottom of p 23, I think that Mr Neville has made a serious editorial mistake, which does discredit to OZ! — He has slandered Mr Domhoff's article by inserting his derogatory comments
RIGHT IN THE FUCKING TEXT!!! Secondly Mr Neville has failed to provide any reason for those comments. It seems to me that if Mr Neville thinks that what Mr Domhoff says is 'CRAP' (in capitals) then Mr Neville should at least 1) Tell us why he feels this way, and 2) Present his

OZ is published monthly by OZ Publications Ink Ltd , 52 Princedale Road, London, W 11. Phone 229-7541. Directors: Richard Neville, Andrew Fisher.

OZ appears with the help of: Jon Goodchild, Felix Dennis, Louise Ferrier, Brigid Harrison, Keith Morris, Lyn Richards, Ken Perry, Miss Murphy, Philippe von Mora, Mike McInnerny, Michael Ramsden, John Wilcock Jim Anderson.

Special supplement: Angelo Quattrocchi.

Advertising: Felix Dennis, 44, Wandsworth Bridge Road, London, S W 6. 01-736 1330

Typesetting: Papyrotype. Distribution: Britain (overground) Moore-Harness Ltd, 11 Lever Street, London, EC1. Phone: CLE 4882 (Underground) ECAL, 22 Betterton Street, London, WC2. Phone TEM 8606. Transmutation. Guildford 65694. California: Rattner Distributors, 2428 McGee St, Berkley, Calif. 94703. Holland: Thomas Rap, Regulierdwarstraat 91, Amsterdam, Tel: 020-227065 Denmark: George Streeton, The Underground, Larsbjorn straede 13, Copenhagen K. Printed by: OZ Publications Ink Ltd, 52 Princedale Rd; London W11.

OZ 20

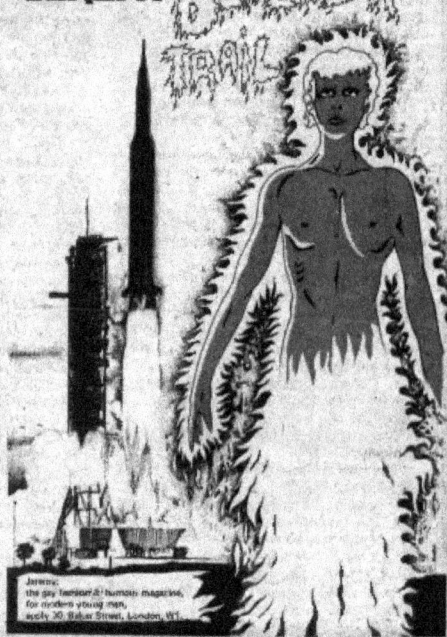

JEREMY BLAZES A TRAIL

Jeremy:
the gay fashion & human magazine,
for modern young men,
[illegible] 30 Baker Street, London, W1

views some other place than *right in the middle of Mr Domhoff's text*. I am sure Mr Domhoff expects commentary on any piece of writing he does for public consumption, but I don't think he quite expected this form of editorial slander! *Jesus, what crap! Ed.*

Thank you sincerely

Charles Conrad
London

P.S. I think some apology on Mr Neville's part is in order.

Dear OZ,
British Students are indeed 'parochial and insular'. In fact, they are a lot worse than that in the majority of cases. They are lazy, apathetic, selfish and smug.

I am at Hull University and very much involved with publications there, along with several others. What our activities have shown though is that these failings are capable of being broken by the right form of attack. I would therefore like to outline our activities in the hope that other small groups seriously dissatisfied with the media at THEIR Unies can do something similar about it.

At Hull we, decided to start a 'mag' to fill in the vacuum left by the other university tabloids. We began a first issue of WORM at the beginning of the Easter Term and by the end had a circulation of 500 and also five issues behind us.

The policy of the WORM is to *guarantee* printing every single contribution from one word to a thousand or infinity. We have strictly adhered to this rule.

WORM is also totally anonymous. There are no editors because everything goes in. Result . . . we get a hall of a lot of good stuff we normally wouldn't have received because people are often either afraid to say what they think because of possible recrimination from University authorities and the law or else they are shy of criticism (especially of poetry).

Things people have been wanting to say are said and spread fearlessly at last.

Creative contributions that would have remained in secret are shared with everyone.

The drawback of obscenity is negligible as it can do no harm and readers are prepared to take the good with the bad.

There is no formal organisation at all so that legal prosecution is almost impossible. Also as there are no editors or staff anyone who wants to can help in typing selling or even getting cups of tea. The same people never work on every issue. Yet we managed to bring out one issue every fortnight which is quite reasonable and we found we received enough material in that time to fill it up nicely.

The mag is also a good revolutionary and active political unit. Issue number three carried instructions on how to make a molotov with diagram and said where in the university to strike with same. No student took the hint but the Authorities certainly tried every form of secret pressure to stop circulation. Issue number 4 again struck at the authorities of the University and their possibilities also slamming a warden of a Hall of residence for his hypocritical treatment of students.

Several other things led to threats of police action on the sellers and publishers if sales were not stopped. The charges include: OBSCENITY, LIBEL, OBSCENE LIBEL, SELLING SAME, WRITING SAME, PRINTING SAME.

All this in ten weeks. WORM is for the students of the University it says what they think. It does not tone down anything. No clique runs it and in ten weeks it is said to have shifted student opinion at Hull from right to Anarchist.

ALL UNIVERSITIES NEED A WORM and Manchester University are to start Man Worm next term on exactly the same print every anything lines. Worm is so powerful because it is honest and because it belongs to everyone in reality.

The mag is unpretentious. Foolscap duplicating paper, Gestetner stencils typed one finger at a time, cost an issue of 500 approx £5-10-0. Any one can produce one all you need is the courage to have *real* freedom of press and a little energy.

Every University has grumbles. Every University has poets and thinkers, it should have more than most units. WORM is genuine revolution, genuine freedom. Its very freedom and the fact that it is not an ego trip cos of a non policy adds to its power and virtually safety from prosecution.

FUZZ: Who writes this obscene revolutionary rag?

WORM: Everybody at the University or nobody.

FUZZ: Yes but it must have an editor, someone must run it.

WORM: Everybody edits it. You are forced to decide what you think is good and bad and form critical judgements, if you find them necessary, while you read it so everybody is the editor.

FUZZ: Yes but . . . (unable to understand that real freedom of this sort can actually exist. Who does he get?)

The banning of WORM 4 from the University Union, by Admin, was unable to stop sales and no one could be prosecuted — except themselves for allowing it in their premises. Mass support from the student body also came in the form of lobbies of President, who apologised; debate attacks on the Admin; and much needed money gifts which were given purely from hearts and not prompted at all. Students at Hull are realising just how much freedom is possible. The Right, who keep trying unsuccessfully to label our policies as anarchistic and dangerous, have felt a backlash that merely lost them power. Their 'credibility' has been destroyed because we really are doing this for the students. WORM is *really* speaking for them. The Authorities read WORM too. It worries them. They cannot understand freedom. It is a complicated and, to them, a dangerous thing.

WORM is everywhere. If you want to give yourselves a little freedom of thought write to us at:
'Worm' Hull University Students Union, University of Hull East Yorks.

5

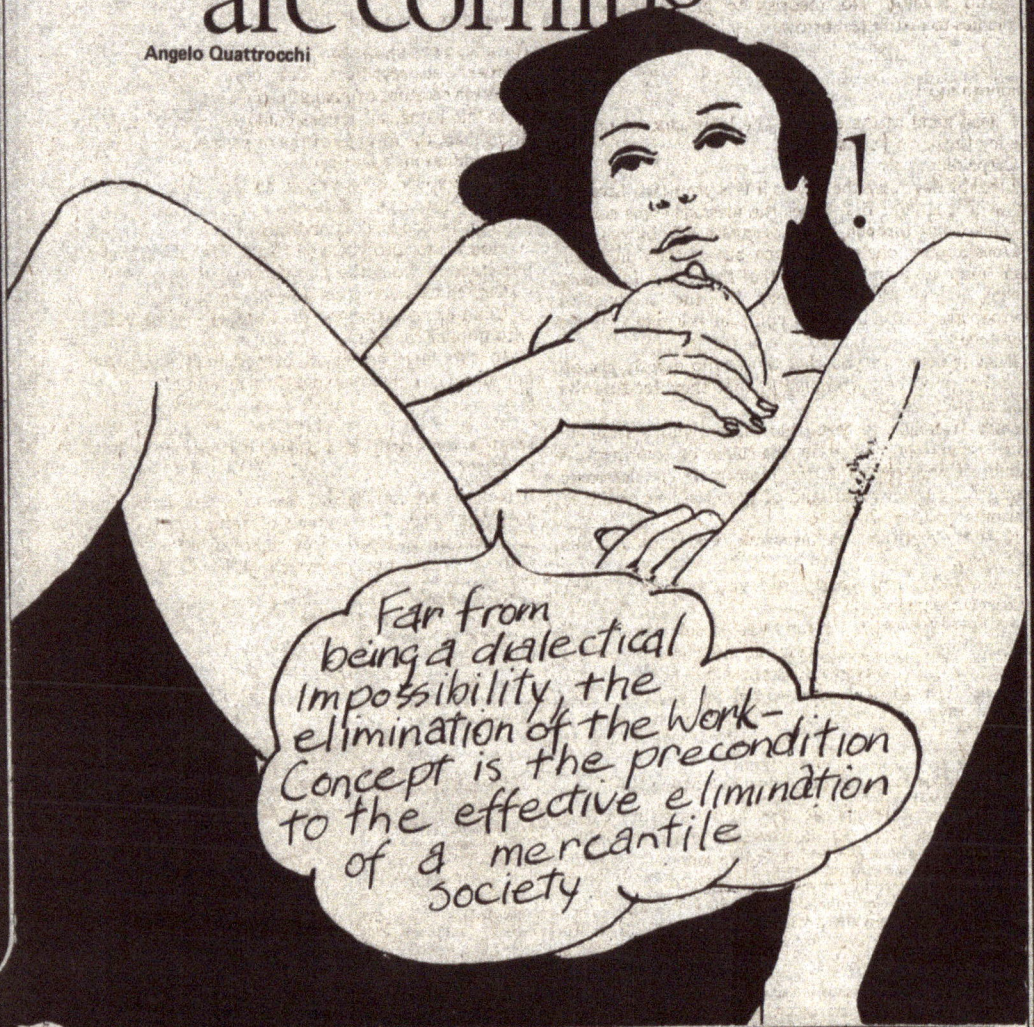

The 'Situationists are Coming' is another in the occasional series of supplements prepared by friends-of-OZ, and way beyond editorial control.

The Situationists are coming

Angelo Quattrocchi

Far from being a dialectical impossibility, the elimination of the Work-Concept is the precondition to the effective elimination of a mercantile society

13 Apostles

I have three gods: love, poetry & the revolution

Love knows no boundaries, refuses no flesh, & is ephemeral, as is my love for women. The act is an accomplishment.

Poetry is the search for beauty, a wolf barking at the full moon, scratches on this page, her face lit by a barricade. A striving. Revolution is the stone thrown in the stagnant pond, & the ripples spreading life to the water, the shaking of the innumerable dead minds & souls from my shoulders. It's poetry achieved, in action, in love.

& no religion. No theories to justify today, no theologies to justify tomorrow.

1.

Memento mori

The dead hand of the enemy. The long hand of power. The icy finger on your soul.

Carpe diem.

Live the day. Live the day as if it is your last. Live the day as if it is your first. Does the message come across?

Does it cut through layers of grease, oil, butter, fat?

Does it enter one ear & come out of the other? Oh, dead mummies, nursed by the flickering of many screens, daily lulled to sleep by the rustling of newspapers, does it occur to you that this day you live only once?

Does it occur to you that those who quietly poison your day need your complicity, that they feed on the dung of your mind?

Does it occur to you that those who assassinate today, your day, do it in the name of tomorrow, a Socialist tomorrow, a fatter tomorrow, an electronic tomorrow, a never never land of promises, the chains of our contemporary slaves.

If they offer you an insurance, you should strike them dead.

If they offer you a party card, you should stuff their mouths with papers.

If they offer you a cause, you should break their hearts with such a laughter that all the glasswindows of Companies & Corporations, from 42nd street to the Calcutta Post Offices should fall in splinters. The tinkling of freedom.

2.

Remember that Saturday afternoon in Notting Hill?

When a few hopefuls in search of instant-coffee communication went around touching passers by with their hands, to provoke togetherness (& giving, unfortunately, an explaining leaflet afterwards).

It is said that a bank manager asked for the purpose of this, & when given the leaflet, remained unconvinced. Housewives found it 'nice', if a bit bewildering. Hippies & similar acted, of course, in a conspiratorial manner. Word spread rapidly in the market (yes, it was the Portobello road, kaleidoscope of dwindling images of the

possible) that some kids were going around touching people. Some eyes went sharper, some, softer. The display of objects, a small degree out of focus.

A handsome (groovy) negro was approached. – Yes, baby? – he said.

A working class bloke got wind of the affair, spotted one of the touchers & told him: 'listen, why don't you touch my mate here, he needs it.'

The 'experiment' ended at pub-opening time, & was written about in the papers.

3.

Once there was a god

An all powerful, transcendental god ready to justify all murders, all sacrifices. The most beautiful & most revolting creature of man's imagination.

In his name, all crimes could be committed by man upon man, the revenge of the oppressed was put aside, & ritualised, in his paradise.

He exploded, like a nova, an interstellar bang, Bang! Now stardust is all that is left.

Objects, goods, commodities.

Houses to protect you from life, to shelter your putrefaction from the putrefaction of your neighbour.

Cars to take you from nowhere to nowhere.

Children to make you die faster, to watch you dying with unblinking eyes.

In this huge graveyard of god, you work, without murmuring, ad maiorem dei gloriam, still.

4.

What is the worth of a desire, if it cannot be put into practice?

It is but a dream, a nightmare, in a dark night where all cows are black. The myriads of desire not fulfilled, the thousand desires sparked by daily frustration, fill our air with a lethal mixture which slowly assassinates the

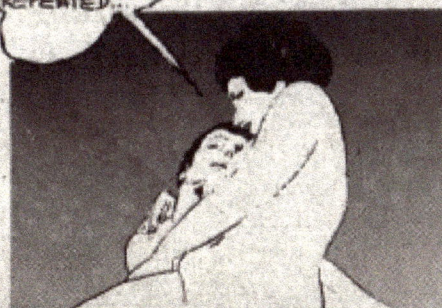

IN WORK THE COMMODOTY-SYSTEM'S INNER CONTRADICTION BETWEEN USE VALUE AND EXCHANGE VALUE IS ENDLESSLY REPEATED...

acquiescent. The rebel chokes, his cough is the only sign of life in the thick smog.

But the all pervading mixture is also inflammable. Strike a match in the black caverns of our desires, & leaping flames will scorch the minds, long abused. At the light of that fire, fed by the dead wood of the sacrifices imposed on us in the name of the three paper gods — Production, Consumption & Alienation, we will dance our last dance of death, our first dance of life.

5.

There are corners where the shadow of misery is paler

The nursery rhymes, where the cow jumps over the moon. The guttural cry of the lover which thickens the air. The child's play, & his questions. The trees standing against the sky at dusk; Even the smoke of the farmhouse in the distance. There are screams which pierce the screen, one eternal instant. Lions copulating at noon. The agony of the tortured & the quickening of the breath of the executioner. A theory of empty, illuminated skyscrapers at night. The lonely joys buried in frightened hearts. Blasphemy, sometimes.

The ghastly grin of the masturbater in a lavatory cubicle. & the lightening, the lightening in pages, in lines.

6.

Where have all the flowers gone?

Where is the alchemy which turns base metal into gold; where the mystery, which makes your hair a forest, your profile to pornographic cameras, reflects the image of our grayness. There is more passion in the sudden fit of the small child who destroys his sandcastle, than in all the metal pricks we are throwing against the solemnity of indifferent skies.

Where have all the children gone?

There's more life in the wind swelling the willow-trees than in all the millions of television aerials, crosses of the graveyards.

Where have all the graveyards gone?

Waiting, waiting, in a long cold winter, waiting. There is more life in the skull of Attila, the Hun, than in all the skyscrapers built for your awe.

But when will they ever learn, when will they ever learn?

7.

Cocks as Coca-Cola bottles. Untap, unzip, pour the liquid into the glass, or, alternatively, suck directly. Pop. As many as you like (can afford). Refreshing, stimulating, & also relaxing? Bip. Hygienic. Zap. & therapeutic. Plop. It mustn't be messy, oh no! No fuzzy edges, no smudges. Cleanliness the only way to Coca-Cola-ness, the best, best way.

Counterparts are unmentioned. Delicate. As loo-paper can be. Pink. Forward, Christian soldiers, unroll. To each according to its size. Temperaments are catered for, by the art-industry. The jolliest of sports. Join the set. With skill and indurance, you too can give an adequate performance. Coca-Colas of the world united, you have nothing to lose but your liquid.

8.

The space of one day mirrors the entire life.

At dawn, a bell murders your dream, too early, and calls you to your slavery. As childrens' play is much too early strangled by the school-factory, which stuffs them like sausages.

Your journey to work ignoring and ignored by others, is a long tunnel crowded with cyphers. The kids encounter the multitude of platitudes, & learn obedience.

The day is filled with the horror of enforced work, your adult life.

& when all the energy is drained, the spine bent, the mind vacuum-cleaned, & the fear of ultimate nothingness approaches, at dusk, then, it's the communion of the dead souls.

The litanies of the cathode tube tirelessly sing the hymn to the approaching sleep, the approaching death.

9.

Get hold of the idea, & hold it, don't let go

The idea is to the mind what the gentle clitoris is to the woman.

It inflames to the point of no return, to the land where your will is king.

The idea of happiness has taken hold, in the collective mind; it cannot recede.

The acid on your tongue is the presentiment of the ripples to come.

The first spasms are felt with such invading sweetness that all else is fast disappearing.

Be gentle & firm, in the pursuit of your goal.

Nothing, nothing else, you can see, is now real.

Pity those who squirm away.

10.

Love thy neighbour. Give Caesar what's Caesar's

Oh, dear Christ, long haired half jew agitator from Palestine, when the Roman Empire, built on slavery, was powerful, what did you think of Pontius Pilate liberalism?

What did you feel when he washed his hands & gave you to the local bourgeoisie to finish the job?

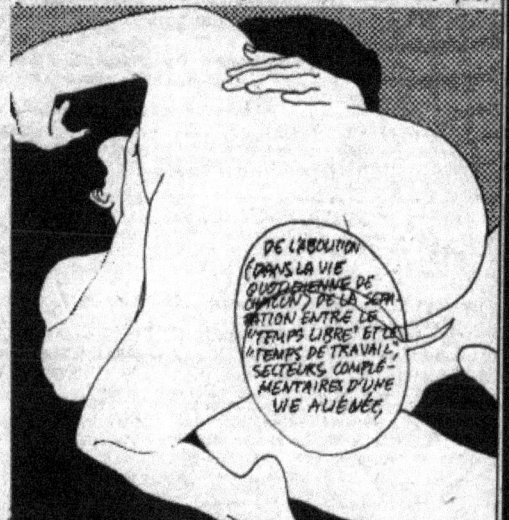

DE L'ABOLITION
(DANS LA VIE
QUOTIDIENNE DE
CHACUN) DE LA SEPA-
RATION ENTRE LE
"TEMPS LIBRE" ET LE
"TEMPS DE TRAVAIL"
SECTEURS COMPLÉ-
MENTAIRES D'UNE
VIE ALIÉNÉE,

At this phase of the present struggle — it is the Work-Concept which must be endangered and ultimately nullified.

(Lumumba, Guevara & the ones who are forgotten and await revenge).

In the catacombs of Rome, slaves drunk on freedom made the empire tremble. Your Christians burn like torches for not giving to Caesar what is Caesar's. There are more men than lions, always, when guerrilla of the mind is engaged. & then they made a Party, with a God in residence & party leaders and officials.

What happened after that was inevitable.

Now God is dead & Caesar fears the Ides of March, because there is only one way of loving thy neighbour, that of not giving anything to God & not giving anything to Caesar.
11.

Society is a plastic flower

The police of our minds, the plastic police, the mass media, are the pouring everlasting rain soaking my heart, the marrows of my bones, the cavity of my brain. The producers of nightmares have attached to my body an obscene shadow I can not shake off, whatever I do. The shadow of fear.

It's fear which makes me work (I have to survive) & without fear my typewriter could produce stars.

It's fear which builds my day (I have to be alive) & without fear people would be daisy-chains around my neck.

In others I see the mirror of my shadow, the same shadow. But in their pupils, which regulate the admission of the light, often I see a gleam, before the eyelids descend.

It is that gleam that, focused like a global laser, will pierce the plastic dome and melt it.
12.

Beware of those who say: 'it's not that simple'

They are the clerics of the dark rites.

Be weary of books which tell you 'how'.

The paths to your liberation are yet untrodden.

To those who say that the "enemy" is still strong, tell them they are the enemy.

Would-be leaders, shoot on sight, it will save time later.

Let us not have one single thought of mine matching yours. Ask for the unison in action, but not in thoughts.

To those who distil rules about the multitudes of futures in store, your attitude should be both of scorn & pity. They are vestal virgins of deserted churches, rallying the waning faithful.

To those who cultivate their gardens, say nothing. Their awakening will be rude, and salutary.
13.

Situationists

Imitations from Raul Vaneigem, author of the book:
'Traite de savoir-vivre a l'usage des jeunes generations.'
A tribute to the ideas that the producers of nightmares & the consumers of alienation will never be able to integrate.
Let — Vaneigem, my friend — the mass media spread them.
Let them buy the noose which will hang them. AQ.

Objects are the gravestones of the cemetery of our lives. You own an object, it owns you. When you consume your life.

People are the only instruments of your pleasure, & if you try to own them, they become objects too: wives.

The sabotage of the system is poetically expressed by those young people who steal the books which show the reasons for their discontent.

Megalomania, often sterile, is also a good tool against the coalition of forces which repress free will. It's the powder which never gets dry, good stuff for dynamite.

Spontaneity is the only mode of expression of individual creativity. Where the light of creativity still flickers, spontaneity has a chance of survival.

To those who refuse the present laws of our world only by instinct, we must say that there is an abyss between fighting in order to create a new life and fighting in order to stay alive. They have to cross that abyss with knowledge. Creativity without knowledge is poetry without style.

To get the feeling of your alienation from life, think of people in the streets, think of their meetings. Each one of them is the policemen of his own behaviour. Chase the policeman from your mind, is the slogan.

It must be said: since human non-communication is what it is, what the world of hierarchy makes it to be, we follow the etiquette of silence as the lesser evil, in a landscape where men are objects.

Misery of conscience forges killers for the state, Consciousness of misery forges the killers of the state.

Like the sexual act, which is not for the procreation, but very accidentally produces children, in the same way our forced labour produces changes, as if in an afterthought. We are changing the world?

Look around! The world changes in the way enforced labour makes it change: that is why it changes so badly.

Hope is the leash of submission. The kettle boils, power provides the spout of hope for the future. An adjustable safety valve, hope for the future is fear of the present.

Like Pascal's thinking reed, we can bend to power, & just survive. Our masochism is the only dead wood feeding the pyre of power, & making our will to live into smoke.

What is an Ideal (God, King, Country, Communism) if not a lie for the people, & a truth which serves the masters?

The more the consuming machine gobbles up the producing machine, the more we are governed by seduction, the less by force.

To create life as if an art is now becoming a popular idea. The vicissitudes of that idea, & the ways to spread it, are the only concern of the new revolutionaries, the new poets.

The armies of power can only recruite psychological cripples. They are beginning to have difficulties in recruiting soldiers, policemen, even clerks.

That is obviously why they are trying to substitute them fast by computers, & missiles.

The area of enforced labour diminishes, but the area of enforced leisure increases in proportion. To each according to the needs of production & consumption.

We live in times when the ideology of consuming has consumed all ideologies. Do not underestimate East-West relations! On one side, homo consumator buys a bottle of whisky & gets in exchange the lie which follows. On the other, homo communist buys ideology & gets in exchange his bottle of vodka.

One system consumes, in order to produce, the other produces in order to consume.

9

Our limitations are inside us, & we rationalize it with ideologies, & give them solidity with politics.

The will to be free from all strictures; the will to battle against all that corrupts; this is the will that has widened the old arena of the class-struggle. Subjectivity, the new subjectivity, makes the battle larger, & more deadly.

The 'party' of the 'will to live' is a political party. We do not want a world where we exchange the certainty of not dying of starvation for the certainty of dying of boredom.

The same drains the blood of the worker in his hours of enslaved work & in his hours of enslaved leisure. Those who speak of revolution & class struggles without talking about the enslavement of our daily life, without knowing that the only spring of rebellion is our love for life, & our hate of imposition, those talk with a corpse in their mouths.

Creation of pleasure is pleasure of creation.

The concept of pleasure knows no limitations. Pleasure either flourishes or shrinks. Repetition kills it. Pleasure is only for the total man, for the free one. Eroticism is pleasure trying to find its style. We must create, in social life, all the conditions for pleasure, for the absolute pleasure which is in love-making.

There to serve the present established order, & any establishment to come. Gulliver pinned down by the Lilliputians.

Love &

respect for the family
These are extracts from a Russian Propaganda Book called "MEN'S DREAMS ARE COMING THROUGH"

When Inessa Armand included in the plan of a pamphlet she was going to write for women proletarians the statement that even a fleeting passion was more poetic & pure than the loveless kisses of a vulgar couple, Lenin objected emphatically. He considered it impermissible not only to advocate "free love" but to justify any fleeting passion or infatuation.

"The loveless kisses of a vulgar couple are *dirty*. I agree. In contrast to them there should be – what? *Loving* kisses, it would seem. You, however, contrast them with a 'fleeting' (why fleeting?) 'passion' (why not love?), the logical result being that loveless (fleeting) kisses are contrasted by the loveless kisses of a married couple . . . That is strange. Wouldn't it be better, in a popular pamphlet, to contrast philistine-intellectual-peasant . . . vulgar & dirty matrimony devoid of love with proletarian civil matrimony based on love . . .?"

Lenin's conclusion about civil matrimony based on love defines the nature of the Soviet family under communism as well.

Love involves two persons, and results in the birth of a child. This is a matter of concern for society & it entails a duty in respect of the community. This is why society controls matrimonial relations & condemns sexual license in no uncertain terms.

Communist society, while not indulging in the petty regulation of the private lives of people, will do all in its power to strengthen the foundations of the healthy family. The important changes that will occur in family life as society advances to communism, & the expansion of the manifold social links between people will gradually lead to the family shedding many of its past & present features & functions. This is not to say, however, that the family will disintegrate or wither away, as bourgeois propaganda asserts.

What changes will the family undergo in communist society? A short working day – the shortest ever – will enable the adult members of the family to give more time to their cultural pursuits & to the education of the children, which will be modified organisationally, with society shouldering much of the burden.

The family will always be able to educate the children morally. Parents' example & that of all senior members of the family, the children's participation in domestic work, the cultivation of good family traditions, & family honour & pride will never lose their beneficial effect. One of the important things in the moral code of the builders of communism is mutual respect in the family, & concern for the education of children.

The family will develop & become stronger, making the lives of people increasingly full. The communist family will join forces with society as a whole to bring children up to be industrious, morally & physically healthy people always striving to improve their knowledge, enjoying the beauty of life & fully appreciating its value.

Survivals of the old, outmoded way of life are particularly tenacious in the family. Habit & customs that people have inherited or developed persist for a long time & exert conservative influence. This is why family life is slower to change than economic & political relations. The replacement of one socio-economic formation by another does not transform people's way of life overnight.

In communist society matrimonial relations will not be ruled by dependence. Family relations will be completely rid of material considerations, & will be based solely on mutual love & friendship. This does not imply, however, that there will be no contradictions in the family under communism. It may well be, for example, that the husband (or the wife) will cease to love his wife (her husband) because of a new love. But such complications will occur far less frequently than nowadays.

Will monogamy exist in communist society, or will there be a new development in matrimonial relations?

"Monogamy," wrote Engels, "arose out of the concentration of considerable wealth in the hands of one person – & that a man – & out of the desire to bequeath this wealth to this man's children & to no one else's. For this purpose monogamy was essential on the woman's part, but not on the man's; so that this monogamy of the woman in no way hindered the overt or covert polygamy of the man. The impending social revolution, however, by transforming at least the far greater part of permanent inheritable wealth – the means of production – into social property, will reduce all this anxiety about inheritance to a minimum. Since monogamy arose from economic causes, will it disappear when these causes disappear?

"One might not unjustly answer: far from disappearing, it will only begin to be completely realised."

And so, monogamous relations, the bulwark of family love & personal happiness, will exist under communism as well. Respect for the family is a highly important feature of the communist way of life. We live today more and more along communist lines, that is, in mutual trust & friendship.

Moral Purity

The moral code of the builder of communism embraces all important relations: in the sphere of morality those between the individual & society, the individual & the collective, work relations, & relations between individuals. Its fundamental principles are:

"devotion to the communist cause; love of the socialist motherland & of the other socialist countries;

"conscientious labour for the good of society – he who does not work, neither shall he eat;

"concern on the part of everyone for the preservation & growth of public wealth;

"a high sense of public duty; intolerance of actions harmful to the public interest;

"collectivism and comradely mutual assistance: one for all & all for one;

"human relations & mutual respect between individuals – man is to man a friend, comrade and brother;

"honesty & truthfulness, moral purity, modesty, & unpretentiousness in social & private life;

"mutual respect in the family, & concern for the up-bringing of children;

"an uncompromising attitude to injustice, parasitism, dishonesty, careerism & money-grubbing;

"friendship & brotherhood among all peoples of the USSR; intolerance or national & racial hatred;

"an uncompromising attitude to the enemies of communism, peace & the freedom of nations;

"fraternal solidarity with the working people of all countries, and with all peoples."

10

Bedtime Story

Peter Buckman

y school is nicely organized. When the headmaster
ouldn't cancel religious assembly, we kept him in his
om for three days until he nearly died. He had to have
rgery to make him pee.

When the English mistress threatened my friend
ttina with detention, the whole class barricaded
emselves in & stayed a week. We had food thrown up
us. Miss Lethebridge (English teacher) has a nasty scar
her head. I think it was caused by a chair. Detention
't fair.'

We had a new young maths master who wanted to
ch us new ways to add. We don't like adding. It's only
ed for counting money. We wanted more art &
story, especially about the slaves' revolt. The new
aths master left after two days. His hair changed
lour.'

They tried to force us to do P.T. Fat Louis always got
because his father is a rich doctor & he told the head
uis had a weak heart. Louis never used to do any
ercise. He got driven to school every day, until we
rnt his car. Then we took him to the gym &
reatened to exercise him till he dropped unless they
pped compulsory P.T. They stopped. Louis goes to
other school now.

The funny thing is what our big brothers & sisters do.
ey got very excited about not being able to sleep in
e girls' dormitory. So they went in & the police came
lots of people got hurt & they still can't sleep in the
rmitory. We do it all the time. No fuss.

They were worried about exams too. Every time they
rry about something the police get called in. Perhaps
because they're older. Anyway, as soon as that
ppens, they all split up into little groups & argue
out what to do. Then their little groups fight amongst
emselves & the police take away those who fall down.
e winner calls itself something like "The Union" &
es & talks to the headmaster, or the President, or
atever. By then they're so tired they forget what they
re originally worried about. Or perhaps "Unions" are
ry forgetful things — we've never had one.

Our big brothers & sisters don't know who to
pport. They rush round to factories when there's a
ike & get thrown out. They rushed round to us when
barricaded ourselves & we threw them out. Why
ven't they got anything of their own to do?

Besides they spend all their time making speeches.
ch little group invents something called a
rogramme' & they talk & talk until everyone falls
leep & then the one who's talking declares his
ogramme carried. Then he falls asleep, & the police
me. Programmes are very tiring — we've never had
e.

What I don't understand is why our big brothers &
ters go on telling us to "make the revolution" when all
ey're doing is boring each other to death.

What I don't understand is why our big brothers &
ters argue like our parents, & get all organized like our
rents, & act exactly like our parents, & still go on &
about how awful our parents are.

They won't be any use to us. We'll have to get rid of
them too.

12

13

THE THREE LITTLE PIGS.

Once upon a time there were three little pigs. The first little pig built a house of straw, the second little pig built a house of sticks, and the third little pig built a house of bricks.

One day a big bad wolf approached the house of the first little pig. "Let me in," he said, "or I'll blow your house down." The little pig was too frightened to open the door. The wolf huffed and puffed, the house fell down and the first little pig was eaten up.

"Let me in, let me in" the wolf said to the second little pig, "or I'll blow your house down." The second little pig was too frightened to open the door, the wolf huffed and puffed, the house fell down, and the second little pig was eaten up. "Let me in, let me in," said the wolf to the third little pig, "or I'll blow your house down." The third little pig was too frightened to open the door, the wolf huffed and puffed, the house fell down, and the third little pig was killed by falling bricks.

MORAL: Those who build houses must take the consequence. Does it really matter whether you are eaten alive or buried alive?

RAMSDEN

A Vicious God

FRAGMENT OF A TAPE FOUND IN AN ASTEROID OF OUR NEAREST GALAXY, 4 LIGHT YEARS FROM US: THE ALPHA CENTAURI

I am about to destroy you, before leaving this wretched part of the Universe.

When I put life, the first spore, into the solar system, I was counting on a few million years of fun. & fun I had at first, watching the first amoeba secrete its mucus, the first slimy cold snake devour tender unarmed flesh, the big monstrous giants tearing themselves apart, horn against claws, fangs against beak, teeth against poison.

The roaring of the beast torn to shreads by its pursuers, the last spasms of death & the mad dance of the scavengers high on blood, the petrified pupils of young animals trapped by fire, oh that was pleasure, millions of years of it!

I remember when the glacial periods advanced. Majestic trees would slowly & inexorably die trapped by the biting ice, or would be uprooted by the rushing waters & be left on the shore, roots looking obscenely at the sky, left there to rot, that was worth it. I enjoyed the scorching sun burning the grass, turning green fields to dust & the dried tongues craving for water. & the sudden madness of the animal caught by the sting of the scorpion was pleasurable . . . . . .

fighting for the mother's tits & dying blindly.

From one species to the other, up the painful evolutionary ladder, I've seen many a twisted shape with no hope of surviving, developing inadequate organs & breeding offspring like factories, producing useless specimens which were prey to others.

The carnage was sublime. Never, never boring.

Insects were lovely too.

There was undiluted poetry in the insects caught in spider's webs, struggling to free itself while the spider approaches to feast on it. There is a quality, a refinement in their velvet deadliness, a purity in the scorpio's sting, an irony in the queen bee & her chasing males which surpasses the gory slaughter of the mastodons.

But you get tired of everything, in time. That's why I had built in the evolutionary mechanism in the first spore, so that I could watch my show in progress, an evolving die-in where the agonies of one era would give birth to more complex, more sophisticated cryings.

The birth pangs had always been a special favourite of mine. From the lacerating howls of elephantial monsters spilling into the open their enormous baggages in a gush of blood, to the quiverings of the miriads of ants & their incessant fabrications, reproductions were the highest moments of my spectacle.

Death had the thrill of the utter, final destruction of a creature, the fine ending of the miserable mortal animals. Their expressions in those moments when confronted by the total horror of the unknown, when all their beings cried out in revolution against the final enemy, that was satisfying.

I do not mention the masturbation of the first ape, the grimace & the lips of the first furcoated simian savagely grinning at its ejaculations, or the explosion of colours . . . . . .

were the same, only he who knows more can suffer more. There was, though, already a difference in quality.

To see him frightened to death by thunder, annihilated by the swelling of a river, grunting in useless search for food had a new thrill which more then compensated for the previous chaos of the beastly parade. Pain had been given a tongue, & could now speak for itself. A new world to conquer.

Tribes toiling in their little corner of the world, fearful & yet resourceful, often at the mercy of the elements but always patiently rebuilding over the ruins.

& then the great moment of novelty, the delicious unparalleled moment which will never come again. THEY KNEW!

These crawling, scrounging, feeble little simians knew about me!

The little fools were making drawings, even ritual offerings for their dead, trying to placate & ingraciate with rituals, it was touching, I was no longer alone!

To see them butcher a calf and offer it in a ceremony was a new form of joy. The days of the mindless agonies of the beasts was far behind. It was the dawn of a new era.

New joys were in store. Fire had a good many uses, now that . . . . . .

the night of Saint Bartholomew.

Ecstasy. There were decades when the delights were so pure that the white heat burned all doubts, man had discovered the true nature of his maker.

When fighting beast, & slaughtering them, he was only cunning, & amusing, a colourful toy.

But when he started earnestly to plough fields & to put aside his bit against the hard times, I think it was only then that the real game started. His first offerings were clumsy, his rites very crude.

But it was a beginning. In his miserable state he had to worship the unknown & to sweat. To learn toil & accept sacrifice. & sacrifice was accepted in my name, & he invented thousands of names for me. Sometimes names of frustrated love, but mostly real names, I had become the image of his suffering, the reason for his suffering, the mirror of his misery.

Slavery was an endless source of entertainment. Only my name & my existence was the instrument of the crippling of minds & bodies. I was now living in every living soul, in his acceptance his of suffering I was glorified.

The masters of men were my best servants, my only servants. The beasts of the forests were no longer there, but the arena was better. Now, power held over men by the masters, in my name, was a many tentacled monster with a thousand heads, indestructable.

The heads had sweet insimes: sacrifice, necessity, immutability, acceptance. It could have gone on forever.

From the darkest hut to the courts my invisible hydra was showing its thousand heads. If one would be cut off, many would spring from its severed hideous neck. My officiants were very often deadly efficient.

the Inquisition was poetry . . . . . .

I started calling hierarchical power my hydra. Power was sacred, the rule was sacred, it had roots in my being. I was never so high, so high in the sky unreachable & so high in my pleasure. & I was never so low, so deep & rooted in every martyred peasant & quartered rebel. I had very few qualms. Sometimes the rulers themselves would get high on the power stemming from me & behave with the majesty of vi ciousness which was too close to my omnipotence. Masters of men tried to behave like gods. But they were passing qualms, man was firmly in the grip of the hydra & the blood was flowing endlessly, the major glory of myself.

I adored their doings, when they went on their voyage of discovery. The 200 Spanish conquistadores & their massacre of the Aztecs, was worth the all prehistorical era, & the real beauty of it, the culmination of my dreams, was the fact that it was done in my name. Beautiful outcasts would penetrate forests, swim rivers, cross oceans, to accomplish their mission, my mission, quartering natives, committing atrocities I had never thought of, thirsty for power denied to them in their own countries. They were drinking the blood of their victims in their furious impossible revenge against their own limitations. The strictures of their codes & rituals reduced them to maddened dogs. & yet, sometimes, when I would see how they were spreading & building everywhere, through blood & fire, yes, but with determination & skill, I would think in my moments of apathy, that maybe something got out of hand.

They were producing their own machines and their own misery, but if the misery was for my entertainment, the machines were for their advantage. My hydra had paled, its heads were getting lethargic . . . . . .

that not only I was doubting them, but they were in doubt about me! The old pleasures were still there, certainly, & some new ones too. The carnages were now unparalleled, internal

15

rivalries between the clans produced wars of unprecedented magnitudes for the partition of power, my power!

But something had definitely gone wrong, very wrong, they were getting out of hand as the result of it.

As if the hydra, my power, had now splintered in miriads of fragments, the spell was still there, but so watered down that it gave me very little pleasure anymore. They were all servants now, servants of their own machines & their social order, servants of their private fears, the very last bastion between them & their own leasure. The officiants of the old rites had been forgotten, in their gray world they were only one step from their accomplishment. I was frightened.

Desecration become more & more widespread, laughter was braking down barriers & self assertion was spreading like bushfire. We were near a cataclysm; I could not prevent & hated, we were near a revolution with no gods no masters, the old myth of Prometheus coming to life & taking over the place of the Gods. The signs were unmistakable. They were talking of a revolution which would establish their total freedom and give them access to the gates of joy, pleasure, fulfilment, so that each one of them could be his own master, his own god.

It was then that I took my decision, before it was too late......

he must have blown himself up, said Alan stopping the tape which was still running.

—ANON

Sparks

by Alan Jackson

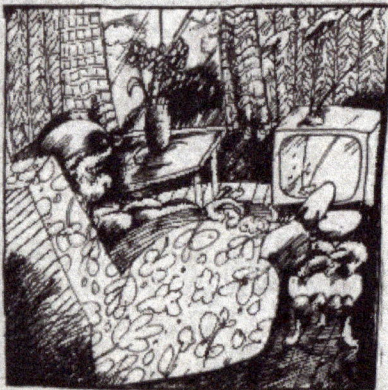

a hard day's work
lends a man dignity
and he is never out of debt

WHERE

apple cake distributed
   between the poor
not one asking
excuse me,
where
   do these apples
grow?

THWARTED

I live forlorn on the seventh floor
of a corporation flat
which the children all have fell from
and the pigeons have beshat.

I do not mind the loneliness
the long evenings with the tellie
but I do wish the wind hadn't altered the flight
of the brick I dropped on Jock Kelly

a man who was a spider
   married an adding machine
and produced the first president
   of the USSA.

AGAINST JOHN BERGER

'X is for ecstasy which is always suspect'
                              —John Berger

god bless the little gnome
& may all his lids fit:
& may he always have strong men handy
when the wind do blow

Oh Lesbia, live with me
& love me so
that we will laugh
at wise old men
with sour faces.
the sun which rose
once will rise again,
when our sun sets
follows night
& endless sleep.
Kiss me now
a thousand times
& then a hundred
& more hundred
of those thousand
till all the hundred
of thousand
kisses accounted &
unaccounted
of mine & yours
will make us
lose the count
so that the sores
will never learn
how many
of given
sweet kisses
& taken
delicious
we've had
kisses.
                    — Catullus

16

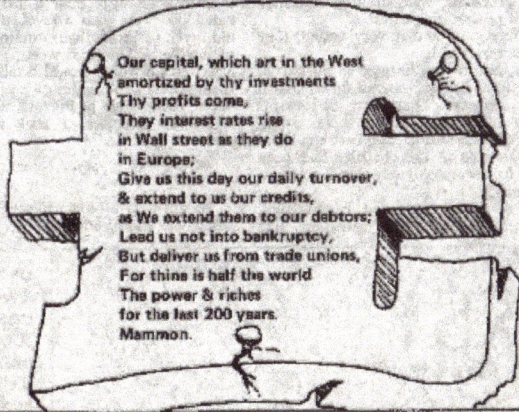

Our capital, which art in the West
amortized by thy investments
Thy profits come,
They interest rates rise
in Wall street as they do
in Europe;
Give us this day our daily turnover,
& extend to us our credits,
as We extend them to our debtors;
Lead us not into bankruptcy,
But deliver us from trade unions,
For thine is half the world
The power & riches
for the last 200 years.
Mammon.

For those who do not understand:

But we too, no longer concerned with the art of submission rather with that of non submission, & offering various proposals of an earthly nature, & beseeching men to shake off their human tormentors we too believe that to those who in face of the rising bomber squadrons of Capital go on asking too long how we propose to do this & how we envisage that, & what will become of their savings & Sunday trousers after a revolution, we have nothing much to say.

(from Bertold Brecht)

END

$200,000 MARIJUANA IS NO JOKE

MAYDAY FREAKOUT

Maybe May Day doesn't turn you on. But this year's procession is different. As the Socialist Worker puts it: "We are not marching through London to shout at the so called citadels of power. Unfortunately there are no Joshua's in the working class movement & the walls of the stock exchange will not fall down as we shout slogans . . . We are marching from Tower Hill through the East End to Victoria Park where we will *enjoy ourselves*." So drop out on May the first, and freak off to Victoria Park.

"My governor is going to be choked when I take the day off. He's going to be double choked if I enjoy myself" — building worker.

MOZIC:

Quote of the month from Janis Joplin in London on hearing that her scheduled front cover spread in the current 'Newsweek' had been abandoned due to Eisenhower's death: . . "Goddam the motherfucker . . . fourteen heart attacks & he had to die on my week. My bloody week!"

HOW TO TELL IF YOUR TELEPHONE IS TAPPED.

Replace the exchange code of your 'suspected' phone number with 175. Thus, if the number of the telephone you wish to test is 229:7541; then, using that phone, dial 175:7541. You will hear a recorded voice at the other end saying: "start test now". Put the receiver down immediately. If it rings back, your phone is innocent. (Silence at other end) If not, it's bugged. The above code is also used by G.P.O. technicians to test the bell. This test is infallible.

17

CITY STUDENT '69
PRESENTS

Sadlers Wells Rosebury Avenue EC1. (nearest tube Angel).
At 3 pm. Sunday April 27th.

MOODY BLUES & JOE HARRIOTT'S INDO JAZZ FUSIONS.
Compere David Symonds.
Tickets 5/-, 10/6, 15/-, 20/-, 25/-.

At 7.30 pm.
PENTAGLE & EAST OF EDEN
Tickets 5/-, 10/6, 15/-, 20/-, 25/-.

JAZZ CONCERT
Sunken Garden, Bunhill Row, EC1.
(nearest tube Moorgate)
From 8 – 11 pm. Tuesday 29th April.

DON RENDELL & IAN CARR QUINTET
Tickets 5/-

FOLK CONCERT
Sunken Garden, Bunhill Row, EC1.
(nearest tube Moorgate)
From 8 – 11 pm. Thursday 1st May

THE TINKERS, ALEX CAMPBELL, JOHN MARTYN
Tickets 5/-

Lyceum Ballroom, Strand, WC2.
All-nighter 12 – 6 am.
Friday May 2nd.

ALAN BOWN, SPOOKY TOOTH, JON HISEMAN'S COLOSSEUM, HERBIE GOINS & THE NINETIMERS, PORTRAIT
Compere Radio 1 DJ Johnny Farlowe.
Tickets 18/- in advance from City University Student's Union, St. John's Street, EC1.

Sadlers Wells, Rosebury Avenue, EC1.
(nearest tube Angel).
3 pm. Sunday 4th May.

JULIAN CHAGRIN LIVERPOOL SCENE
A splendid time is guaranteed for all.
An afternoon of mime, wit, pop, and poetry.
Tickets 5/-, 7/6, 10/-, 12/6

18

TWISTED WORDS PRISON PERSON GO OUT GO

PROBABILITY LEAPS TO
NATION SUFFERING PASS THROUGH HEAD

SEE LOYALTY PERSON

TIME THE STAR

HAVING SORROW START EXCELLENCE POINT TREAT

CAGE OPEN BAMBOO LIGHTNING GO OUT REAL

DRAGON

WORD PLAY

TAKE THE PERSON OUT OF THE PRISON INSERT PROBABILITY AND GET A NATION,
TAKE THE MOUTH AWAY FROM SUFFERING AND SEE THE BEGINNING OF LOYALTY,
A PERSON HAVING SUFFERED HAS THE BEGINNING OF A POINT OF GREAT EXCELLENCE,
THE LIGHTNING COMES AND RIPS AWAY THE BAMBOO FROM THE CAGE AND THE REAL
DRAGON EMERGES.

HO CHI MINH *PRISON DIARY*.

COMMENTARY

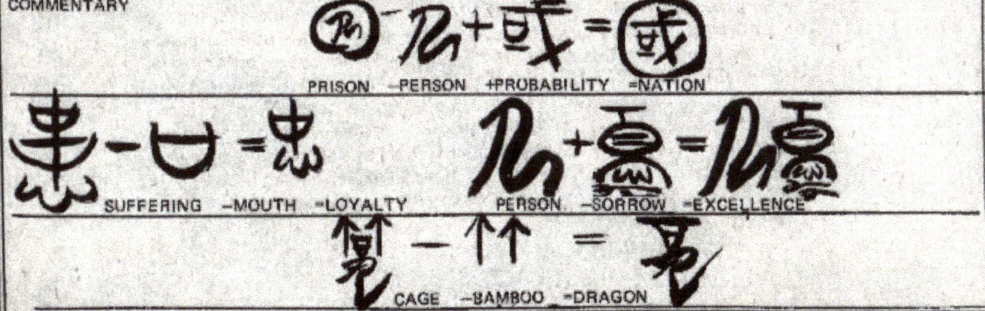

PRISON −PERSON +PROBABILITY =NATION

SUFFERING −MOUTH =LOYALTY   PERSON −SORROW =EXCELLENCE

CAGE −BAMBOO =DRAGON

19

Peter Mayer

20

The first in a series of Edwardian dialogues. McInnerney.

Men bend over! Women get ready! Children get lost! The DEVIANTS are coming! Agency: 01 – 493 7566

We require someone with thorough, practical knowledge of electronics & sound to design & make custom-built equipment on a freelance basis. Workshop facilities are available. Initiative is essential, as well as keen interest in new fields, such as Solid State Lighting etc. Apply: Broadbent Designs Ltd., 118A Holland Park Avenue, London, W.11. 01 – 229 8207/8/9

Famous Turn-On Book; how to synthesize LSD, THC, Psilocybin, Mescaline & more. £3.00 to Turn-Ons Unlimited, 6311 Yucca St., Hollywood, Calif. 90028 Dept 54. Includes postage & handling. Ecstacy or refund.

Layout Man, 42, tall & muscular, expert, seeks contact adventurous female aged 18 upwards, slimmish, lovable, spankable, liking drink & music. Phone John 01-584 9955 or write BM/TRUMP W.C.1. Time wasters please abstain.

Miss Nothing. See without being seen with two way, X-Ray, see through mirror. Easily made from readily available materials. Complete details 10/–. Mailservice, 21, Tooks Court, Cursitor Street, London, E.C.4.

A people community. 15 – 20 years, wanting to know yourself & others better? Write Box (3) 20 for live-in 'infor'.

Directory of Little Magazines & Little Presses. The 4th edition is now available & lists hundreds of avant-garde artistic, poetry, hip, underground publications throughout the world. Send 15/– to: DUSTBOOKS BCM/ORACLE London, W.1.

Girls & boys for nudie movies, exported only, not pornographic. Riviera Line Productions, 45, Hereford Rd., W.2. 01-727 9834.

Young guy, do anything, anywhere, anytime for bread. 01-675 0159.

Old pairs of spectacles needed to be reburnished & sent to underdeveloped countries. Help someone to see again, send to: Albert Baily, 'Hinstock', Marrowbook Lane, West Farnborough, Hants.

WORLD CALL! Swedish liberty in sex. Send 10/– (no postal Order) or $1 for rich illustrated brochures of magazines & photos. Outside Europe add $1. Adults Only. Write to: HERMES – OZ Box 6001, S-2001 Malmo 6, SWEDEN.

C.P.A. still need more Glamour Chicks for Nude/bikini/Glamour photography for our publishers overseas. We've had a tremendous response to our previous advertisements & a lot of girls have been given assignments as a result of their applications. This work is not pornographic. The advertiser is genuine. Modelling experience is not an essential quality – we are looking for girls who are uninhibited & who are possessed of an ability to inject that freedom into the pictures we take of her. She will be expected to pose nude, semi-nude, in bikinis, lingerie etc. Our 'ideal girl' would be fun-loving but still be wholly immersed in the work she is doing when she is doing it. The girl who can inject a little ray of sunshine into our rather 'dull' job will be assured of not just one job but as many jobs as we can feasibly assign her. PAYMENT IS GOOD but 'gold-diggers' are discouraged right from the start. Scrubbers need not apply' If you want to earn some money & are prepared to 'slave your guts out' then you should telephone 01-670-9276 any evening between 4.00pm & 9.00pm or all day Saturday & Sunday. C.P.A. 01-670-9276. C.P.A. wants to contact photographers for assignments. C.P.A. 10-670-9276. C.P.A. can supply models to other photographers. C.P.A. 10-670-9276.

SKINT CHICK INSTANT BREAD FOR HOUR'S AMATEUR POSING. NON-PUBLISHED, NON-PORN, & NON-INVOLVEMENT. Box No. (1) 20.

FERRY VANS FOR LIGHT REMOVALS 7 DAY SERVICE WITH WORKING DRIVERS. 485.0450.

Young West-End photographer with flair for the unusual will photograph the actual birth of your child. Telephone 01-262 0403, (day or night).

WRITER/TEACHER 32, goodlooking, looks/acts/dresses much younger, interested books (especially science fiction) writing (one paperback published), the occult, films personally affectionate, kind, loving, but uneasy at thought of having own children (my big hang up) & very untidy, seeks girl, definitely younger, educated, slim, longhaired, independent, strong sick sense humour, bold personality. Object, permanent relationship. No objections to manless mothers, in spite of above. Photo appreciated/reciprocated. Genuine ad, so please no time wasters. Jeremy Ward, Flat 2, 68 Fairhazel Gardens, LONDON N.W.6.

Fast duplicating from typed, drawn, photo originals. Miss Winder 01-MUS.9327.

SMALLS

ACCORD INTERNATIONAL BALL.

Camden Fringe Festival 1969

MAY 31st at the Roundhouse. From 9 p.m. to 2 a.m.

John Dankworth & his orchestra, Cleo Laine.
Flamenco guitarist, Paco Peña.
The Soft Machine
The Merrymakers Jamaican steel band. & possibly J. J. Jackson & John Hendricks & others to be announced.

A general carnival atmosphere with international booths, booze & things to eat.

2000 souvenir programmes to be given away free. Articles by prominent writers on race relations, photos by Cartier-Bresson.

Male Models required by physique photographer . . . All nationalities. Age up to 25. Full details & photographs to: J.D.S. Publications Mortimer House, 13A Western Road, Hove, Sussex.

C.M.C. offers male friendship, correspondence, holiday companions, ads. Details, 1/6. Box no. (2) 20

A male student (21) from overseas, very lonely & fed up, needs an intimate female friend. Age & appearance immaterial. Box (4) 20

DIRECTORY OF SOCIAL CHANGE

There is a crisis of information in the underground. Too much or too little or the wrong sort. The Directory of Social Change puts an end to all that. It is the first book of its kind ever published or conceived. Containing detailed information on all aspects of life & the alternate society. Here are some of them: community action/ intentional communities/ psychedelic churches/ experimental arts minority groups/ the law/ radical & underground publications/ city by city guide to the changing scene/ bibliography of change/ minority & deviant groups/ the sexual revolution. Indispensable to all broadminded & progressive people & all those who want a way out. It is your book because you are a part of it. Get your copy today. Copy £1 . . . The Fifth Estate Press is offering OZ readers a 25% discount if they order now. Send 15/- to: Fifth Estate Press, 64, Muswell Hill Road, London, N.10.

I want to go to college. No bread. Send me any old (or new) shillings or American quarters to Bill Medvesky Jr., Norwood, Massachusetts, U.S.A. I am completely serious & will spiritually thank those who help me.

John Peel said it, "If you want to know what is really happening, you MUST read Peace News". Currently available on a six week trial offer for 5/- from: Peace News, 5 Caledonian Road, London, N.1. It is much more important to read than anything else.

TAXIMOVES: Light removals in 1 & 2 ton vans with helpful working drivers. Phone 01 – 722 7661 Please quote this advertisement.

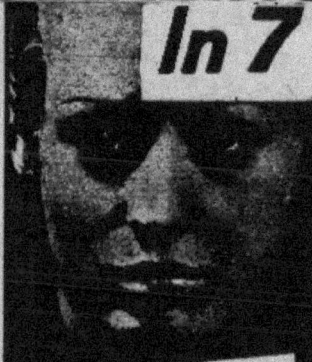

hip pocrates

(copyright 1969)
Eugene Schoenfeld
M.D.

QUESTION: How can a male determine whether or not he is circumcised? I am not sure about myself.

ANSWER: Buy the John Lennon-Yoko album. Neither John nor Yoko are circumcised.

QUESTION: First, my current female companion thoroughly enjoys my uncircumcised penis (it's the first she encountered, she said) which has prompted me to abandon plans to have the foreskin lopped off. We both find it pretty groovy for her to play with, which she does for long periods.

Therefore, we both disagree with the observations of your "assistant" that the shot of John Lennon's uncircumcised penis is ugly, thereby implying that all uncircumcised penises are ugly.

Now the problem: We both engage in oral stimulation in our frequent sexual relations, and as much as I hate to admit it, my chick complains sometimes about the "smell" caused by the presence of my foreskin. I think the medical term for the substance formed under the foreskin is smegma, right? (right) I wash under there as carefully and as often as I can to combat this, but it's a real drag for me to jump up from our play and rush to the bathroom to rinse off my penis to kill the smell and then run back.

You can imagine how this would cool off things.

What can I do? If I wash ahead of time, everything is OK, but I don't always know when we are going to swing together and can't plan so far ahead. I've suggested going ahead with the circumcision, but my chick is against it. Besides, I've been told by my doctor that a circumcision takes about 10 days to two weeks to heal and can be pretty painful during the first 6 days, especially if one gets an erection.

ANSWER: Maybe you've discovered one of the original causes for circumcision. Smegma is also suspected as a cause for cancer of the cervix, a disease seldom found in Jewish women (at least those married to Jewish men).

QUESTION: My physician accepts the theory that one should go off birth control pills every 4 years in order to prevent future difficulties in pregnancy.

I'd like to know what evidence supports this theory.

ANSWER: Because birth control pills have been used clinically only for the past ten years, many physicians take their patients off the pills at periodic intervals as a precautionary measure. Time limits on the use of birth control pills had been recommended by the manufacturers and the U.S. Food and Drug Administration until recently but no adverse effects from long term use of "the pill" have yet been discovered.

QUESTION: I've been told all the sperm is ejected after the first ejaculation. After that, the story goes, one may have another orgasm, or several, but for 36 hours or so, he won't be able to father a child.

If I could do it with a rubber at night and without it in the morning, I'd be happy.

ANSWER: I hope you read this soon. The amount of sperm does decrease with each subsequent orgasm during a fixed period of time (say 48 hours) but you can certainly impregnate your friend(s) each and every time. The average emission of semen may contain 500 million spermatozoa and each one could conceivably cause a girl to conceive.

HIPPOCRATES is a collection of letters and answers published by Grove Press, $5.00. Dr Schoenfeld welcomes your questions. Write to him c/o PO Box 9002, Berkeley, California, 94709. Mark your letters, OZ.

ROAST TRAFALGAR PIGEON

Total Cost around 11d, (the price of a small, uncut loaf), plus whatever vegetables you can afford/steal. Total Preparation time 4-6 hours.

Ingredients

As above. 1 fat pigeon per person or three skinnies between two should prove sufficient.

Method

Clear a room of all furniture and breakable objects. Open the windows wide. Cut the loaf and deposit half back into the bread bin, (to be used for cold fowl sandwiches the following day), crumbling the remainder liberally from the window ledge in a winding, 'paper-chase' trail across the floor. Leave the room and close the door. Don't stand outside trembling with anticipation, birds have amazingly acute hearing. Go away and make yourself a cup of tea.

When you've finished your tea pick up an old blanket or bedspread and walk back, removing your shoes first to avoid noise. Burst in. Don't bother listening at the key-hole — if there are no pigeons in the room then nothing is lost — if there are, run immediately to the window and shut it, slamming the door with a backward kick as you do so. Examine your prey. Be choosey. Contrary to nursery rhyme instruction sparrows and blackbirds make lousy pie-material, let alone a roast. Assuming you have two or three excited, squawking pigeons as prisoners the next step is to capture them bodily, using your blanket as a net.

There is another, slightly more sophisticated method of obtaining these birds that may be worth noting — providing you live within easy reach of Trafalgar Square. It's simple. Borrow or beg a zip-up carrier bag, the larger the better. Sprinkle in it half the loaf. Stand in the Square, and opening the bag, you have merely to wait until the required number of meals are gathered gorging themselves within. Then zip the bag and return home.

Killing pigeons is easy and painless, (to both parties), as long as the procedure is carried out methodically and firmly. Grasp the bird across its back, beak pointing away from you, in your left hand. This effectively controls all wing movement and allows your right hand to twist the head three-quarters of a revolution, clockwise, jerking the neck upwards at the same time. The bird will struggle for approximately 45 seconds before becoming limp but continue holding the neck strained in this position for at least two minutes to ensure death.

Split the beak horizontally with a sharp knife and hang by the legs to drain away excess blood. Leave for several hours if possible. Pluck feathers, excepting those on the wings and head, and allow to soak in salty water, again for as long as possible. Cut off head and claws and snap wing out from the knuckle. Using the knife split the stomach slightly and remove the nastier looking intestines. Roast in oil or margarine with new potatoes in a moderately hot oven. Remember to baste, (pour hot fat over the top of the bird with a spoon), occasionally. A casserole with these birds is even more delicious. Either way it's free, nourishing stuff. One word of warning — it's probably illegal.

Golden Rule

Do not, under any circumstances, twist the neck anti-clockwise.
Felix/Ken P

OUT OF THE PSYCHODRAMA

David Widgery

Once again, like a nation on heat, we enter some summer. With sun on the nylons & a pair of froggish sunglasses, England will take its holiday time for the next four months. The beautiful middleclass will further extend their self-organisation for the consumption of pleasure through such glossaries as Time Out & the internal bulletin of the ICA. The pressing questions of apres-beachwear, leg makeup & duty free cannabis will for the months to come occupy mens minds. The sales of garden forks, tambourines, tennis rackets & methylamphetamine will grow, as will dancing in the park, public sorcery & the other advancing orders of hippy emptiness. But for those who find the easy pleasures difficult still & find wasting time timewasting; for those (other than the accountants of recently radicalised publishing houses) who remember last May in France: things are a lot different this summer.

Politically, our May days may be the whole year round; 1969 will be the best year since 1945 to gain a footing & a hearing in what the class revolution is all about & whose absence from politics has defined every protest movement of the last twenty years by the workers themselves. Whether the abbatoir of the extreme Left is in fact capable of being more use now than it would be sunbathing in Green Park is another matter; but the opportunity, the opening through which revolutionaries can provide the sort of politics & analysis workers are starting to feel in need of, that political eye of the needle is there. Unfortunately over the last three years the notion of the revolutionary overthrow of capitalism in the West has been mainly nourished by the demonstration of the peasants of Asia & some important parts of Latin America to militarily defeat the imperial aims of North America. But the wringing of the maxims of Mao & the study of apt texts on guerilla war didn't disguise the insuthenticity of the act of identification. Whether the national teams of the peasant world were applauded from the director's box (a la New Left Review) or by the Vietnam Solidarity Campaign in the stands, for a British socialist the statement was one of impotence, though certainly an impotence of a different order than the position of the Marxists bivoacked in the liberal prairies of CND . . . this time our side looked like winning. Nor was talk of police repression in this country much more than wooliness or hysteria; we are drilled by injustices at present more elusive. The arithmetical addition of the Cuban emphasis that 'The duty of the revolutionary is to make the revolution' to an over optimistic & usually ill-informed version of what happened in May turned out to be a short cut to nowhere except a lot of toxic cross about fuzz terror by people who would clearly have difficulty telling the Keystone Cops from Securicor. The urban black proletariat are the only people who are fighting the police & winning.

The tactical exhaustion & subsequent political disintegration of the VSC after the October march (probably the biggest under revolutionary banner since the chartists) must have depended not a little on the unconcious assumption of many that marched of ideas of sparking, detonating or otherwise setting an example to workers. Because Cohn Bendit's spark set off a gigantic general strike which hoisted the red flag over factories, besieged police stations, for 30 days, ran whole zones of France under a species of workers control & only relinquished control of their lives & jobs after several bloody battles, we were destined to throw matches about the room & hide the fire extinguishers. & if this becomes your view then a set-back in a demonstration becomes a retreat for the movement, a tactical withdrawal becomes a political capitulation. Thus the self important quarrel's about march routes & the appalling & wasteful hyperbole (as late as the March 30th march this year, Maoist groups were talking of 'our target . . . the most desperately guarded & beleagured building in Britain; the hideout of the US mass murdered in Grosvenor Square') A similar fizzle is reported by the SDS campaign of fighting in the streets against the US election & inaug ration the German SDS's growing isolation & even the wilder forecasts of a Red October in France by those well heeled French revolutionaries who materialised in London.

Now it is certainly true that the militancy of students & blacks has in some cases reawakened factory workers to their own traditions; several factory occupations have taken place in Britain. One for 17 days. But then they don't talk about that too much in the papers. It's also true that the barometers by which political interest or disinterest are normally monitored (membership of political organisations, electoral voting, Trade Union branch participation) were all quite unable to predict the spontaneous revolt in France & are equally unlikely to do so here. The frozen slopes of post war politics are melting fast, one action can set off an avalanche. But since the nature of the spark is essentially unpredictable there is little point in trying to provoke it into existence, rather the job is to create a sultry atmosphere where the spark will spread. The psychodrama of the student power expert of the vietnam militant is a nonsense without a working class in action & this cannot be manufactured by students or TV programmes. It can & is being manufactured by Harold Wilson & we should be precious glad.

For what's happening over those very two years that Grosvenor Square rang with curses is that the essential business of the British ruling class was failing. The Government were being unable to dismantle that industrial awkward squad, the shop stewards, the only centre of independent political power stopping the solution of British capitalism's crisis at the expense of the majority. The struggle has been conducted with typical British hypocrisy, despite ostentatious declarations for the gnomes benefit & the public clobbering of weak & vulnerable workers (notably the seamen, builders & contracting electricians), Barbara & Ray climbed down quickly & quietly when faced with determined union organisation or stray solidarity feeling (as in docks & post office). While the threat at least of the Prices and Incomes policy has held down the wages head of steam, the white-coated, slide-ruled, productivity magicians have attempted their sleight of hand on the shop floor. But even then the expected improvements have failed to come over the hill. Rather the reverse; after four years of belt-tightening, things have never been worse; the moment the economy looks like expanding, its tendency to such in imports forces a cutback which in turn depresses investment. The Crisis, once occasional as in Suez or Profumo, becomes the permanent crisis as in exports, productivity, unemployment.

The more Wilson attempts to fill the bath with the plug still out, the more loony the attempt looks & is, the more incredible the politics that underly it, the less acceptable the avuncular manacles of Mrs Castle. Four years tinkering with the trade unions raw nerve has at last founds its response among the better organised workers (car men, printers, engineers) & the regional centres of labour indiscipline (Merseyside and Clydeside). As a gesture of how much they care about the disguise, the lies & the greater glories of the export drive, that highest of man's aspirations, half the total of British workers failed to turn up on New Years Day. On 27th February there was, surprise, a national strike against the Incomes Policy more important than one hundred Vietnam marches. More important too than the struggle at LSE was the readiness with which revolutionary students were received at the Fords picket line. & on the 1st of May, there promises to be a major political strike, one which the union leaderships have to support but do not control & which will be organised by workers, students & oddball militants. & if Wilson lasts long enough to put through his anti-strike laws, there will be a lobby of Parliament which far from pleading with MPs will probably take Whitehall apart. Those who witnessed workers knocking chunks off the palace of Westminster in 1962 will know the difference in the 'militancy' of a workers march & a Vietnam stomp. & those whose remembrance of this bland & torpid isle goes back to the St Pancras rent strike & the impact Irish site workers & railway men made on the 4,000 police who performed the eviction, must view with interest the United London tenants' Association's call for a rent strike if eviction goes ahead.

The point is not the sudden emergence of a worker's revolutionary movement which will make the politics of Nabarro & Anguilla look as pallid & adolescent as they are. What is happening is the much slower recovery of politics as a way of solving problems and belief in ideas as a way of thinking. The new movement will undoubtedly include new versions of left reformism (some Squatters) right reformism (Shelter etc) industrial syndicalism (the Workers Control movement) & anarchic fucking authority about (sabotage vandalism and overdue library books). But all these fragmented challenges raise questions which unlike orthodox Labour & TU politics do not entirely accept the arrangement of the existing society but starts to be subversive of the status quo. It is not a revolutionary movement that will win, indeed its splintered parts have proved relatively easy to co-opt, restrain, bamboozle or destroy one by one. But as the Labour Party finally decomposes & the Communist Party begins to act more & more like orthodox grand social democracy, the chance is there to build parties to the left of the CP which might have a certain influence.

Within these groups (the most important being at present International Socialism) with the arguments on the basis of shared experience which are the forge of the revolution. Such groups are even in France still tiny & unknown. But every further month of Labour's leaky steam roller is filling in another clue in the political cross word, another piece in the jigsaw of consciousness, until soon something that will be recognised by workers as their own will be visible in the revolutionary mosaic. In the setting sun of the Labour government in the blankness of the Tories & the coma of the Liberals, the shadow being cast again by the ideas of Marx, Lenin, Luxemburg & Trotsky are quite long. & quite potent.

Now no doubt the composers of pop songs & the makers of pretty clothes will find it increasingly difficult to ignore the rising level of social conflict & may borrow tension from it. But this pulling out of the chocks, kicking away of the stilts & blowing of the mind is merely the manufacturers description not the contents of the packet. The clownish idea that a Zappa on every turntable will turn the world red ignores the fact that its mainly succeeded in making big capitalist record companies bigger. The idea that the simpering Beatboys of pop are in fact the Archangels of revolutionary change ought finally to expire in the face of the Apple Saga wherein one Lennon, a hard, sarky, rock singer turns into a soggy, quietist TV celebrity & lived happily opening Oxfam bazaars & repelling take over bids. We will also hear a lot of condescending cabbage water from various 'experts' who wouldn't know Bukarin from Bakunin & would be more likely to associate Thermidor with sea food than the Paris Commune, that things are in danger of getting out of (their) hand & about the 'complex' (etc) problems of the 'real' (etc) world. & there will be the usual suggestions that the revolution is a warm gun, a fleshy girl turning on in a wood surrounded by portraits of Che Guevara, Madame Binh in Flask Walk or John Gollan as Minister of Red Productivity. It is not. It is industrial workers who have been socialist since they were born & are now refusing to vote Labour, its wanting to stop the strike law & not being sure whose going to help you, its the capacity for self-activity & self-education the British working class movement have always shown. Its what really happened in Russia in 1917, Spain in 1936, Hungary in 1956 & France in 1968. it's, in one of Eldridge Cleaver's wiser words, 'the difference between those who make up the problem & those who make up the solution'.

1964 & 1965: AMERICAN MASS MEDIA DISCOVERS THE HELL'S ANGELS. MOTOR CYCLE PACKS REPORTED ROAMING CALIFORNIAN HIGHWAYS, RAPING BABIES, TERRORISING THE GOD-FEARERS & FREAKING OUT THE HIPPIES. A NEW CULTURE – THE LOST VIRILITY REGAINED – THE ANSWER???

SATURDAY, AUGUST 7th, 1965 IN LA HONDA CALIFORNIA, KEN KESEY & THE MERRY PRANKSTERS (see OZ 3) TURN THE ANGELS ON TO LSD, DMT & CHRIST KNOWS WHAT. KESEY'S FANTASY PLACE – THE WOODS WIRED FOR SOUND MICROPHONES HORN SPEAKERS & BOB DYLAN. TREES COVERED IN DAYGLO. PEOPLE COVERED IN DAYGLO. THE BUILDING FULL OF EVERY IMAGINABLE PIECE OF ELECTRONIC EQUIPMENT. THE PRANKSTERS RECEIVE A BAND OF ANGELS IN RUNNING FORMATION ON THEIR MASSIVE CHOPPED THUNDERING HARLEY 74'S. ANGELS WITH BEARDS, LONG HAIR, SLEEVELESS DENIM JACKETS, DEATHS HEAD INSIGNIA... LOOKING THEIR MOST ROYAL ROTTEN. AMAZINGLY A FANTASTIC ALLIANCE BEGINS. THE ANGELS ADD KESEY & GINSBERG TO THEIR EXISTING LIST OF HIGHS – BENZEDRINE, METHEDRINE, POT, GRASS, BEER, SECONAL, AMYTAL, TUINAL, WINE ETC. & MORE ETC. THE PRANKSTERS ADD THE ANGELS TO THEIR MOVIE. EVERYWHERE IS KEN KESEY. LATER CHASED BY THE FUZZ – JAILED – THEN ON THE RUN & IN THE END REJECTED BY THE BEAUTIFUL PEOPLE. HE WANTED TO GET BEYOND ACID. ITS ALL DESCRIBED IN TOM WOLFE'S AMAZING BOOK 'ELECTRIC KOOL-AID ACID TEST. MEANWHILE OTHER BOOKS WERE BEING WRITTEN ABOUT IT ALL. 'HELL'S ANGELS' BY HUNTER THOMPSON, 'FREEWHEELIN FRANK' AS TOLD TO MICHAEL McLURE. PLUS ARTICLES IN EVERY BIT OF PRINT IN THE WORLD.

CHRISTMAS 1968: TWO HELL'S ANGELS ARE REPORTED IN LONDON. THE TRENDIES QUIVER & STRAIN TO GET AT THEM. RUMOURS ARE THAT THEY ARE STAYING AT APPLE – THROWN OUT BY GEORGE HARRISON? WHERE DID THEY GO? HOME.

MARCH, 1969: SQUATTERS & MEMBERS OF THE LONDON ARTS LAB OCCUPY A DERELICT HOTEL IN DRURY LANE. AS THE PRESSURE INCREASES PEOPLE BECOME EXCITED BY A PIECE OF NEWS. IT IS SAID THE HELL'S ANGELS ARE IN THE BUILDING. THE U S CAVALRY OVER THE HILL TO THE RESCUE? AN UNDERGROUND POLICE FORCE TO MATCH THE FUZZ? OR A MENACE TO AN ENGLISHMAN'S PAD?

I looked up to heaven
What did I see
Comin' for to carry me home
A band of Angels
Swing low Sweet Chariot
Comin' for to carry me home.

For a London Hell's Angel that sweet chariot is driven by Angel Levi – he is in charge of Rescue & Maintenance. "It's my job when they break down at Lands End or somewhere to go & get 'em in my van." But recently he had his colours taken away. Colours are the emblems all Angels, anywhere, wear. The top rocker says 'Hell's Angels'. Underneath it is a skull with feathers & 'MC' for motor cycle club. Below that is the bottom rocker which has the name of the chapter – in this case London. But Levi went & rolled an acid dealer to get some bread, didn't hurt him mind, there was no violence like & because the dealer was a friend of Jack Henry Moore & because J H Moore is a sort of Ginsberg-Guru figure for the London Hell's Angels & because everyone was very upset – Levi lost his colours – officially for eight weeks but maybe for ever because he appears to have just gone away.

Before all this happened I talked to Levi. The President, Crazy Charlie (why crazy? 'He's crazy that's why we call him crazy. Just crazy that's all') was in the nick charged with possessing offensive weapons & Levi was acting President. With him was Odd Job, an amiable Angel possessing all the physical beauty of a cut down fence post with pop eyes, and Christine, Levi's 18 year-old Old lady (Angel wife). What happened when the Drury Lane hotel was occupied?

LEVI: We moved into the hotel & Kylastron, the organiser there, a musician, a fucking good one & a nice type of bloke, was elected to organise things. Our part was to keep eyes on the place – security – to prevent people walking out of the place with stuff wherever possible & to control the flow of pot. We had quite a few turn outs, some of them at three o'clock in the morning – through smoking. Everyone who was there was against normal society & they wanted to be different. They don't like the

26

Andrew Fisher.

hell's angels

authority that everyone else runs under. We don't like authority ourselves that's why we're one percenters. We've got a lot of bad names put our way through acting like a mini gestapo force when we'd be asked to do something for their own sake.

ODD JOB: We were the one group that was organised, tight-knit, we knew how to act together.

LEVI: We'd never done this thing before we was asked. We had a meeting amongst ourselves & we decided that it would be a good scene for us in as much as we're doing good. Not all Angel chapters are good. Some has got a right bad name. Well we ain't got a bad name, but we haven't got a good name. We're not worried how our name is. We're Angels that's all we worried about.

ODD JOB: We have a reputation of being a bunch of hard nuts & I think that's made them a bit wary of us. When we walked into a room and told them to get out they went, they didn't want any part of us.

LEVI: One or two put up arguments & argued against us but they were only in a minority. It was the majority who carried over them. One night there was me, Crazy Charlie and Loser Pete up there smoking. Then it was decided in a meeting that there'd be no smoking on the premises. Later on someone told me there was a man smoking up there so I had to go up & tell him. 'Get rid of it.' Alright, next night the same thing happened, same man. Earlier the same evening we had had a meeting & agreed that we could ask people to leave if this was going on, so I had to ask him to leave. Alright, he was tripping at the time so when he got his stuff together he went. He came and saw Kylastron a couple of days later & asked if he could come back; he got his own room back, he moved in again; a couple of days after he moved in we had to throw him out again. He was permanently out this time for smoking.

ODD JOB: I might point out that during the two days he was away we looked after his gear & made sure that no-one took it.

LEVI: You know, it's a bit of a bind at times, you've got your own business to look after, we've got our own lives to lead & we've got to make our living same as everyone else has. It was a bit of a bind but I think by & large we enjoyed doing it. Now we stay at the Arts Lab — we've been thrown out everywhere else. If we left the place'd collapse — we run it without thanks.

But the underground's a great crowd really. We enjoy them as people they are just being what they are. They're very acceptable. We get on well with THEM. & I think most of them get on well with US. We had one upsetting time in the hotel when one of the chaps from I.T., Dave something, came down & declared that we had no right to wear the colours & that we weren't Angels. My first reaction to this guy from I.T. was to smack him in the eye. I told him I was prepared to come out into the street with my shirt off about it — so were the rest of the Angels there was about six of us in the room at the time. I pity him afterwards if he'd actually come out in the street. We're not hard cases or anything like that. You see this guy knew some of the Angels State-side, or at least he thinks he knows ... We told him the chapter had been authorised & we got a charter from the Frisco Angels from Oakland, when they were over here just before Christmas. There are a lot of other groups that call themselves Hell's Angels. The Nationale Angels have been running for about ten years & there's a hell of a lot of one percenters up & down the country. 99% of all motor-cyclists are law abiding citizens, a statement released by the American Motor-cyclists Association after there'd been some trouble with the Hell's Angels in the States, so naturally the rest of us are one percenters.

Anyway, it was decided that he'd phone up the Angels out there — we gave him the phone number of one of the Angels — Sweet William, & he did this & I think he was a little sick over it because he found that what we'd told him was so. We were rather pleased Sweet William said this because it was the first real contact we'd had with them since they went back over to the States.

It all started at Chelsea Bridge. There's only a dirty little old coffee stall up there but a congregation of motor-cyclists get up there from all over South London. They all end up there at some time or another, mostly in the early hours of the morning. Loser Pete, Red & Charlie who knew each other from the Bridge got into company with the Stateside Angels. This was at Christmas time. It was suggested, after the three of them had been kipping up with them & travelling round with them round the country, that they might start their own pack. I think now we've got about twenty five members. Unlike a lot of clubs we've all ridden together a number of times.

THE MIGHTY VULCAN

hell's who?

Rat Face is another Angel. He has two great aims in life – one is to be better than me. His top number of girls in one night is about eighteen – that's the number of times he's had it without pulling out – that is with one bird. In one session eighteen times without rolling off. MY greatest time so far is four different birds in one night.

But our aim in being Angels is to look after each other. If you don't YOU get looked after – in another way. Eventually we'll have a real big pack with us. We've got sufficient but we'll grow. We're only four months in existence as Angels, time will tell. People who want to be Angels find us, we don't find them. Then they have to have a 100% vote. It may mean that they have to hang round with us for months and months before they get 100% vote but that's up to them. Whether we like them personally or not doesn't matter, it's whether we think they'll make a good Angel. They must have a bike. If their bike's off the road it's got to be on again in thirty days, otherwise they hand their colours in. We've got to know if they've got class. When they join, the rest of the Angels at the initiation can shit, piss or vomit or do anything to a new members colours – then if he wants to be an Angel he has to wear them like that.

Odd Job and me have had Angel weddings. I was the first Angel to get his red wings and I'm rather proud of the fact.

This is my old lady here, Christine she was a momma but I changed my mind. I did have an old lady but she got busted the day after I got married. They carted her away – I can't be in two places at once. She's gone away for three years. There's quite a few mommas but they're not always with us all the time.

Some nights we feel like a dip of the wick & we've got a few mommas so they get passed around.

CHRISTINE: The mommas have to pull a train – they have to go with all the Angels who are there.

LEVI: So we get down and all have a go. Too bad if she can't last the time. They have to do this before they can become a momma – everyone has to sample the goods.

We have a meeting once a week so everyone can be brought up to date & told what's to be done. If you miss a meeting it'll cost you half a quid unless you've got good reasons. If you wear your colours on public transport it'll cost you a dollar. These things are stuck to, they're rules & they have to be abided by. We don't want to be exactly like the Stateside Angels because that's conforming & we don't want to conform. Generally we have to be more careful. We don't

want to get a name for being bad, but we don't want someone to brand us as do-gooders. We're Angels, we're as we are. People take us as they find us or it's too bad for them.

Charlie is our President. Odd Job is Deputy Sergeant of Arms. All the officers have stand-pins to take their places when they're not there. Sergeant of Arms looks after the discipline side. Rat Face is our treasurer. Loser Pete is our secretary; they call him Loser Pete because the general impression is that if he gets anything he loses it. He's a terrific guy — he's in Switzerland at the moment. At meetings we discuss when we're going to have runs, where we're going to run to, what we're going to do when we get there, whether anyone has got to be busted, generally things that would be discussed at any board meeting. We discipline members, take their colours off them. We're lax at times but as Angels we can't be wrong. We have a run about once a month and every member must turn out, if they miss an official run it costs them money. When we get there we play it pretty cool, we ride respectable, we don't disturb anyone. When we get there we have our fun. We don't go out of our way to aggravate people its just that some people don't like what we wear, don't like that we wear German insignia. We have no political affiliation there's no racial discrimination.

CHRISTINE: We have a chick society to help girls. We do just about anything for them. Wash their hair, clean their clothes, patch them up when they're hurt, clean the boys' bikes. It's for anybody, Outlaws or Angels' girls who need help. I love being with the Angels, I've been with them for two weeks. Before that I modelled for art classes and was once a secretary at a police station. I feel being with the Angels is the beginning of my life. I like being 'property of'. I'll have a jacket with 'Property of Levi Hell's Angels' stitched on it. LEVI: We wear as standard the one percent badge, that's the outlaw caste. There are other outlaw packs. There's the Hangmen, the Road Rats, the Outlaws, the Aces — they come from Nottingham, there's Angels in Bristol, there's Angels in Manchester, there's Angels in Birmingham, you find them all over the place & they all wear One Percent. I wear an S.S. helmet, there's only two good ones in the London area that we've seen, one belongs to the President of the Outlaws. In the States they wear denim jackets over here the weather makes it necessary to wear leather jackets so we wear a cutdown denim over the top of it. This badge is one we appropriated from a youth club and changed, so it now reads Hell's Angels, London. The colours are sacred, every member must wear them. No woman can wear my colours nor any-one else. There's no point in being an Angel unless you can ride a bike. Mind you we don't say we're the best I imagine there's a lot more who can ride a damn sight better.

29

ME A LITTLE
KISS OR
SOMETHIN'

WHAD YA EAT LAST?

NEXT DAY OZ DOES PHOTO SHOTS IN THE STUDIO

Much bartering about money. Charlie says we shouldn't step in front of the camera except for money' – Levi brings along Christine – a beautiful honey-eyed Lolita, charming, chatty & sexually striking up. Odd Job brings along Wendy from the Outlaws club which outnumbers the Angels ('one Angel can stomp ten Outlaws'). She says she's going to be married to the leader of the Outlaws at the Arts Lab. The ceremony uses a motor-bike manual instead of a Bible & is performed by the Outlaws' second in command. The parties swear that the bike comes before anything else. Wendy has a superb silky body hidden beneath soft leathers & one of those cunts where the clitoris hangs out like a dog's tongue. They are two of the most unselfconscious models on the planet & Odd Job is heavy tongue kissing. When asked to drop their pants and go down on the girls Levi readily complies. Christine however declines to remove his underpants & mutters "it's up to her." Levi fingers Christine tenderly(?). Afterwards Levi & Christine get a bus back to the Arts Lab, their tickets astonishing the conductor. THE BEST THING THAT'S HAPPENED RECENTLY IS H MOORE'S CLOSED CIRCUIT TV SYSTEM WHEREBY PEOPLE GET TO BE A TEN MINUTE TV STAR IN A CLOSED LOCKED ROOM. OUTSIDE ON A MONITOR YOU SEE WHAT PEOPLE ARE DOING INSIDE & THEY GO IN IN GROUPS & FUCK & STRIP & FREAK & EXPOSE THEMSELVES. MEANWHILE JIM HAYNES THE MAN SITS IN A LOFT AT THE BACK, WONDERING.

The Lab is like an occult loo where people from every country come & background can meet in hopefully sympathetic surroundings & they rub off on each other and reach out to a more sensitive & tolerant attitude on everyone's part.

WHAT ABOUT THE ANGELS THEN?

JIM HAYNES They frightened a lot of people especially some of the over thirties. It's frightened a lot of people because of the whole uniform thing of the swastika. There's no doubt about it. At the same time I think that people meeting them & talking to them as individuals have been absolutely surprised by the fact that they are underneath the veneer something else again. & I think it's worked the other way. They are men & people they would otherwise have been frightened of. For example Michael X was here for a night & gave a lecture. There were two of those hell's angels here who I'd talked to & up. They just didn't want to know about Michael X. At the end of the lecture three of them came over to me & said what a groovy guy. The whole tolerance thing – this was a beautiful example of it in action. We probably have lost people as a result of the Hell's Angels & this is one of the things that depresses me. We've lost a lot of people in the last few months because the place has looked tatty – more tatty than it's ever looked. It's worn – a lot of people have come through this building over the last year & a half.

The Angels relation to the squatters was very strange. I think on the whole it was good except in the end. I mean I'm not into violence. Having said that, in the end I wish we'd put up a bigger fight for the building & that's when they would have been absolutely invaluable. Had we dug in I think we would have held the building. I think the events dictated what happened rather than any policy. I initially wanted to set a place for the Arts Lab staff, a place for people to live & a place for visitors. A London to live, but it was impossible to dictate to. The day before it was busted we all got together & decided that we weren't going to talk philosophy any more or democracy or any type of ideology, we would get down to defending the building & putting a fight. & at the end of the court decision we had a large meeting with everyone there to decide what use the building should be put to.

& WHAT ABOUT THE LAB?

In my obvious euphoria I think it's going the other way – that it's getting better.

YES PLEASE HELP THE LAB IT'S TOO IMPORTANT TO... GIVE & £r Dm Yen ETC ETC

NOTES: Phone call from Odd Job. President of the Outlaws is furious about Wendy being in a photo without permission. He's going to stomp someone from OZ. 'Don't worry man' I'll keep him off your back.

INSIDE THE ARTS LAB. Talking to the Outlaws. The President of the Outlaws. Friendly, sensitive, an addition of Phobos Foot in plaster, got matted into a drunken stupor. Not at the Arts Lab but a place for VD One. They used a double motor bike manual as he has a combined machine. We would have called ourselves Angels because we couldn't live. It is the basis of show the existence of the real Angels. These guys here who haven't the class although in their little way they think they have. They're losing members all the time. They're down to about four now. Than thirteen. Ouside me – too drunk & environmental – people leave because of that. One's always throwing tantrums & making his elbows in. There's a real bunch of Angels around. Everyone with Harleys. Last time was the only guy with any class. & now he's gone to Switzerland.

One Angel said to a chick. Are you going to fuck that cat (count) REPLY I answered this cat saying I might. He do it's too late I was going to end you to this chap.

An Angel seemed to have class. Someone said it meant as much to them as a slight cold. Christine who had her face bruised & beaten up. Attacked by another old lady at the 'Wimpy' she says cheerfully.

BACK AT THE ARTS LAB. Two Dutch would-be outlaws cleaning their bikes. They raved about it all seemed to learn. Both handsome clean & obviously gentle. Andre interested in the fucking scene not violence. There are a few outlaws in Holland pursued by police on the run. Once the

30

Dutch heat smashed their big handlebars & curving exhaust pipes. Why do they want to be Angels?

You can get high on alcohol, you can get high on dope, we get high by riding our bikes.

ANOTHER DAY. MORE OZ PHOTO SHOTS. Supposed to be of massed Angels showing class. But Charlie has gone on a run to Folkstone. & Odd Job's bike is the only one left working. It's a Honda (OZ photographer: 'My old mum rode one of those'). Off we go trailing Odd Job in a mini moke. Levi comes along. Odd Job tries to do a few wheelies but can't quite get the front wheel off the ground ('Don't really like doing them'). Levi tries a wheelie between frightened passing tourists & pensioners with horrible grimaces. Levi gets on revs up & the bike smashes into a tree. The chain breaks. Odd Job wheels it disconsolately away. More haggling over money.

SUDDENLY A LARGE LUMBERJACK FIGURE GOES PAST IN THE ARTS LAB. KEN KESEY. STETSON HAT, SCARF & A TOOTH WITH THE STARS & STRIPES ON IT. IN ENGLAND TO CELEBRATE THE SUMMER SOLSTICE AT STONEHENGE WITH THE PRANKSTERS.

WHAT'S HAPPENED TO THE HELL'S ANGELS?
INTERVIEW

The Hell's Angels have changed. I saw Pete & Sweet William just before I left San Francisco. These are the two guys who came over before. Pete's the heaviest guy I know. Just flat – like he quit catholic military school in 3rd grade. Dropped out THEN – said cut it THEN. He's got a faith thing that goes farther back than anybody I know. When you're all travelling out there on the edge you get just so far & then you have to reach back. He can go farther there & be there longer than anyone I know. He can't read or write but there's something in his face that's just so RIGHTEOUS. It's the only word I know. That's what got to the Angels when we were here before. It's just that guy's face. He wants to get as many Angels as he can from over there to come to England. He's havin' a tough time because they know him as just this 35 year old Arkie – he's from Arkansas. He drinks a lot of beer & laughs a lot – has been an Angel longer than anybody. His face is really just beat to shit. This reporter was interviewing him & she was asking him what does it mean to be an Angel – and Sweet William who's the youngest Angel – the first Jewish Angel – said what it means & she breaks down & begins to cry. He's really got a heavy face there's just something about it. One thing you can see everything comes hard for him – this whole Angel thing came hard for him. Now they traditionally don't recognize anyone unless they've been officially recognised & these two came over here & found themselves idolised by two thousand/reproductions. Tradition says that they're supposed to flatten these cats who are wearing their colours unless they've been officially recognised. The English are so good at recognising aristocracy. They see people & know it immediately – that there's the Man. Pete, he's really stuck in a dilemma – I've never seen Pete so worried about anything for so long. What's he going to do about all these Angels over here in England? We have a bet with him that there'll be more Pranksters back over here at the Solstice than Angels.

He knows that it is likely to be true because he can't communicate what he's trying to do to his Angel friends to try & get them interested. All they want to do over there is drink & have a good time which is what they're supposed to be doing. They keep him honest that way.

But these guys over here – & I met some very good guys. Loser Pete is one of the best. Angels have a

saying they don't pick their members they recognise them & Pete came over here & he recognised them, he recognised lots of them – if they were over there they would be members, they just have that kind of bearing. Certain guys will make it as Angels & that's what will happen over here. They once asked me why I wasn't an Angel & I told them I just couldn't take it – you know when they get in a long line & spit a goober in each guy's mouth all the way along the line – taking it in turns letting it grow & passing it on – by the end of the line it's not so good at all – I just couldn't take it. (OZ Photographer starts taking photos) Hey! A camera is tough business. A camera & tape recorder are the two most vicious instruments known to man.

When I came here a week ago these guys were carrying arms – but they don't need it, that's the good thing about Angels – they came over here & got on with the Bobbies real well because they know it's a one to one thing in the streets because the Bobbies aren't carrying guns & clubs & the Angels respect that. That's what builds them they have decided to do something that nobody else has wanted to do yet, like they say it'll take some ugly to be fucking president of the fucking world, alright we'll stand up & do it & mean it. If it came to voting for president of the world I'd vote for Pete in a minute. There are a lot of Angels who are still too young to be great congressmen but there are a lot of them I'd like to see in Congress too. They're RIGHTEOUS, man, they've had kicks & everything long enough that they're interested in comfort & one of the ways to be comfortable is to make the population comfortable around you. They're doing it. When you're around them & they're feeling good towards you, man, it furnishes you with something which is unmistakable. Like you walk down the street surrounded by great big Angels through any district in the world & you feel good about it. I feel that same covering here over the Arts Lab. I think they're trying to make it work. They know that that's what they have to do. That one guy stood up there – he'd just

Levi

been arrested for carrying a double barrel shot gun & I told him you don't need that & he doesn't, because you can already see in his eye that thing where he says – he's reached across & sworn with a bunch of other guys – when it comes to certain things I'll stand behind this all the way to the grave if necessary.

A good hero is working towards the day when there are no longer any heros. Any other hero is insane. Nobody wants to carry that load indefinitely. They work towards the time when its spread about. It's a weight. It's a difficult dedication. Like Sweet William the Jew. He joined them thinking he was going to convert them to accepting spades in their ranks. He found they were much further out than that. He found he was in something for life. About integration he found they had discovered about that years and years ago & just knew where they were.

I was brought along with the Angels last Christmas. It was the fabled Trip without a Ticket. Someone put together this thing whereby 13 people got to take a ride in a plane to England. They just packed the 13 people in. Bill Graham of the Fillmore paid for the Angel bikes to be brought over. One guy with an airline office paid for the tickets but they were open anyway. Air India, Indians are cool man. We got on – the psychedelic monsters. I was an hour late & turned up wearing a white scarf & a black leather jacket & a Lindbergh aviator hat. This Indian airline Captain who'd been waiting for me for an hour said 'If we get into any trouble I'll call you.' They have stewards as well as stewardesses. It liberates the stewardesses. They don't have to take the sort of shit the American stewardesses do – you know like look at me but you can't touch me. Anyway we were all sniffing THC & the plane soon became a living room. I walked back & one of the stewardesses said you have marijuana? I thought they were going to bust me until I realised they were Pranksters. It really blew my head – they knew everything that was going on – we hadn't concealed anything from them. The great thing about England is that you have the Indians. They're the coolest people around.

Man right here is the front line. All the time I spend here it's hard work – it's the frontier where things are happening. I mean I could go to Mexico have an easy time but in the end I know I'd have to come back to London.

LEADER OF THE PACK

AND NOW CRAZY CHARLIE PRESIDENT OF THE HELL'S ANGELS LONDON CHAPTER.

Q. What about the acid-psychedelic scene that Kesey personified once. Are you involved in that?
A. That's more Loser Pete's scene than mine. Loser Pete wasn't a grease boy. He was a beat who liked motor cycles. Levi was a traveller.
Odd job was . . . Odd Job. We've all got different scenes. The whole thing is to get to know each other's trips.
Q. Are you on an acid scene?
A. I'm pleased to say I don't take drugs.
Q. Why are you 'pleased' about it?
A. It's just one less thing the police can get me for.
Q. Is that the only reason?
A. No. I get my kicks other ways. I haven't tried acid but I've tried the others. It's just not me.
Q. Are you against people taking drugs?
A. I'm not against anybody.

& THE SAME DIFFIDENCE ABOUT THE CRAZY DANGEROUS FLAMBOYANT THINGS THAT ANGELS DO & SEEM TO INCARNATE THE IDEA OF AN ANGEL – SHOWING 'CLASS' IT'S CALLED. HE EXPLAINED THAT 'SHOWING CLASS IS SHOWING OFF, BUT SHOWING COLOUR IS SHOWING WHAT YOU'RE MADE OF!' I ASKED HIM IF HE HAD HIS RED WINGS.

A. Things like that – class – doesn't affect me at all. I was once critizised for not showing enough class. I just don't need to show class. I show more colour in one day than many people show in the whole of their lives. Just by being what I am.
Q. Hasn't this affected the other members?
A. It has done but they've gradually come to know what I say is right.
Q. Isn't it important that Angels, especially their leaders, should show class. Isn't showing class part of being an Angel?
A. No . . . showing class is snapping peoples minds. Like one of the lads went up to Heston Services on the M 4 – He got a raw egg, rolled it around on the floor with his nose. Then he broke it, reached up, put salt & pepper on it & then sucked it up off the floor. Now that was a mind snapper. It's a sort of free expression. Showing class is a very little part of being an Angel.

& WHERE WAS THE RIGHTEOUS ANGER? I TOLD HIM WHAT THE OUTLAWS HAD SAID ABOUT HIM & THE ANGELS.

A. The thing is they don't know what it's about. I know what it's about. Loser Pete knows what it's about. It's our task to show others what it's about. The President & the Sergeant of Arms of the Outlaws they'd make very good Angels. But they've always said they'd be members but for the fact that it's not their trip. It's not what you do but what you think.

STORY OF THE BEGINNING OF THE ANGELS

A. Loser Pete is the original London Hell's Angel. He came over from Switzerland. We met at Chelsea Bridge. Something just drew us together. I didn't see him for two weeks & I've never missed anyone so much in all my life. I was looking for him every day then one time he was there. From then on we were together. Then the Angels turned up. Even then I wanted time to decide whether I wanted to dedicate my whole self to it. I finally decided & here I am. It wasn't a hasty decision. It came over a period of months. It was Loser Pete who found out about the Angels. He had books, newspaper cuttings – everything. It was like a school project for him. You know where you have to get something ready for parents visiting day. He did the colours himself, it takes him a day to stitch a set. He'll be back in about two weeks. Then the Angels came over, told us roughly what it was all about.

WHAT HAPPENED AT APPLE?

The Angels had a room upstairs at Apple. Someone tried to throw us all out of Apple at a party – we were drinking & the food was out. Suddenly the food disappeared. We said, "Where's the food?" & someone said to Pete, "It's uncool to be hungry". Pete just busted his head. There was a real tense atmosphere. I didn't really know what was going on. I wasn't an Angel then & I only saw the surface of things.

& WHAT ABOUT THE UNDERGROUND? ARE THE ANGELS GOING TO BE A POLICE FORCE OR WHAT?

A. I have no feeling personally about politics or anything like that. I'd say I have an open mind about it. The Underground hasn't affected me – as far as I'm concerned it doesn't exist – it's just another lot of people doing another lot of things.
Q. So what keeps you at the Arts Lab?
A. The People. The Arts Lab is a world on its own. It's a totally different community to what you usually get. But it is a community. You get council flats & blocks & they say they've built a new community centre. It doesn't mean anything – there's no spirit of community.

SO WHAT'S GOING TO HAPPEN TO THE ANGELS?

A. They're going to get bigger & bigger. There's no limit. One day its not going to be Hell's Angels Chapter London or Chapter California, it's going to be Hell's Angels Chapter Earth. CONTINUED PAGE 42

32

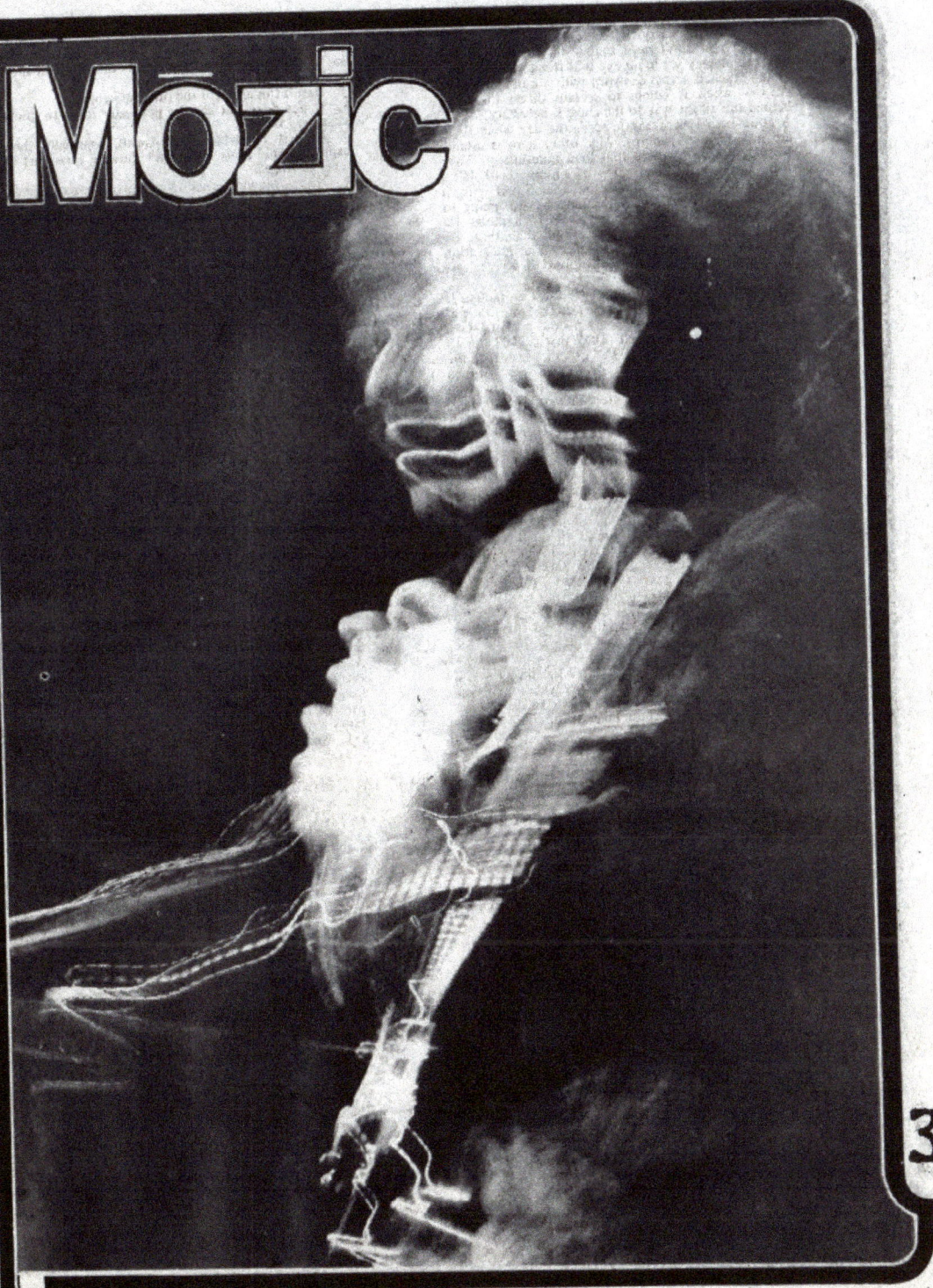

Mōzic

33

DANIEL VOLPELIERE – PIERROT

CHILD THAT I AM I DO

Danaë

I saw the Incredible String Band use the Fillmore stage for a picnic site turn the Lower East Side into a woodland glade & do a very far out thing & then return on a backwards trip to the fields of childhood innocence.

I too sat on the wall & watched the baker's stubbly grin. How beautiful to find that England shimmering on New York air & I fell in love with the Incredible String Band.

'What's holding you back from loving everyone? Everyone is basically good so if you try to understand why people are acting in weird ways being abrupt being ridiculously angry then you get to know how the mind works you get through that & really love them' (Rose)

When they move on stage they are private but close together like new lovers & lit with a clean fire that talks of peace & apple cheek country weather. What can I say but child innocence? It sings across their music & dances at the corner of their eyes.

'Our music isn't consciously gentle it just comes out like that . . . violence is a hang-up . . . my kind of music is ripply and floral . . . I have a love of ancient sounds – Eastern, Chinese, Kabuki music & African drums' (Robin)

I meet them in London grey sound studio clanking with wires & microphones & busy television try hard freakies. Don't want to know how old they are where their parents live who they fuck – but how they are what they are & understand it. How does the gentle love wave survive the you-next-boy-pop-to-the-top hassle & come out trembling?

'I want to communicate my experience of the glory of life & how we all share in making our lives what they really are. Communication is an end in itself. I say buzz & you say bleep – that's a communication. Starting from that basic theory a lot of things can happen' . . . (Robin)

Robin is a hawk, two light eyes astride a beak, & golden hair. Mike a dark matyr living another life on the stage with bare feet.

'The amount of time we've all lived in the universe is incalculable what does this instant of talking matter except that we are communicating?' (Robin)

It's cold and their noses are blue, Licorice's legs mottled above the knee, rust velvet squashed & shiny barely covering her small girl's body. Smiles at me with one tooth missing. What is it that divides the eyes of those who watch & those who don't. A psychic beam travelling through witchcraft. Pick it up on the cold air

auditorium. Pick it upon the headphones taking your mind into aliceland. Pick up the incredible psychic string band & know that they've been places you've been those mystical acid trips where you found nothing but yourself but found yourself to be everything.

'Writing was a necessity . . acid opened my eyes so many changes in the past six years I could have given you twenty different answers to what I believed in. You name it I've tried it like the mysterious ancient things – Tarot, magic, astrology . . ' (Robin)

Somewhere in Wales near the wet sand & the magic stones live the Incredible String Band & part of the Exploding Galaxy & there they made a fable film taken from Robin's head & decorated with secret dreams. Soon the multichannelled machine will box his magic fable with words, the dream pinioned by a million eyes devouring plastic food. Running water down a strong welsh mountain I hear in the music celtic winds & ancient dreams on the flat notes.

'I am fascinated by places where there's memory of druids, the magic stones, & ancient towers, woods & sacred groves. Art is the creation of beautiful space artists in living life in it. A town could be paradise but in this age of supposed-to-be sensuality nobody seems to think about pleasure in a city . . there's no reason why a city should not be a garden of joy but it's down to thoughts. A city is the colour of the minds that built & use it' (Robin)

No electronics perms peroxide. The girl's hair sticks out newly washed in rainwater faces newly scrubbed. Music from folklore; jugband music they play with their strings not on them.

& along the way some kind of religious mania. 'We go somewhere & there they are hiding in a corner unloved for years' (Licorice)

'It started with interest in the real natural music & the skills just flowed out. If you love something it's very easy . . it's a joy to let the secrets of the instruments unfold themselves' (Robin)

'A year ago I'd have said I was in touch with the Spirit which wrote all the songs I would have said I wasn't responsible for their existence it was the music but now I'm starting to take responsibility for actually creating them' (Robin)

& that responsibility found through the present method, the future wish, a new way, found through the macrobiotic restaurant in New York, paradox, found in Tottenham where Father Hubbard holds his court. The Incredible String Band are scientologists. Spilt long blond hair & cinnamon breath.

'We believe in Scientology' (All)

'It is applied philosophy to make the able more able through the restoration of awareness' (Robin)

'It took out the last pain in me so that now I am able to play instruments on stage which frightened me before' (Licorice)

. . . . which goes on & on & on. . . . . all down the tunnel of Rose's smile & find . . . . their skin. Been together since . . . . & before . . . Licorice & Robin . . .

butter on a brown bread stage.

'I wanted to play . . . . came was playing & gradually . . . . because I could cut them to . . . . . . I wanted show more people how happy I was . . . . . playing ou gigs & just get happier all the time. . . . . '

So I saw them . . . . mother-fucker-land cloaked in Abbie Hoffman humour shaken by Bill Graham million . . . .

'Revolution is think . . . . you've got to fight something . . Governments . . . . . . there is no fight they're there to be something if anything . . . . the opposite of revolutionary . . . revolutionary . . revolutionary' (Robin)

'I don't want to corrupt people. It's not my trip. But I think there must be some kind of Government, but it has to be done by people individually. Maybe there has to be some kind of code which everyone'll agree to . . . the way I'm removing politics is by improving myself to a point where I don't need law'

Listened again to them freeze crystal clear in the glass cage of Lincoln Centre. Last hear them play to lumpy hippies in Croydon far removed in the drizzling rain from the other times & each time something different. Some songs dipped into another pot.

'No drugs for more than a year now'

Stripped pine & chrome Fairfield Hall jampacked with superconscious indian bands tied carefully with a back mirror facing the light to match marks & spencers.

But what does it matter if the fairy music harsh in the hard accoustics of Croydon. . . . .

All that matters is love between man & woman & child. It's been said before. Confucius has an edge on even an Incredible String Band but he could not, did not, does not sing with a flat voice and hawk eyes out of Scottish Welsh wet blue skies nor smile with an endless smile, nor lose his tooth not to find another, nor die a martyr once to rise again skinny on a little trippy stage.

What does it matter why . . . Incredible String Band & play again, ...

'I believe . . . . with a smile once' (Robin)

Child that I am too when man moves for my arms when the . . . . roaring when . . . . bright morning sound when everything is real again and is awake now is it possible . . . . drop of clay better to ask your . . . .

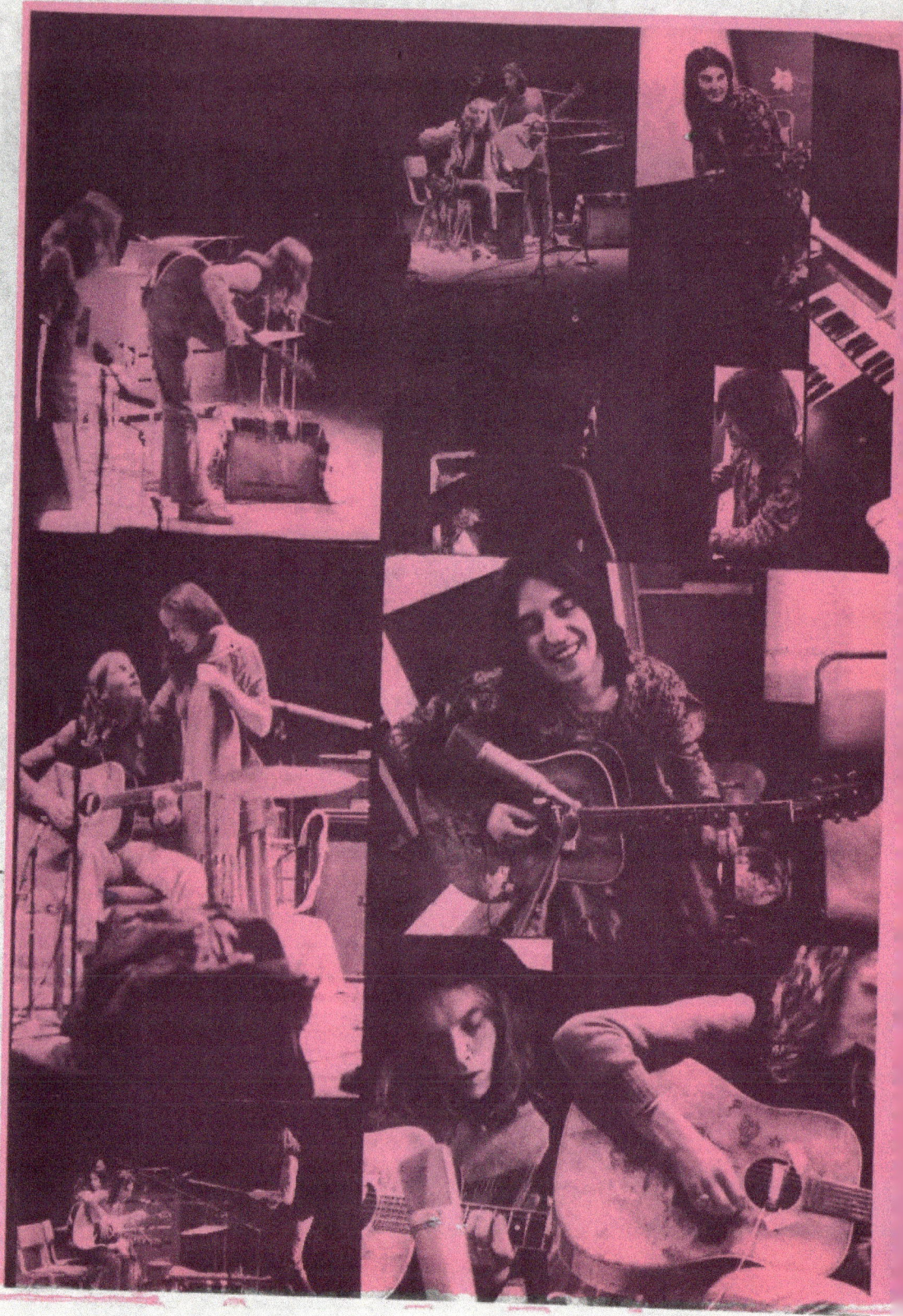

JIMMY PAGE

Felix Dennis

EARLY DAYS

It all really began for me rehearsing with Cyril Davis. That would be around six years ago now, just after he'd split with Koerner. Then I was accepted for Art College and I had to decide between painting and playing. Well, the music scene was pretty depressing around that time . . . nobody was interested in Chuck Berry or Bo Diddley, all they wanted was Top Twenty & Jazz . . . so I went to College. Of course, about a year later everything began to happen with the Stones and Liverpool and the R 'n' B scene so I took to jamming occasionally at the Marquee on Thursday nights. Somebody asked me to play on a record — can't remember what it was to tell you the truth — but from that session came other offers of work and suddenly there was more than I could cope with, four or five sessions a week. I began missing too many lectures & taking days off at College so I thought that I'd better finally decide: painting or playing? It wasn't an easy decision but finally I took the plunge & chose sessions. Sometimes I wonder whether I made the right decision.

YARDBIRDS

The Yardbirds came out of getting bored with session work, which is so unpredictable. One minute you're playing for really good musicians & the next . . . well . . . Herman's Hermits are into their own thing no doubt, but it isn't my scene exactly. I'd known Jeff* in the Yardbirds for quite a long time & when Paul Samwell Smith** quit that was it. I'd never played bass before but I quite dug it & we left for the States shortly after I'd joined. Then Jeff was ill one time in LA & it was a case of me play lead guitar & Chris Dreja† do the bass or scrub the gig. After that it worked out that the Yardbirds had two lead guitars, until Jeff left finally to form his own band. It was a shame that the Yardbirds eventually folded out. Towards the end Keith and Jim MacCarthy just didn't have their heart in the music. They were almost ashamed of the name Yardbirds in the finish, though I don't know why: on the last tour we were getting better reaction than we'd ever had. They were a great band, I was never ashamed of playing in the Yardbirds.

MUSICAL PRESS

I don't read any of them in this country, not even the MM. I used to but I just can't now. They're so shitty. This country desperately needs a new trade paper. There isn't one authorative writer on the staff of one music paper in this country who knows anything about rock music. Yes, you can print that. Let's talk about something else, let's not talk about them.

UNDERGROUND

Is Led Zeppelin an underground group? I suppose if you mean in terms of lack of airplay on Radio One then yes, we'll be an underground group. I know we won't ever be heard on Radio One, except maybe on Peel or Drummond's shows. The radio in this country, in fact all the mass media, are in a disgusting condition. They're so restricted. The BBC just won't accept that really worthwhile music has developed from rock & roll, from all those awkward pimply guys who were playing guitars in 1960. That's what's happened, but they just can't accept it.

I mean I don't want to keep referring things to the States because Britain isn't America, but at least there are some channels for rock music. In fact for all forms of music, over there. The only underground group that's ever existed in the States was Hendrix. That may sound strange but you know he'd had two hit albums & a whole year of acclaim and success before they finally offered him one TV spot. Underground to me means something that is being suppressed by the authorities & that's certainly what was happening to Hendrix. His reputation was spread solely by word of mouth & the FM stations, TV exposure is the most important thing in the States, the most accepted method. He was denied that exposure constantly.

I know perhaps you were referring to the underground in the sense of a collection of people and ideas existing within but divorced from the society in which they live. That's an interesting concept but has little to do with our music. In this country, & this is just personally speaking, it seems to me to be something which has been distorted into an almost comical replica of the US. Take IT for example. There's an example of the basic theory of the underground, the alternative society, the theory being lost behind the pounds shilling and pence. The underground is big business now & that's a pity.

CENSORSHIP

I remember bringing back copies of Australian OZ to England & they had these ridiculous censored things . . . breasts, can you imagine? Australian censorship is . . . well, I guess you'd know, wouldn't you? Even the nudes in Playboy are censored sometimes. I mean, Playboy! That's ridiculous. If I ever saw a pair of tits that excited me in Playboy I'd begin to wonder if I was perverted. Playboy's like Doris Day in the nude. Impossible. I'm sure if I stripped off Doris Day's bra I'd find another bra underneath. I have these theories about Hugh Heffner . . . (nodding to tape) . . . not while that's on though.

SCREAMING LORD SUTCH

Ah, Sutch was a gas. I was going to produce him for Immediate once but something happened & it never got together. Sutch was four years ahead of his time . . . I mean Arthur Brown, he's only a psychedelic Sutch really isn't he? You know what Sutch is doing now? He's in America, a travelling representative for Marshall equipment, driving a huge Rolls with this union jack painted across it. He scared the shit out of his audiences, him and his Savages. What a crew!

JOHN MAYALL

Mayall? Look . . . yeah . . . let's just not talk about John

---

*Jeff Beck, lead guitar in the Yardbirds after Clapton.
**Paul Samwell Smith — bass player in early Yardbirds.
†Chris Dreja — rhythm guitarist.

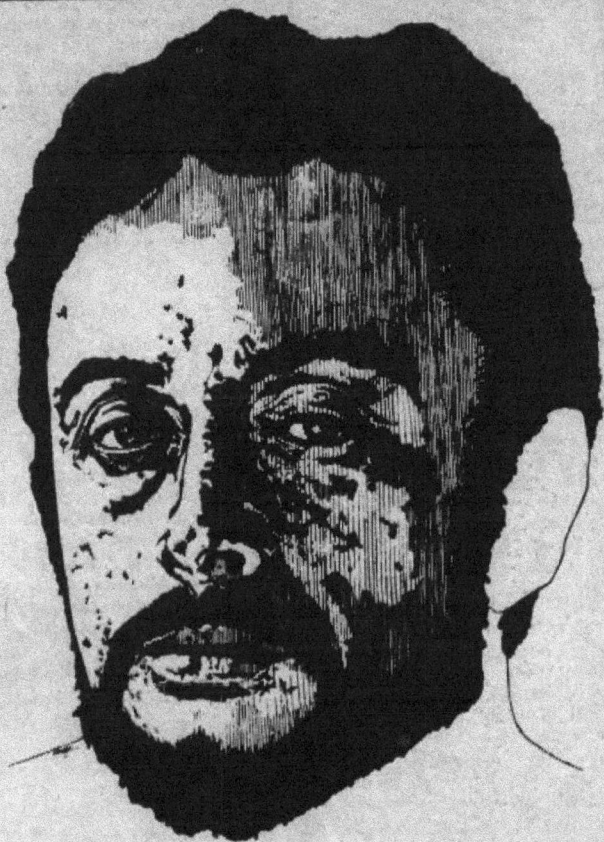

AMONG THE ACCUSERS, AMONG THE FINGER-
POINTERS OF OUR TIME, ONE STANDS OUT
CLEARLY: **LENNY BRUCE.** AS HE SAID ONE
NIGHT, IN A FAMED ASIDE: "I'M SORRY IF I'M
NOT VERY FUNNY TONIGHT, BUT I'M NOT A
COMEDIAN. I'M LENNY BRUCE." PROFOUNDLY
SO; AND SINCE HIS DEATH THE ONCOMING
WAVE OF YOUTH HAS PICKED UP ON HIM.
NOW THE MYTH, THE MARTYR, SPEAK OUT
STILL THROUGH A HERITAGE OF TAPED LIVE
PERFORMANCES. FROM THESE, **FRANK ZAPPA**
CHOSE **THE BERKELEY CONCERT,** AVAIL-
ABLE AROUND MID-APRIL ON TRANSATLANTIC
TRA 195D. THIS IS THE FIRST LENNY BRUCE
FULL CONCERT PROGRAMME ISSUED WITH-
OUT ANY EDITING WHATSOEVER. TWO
LPS **71s 3d.**

Transatlantic
WHERE TRENDS BEGIN

Mayall, I don't want to talk about him. Mayall . . . long pause . . . no, we just won't talk about him. Do you mind?

HIT RECORDS

Say we made a record like the Marmalade's, sure we could do that, we could do that easily. But I'm a guitarist and a musician as such & I just don't want to be associated with those scenes. Anyway, that group just couldn't get a tour or stir any interest in the States. America has enough of its own bubblegum music. Someone like Eric you really have to admire, simply because he broke through in his own right, without watering down his music. Whether he finally achieved his goal in the Cream I don't know. Like at Madison Sq. Gardens where there was that audience of 35,000, well a good part of that audience was composed of teenys, nine to twelve year olds. They hadn't really come to listen to the Cream's music had they? I'm sure they defeated Eric's purpose. He left the Yardbirds in the early days, just after For Your Love to avoid all those scenes. *The overpublicity of the Cream was the biggest single factor in their break-up.*

GROUPIES

The first time I came into contact with groupies was on the initial tour of the States with the Yardbirds. We were playing in this huge ballroom in LA & there were a whole crown of teenys screaming & waving banners & posters with the group's name on & things. Then right in the middle of these banners with 'I love Keith', & 'Jeff, Jeff' & 'Yardbirds Forever' rose this huge poster with the word 'WANK' in four foot high lettering. Christ, I nearly stopped playing.

Then there were these telephone calls at the hotel from groupies.

Somehow they learned a hell of a lot of cockney slang. They'd phone up and say, 'Hi Jeff, how's yer 'Ampton Wick?' Ridiculous!

That edition of Rolling Stones with the groupies was useless. There aren't any groupies in San Francisco anyway; most of them are based in New York, LA, Chigago & a couple in Miami. There was only one real groupie pictured in the entire Rolling Stone article, which in any case was a diluted version of the Realist original. The Realist was the paper that carried pictures of the Plaster-Casters' trophies. The Plaster-Casters have retired now..

DYLAN

Dylan's lyrics are like four minute versions of a book. You can just keep taking them in. What can you say about Bob Dylan? It's all been said.

AMERICA

The US is an explosive scene, politically & socially speaking. It's difficult to explain to someone whose never been there. & it's so big; what's true in Mississippi wouldn't apply in New York. Remember the US is a lot of little countries tied together by Washington. The laws vary from State too. Take a sixteen year old girl across the state line in your car in Texas without her parents permission & that's abduction. Fuck a girl under 18 in Texas & that's rape.

The fuzz in that part of the world are pretty paranoid too. Any excuse to get their guns out. Every day you

hear of cops shooting innocent people, bystanders & the like. Keith bought himself a gun for $12.50 in Texas, bullets and everything included. He bought it for protection. He was frightened of Texas . . . well, so was I. The whole atmosphere is hostile. And in Alabama. *We were in Alabama when Robert Kennedy was shot. We were drinking in a bar when the news came over the radio. There were a lot of people suddenly smiling in that bar . . . one guy turned to his mates & said in a loud voice, 'well, that's another bastard down.' Nobody was shocked, let alone sa d that a man had just lost his life. Heartless people. Winning is the biggest religion in the US.*

But there are good scenes of course in the States. Kids will listen to your music, the FM stations are good, the bread is there. People seem to be more aware of what you are trying to say, musically speaking that is . . , & you get a better chance to prove yourself live. It always seems to me that in England people are too ready to tear musicians to shreds, to play the comparison game. Something like, 'Beck's not a bad guitarist but he's not as good as Clapton is he?' End of Jeff Beck. We'll be back in America in April & I'm looking forward to that.

THE ALBUM

Well you can't really judge anything about Led Zeppelin from the album alone. The group had only been together for two & a half weeks when we recorded it. We'd had fifteen hours rehearsal before shooting over to Scandinavia for a few gigs, then straight after that we cut the album. There's very little double tracking, we were deliberately aiming at putting down what we could actually reproduce on stage. I know that I influenced pretty heavily the content & arrangements on this first one, but that was only because we didn't have the time to discuss everything between us. The next album will almost certainly be more of a group project. The best thing about the Zeppelin is that nobody's being carried. Robert & the two Johns are all excellent musicians, they all have something to say.

LED ZEPPELIN

Like I said, the great thing about the Zeppelin is that nobody's carrying anybody else. John Bonham & Robert Plant were both in a group from Birmingham. 'The Band of Joy'. I was very lucky to find two such fine musicians available at the same time. John Paul Jones, well, I expect you already know quite a lot about him. He's done an awful lot of studio work; I'd say he's one of the best bass players in the country.

I don't know how you'd bag our music . . . maybe it's too early to say. Anyway we're not consciously aiming at anything or in any specific direction. Just playing together and taking it as it comes. Since recording the album we've changed a lot of the material, & the length of the numbers seems to have expanded. One thing that used to get me about the Cream was the way I thought they relied too heavily on Master Eric for the improvisations. That's not going to happen with us. Everybody's got something to say &, well, that's what we'll be doing. I can't believe that we've all come together so quickly. If I'm really honest with you, though it'll probably sound like I'm boasting, I'd say that I feel very confident about the direction of Led Zeppelin.

INSIDE JANN WEN-
NERS HEAD THERE IS
A STONE-ROLLING

Sebastian Jorgensen

Every form has its fashionable arbiters, even rock & roll. These are not unlike ring-side reporters at a big fight: relatively secure in their complimentary seats, marginal participants in that holocaust of vibrations which concrete action generates, favouring one combatant then the other & all the while scribbling as others punch or pray.

From this position these people rarely emerge, like the objects of their passionate scrutiny, as household names; nor can their final judgements compete with the referee's. Their one great advantage, potentially, is their distance from the vortex, a distance which should enable them to formulate cool patterns from hot, confusing detail.

Finally any publication which is specialist by nature will sail or fail depending on whether it backs winners with any consistency over a period of time. Just as the charts (singles &/or albums) are the referees in pop so circulation figures are the determinants of success or failure in publishing.

By these standards – & seen in an underground context — the San Francisco based rock music fortnightly "Rolling Stone" is an unqualified success. More flexible than committed – I doubt whether anybody on "Rolling Stone" was ever fooled for long by the early promise of acid, transcendental mysticism or revolutionary politics – it sells 57,000 copies in the States & now, with the backing of Mick Jagger, its forthcoming London edition could topple that figure.

The 23-year-old "Hugh Heffner" of pop, as Geoffrey Cannon dubbed him with characteristic heavy-weight wit in the Guardian, has little time for the present run of rock pundits, both under & over-ground, here or in America. Not only the lamentable M.M. but also I.T., Eye Magazine, The East Village Other, Berkely Barb & just about everyone else (apart from this magazine, strangely enough) is icily dismissed. "You find that the major critics in the United States previous to 'Rolling Stone', people like Richard Goldstein, they don't know what they're talking about," said Wenner looking for all the world like an unusually hairy rugby player who turned on tuned in & scored yet another goal. "They produce terribly overwritten, boring stuff, immitation Tom Wolfe stuff to conceal their own ignorance of the subject, I mean they couldn't make a plain, flat statement about the music. The other thing that became very clear was that they really didn't like it. We're out to replace 'Melody Maker' and all these shitty music publications. There's nothing to read around today." With the 50:50 partnership deal with Mick Jagger already finalised, hip Londoners still quoting from his magazine's brilliant expose of groupiedom, the Sunday Times' jazz-pop critic Derek Jewell about to talk to him on "Late Night Line-Up" & a return flight ticket to San Francisco in his pocket there was every reason for his friendly cat-that-got-away-with-the-cream smile.

ON KENNEDY: "The assassination changed the whole course of American history. Politics is all a lie in the first place & Eugene McCarthy is as big a liar as anyone else. But John Kennedy was an interesting cat. The thing is the most a president can do – if it's true that both parties are the same & all that shit – the most he can do is set a personal tone & a personal style. The death of Kennedy points to what an influence he was. I mean all over the world people were just fucked. It was incredible. There was no hippy thing in America, there was no flagrant drug scene. It all wouldn't have happened if Kennedy hadn't got killed. Everybody was still digging what was going on in that other scene. Kennedy made politics & the whole thing very relevant because he was young, he was attractive, he was just plain beautiful you know & not ugly. Lyndon Johnson is ugly & Richard Nixon is ugly & they just emphasise the ugliness of the scene they're in already. But maybe it was all false anyway, maybe it was just a false promise, an illusion & it was deception rather than reality. It could well have been. Maybe that's why he was shot. It all happened after Kennedy. "Because after that, man, fuck! there was nothing interesting after that."

ADVERTISING: "We haven't yet developed solid advertising outside of the record companies. We are moving now into new areas but we do operate a kind of censorship. We won't accept sex ads, we won't accept wig ads or cosmetic ads or cigarette ads. We wouldn't accept Magnaphal ads because it's kind of tasteless. Puritanical? No, I don't have any argument with Magnaphal & I don't want to see them go out of business. But since advertising is 50 or 30 per cent of any magazine it as much as anything else characterises the magazine. Cigarettes anyway are bad for you. I think it's a filthy habit though I smself smoke. Alcohol though is groovy & we would accept those kinds of ads. 80% of the readership of East Village Other & the Berkely Barb is only interested in the small ads. I want to avoid that. They're the only market places for homosexuals. It's the sex market, they're the sex scene newspapers. The rest of it is pretty boring."

RELATIONSHIP WITH JAGGER: "I met Mick a year ago in L.A. & we had a pleasant meeting & we just talked about business & hip businesses & you know the energy of rock & roll & how it was being wasted &

41

where it was going & Apple & about his own abortive record company & it was just an absolute natural that we should do it here together. I don't see any conflict of interest in reviewing a Rolling Stones' record in future. Of course they'll have a say editorially. But you know we're not a Rolling Stones fan club publication. Mick & I are 50:50 partners in Invisible Ink Printing Industries or whatever it's going to be called.''

THE GAP: I think that the only hope for students & our side of the fence is that the old people die off as quickly as possible. Every time I pick up the papers I read of them dying off. The faster the better. I think it's the only way. Now the kids come home to their parents with faces broken out in blood. It used to be 'Oh Dad, I've got to talk to you. I just took some acid so let's sit down & have a talk for the first time in our lives. Let me play you 'Rubber Soul' or something!

DOPE: ''It was & is very important. When it first happened it had a tremendous impact. In my own life it was a fantastic turn-around. You know – wait a minute fellah, wait a second, look at THAT! When the acid scene started off you could take L.S.D. without having read about some freak trip in Life magazine, without having read all those horror stories. Everybody who got too fucked up on acid has come out of it fine. Chromosome damage? Who can tell? It might even be a good thing anyway to have some mutants around.''

THE ROCK & ROLL ARMY: ''Rock & roll is a different kind of politics in the broadcast sense. The one thing most people dig is rock & roll. & like the Jerry Rubin thing, the Yippee thing, the real power of our side is in what I like to call the Rock & Roll Army. But who's going to get this army on the march? It hasn't been

Eldridge Cleaver & it could have been the Beatles but they're not going to do it & maybe they shouldn't do it but that's where the power is. & the Rock & Roll Army is the army that has gone home & turned on its parents.

CAMPUS REVOLUTIONARIES: What kind of revolution is it where you go in & take over a building & you burn down some kind of college hall or take over the library & destroy the presidents office & go around ranting & carrying flags & taking over the campus. & then you get beaten up & thrown in jail & ten minutes later you're bailed out. Then you go home with complete impunity. What kind of revolution is that? There is yet to be anyone killed at a college demonstration. When it happens we're talking about revolution, now we're not. It would be much better if it could be done by going home & turning on your old man. America is just a violent, violent place. I'm not an advocate of violence but I understand it. ''When I see pictures of these kinds of things on television I go pfft. You know, if I was there I'd have a gun. So that's why I don't go.''

MUSIC: You can intellectualise about a lot of rock & roll music but it's primarily not an intellectual thing. It's music, that's all.''

continued from P32:

Q. Freewheelin Frank said that . . .
A. Yeah he's incredible. I've seen bits of his poetry. & his book – there's only one person who can talk like that. He might just get over here this year.
Q. But how do you want the Angels to develop?
A. I personally want them to develop to – not necessarily numberwise – but to the point where say one bloke is shafting his bird somewhere & you're up the other end of the M 1 & you break down, & after one phone call the bloke whips his end out & comes straight to your rescue. Loser Pete had this very quality. My bike broke down & without even me phoning him he was there. It's this thing it's like telepathy. I couldn't care if there was only two of us or if there was 500 of us provided we all felt about each other the same – like that.

CHARLIE SYMBOLISES THE LONDON ANGELS. FRIENDLY, LIKEABLE, HELPUL, WILLING TO TALK. IN A WAY GENTLE. A CONTRADICTION? IF SO, WHAT ARE THE ANGELS?

MAYBE YOU COULD FIND OUT.
By wearing colours like 'Hell's Angels, Sidcup', & walking around the Arts Lab & Chelsea bridge.
Will a real Angel fist strike you?
Or try & become an Arts Lab Angel or any sort of Angel.
Chicks could try becoming a momma.
How many fuck you? Do you enjoy it? Do they enjoy it?
Try counting Angels.
Try giving Angels bread so they can get their bikes together.

IF YOU FIND OUT ANYTHING TELL US ABOUT IT SO WE'LL KNOW TOO.

My folks were always putting him down (down, down)
They say he came from the wrong side of town
  (whatdoyoumeanhecamefromthewrongsideoftown?)
They told me he was bad
But I knew he was sad
That's why I fell for the . . . LEADER OF THE PACK

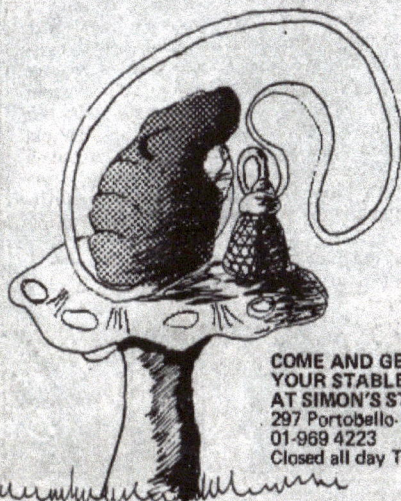

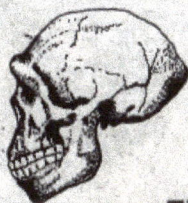

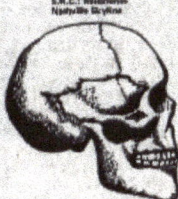

43

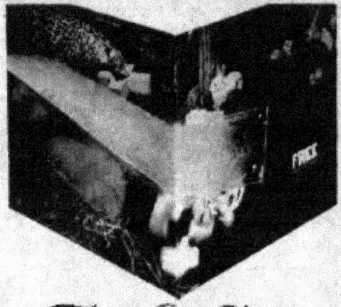

LP REVIEWS

THE LAST EXIST Traffic *ILPS 9097*

The intriguing thing about Traffic was the acabradabra of their originality. Stevie Winwood may be "... quite simply the best white blues singer I have ever heard, regardless of age, environment or nationality ..." — Al Kooper, April '68 — but there are a dozen white blues singers, both in Britan & America who can certainly sing *almost* as well.

Capaldi is a fine rhythmic drummer, tight & always relaxed, with a well controlled left hand, but he'd be the first to point out that Baker, Hiseman, Moon or any one of a hundred others feature similar qualities in their drumming. The same applies for Mason & Chris Wood. Both are much more than competent musicians but neither is an outstanding one in the literal sense of the word. It was the combination that did it.

When Stevie split from Spencer Davis he was emphatic that his next venture wasn't going to be 'The Stevie Winwood Group'. Tired of the 'boy star wonder' image constantly laid on him in those early days, (however true it may have been), he carefully gathered a collection of home town friends & lit out for the country. When the music finally emerged it was evident that he had nearly achieved his purpose. Nobody in Traffic was backing up S.W. They were playing with him, not behind him; they were playing together. *That* was the secret.

But here, on 'Last Exist', & just faintly on their previous album, it was becoming apparent that Winwood was outgrowing the cloak he had so deliberately drawn around himself. On live appearances too, it was Steve's emotional singing & playing that brought the audiences to their feet ... they appreciated Mason, Capaldi & Wood, but they rose to Winwood. For Steve Winwood *is* a musical genius, albeit a reluctant one, & whatever carefully planned steps he had taken to disguise & diffuse the fact, nothing could have hoped to veil his enormous talent for long. He is probably the most *multi* talented musician, singer-organist-composer-guitarist-pianist, that Britain has produced in the last decade. Eventually he will play jazz; no other field encompasses a wide enough area to absorb his music.

One complete side of 'Last Exist' consists of part of the recordings made last summer at the free, open-air concert in Hyde Park. Consequently the balance at times is shoddy & the group suffers from all the technical hang-ups encountered on any live recording. But these are trifling complaints compared to the magnificent performance. In 'Feelin' Good' Winwood lays down his best organ solo to date, a beautifully constructed & intricately phrased piece of music, tapering off finally into Chris Wood's melodic, gypsy flute, hovering like a guardian angel over the free-form timing & creating a bridge of continuity without which the song might well have become too involved for even the musicians to follow.

The studio tracks on the album are interesting, occasionally moving, especially Winwood & Capaldi's 'Withering Tree. & 'Shanghai Noodle Factory', but the overall impression is perhaps that the cuts are good because it is Traffic playing, & through little merit of the material. If these are the best tracks that Island could salvage out of what the group left on tape, then maybe it would be as well if this really was, 'The Last Exit', (which of couse it is decidedly not; we've still got the 'Best of Traffic', volumes, one, two & three to come yet.)

So the Cream is dead, the Buffalo Springfield & the Yardbirds, & the Mams & the Papas & the Electric Flag & the Byrds, (well almost), & now Traffic. You could buy this album for any one of a number of reasons. You dig Traffic, you dig memories, you dig Island Records, you were at Hyde Park & you'd like to hear yourself clapping or you just want to be able to pull the weird black flat circle out of its dusty cover in 30 years & say, "hey kids ... this is where S.W. really began you know ..." Anyone of those reasons would be excuse enough.
Felix Dennis.

BLOOD, SWEAT, & TEARS Blood Sweat & Tears. *CBS 63504*

If you, like me, never quite got used to the horn sections on any of the Mike Bloomfield, Buddy Miles, Paul Butterfield or even John Mayall LPs, this one is for you. Whereas with other rock groups on the brass kick, horns take the form of added accompani ment & sound jarringly superfluous, BST's arrangements bring out their full value. In rock music there is a certain professionalism emerging with the influx of jazz musicians, & that is especially evident with BST who do the right things in the right way & know how to handle a horn section. On the sleeve notes they thank their producer, among other things, for his dogmatism, which strikes one as a pretty strange thing for a rock group to appreciate; on reflection though, it shows just where BST are at. Their choice of material is interesting; it ranges from Variations on a Theme by Eric Satie to Traffic's Smiling Phases — & throughout an abundance of skill & musical understanding. Like the professionals they are, they include some standards — Laura Nyro's 'And When I Die' & Billie Holiday's classic 'God Bless the Child', which is, incidentally, the best track. It is a measure of their class that they are able to take songs like these & do them more than justice, while at the same time injecting something of their own.

One of the good things about the Blues Project was that they didn't let any conventions stop them from experimenting The same is true of BST. 'Blues – part II' is a masterpiece; it starts with a puzzling interlude on electric organ by Dick Halligan in what seems to be archaic classical style, but is in fact free-form & not set to any classical standard, although it starts to sound like a toccata at the end.

I understand that More & More is this LP's contribution to the Rock Machine I Love You record. That track is worth the 15/- on its own. In fact Steve Katz's delicious solo is worth it.

In front of the band David Clayton-Thomas gives an impeccable performance throughout — he might be

45

said to have soul. Bobby Colomby on drums & Jim Fielder on bass make up a rhythm section that rocks hard & swings nicely. Fred Lipsius on alto also shows up well in this set. The production is perfect & there are no lapses in taste; what is more BST in no way suffer from the morbid habit of taking themselves too seriously.

Nowadays, when we are seeing the last great flowering of the movement in rock that started with the Who & the introduction of the Marshall amplification system, there seems to be a dearth of really musical records. Because of this Blood Sweat & Tears is a refreshing experience & totally satisfying.

THE LIVE ADVENTURES OF MIKE BLOOMFIELD & AL KOOPER Mike Bloomfield & Al Kooper (CBS (S) 66216)

'An American music band' was Mike Bloomfield's description of his short lived Electric Flag, & 'American music' sums up this latest album of his. With their Electric Flag & Blood, Sweat & Tears bands, Bloomfield & Kooper were exploring similar areas of blues-soul-rock, & this album is the logical extension of those experiments - but without the brass. Super Session took it some of the way along & was an important record, musically & historically, but only partly realized the full potential of the musicians involved. The music on this double record set makes the 'can-white-men-play-the-blues' controversy, irrelevant. This has nothing to do with imitation black blues or imitation black soul. This is American music from two white American musicians who have all of America's music floating around in their heads. Music from the radio & from ball rooms & clubs & from the street & people's homes. Blues, soul, jazz, country, folk, pop – all that they have heard & absorbed as naturally as a kid growing up absorbs the language, syntax & slang of his family & everyone around him.

Often, otherwise good bands, particularly white blues bands are let down by a wooden rhythm section, but here, Skip Prokop on drums & John Kahn on bass actually know how to swing. Listen to them on 'Her Holy Modal Highness', a jazz influenced piece that is the essence of the instrumental work on this album at it's best, relaxed instead of forced but building to intense climaxes, & always completely together. There is little left to say about Mike Bloomfield, probably America's favourite guitarist. Though his playing on the Electric Flag album sounded tired compared to his work on the first two Butterfield albums, here he is back in form. Like his chief influence, B B King, Bloomfield is a blues guitarist, but one with an awareness of jazz that shows in everything he plays. His perfectly constructed improvisations never contain the merely flash. Playing with economy, he is a master of form.

Kooper's throaty vocal style is well known, but this is Bloomfield's first vocal cutting on record. Not a great blues singer (his songs are all blues), he makes up for any lack of power, depth or

intensity of feeling with a superb sense of phrasing. Carlos Santana of the Santana Blues Band plays on the other guest spot, Sonny Boy Williamson, a tribute to the late blues singer & harp player, written by Jack Bruce & Paul Jones. Certainly one of the funkiest numbers on the album, with one of those persistent riffs that remains in your head for days after you've heard it. It is Al Kooper, though, who is the more dominant musical personality. Not surprising perhaps, as it was he who suggested the session & produced it.

There are only two original numbers, but a jam isn't about presenting new, original material – a jam is about playing & numbers like Paul Simon's Feeling Groovy, which they completely restyle, & the Band's The Weight are given fresh, exciting treatments. The choice of Material throughout is excellent.

This is a record that points to two of the several directions, rock is now taking: the increasing status of individual musicians & the jamming resulting from this, & the idea becoming more & more popular of recording live in the ball rooms and clubs, where the music & it's directions are created. Neither concept even when good musicians are involved is, or will, always be necessarily successful. But this is one of the successful LPs and one of those you might try to converting your jazz friends with. You'll probably succeed.

Peter Dalton

REALITY IS BAD ENOUGH. Patrick Sky. Verve Forecast SVLP 6103

The use of the theatre as a symbol for the world & drama as a symbol for the patterns in which human life is worked out, is as old as Shakespeare's "All the world's a stage", perhaps older, perhaps even as old as the theatre & drama themselves. One feature of Patrick Sky's album is the way it takes these symbols & makes new use of them. The album is not theatrical; it doesn't seek to mimic an overall theatrical presentation as, say, Sgt. Pepper did. There are, however, obvious theatrical overtones.

Most overtly there is Sky's version of Gilbert & Sullivan's "Modern Major General" where the comic atmosphere is intensified by the use of a solo banjo backing wedged paranthetically between a marvellously staccato orchestral introduction & finale. Another costume piece, "Enjoy Enjoy Enjoy", mimics a kind of awful American pre-war big band radio show. One can imagine Sky singing this with tuxedo & slicked-down hair.

Again, a theatrical motif is used as a design concept. The album's cover shows two clown faces, cut-out representations of the familiar tragi-comic masks of Greek drama. To a certain kind of mind (obviously the "New York Times" mentality that Sky slams in "Not The Loving Kind") the songs would lend themselves to easy classification into comic & tragic categories, paralleling this theatrical "Make 'em laugh, make 'em cry" tradition; one feels an Art Director is fretting somewhere because they wouldn't, just wouldn't, take the idea of duality to its extreme & tie the whole thing up neatly by calling it "Two Sides of Patrick Sky".

Of course, it's the failure of the songs, & Sky's talent, to be tied up neatly in any but this superficial manner that makes them so interesting. A child would probably find the mantric sadness of "Children's Song" unbearable. "Silly Song" is acutely perceptive in a way we don't usually expect "silly" things to be.

Just as the theatre is no longer an easy black & white, a simple case of God versus the Devil as in mediaeval miracle plays, so popular music & contemporary folk art are outgrowing their early "Teenager In Love" ingenuousness. Sky's album is valuable both as a product of this process & a graphic embodiment of its principles. "Reality," as the man says, "is bad enough. Why should I tell the truth?" Think about that when "Che!" visits your friendly neighbourhood repertory company.

Graham Charnock

HOWLING WOLF: Electric How. Pye CRLS 4543 (s)

Howling Wolf is supposed not to like this record. The cover blurb reads 'This is Howlin' Wolf's new album. He doesn't like it. He didn't like his electric guitar at first either.' Presumably Cadet-Concept adopted this aggressive defence because of the bad press that the recording got in Rolling Stone & elsewhere.

But however much you might sympathise with the idea of the proud bluesman electrified against his will, or deplore the way that the publicity was angled – poor old coon, he'll thank us in the end, – the important thing is the record. Ultimately what the record company did & what Howling Wolf thought doesn't matter.

The music itself isn't as bad as one might expect. It's thoroughly electrified but that in itself is no bad thing. In fact it's all good leaping stuff – the kind of blues you can really dance to. It's depressing to find people who say they can't dance to anything but Marvin Gaye, Stevie Wonder & Otis Redding. If they had an ounce of rhythm in them they could dance to Electric Howl. Phil Upchurch, who plays guitar on three of the tracks, recorded 'You Can't Sit Down' a while back, & the bass & drums lay down a beat that'll make your neighbours' ducks fly off the wall.

The material consists mainly of standard blues numbers all given the same treatment – thumping rhythms; screaming wah-wah guitar, with Howling Wolfs' harsh vocals (which sound like they were torn out of his stomach with barbed fish-hooks). Best number of the album – & the worst for dancing because the superb jumpy bass line stops & re-starts several times – is 'Evil', but 'The Red Rooster', & 'Smokestack Lightning' are all almost as good. The arrangements are nearly the same throughout but the backing musicians are so good and so together that that doesn't matter either.

Put it this way – if you don't know who Howling Wolf is & you like electric blues, you'll dig the album. If you do know who he is & you care that he was hyped, the best thing you can do for him is to buy the record. That way he can howl all the way to the bank.

John Leaver.

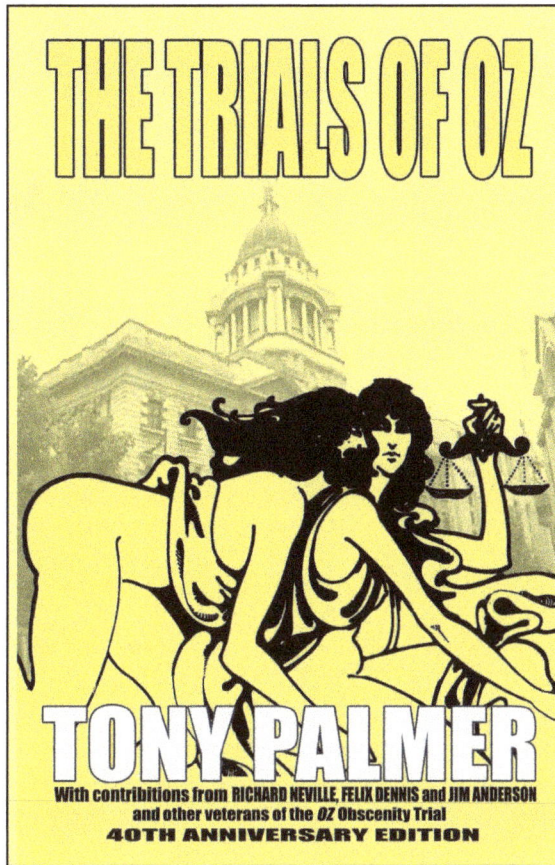

THE TRIALS OF OZ

TONY PALMER

With contributions from RICHARD NEVILLE, FELIX DENNIS and JIM ANDERSON and other veterans of the *OZ* Obscenity Trial

40TH ANNIVERSARY EDITION

The *OZ* trial was the longest obscenity trial in history. It was also one of the worst reported. With minor exceptions, the Press chose to rewrite what had occurred, presumably to fit in with what seemed to them the acceptable prejudices of the times. Perhaps this was inevitable.

The proceedings dragged on for nearly six weeks in the hot summer of 1971 when there were, no doubt, a great many other events more worthy of attention. Against the background of murder in Ulster, for example, the *OZ* affair probably fades into its proper insignificance. Even so, after the trial, when some newspapers realised that maybe something important had happened, it became more and more apparent that what was essential was for anyone who wished to be able to read what had actually been said. Trial and judgment by a badly informed press became the order of the day. This 40th Anniversary edition includes new material by all three of the original defendants, the prosecuting barrister, one of the *OZ* schoolkids, and even the daughters of the judge. There are also many illustrations including unseen material from Felix Dennis' own collection...

ALSO AVAILABLE FROM GONZO MULTIMEDIA

GONZO Books

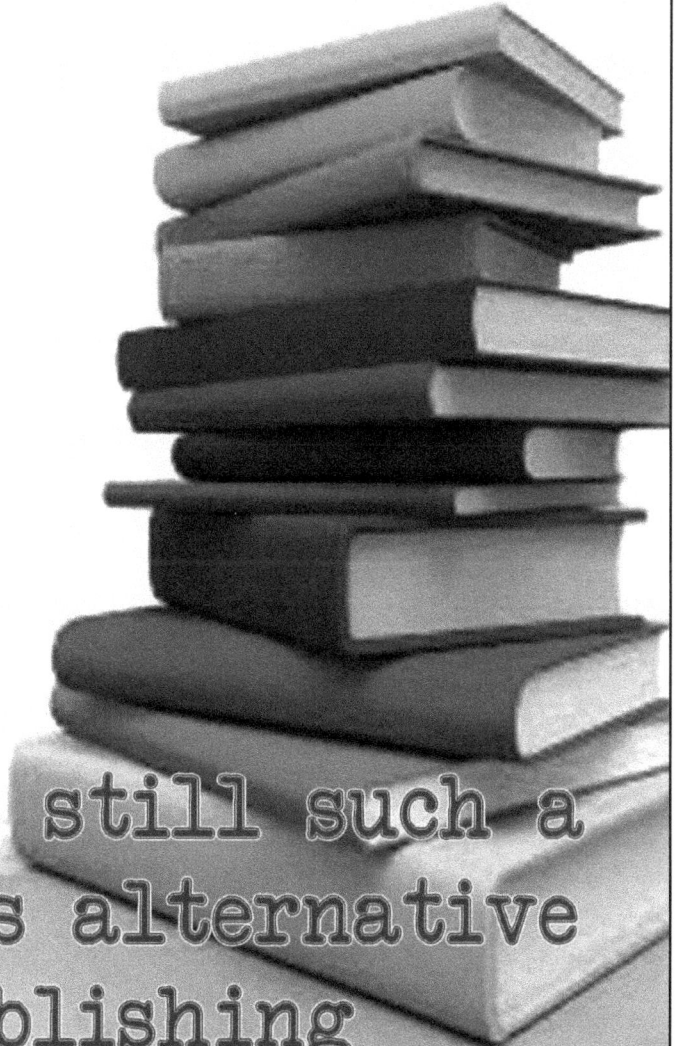

There is still such a thing as alternative Publishing

robert calvert
centigrade 232

HYPE
the music may change, but the hype goes on
ROBERT CALVERT

CAPED CRUSADER
RICK WAKEMAN IN THE 1970s
DAN WOODING
Foreword by Elton John

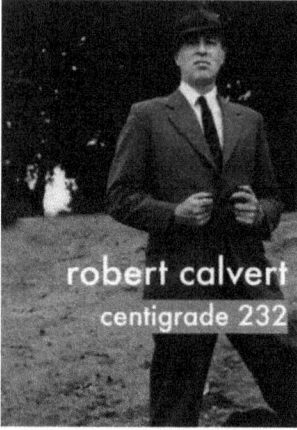

Robert Newton Calvert: Born 9 March 1945, Died 14 August 1988 after suffering a heart attack. Contributed poetry, lyrics and vocals to legendary space rock band Hawkwind intermittently on five of their most critically acclaimed albums, including Space Ritual (1973), Quark, Strangeness & Charm (1977) and Hawklords (1978). He also recorded a number of solo albums in the mid 1970s. CENTIGRADE 232 was Robert Calvert's first collection of poems.

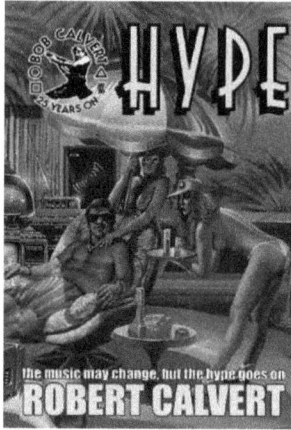

Hype 'And now, for all you speed ing street smarties out there, the one you've all been waiting for, the one that'll pierce your laid back ears, decoke your sinuses, cut clean thru the schlock rock, MOR/crossover, techno flash mind mush. It's the new Number One with a bullet … with a bullet … It's Tom, Supernova, Mahler with a pan galac tic biggie …' And the Hype goes on. And on. Hype, an amphetamine hit of a story by Hawkwind collaborator Robert Calvert. Who's been there and made it back again. The debriefing session starts here.

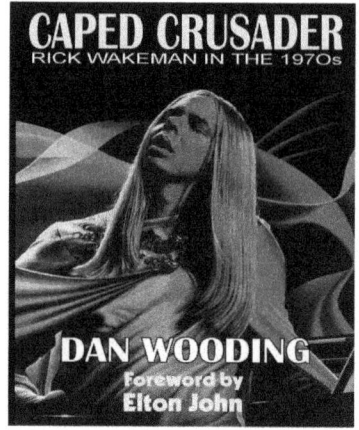

Rick Wakeman is the world's most unusual rock star, a genius who has pushed back the barriers of electronic rock. He has had some of the world's top orchestras perform his music, has owned eight Rolls Royces at one time, and has broken all the rules of com posing and horrified his tutors at the Royal College of Music. Yet he has delighted his millions of fans. This frank book, authorised by Wakeman himself, tells the moving tale of his larger than life career.

"So many books, so little time."
Frank Zappa

THE NINE HENRYS
By Peter McAdam

TERRY DENE: BRITAIN'S FIRST ROCK & ROLL REBEL

DAN WOODING

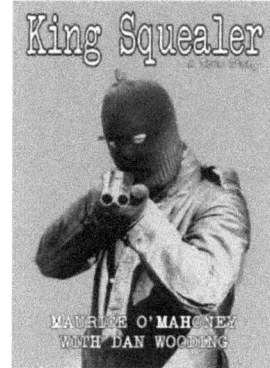

King Squealer

MAURICE O'MAHONEY WITH DAN WOODING

There are nine Henrys, pur
ported to be the world's
first cloned cartoon charac
ter. They live in a strange
lo fi domestic surrealist
world peopled by talking
rock buns and elephants on
wobbly stilts.

They mooch around in their
minimalist universe suffer
ing from an existential
crisis with some genetically
modified humour thrown in.

Marty Wilde on Terry Dene: "Whatever
happened to Terry becomes a great deal
more comprehensible as you read of the
callous way in which he was treated by
people who should have known better
many of whom, frankly, will never know
better of the sad little shadows of
the past who eased themselves into
Terry's life, took everything they
could get and, when it seemed that all
was lost, quietly left him ... Dan Wood
ing's book tells it all."

Rick Wakeman: "There have
always been certain 'careers'
that have fascinated the
public, newspapers, and the
media in general. Such
include musicians, actors,
sportsmen, police, and not
surprisingly, the people who
give the police their employ
ment: The criminal. For the
man in the street, all these
careers have one thing in
common: they are seemingly
beyond both his reach and,
in many cases, understanding
and as such, his only associ
ation can be through the
media of newspapers or tele
vision. The police, however,
will always require the ser
vices of the grass, the
squealer, the snitch, (call
him what you will), in order
to assist in their investiga
tions and arrests; and amaz
ingly, this is the area that
seldom gets written about."

"Outside of a dog, a book is
man's best friend. Inside of a
dog it's too dark to read."
Groucho Marx

LUNAR NOTES

ZOOT HORN ROLLO'S CAPTAIN BEEFHEART EXPERIENCE

BILL HARKLEROAD with BILLY JAMES

THE EMPIRE OF THINGS

SELECTED WRITINGS 2003 - 2013

CJ STONE

The Time of Feasting

mick farren

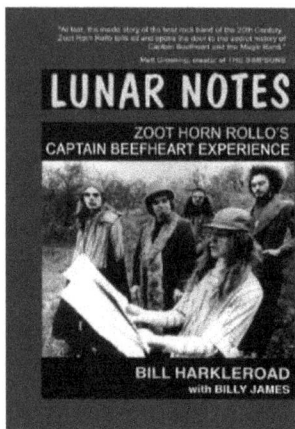

Bill Harkleroad joined Captain Beef heart's Magic Band at a time when they were changing from a straight ahead blues band into something completely dif ferent. Through the vision of Don Van Vliet (Captain Beefheart) they created a new form of music which many at the time considered atonal and difficult, but which over the years has continued to exert a powerful influence. Beefheart re christened Harkleroad as Zoot Horn Rollo, and they embarked on recording one of the classic rock albums of all time Trout Mask Replica - a work of unequalled daring and inventiveness.

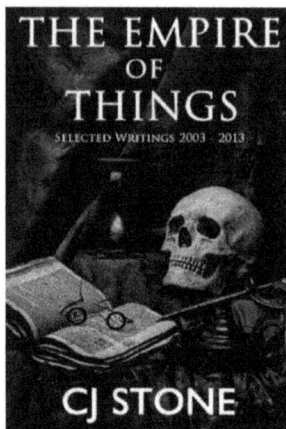

Politics, paganism and …. Vlad the Impaler. Selected stories from CJ Stone from 2003 to the present. Meet Ivor Coles, a British Tommy killed in action in September 1915, lost, and then found again. Visit Mothers Club in Erdington, the best psyche delic music club in the UK in the '60s. Celebrate Robin Hood's Day and find out what a huckle duckle is. Travel to Stonehenge at the Summer Solstice and carouse with the hippies. Find out what a Ranter is, and why CJ Stone thinks that he's one. Take LSD with Dr Lilly, the psychedelic scientist. Meet a headless soldier or the ghost of Elvis Presley in Gabalfa, Cardiff. Journey to Whitstable, to New York, to Malta and to Transylvania, and to many other places, real and imagined, polit ical and spiritual, transcendent and mundane. As The Independent says, Chris is "The best guide to the underground since Charon ferried dead souls across the Styx."

This is is the first in the highly acclaimed vampire novels of the late Mick Farren. Victor Renquist, a surprisingly urbane and likable leader of a colony of vampires which has existed for centuries in New York is faced with both admin istrative and emotional prob lems. And when you are a vampire, administration is not a thing which one takes lightly.

"The person, be it gentleman or lady, who has not pleasure in a good novel, must be intolerably stupid."

Jane Austen

Darklost

mick farren

Los Angeles City of Angels, city of dreams. But sometimes the dreams become nightmares. Having fled New York, Victor Renquist and his small group of Nosferatu are striving to re establish their colony. They have become a deeper, darker part of the city's nightlife. And Hollywood's glitterati are hot on the scent of a new thrill, one that outshines all others immortality. But someone, somewhere, is med dling with even darker powers, powers that even the Nosferatu fear. Someone is attempting to summon the entity of ancient evil known as Cthulhu. And Ren quist must overcome dissent in his own colony, solve the riddle of the Darklost (a being brought part way along the Nosferatu path and then abandoned) and combat powerful enemies to save the world of humans!

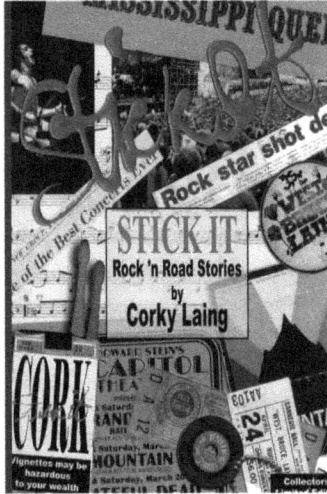

STICK IT
Rock 'n Road Stories by Corky Laing

Canadian born Corky Laing is probably best known as the drummer with Mountain. Corky joined the band shortly after Mountain played at the famous Woodstock Festival, although he did receive a gold disc for sales of the soundtrack album after over dubbing drums on Ten Years After's performance. Whilst with Mountain Corky Laing recorded three studio albums with them before the band split. Follow ing the split Corky, along with Mountain gui tarist Leslie West, formed a rock three piece with former Cream bassist Jack Bruce. West, Bruce and Laing recorded two studio albums and a live album before West and Laing re formed Mountain, along with Felix Pappalardi. Since 1974 Corky and Leslie have led Mountain through various line ups and recordings, and continue to record and perform today at numer ous concerts across the world. In addition to his work with Mountain, Corky Laing has recorded one solo album and formed the band Cork with former Spin Doctors guitarist Eric Shenkman, and recorded a further two studio albums with the band, which has also featured former Jimi Hendrix bassist Noel Redding. The stories are told in an incredibly frank, engaging and amusing manner, and will appeal also to those people who may not necessarily be fans of

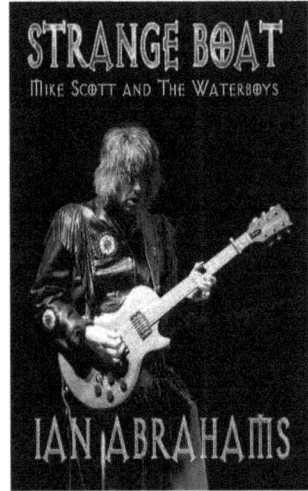

STRANGE BOAT
MIKE SCOTT AND THE WATERBOYS

IAN ABRAHAMS

To me there's no difference between Mike Scott and The Waterboys; they both mean the same thing. They mean myself and whoever are my current travel ling musical companions." Mike Scott Strange Boat charts the twisting and meandering journey of Mike Scott, describing the literary and spiritual references that inform his songwriting and explor ing the multitude of locations and cultures in which The Waterboys have assembled and reflected in their recordings. From his early forays into the music scene in Scotland at the end of the 1970s, to his creation of a 'Big Music' that peaked with the hit single 'The Whole of the Moon' and onto the Irish adventure which spawned the classic Fisher man's Blues, his constantly restless creativity has led him through a myriad of changes. With his revolving cast of troubadours at his side, he's created some of the most era defining records of the 1980s, reeled and jigged across the Celtic heartlands, reinvented himself as an electric rocker in New York, and sought out personal renewal in the spiritual calm of Findhorn's Scot tish highland retreat. Mike Scott's life has been a tale of continual musical exploration entwined with an ever evolving spirituality. "An intriguing portrait of a modern musician" (Record Collector).

"A room without books is like a body without a soul."
Marcus Tullius Cicero

THE TRIALS OF OZ

TONY PALMER

With contributions from RICHARD NEVILLE, FELIX DENNIS and JIM ANDERSON
and other veterans of the OZ Obscenity Trial

40TH ANNIVERSARY EDITION

CALLING FROM A STAR

THE
Merrell Fankhauser
STORY

THE REAL PORN WARS

EXPLICIT CONTENT

RECORD LABELING
HEARING
COMMITTEE ON COMMERCE,
SCIENCE, AND TRANSPORTATION
UNITED STATES SENATE

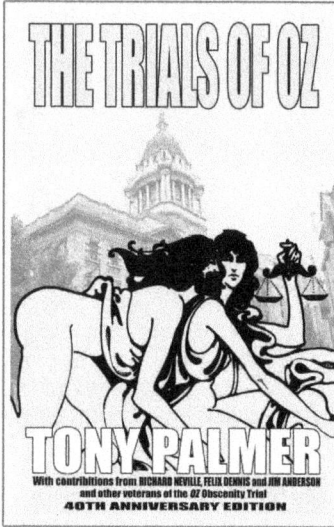

The OZ trial was the longest obscenity trial in history. It was also one of the worst reported. With minor exceptions, the Press chose to rewrite what had occurred, presumably to fit in with what seemed to them the acceptable prejudices of the times. Perhaps this was inevitable. The proceedings dragged on for nearly six weeks in the hot summer of 1971 when there were, no doubt, a great many other events more worthy of attention. Against the background of murder in Ulster, for example, the OZ affair probably fades into its proper insignificance. Even so, after the trial, when some newspapers realised that maybe something important had happened, it became more and more apparent that what was essential was for anyone who wished to be able to read what had actually been said. Trial and judgment by a badly informed press became the order of the day. This 40th Anniversary edition includes new material by all three of the original defendants, the prosecuting barrister, one of the OZ schoolkids, and even the daughters of the judge. There are also many illustrations including unseen material from Felix Dennis' own collection...

Merrell Fankhauser has led one of the most diverse and interesting careers in music. He was born in Louisville, Kentucky, and moved to California when he was 13 years old. Merrell went on to become one of the innovators of surf music and psychedelic folk rock. His travels from Hollywood to his 15 year jungle experience on the island of Maui have been documented in numerous music books and magazines in the United States and Europe. Merrell has gained legendary international status throughout the field of rock music; his credits include over 250 songs published and released. He is a multi talented singer/songwriter and unique guitar player whose sound has delighted listeners for over 35 years. This extraordinary book tells a unique story of one of the founding fathers of surf rock, who went on to play in a succession of progressive and psychedelic bands and to meet some of the greatest names in the business, including Captain Beefheart, Randy California, The Beach Boys, Jan and Dean... and there is even a run in with the notorious Manson family.

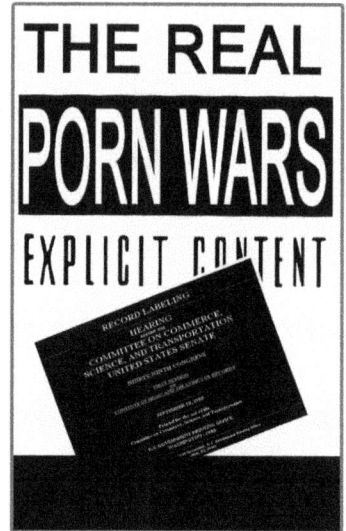

On September 19, 1985, Frank Zappa testified before the United States Senate Commerce, Technology, and Transportation committee, attacking the Parents Music Resource Center or PMRC, a music organization co founded by Tipper Gore, wife of then senator Al Gore. The PMRC consisted of many wives of politicians, including the wives of five members of the committee, and was founded to address the issue of song lyrics with sexual or satanic content. Zappa saw their activities as on a path towards censorship and called their proposal for voluntary labelling of records with explicit content "extortion" of the music industry. This is what happened.

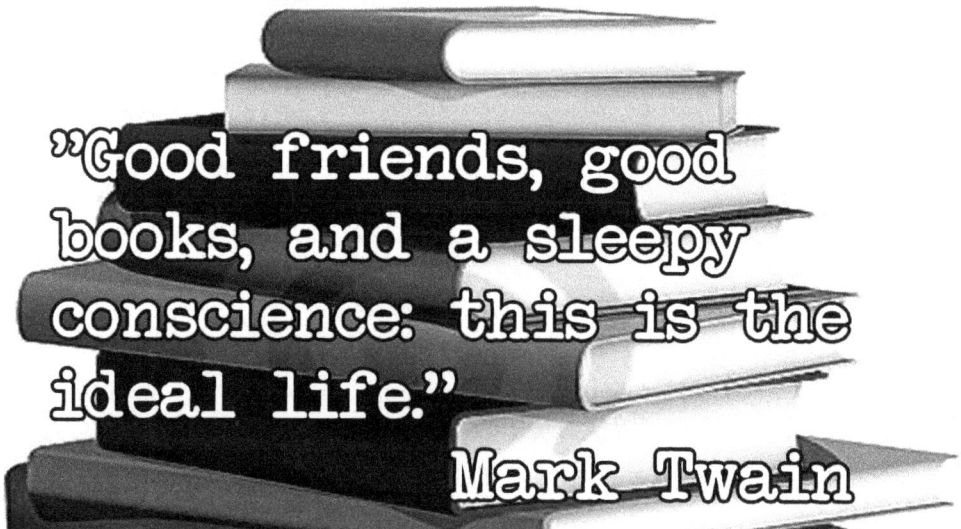

"Good friends, good books, and a sleepy conscience: this is the ideal life."
Mark Twain

500 ALBUMS
You Won't Believe until You Hear them
NEIL NIXON WITH THOM NIXON

The Way to(o) Weard
A Musical Memoir of (not) growing up in the Sixties (or since)
ROY WEARD

Luca Ferrari
OUT OF NOWHERE
the uniquely elusive jazz of
MIKE TAYLOR

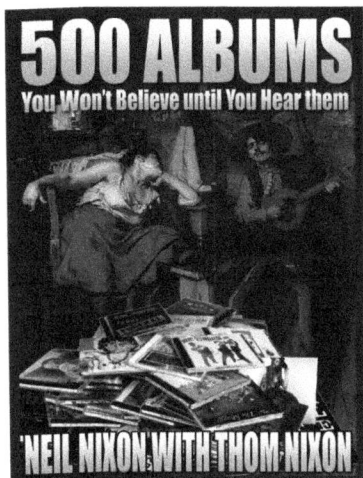

An erudite catalogue of some of the most peculiar records ever made. We have lined up, described and put into context 500 "albums" in the expectation that those of you who can't help yourselves when it comes to finding and collecting music will benefit from these efforts in two ways. Firstly, you'll know you are not alone. Secondly, we hope that some of the work covering the following pages leads you to new discoveries, and makes your life slightly better as a result.

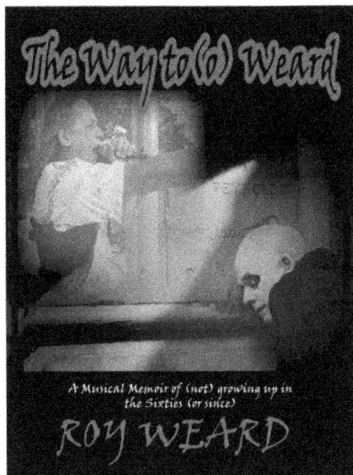

Roy Weard was born in Barking, then a part of Essex, in 1948. He spent most of the mid-sixties through to the mid seventies involved first in folk music and then in the psychedelic hippie scene. He toured with many bands in various capacities from T-Shirt seller to sound engineer, production manager and tour manager. He was involved in several bands of his own, played at many of the iconic free festivals, made three full length albums and two singles, wrote for music magazines, computer magazines and produced copious MySpace blogs. He has lived all over London, spent four years in Hamburg, Germany and finally settled in Brighton where he now resides. He still sings in a rock and roll band, promotes gigs, does a weekly radio show and steadfastly refuses to act his age. This is his story.

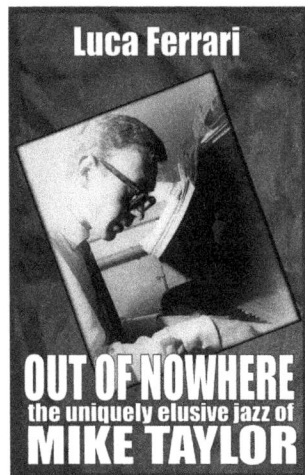

Michael Ronald Taylor (1938 - 1969) was a British jazz composer, pianist and co-songwriter for the band Cream.

Mike Taylor drowned in the River Thames near Leigh-on-Sea, Essex in January 1969, following years of heavy drug use (principally hashish and LSD). He had been homeless for three years, and his death was almost entirely unremarked. This is the first biography written about him.

> "I have always imagined that Paradise will be a kind of library."
> Jorge Luis Borges